Mass Media and
the Environment

David M. Rubin
David P. Sachs

The Praeger Special Studies program—utilizing the most modern and efficient book production techniques and a selective worldwide distribution network—makes available to the academic, government, and business communities significant, timely research in U.S. and international economic, social, and political development.

Mass Media and the Environment

Water Resources, Land Use and Atomic Energy in California

PRAEGER SPECIAL STUDIES IN U.S. ECONOMIC, SOCIAL, AND POLITICAL ISSUES

744544

Praeger Publishers   New York   Washington   London

PRAEGER PUBLISHERS
111 Fourth Avenue, New York, N.Y. 10003, U.S.A.
5, Cromwell Place, London S.W.7, England

Published in the United States of America in 1973
by Praeger Publishers, Inc.

Library of Congress Catalog Card Number: 72-85982

Printed in the United States of America

To Our Parents, for Their Constant Faith and Support

For the citizen's engagement in his new concern with applied ecology, this book supplies effective tools and even weapons. Science, technology, progress, selfishness, and population are the usual villains of popular anxiety about the environment. In place of such abstractions, the authors give the leading roles to live actors. They examine the behavior of the institutions—business enterprises and government agencies—by which our society turns technology to the exploitation of resources and the concurrent transformation of the landscape. Throughout, they keep the spotlight on the press, that crucial institution on which the founding fathers counted to keep our society self-governing.

Today, self-government often is regarded as a term of romance and, at worst, as a camouflage for the real sources of power in our land. The bigness that is associated with efficiency in the industrial system and the interdependence that so tightly interlocks the flow of energy, food, materials, and other wherewithals seem to have concentrated power in remote centers beyond the reach and out of sight of the citizenry. A pall of secrecy hides the decision-making, which in any case appears to rest upon considerations too complex and arcane for comprehension by the ordinary individual. Learned treatises have argued that the technological order has become autonomous and self-actuating, seeking its own impersonal ends beyond all human control. The citizen, it seems, has followed other sovereigns into retirement.

This book is testimony that significant power lies within the grasp of enterprising and responsible citizens. The authors have chosen an important public interest: the exploitation of water and land resources. Water is a scarce commodity at the western edge of the Great American Desert. The experience of the West in this regard, however, soon is to become common in other parts of the nation where water hitherto has been thought as free as air. The fragility of the life community in the West holds portents for other regions that have been no less improvident and heedless of the resources that originally placed them on the map. The issue gains another dimension of significance as the authors show that government agencies, motivated by bureaucratic aggrandizement, can be as feckless as business enterprises driven by profit.

As the first lesson for consideration by their fellow citizens, the authors show that the pall of secrecy can be lifted—that it hangs where it does by lack of initiative on the part of citizens who ought and need to know better. The public record is rich in information mandated by law. This information includes not only the data on which business enterprises and government agencies act but also intelligence on the interlock of interest relationships that, in addition to tying business enterprises together, cross the line to government agencies charged with responsibility for resources and the public interest. Where government secrecy and corporate privacy resist the law and claim privileges beyond it, the authors show that ingenuity and persistence can circumvent these obstacles. There then remains the obstacles referred to under the rubric of "public understanding of science." The authors show that this, too, can be made to yield to humility on the part of the popularizer and sufficient motivation in the reader.

The record developed in this book stands as a rebuke to the press for chronic failure in its constitutional function. Many questions come forward not only for study by scholars but for introspection by the professionals of the press. What legal and ethical standards should govern advertising addressed to public issues by private interests? What influence does corporate public relations exert upon news coverage? In what ways has the press contributed to the promotion of unplanned development and resource wastage? How does a topic—now so obviously of public concern—like deterioration of the environment go so long neglected by the press? What role has the activist public played in awakening the press, as well as the public at large, to the issues implied by environmental deterioration?

The last question is one not only for the professionals of the press but for the practitioners of the learned professions upon whom contemporary society now depends so heavily for its welfare, protection, and amenity. This book is the work of young scientists, engineers, physicians, lawyers, and journalists still engaged in their undergraduate and graduate education. What they have accomplished is an example and a model, ready for replication by the seniors in their professions. A society that depends upon science and technology must look to its scientists, physicians, and technologists for wisdom and conscience in the management of the extraordinary power that objective knowledge has placed in the hands of man.

Within recent years, Americans have found themselves caught up in the cyclical awakenings that have swept the country, forcing new directions in thought. In the 1950s we were preoccupied with the Cold War abroad and the Communist menace at home; in the 1960s attention swung to the divisions between black and white Americans. Now to these two specific problems a third has been added for the 1970s—the deterioration of the environment.

Mass media have played a crucial role in establishing a framework for discussion of these problems. The difficulties the news media encountered in accurately reporting the victory of Mao in China and the charges of Senator Joseph McCarthy helped produce the American fear of monolithic Communism. The report of the Kerner Commission (Advisory Commission on Civil Disorders), undertaken in the wake of 1967 ghetto rioting, emphasized that one reason for American racial tensions was the failure of the media "to analyze and report adequately on racial problems in the United States and, as a related matter, to meet the Negro's legitimate expectations in journalism."

It is yet too early to assess completely the impact of press performance on the environmental protection movement. This volume investigates the role of the press at a comparatively early stage, while there still may be time to modify performance. Political events since 1969 show that the news media already have played an important part in educating the public to environmental problems: witness passage of the landmark National Environmental Policy Act in 1969, defeat of the SST, and recognition by many segments of the population that "bigger" is not necessarily "better" and "growth" does not always presage "progress."

The studies in Mass Media and the Environment were developed at Stanford University from June 1970 to September 1971 by three dozen graduate and undergraduate students in communications, law, medicine, geology, physics, and biology. The National Science Foundation supported the research within Grant GZ-1777. While the results are of national interest, much of the research necessarily was rooted in California, particularly in the nine counties known as the San Francisco Bay Area. A word about this region's people, media, and environmental problems will aid the non-California reader to interpret our findings.

Perhaps because they are surrounded by so much natural beauty, the five million people of the Bay Area organized earlier and fight harder than people of other areas to protect the quality of their environment. The Sierra Club, the most important national citizen organization lobbying on environmental questions, was founded in California and roughly 39,000 of its 114,000 members live in the Bay Area. Another 7,000 residents are politically organized in the Save Our Bay Action Committee, and 3,000 more comprise the Committee for Green Foothills.

Over the years these eco-activists have fought, with success toward the following goals: (1) to stop the filling of San Francisco Bay by developers, creating the Bay Conservation and Development Commission as a watchdog; (2) to halt construction of one of the first nuclear power plants in the nation; (3) to preserve the redwood forests north of San Francisco; (4) to curtail construction of urban freeways and bridges; (5) to prevent construction of skyscrapers portending the "Manhattanization" of San Francisco; and (6) to pass legislation preserving as much of the California coastline as is not already desecrated by developers. These Californians are especially sensitive to the need for open space, preservation of coastal beauty, and prompt action on air and water pollution problems.

The nine-county Bay Area is served by 28 daily newspapers (with a total circulation of 1.6 million) and numerous weekly and monthly publications. The San Francisco Chronicle dominates the morning newspaper field, with some competition from the San Jose Mercury in the South Bay. The afternoon market is highly fragmented, with much circulation falling to suburban dailies in such cities as Palo Alto, San Mateo, San Rafael, and Santa Rosa.

The television market is divided among the three network affiliates licensed to San Francisco, but the area does have a strong noncommercial station and a profitable independent station. The radio audience is split among KCBS (an all-news CBS station), KGO (an all-talk and news station owned by ABC), and KSFO (a sports and pop music station). Cross-media and chain ownership are as prevalent in San Francisco as in other cities, but on the whole newspaper and broadcast quality is somewhat higher than in other urban areas, with the exception of New York, Los Angeles, Washington, and Chicago. We are confident that the trends, obstacles, and problems detailed in this volume are not limited to the media in northern California.

In presenting our results we have included some methodology to make the data analysis more useful. For those who wish to replicate these studies or more closely study our methodology, we have provided complete mail and telephone questionnaires, content analysis coding procedures, and similar material in the appendixes. The reader also will find a bibliography on the media and the environment.

Our purpose was not simply to evaluate media performance and apportion praise and blame. We hope our findings will be used by journalists, environmental activists, corporate and public officials, physicians and public health officers, and others who hope to improve communications on this vital topic so that every American can, at last, learn how to live in harmony with the world.

For their faith we would like to thank M. Joan Callanan of the National Science Foundation and Fred Honkala, formerly with NSF and now president of Yankton College, South Dakota. For their sponsorship and guidance, many thanks to Williams L. Rivers and Joshua Lederberg, Stanford professors; to Niels Reimers, Frank Newman, and Glen Barber of the Stanford administration; and to Don Stuedeman, our grant administrator. We also are indebted to Elliott Leventhal and David L. Grey for their cooperation and advice. For tracking down difficult references we would like to thank the staff of the Stanford Falconer Biology Library: Peggy Craig, Ferne Barr, Clair Shoens, and Margaret Fuhrman.

For their valuable assistance throughout the project, we wish to thank Stephen and Janice Fortmann, Glenn Lopez, Ellen Macke, David Sachsman, Martha Press, Lynda Weisberg, Muriel Allan, Marilyn Benefiel, and all the other members of the Stanford community who worked long hours, far beyond reasonable expectations, to bring this project to a successful conclusion.

Special thanks to James B. D. Mark, M. D., professor of Surgery and associate dean for student affairs at the Stanford University Medical School, for his insight and personal understanding of this project's importance and value to American medicine.

In completing this report we frequently resorted to research techniques that can only be compared to Chinese water torture in their effects on the unfortunate victims. Literally hundreds of working journalists in and out of the Bay Area cheerfully submitted to our mail questionnaires, telephone interviews, requests for information and access to files, and various other tools of the trade. To all, our deepest thanks. We can understand why some may never want to hear the word "environment" again. And special thanks to Tom Harris of the San Jose Mercury, who should be awarded some sort of medal for bravery in the face of academicians.

CONTENTS

LIST OF TABLES

LIST OF FIGURES

Mass Media and the Environment

Scores of polls and opinion surveys over the years have demonstrated, to the concern of social scientists, the low level of public knowledge on most issues of national significance. Throughout the twentieth century this has been especially true of scientific matters, particularly those with a direct bearing on national policy.

The usual interface between scientific discovery and the public is the mass media. In the first part of the twentieth century scientific advances came at a slower rate. Their impact on public affairs and policy was perceived only dimly. Since World War II the pace of science has shot up at an exponential rate with such developments as nuclear energy, antibiotics, chemical pesticides, high octane gasoline, solid state physics, and transplantation surgery. These basic scientific advances produced technological spinoffs that radically altered the style of life and government in the United States. Consequently, it has become increasingly difficult for the average citizen, leading his own busy life, to fully perceive the significance of these changes.

Many thoughtful scholars and political leaders have addressed themselves to this problem. They fear that democracy, as we have endeavored to define it over the past 200 years, cannot survive unless each citizen can judge intelligently what will define his best interest, what will enhance his life, and what will erode his freedom. Democracy depends on an enlightened citizenry.

Material for this chapter on the history of the California Water Project was prepared by Lloyd W. Lowrey, Jr. Mr. Lowrey is a 1971 graduate of Stanford University Law School where he worked for the Environmental Law Society. He intends to work for the General Counsel's Office of the U.S. Post Office following his army discharge.

The lag in cultural and political thought produced by this century's scientific progress already is having serious global consequences: leaders apply nineteenth century militarism with twentieth century armaments. Domestic consequences of a different nature already are emerging. We cannot long remain on this sphere called Earth if we continue to be a world of pre-seventeenth century theologians, eighteenth century philosophers, nineteenth century generals, politicians, and newspapermen, twentieth century social and cultural theorists, and twenty-first century scientists. This problem is magnified when scientists do not realize how far apace they are from the rest of society.

SCIENCE AND THE MEDIA

Obviously, in post-World War II America the reporting of science to the public has been difficult for a media network oriented toward a much simpler time when a general beat reporter could be assigned any topic and produce an intelligent, understandable, readable story. Scientific writing crosses many traditional boundaries, involving not only the technical field in question but often economics and politics as well.

Reducing complex scientific arguments to lay language is no easy task; it is most difficult for the reporter with little background or interest in science. The quality of coverage hinges on both the training and abilities of reporters and editors as well as on the scientific nature of the story. For these reasons, before moving on to a more specific discussion of environmental coverage, it is worth reviewing the considerable literature on challenges to the mass media in communicating science to the public.

A 1957 questionnaire employed by the National Association of Science Writers and the Survey Research Center of the University of Michigan to gather information from science writers and editors contains a comprehensive definition of science news: "Science includes everything scientists discover about nature—it could be the discoveries about the stars, or atoms, or about the human body or the mind—any basic discovery about how things work and why. But science also includes the way in which this information is used for practical uses—it might be a new way of curing disease, or the invention of a new auto engine, or making a new fertilizer." This definition adequately recognizes the two primary divisions of the scientific endeavor: basic research and its handmaiden, applied research.

"The Continuing Study of Newspaper Reading" makes clear that, at least until the early 1960s, the reading public had a comparatively active interest in science news although editors were inclined to downplay its importance.[1] Only 0.6 percent of 40,158 news-editorial-feature items appearing in 130 daily newspapers from 1939 to 1950 were categorized as either science news or invention, making it among the least important of some 40 news categories. Yet interviews with about 50,000 adult readers revealed that science and invention news ranked twelfth in interest, surpassing such bread and butter items as news about accidents, local and national government, and sports, as well as the fine arts and religion.

Although we do not have comparable research data for the past 20 years, it seems likely that reader interest in science news has remained high and the gap between interest and the amount of information presented by editors has narrowed. Further, with the increased specialization of newspapermen since World War II has come the science writer, who covers such stories on a regular basis.

A University of Michigan Survey Research Center study in 1957 queried 1,919 adults about the number of science and medicine items they could recall and the medium from which the information came. The table below illustrates the importance of newspapers by showing the percentage of respondents citing different media as major sources of science items they recalled.

	Newspapers	Magazines	Radio	Television
Science	14.1	4.0	1.9	6.3
Medicine	28.9	2.1	1.0	3.9
Total	43.0	6.1	2.9	10.2

When newspapers were not named as the first source of science news, they almost always were the second choice. Such data led the researchers to conclude that "Newspapers are the major primary and a strong supplementary source of science news for the public."[2]

In a more recent interpretation of these and other public opinion data, Wilbur Schramm and Serena Wade concluded that newspapers and magazines are used to a greater extent than television as sources of public knowledge regarding science, and that newspapers dominate the science news field as television dominates political campaigns.[3]

Reporters with regular science beats and those sporadically assigned to science stories must cope with problems that usually do not trouble other reporters. Many science stories are complicated and demand extensive background knowledge on the part of the reporter. While criticizing coverage of the U.S. space flight program, a story that attracted most of the science-writing fraternity, James Skardon admits in a 1968 Columbia Journalism Review article, that "reporting such vast and complicated operations as NASA presents almost super-human challenges."[4] Newsmen in Houston and Cape Kennedy often were at the mercy of NASA technicians to understand what was happening during a flight, and most information between flights was channeled through NASA public information officers. In reporting almost any scientific discovery, the newsman acts principally as a conduit for the scientists involved: he either rewrites a journal report or paper delivered at a convention or he interviews scientists firsthand. Unlike the political writer, he usually cannot provide a summary and analysis of events with an assessment of various alternatives. The science reporter can do little more than give all sides a hearing and hope for the best.

Defining what constitutes "news" in science reporting is quite elusive. The scientific "breakthrough" is more a fiction of the news pages than a laboratory fact. It results from bending the pace of science to fit the press' daily deadline and demand for "timeliness." Particularly in handling an environmental story, the science writer, often is dealing with an event that has been months or years in the making; he has no specific news peg, no natural lead paragraph. "Localness" is another criteria that helps a reporter determine whether a story is newsworthy. But at a scientific convention one obviously would not report only papers from local researchers, nor necessarily give them greater prominence. Tailoring science stories to the traditional conception of news is a problem for both editors and reporters.

Because the science writer is legitimately concerned with the uses to which technology is put, many science stories contain strong elements of politics and economics. Carl Heintze, former science writer for the San Jose Mercury-News, says of the demands of science writing:

> It means you supposedly know something about local medical politics; the confusion which spreads around county hospital administration, and the three new hospitals which have suddenly sprung up in a mushrooming population like the subdivisions around them in uncertain provisions for the future.
> It means . . . coping with space and technology, for both are important words in California, not because of science, but because of business dollars, payrolls and the harder realities of getting to the moon.[5]

As a corollary, Victor Cohn stated in a recent Science article, "Politics today is mainly a response to the pressing and bewildering advances of science and technology and the social changes they work."[6] Although in the context of news reporting the science writer is a specialist, his topic makes him a generalist in a very complex field.

Because the science beat is not isolated from these larger world concerns—and may really be at the center—demands routinely made on political writers by the social responsibility theory of the press extend to the science writer as well. Just as the political reporter has a watchdog function to perform, so the science reporter must act as a watchdog and provide early danger signals to the public. Earl Ubell, science editor for CBS and formerly for the New York Herald Tribune, says, "What we have to do is act as an alerting mechanism."[7] James Skardon writes that his criticism of the science press corps' reporting of the NASA-Apollo program boils down to the belief that they "could have been expected" to "have 'flashed the light, rung the bell, and blown the whistle' more effectively."[8]

Because of the complexity of many scientific stories, the difficulty in obtaining accurate information, and the dependence of the science writer on news sources directly involved in the success of a project, the science press corps often has difficulty performing the watchdog role. Karl Abraham, science writer for the Philadelphia Evening and Sunday Bulletin, summed up these problems in his reply to Skardon's criticism of the lack of watchdogging by the press on the NASA space flight program:

> The assumption that a newspaperman might have affected
> a redesign of Apollo—in a project more than five years
> old and involving thousands of technical experts—is pure
> Walter Mitty. . . . Mr. Skardon asks whether the press
> performed its traditional watchdog role. It did, in the
> traditional way, and that is precisely what has proved
> to be quite inadequate to coverage of the space program.
> It will prove equally inadequate in the coverage of pollu-
> tion abatement, the future miracles of medicine, new
> transport systems, and many other technologies. . . .
> This problem of technical obscurity bred by technical
> complexity is not unique to the space program. Where
> was the press while German babies became deformed
> because of thalidomide? . . . The traditional watchdog
> role of the press is not irrelevant to these problems,
> just inadequate.[9]

The President's Science Advisory Committee noted in 1959, in Education for the Age of Science, that such problems as air and water pollution, the population explosion, and uses of nuclear energy are too urgent to "await the enlightenment of the electorate that will slowly come about with improvements in the nation's educational system."[10] This puts the burden of educating the public about scientific and technological challenges squarely upon the mass

media—particularly newspapers, the chief source of science information. If a willingness to fulfill the watchdog role is not alone sufficient
to the task, then perhaps science writers should be given more tools—
at a minimum more scientific training—with which to do the job. As
Harvey Wheeler of the Center for the Study of Democratic Institutions
points out, "We either have to invent new procedures for handling
science policy or be ruled by technology."[11]

SOCIAL CONTROL IN THE NEWSROOM

The philosophy of news held by many editors and broadcast
executives also can force the science reporter to do less than his
best work. Editors who still are trying to boost circulation through
the Hearst approach to journalism often find scientific matters too
bland to conform to a bold-face, banner headline format. The editor
who maintains this attitude is likely to assign few scientific articles,
and those he does assign often may be distorted through an attempt
at sensationalism. The able science writer not infrequently finds his
own conscientious efforts subverted by uncomprehending editors.
This dilemma was illustrated by the consequences that befell Donald
C. Drake, the veteran, award-winning science and medical writer for
the Philadelphia Inquirer, following the 1971 Philadelphia convention
of the American Association for the Advancement of Science (AAAS).
Demonstrators and picketers had heckled some political speakers
at the convention, including Hubert Humphrey and McGeorge Bundy,
to protest the Vietnam war. Media coverage of the convention centered
almost exclusively on these demonstrations and the near-violence
that resulted. Drake's thoughtful analysis of the events, originally
published in the February 1972 Philadelphia Journalism Review and
reprinted in the April 1972 AAAS Bulletin, pointed out that this type
of coverage gave the reader a totally erroneous impression of the
convention. The news media generally ignored the more than 1,500
papers and 120 symposiums, only a handful of which were disrupted
by demonstrations. Also ignored was the content of these papers,
many of which would have interested the general newspaper reader.
Deriving their information from their news staff, the editors of the
Philadelphia Inquirer sardonically and self-righteously "attacked the
demonstrations saying they couldn't understand 'how science was
advanced by this juvenile display of bad manners.'"[12]
Drake further pointed out that the science reporters at the
convention were not impressed with the demonstrations, did not find
them particularly newsworthy, and spent little time discussing them.
Rather, they reviewed some of the more significant scientific sessions,
discussed the content of the talks by Humphrey and Bundy, and analyzed

the general status of science and international affairs. Nonetheless, with the exception of the New York Times reporter, all the science writers, including Drake, filed stories beginning with a demonstration-violence lead. Why? Drake's own admission is significant and reveals an important defect in the editor-reporter relationship:

> I wrote the story that way because I knew, without asking, that that's what the desk would want and I wanted good play for the story. I didn't want to see a wire story substituted, nor did I want to argue with an editor after an exhausting week. And finally I felt that the facts, using conventional journalistic criteria, supported the lead regardless of whether it was the right lead.
>
> In effect, I gave them what they wanted. In doing so I became a hack, a whore, not only to my profession but to my paper.
>
> I could hide behind the fact that practically every other reporter at that meeting filed a demonstration lead, but for me this is an inadequate defense because I thought the demonstration was not significant. . . .
>
> I realize that ideally editors may have better judgement on a given story than a beginning reporter or a bad reporter, but I insist that an experienced and good reporter, who is more familiar with the story than anyone else in the newsroom, is the best one to judge what the story should say. He may or may not benefit from a discussion with an editor, but contrary to usual practice I believe that after the discussions and after the written story has been challenged, the final decision on what the story says should rest with the writer.[13]

And, Drake might have added, not with an editor with less scientific insight than the writer.

For his confession, Drake was removed from the science and medicine beat, which he had covered in generally superb fashion for six years, and made a general assignment reporter. The Inquirer's executive editor told the AAAS that "the change in assignment is an 'internal' matter that is not appropriate for public discussion."[14]

Although this assignment shift currently is being reviewed by the American Newspaper Guild and the Inquirer, the incident underscores additional problems that confront the capable science reporter as he attempts to communicate some of the most vital issues of our time. Drake's story illustrates what we call internal or social control in the newsroom. As a result of working with a specific editor, the writer will present a story in a way that conforms to his editor's

values and orientation in order to avoid uncontrolled modification or
complete deletion of the story.

There is another equally subtle manner in which newspaper
policy can undercut, sometimes unintentionally, the educational
efforts of science writers. For much of newspaper history, editors
depended on newsstand sales for their existence and therefore developed
the banner headline to attract buyers.

Times have changed, though, and today newspapers derive their
revenue from advertising and home-delivery subscriptions. This
means that any civic policies that promote subdivision developments
also should increase newspaper circulation—and revenue. Furthermore, the growth of shopping centers and industrialization that
can accompany population increase will boost newspaper advertising
revenues. Thus it is very easy for some newspaper executives to
develop policies that make the paper itself an instrument of the
growth establishment, presenting to its readers a biased perspective
on a wide range of scientific and environmental issues, from airport
and highway development to water supply projects. We explore the
far-ranging consequences of this orientation in a case study of the
newspapers in San Jose, California, in Chapter 7.

ECOLOGICAL MEDICINE

Communicating environmental science to the public is as
difficult as general science reporting. Indeed, there are further
complexities that make it even more challenging. Invariably, environmental affairs have direct and indirect human health effects.
Sometimes it is difficult to appreciate even the direct health effects,
let alone the indirect ones.

Some of us can readily perceive that the nitrogen oxide-oxidant
smog in Los Angeles is unhealthy. Manhattan's smog, which contains
a relatively high percentage of sulfur dioxide, is even worse. The
sulfur dioxide in the air combines with water in the airways, producing
a dilute solution of sulfuric acid sloshing around in the lungs.

For physicians trying to practice medicine from a preventive
standpoint, such conditions are anathema. For medical and science
writers trying to present these complex interrelationships to a public
ignorant of basic anatomy, the job is herculean. For physicians,
other scientists, and science reporters who do attempt to orient the
public to the concerns of ecological medicine, the task is fraught with
frustration even though the environmental health problem is obvious.
For problems that are not as obvious, the challenge is even greater.

At this point it will be helpful to clarify two concepts we shall
use throughout this book. Ecology is the study of the mutual

interactions of organisms with their physical and biological environment. The environment of a specific biological species includes the amount of solar energy reaching its habitat, the temperature, amount of moisture, geologic structure, meteorologic conditions, the other plant and animal species present, and numerous other factors.

Environment might well be viewed as setting the stage for the drama of life, while ecology is that drama, depicting the constant interaction between the multitude of elements comprising the environment. This interaction creates a wide range of positive and negative feedback loops affecting the organism as well as its environment. A given species can be affected by environmental changes produced by other organisms or by changes it induces itself. Although he often loses sight of this fact, man, too, is a part of the ecosystem—subject to, and not immune from, the feedback resulting from self-induced environmental change. The entire urban phenomenon is an excellent example of this.

Within this context, the role of ecological medicine is to delineate the interrelationships between the human environment and human physical and mental health. It should assess the impact of man's urban and environmental changes on his own well-being, fully exploring the multiple feedback loops involved in order to develop rational, balanced therapeutic procedures. Ecological medicine therefore is intimately related to the environmental, sociological, and psychological sciences, and to medicine.

Although he probably never heard of ecology, Harvey Cushing, the distinguished, early twentieth century physician and neurosurgeon, prophetically expressed the basic tenet of ecological medicine when he said that a physician is obligated to consider more than a diseased organ, more even than the whole man—he must view the man in his world. The goal implicit in this objective is the prevention of disease, whether it be disease affecting an individual, a family, or a society.

The Environment and Human Health

Finite resources cannot support a continually growing population. This idea is pertinent whether we are discussing a city, a state, the United States, or the world. Generally speaking, overpopulation exists when the biological community requires resources the environment cannot provide. From this perspective, most urban regions in the United States are as overpopulated as the underdeveloped countries throughout the world. These environmental limitations need not originate from natural or food resource shortages alone. They also arise from the inability of our urban environment to provide adequate housing, sanitation, transportation, educational and medical services,

and cultural resources. Shortages in these areas can have as great
an impact on the inhabitants as shortages of food, fossil fuel, or
mineral resources.

A variety of environmental factors can impinge upon the urban
dweller with potential health impact. For example, disease-carrying
bacteria can spread with greater ease in a more crowded area. The
city provides such a nexus: bacteria responsible for typhoid fever,
cholera, and amoebic dysentery all encounter more potential victims
in an area with a highly concentrated population, especially where
waste water and drinking water facilities are poor. Public health
specialists, working with engineers, chemists, and biologists, developed
both the theoretical framework and the practical procedures for
preventing these diseases. Once their bacterial origin had been
established and accepted about one hundred years ago, it was possible
to design an empirically-based sanitation system that would prevent
these water-borne diseases from taking hold. On the whole, medicine,
public health, and engineering have done rather well in coping with
this type of environmental health hazard.

Global Health: Albedo and Air Pollution

Other factors influencing health are not so obvious. Earlier we
mentioned the idea that man's urban activities generate feedback that
affects both man himself and other organisms in the environment.
The amount of solar energy available at our planet's surface is
obviously of vital importance: not only is this the source from which
all life derives its energy but it is crucial for maintaining planetary
climatic and water balance. Alteration in any of these factors would
have cascading effects on living populations and might well directly
influence human disease rates.

A certain percentage of incident solar radiation is reflected
at the earth's atmosphere by planetary albedo. Albedo can be visualized
as a thin shell of small particles, one micron or less in diameter each,
encircling the planet. Clouds, for example, form part of the albedo
and are responsible for reflecting solar energy away from earth.
Their presence has been relatively constant over time. We are more
concerned with additional factors that could increase albedo, since
such changes would lower the energy available for photosynthesis
and could alter climatic conditions. Have pollutants from human
activity, released into the air, altered the earth's albedo?

Initial efforts to answer this question examined conditions
following major volcanic explosions, such as Krakatoa in 1883 and
Katmai in 1912. Generally speaking, following such cataclysms
atmospheric turbidity increased as billions of microscopic particles

were shot into the upper atmosphere. Turbidity and albedo returned
to normal after approximately three years, depending on the explosion's
severity. This caused planetary albedo to increase. Most people
were aware of this only because of the flaming red sunsets that followed the Krakatoa explosion for about one year. They probably
did not realize that other changes occurred during the period following
these explosions. Over widely separated areas of the globe, populations
of certain insect and mammalian species dropped. Influenza outbreaks
in England and Wales increased sharply. Even after other factors that
could have caused such fluctuations had been accounted for, these
biological changes retained validity and statistical significance. Such
volcanic explosions also may explain large-scale temperature changes
during these periods including drops of as much as 0.5°F.[15] Because
this drop is in annual <u>mean</u> global temperature, it is highly significant.

The effects of decreased solar radiation at the earth's surface
discussed above result from acute, specific events: volcanic eruptions.
But what of the long-term changes? From 1930 to 1960 dustfall in
high mountain regions of the U.S.S.R., well away from local pollution
sources, increased 20 times. The concentration of sub-micron-sized
particles in the upper atmosphere over the rural and urban United
States increased, on the average, by a factor of 10 during the 1960s.
Moreover, following the volcanic eruption of Mount Agung in the East
Indies in March 1963, the global turbidity in the upper atmosphere
had not returned to normal five years later. This caused some consternation in professional circles since the increased turbidity that
followed Krakatoa, a much more violent explosion, lasted only three
years. Not surprisingly, considerable data appear to support the
contention that we are witnessing superimposition of this explosion
over a longer-term trend toward increasing turbidity and albedo
caused by man-made air pollution. Indeed, careful analysis of the
data collected both preceding and following the Mount Agung explosion
reveals a general global turbidity increase of about 80 percent per
decade since 1950. However, the overall increase per decade since
the start of the twentieth century has been only about 20 percent.
This evidence confirms a sharp rise in albedo during recent years.

An analysis of world temperature data shows that average
global temperature, from the mid-nineteenth century until about
1940, increased by 0.7°F. But since 1940 mean world temperature
has decreased by 0.2°F.[16] As would be expected, there are several
schools of thought that attempt to account for these observations.
Increases of carbon dioxide in the atmosphere, from the burning
of fossil fuels, are thought responsible for the temperature rise
until 1940. Changes in the amount of energy leaving the sun do not
seem to account for the temperature drop since that time. Since
residual sub-micron particles have been increasing gradually since

the turn of the century and much more rapidly since about 1950, it is appealing to postulate that the increase in albedo, with a resultant drop in absorbed solar radiation, is a major factor behind this temperature decrease. If this hypothesis proves correct, then one man-made factor—burning fossil fuels—would account for a temperature increase while increasing albedo from particulate air pollution has been reversing that phenomenon. In any case, a man-made geophysical experiment of such magnitude certainly should concern us.

This discussion shows that pollutants discharged into the air and not recycled might have feedback effects above and beyond their direct toxicologic consequences. Professionals generally agree that certain chemicals released into the air also can aggravate existing pulmonary and cardiac diseases, particularly in elderly or debilitated people. Sulfur oxides, nitrogen oxides, and ozone, all common components of urban air pollution, can destroy most of the body's normal defense mechanisms against air-borne invaders. Hence, rates of influenza and pneumonia often increase with severe air pollution levels. There is accumulating evidence to indicate that these same compounds may destroy portions of the lung, making it more difficult for oxygen to enter the bloodstream. Specific diseases, such as emphysema, bronchitis, bronchiectasis, and bronchial asthma all are thought to be worsened by urban air pollution.[17]

Pollutants that enter any of the major environmental components— air, land, or water—can have multiple feedback effects on human society and health. Pollution problems are not unique in this regard; many other types of urban phenomena can exert similar influences, both advantageous and deleterious, which we shall not have time to discuss in this volume.

It is important that we not lose sight of the fact that, although these environmental changes can have immediate direct and indirect personal health effects, such changes also involve economic tradeoffs that are invariably more complex than they appear at first glance. Thus, for example, while hundreds of thousands of acres of east coast salt marsh could be transformed into industrial centers, Virginia alone would lose a commercial fishery valued at $22 million per year.

THE TIME FACTOR: EUTROPHICATION

As the example of turbidity and albedo indicates, the environmental news reporter is faced with issues developing over prolonged time periods. The classic example is the eutrophication of Lake Erie. Generally speaking, when a lake is formed its waters are low in dissolved phosphates and nitrates. Consequently, algal populations are small, the waters are clear, adequate oxygen is present throughout all levels of the lake, and the lake is rich in game fish—trout, walleye, and pike. Because of the low concentrations of plant nutrients, the nitrates and phosphates, the lake is termed oligotrophic, from the Greek words meaning "little nutrition."

Over the course of thousands of years, rivers deposit silt and soil is leached by erosion. Consequently, the plant nutrient content increases, enabling colonies of suspended plankton and algae to grow. With time these colonies increase tremendously and the water takes on a murky green cast. Algal decay exhausts the dissolved oxygen in the water, killing off such important fish-food organisms as mayfly larvae. With the loss of primary food sources and the reduction in oxygen, consequences cascade down the food web, forcing the game fish to seek out a different environment. In their stead come the so-called coarse fish—carp, catfish, smelt, and alewives. This type of lake, with high concentrations of dissolved nitrates and phosphates, is called eutrophic, also a word of Greek origin meaning "good nutrition." With the passage of several more thousand years, this lake will pass through the distrophic stage and ultimately become land.

The entire process of birth, transition from oligotrophy to eutrophy to distrophy, and eventual death of the lake usually occurs over many thousands of years. We must remember that all organisms pollute their environment to some extent. Fish, birds, and other wildlife pass wastes into the water; aquatic organisms add chemicals and biochemicals. The effects of this pollution are minute, but they are cumulative factors in a lake's transition from oligotrophy to eutrophy. Man alters this pattern, primarily in a quantitative sense, by speeding up the sequence several orders of magnitude.

In 1953 scientists reported the sudden, virtually complete disappearance of the formerly huge mayfly populations in Lake Erie. Shortly thereafter the commercial fisheries went on the verge of bankruptcy as catches of bream and alewives replaced whitefish and trout. In the mid to late 1950s scientists reported that since 1930 algae in Lake Erie had increased thirtyfold. Between 1930 and 1960 nitrates and phosphates increased nearly tenfold. While the lake hardly could be termed "dead," it had rapidly accelerated into the eutrophic stage. By the late 1950s scientists familiar with Lake Erie were reasonably convinced that these sudden changes, wrought in a scant three decades, were a consequence of the heavy urban population concentrations around the lake.

Unfortunately, this was well before the "age of ecology." The public was much less interested in such matters and most governmental officials still were caught up in the notion that all growth was good and that smoke belching forth from factory stacks was a welcome sign of a sound economy.

Robert C. Drake, veteran science and nature writer for the Cleveland Plain Dealer, waged a one-man campaign in 1959 and 1960 to alert the public to the profound changes occurring in Lake Erie and to prod city and state governments out of their lethargy. Unfortunately, he was alone in his warnings, his voice lost in the cries of "progress" and the deadwood of bureaucracy. The emergence of the eco-activist was ten years in the future. Few people really understood what Drake was trying to tell them; he spoke too early, yet at the same time not early enough. By the time he began outlining the changes that had been thirty years in gestation, the problems were serious, with much more extensive effort required to reverse them than would have been needed to prevent them three decades earlier.

The Plain Dealer published Drake's extensive investigative effort in a magazine supplement. In the early 1960s the paper apparently did not feel that the topic warranted day-to-day treatment; rather, it received one-shot coverage. Following the 1965 Federal Water Pollution Control Administration hearings in Cleveland, which established beyond doubt that man's pollution had accelerated the eutrophication of Lake Erie, both Cleveland newspapers, the Plain Dealer and the Cleveland Press, began printing special boxed articles, with an identifying logo, several times per week. This editorial policy is still in effect; it could have been employed to advantage earlier, placing the press in the role of initiator and educator.

As we shall see from interview data with reporters in Chapter 2, the press is reluctant to perform in this capacity. It prefers to report events (or pseudo-events) of someone else's making—particularly when that someone else is government. Few editors feel it appropriate or possible to develop coverage on a problem such as the eutrophication of Lake Erie without help from government, business, and citizen groups. While Drake was alive, the Plain Dealer had a reporter with unusual scientific acumen. Had the paper modified its editorial policy in 1960 to permit regular coverage of Lake Erie, with Drake's help it would have been in the vanguard of environmental reporting. But that is now history.

THE MEDIA AND THE CALIFORNIA WATER PROJECT

During this period, another environmental story involving water resources was developing in California. This involved legislation and a public vote on a massive plan to move millions of acre-feet of water from water-rich northern California to water-poor (but people-rich) southern California. As will be made clear, the California Water Project was fraught with confusing economic arguments, political deals, conflicts of interest, secrecy, and unknown environmental consequences. Unlike the Lake Erie story, the water project was a major topic of political conversation in California, the sort of story the press usually can report in detail. Yet the complexities of the story defeated the media's best efforts at outlining the issues prior to a vote by the public on funding the project.

Even "active" environmental stories (as opposed to the "passive" Lake Erie story) create unusual problems for the press because they demand background knowledge in many fields. While the citizenry generally was more alert to environmental problems in California than in Ohio, it unfortunately had no journalistic synthesizer to clarify the issues of the state water project. Had Drake lived in Los Angeles or San Francisco, instead of Cleveland, and had a newspaper editor given him space, perhaps the legislative history of the water project might have been considerably different.

The story is a long one but worth considering for the further insight it can provide about the problems posed by technology and the difficulties in communicating technology's environmental impact to the public—issues that will shape the living conditions, and therefore the overall health and welfare, of millions of Californians.

California is a semi-arid state with a population-water supply imbalance. About 90 percent of the people live south of the San Francisco Bay Area, while 75 percent of the fresh water runoff occurs north of that region. This uneven distribution of the 190 million acre-feet of water that fall on California each year produces a similar uneven usable surface water distribution throughout the state.* About 71 million acre-feet per year become natural stream runoff, which is distributed throughout California approximately as follows (see also Figure 1.1):

	Percent of Total
North Coast and Sacramento	67.6
Central Valley	15.5
San Francisco Bay, Central and South Coast Area (including Los Angeles)	10.5
Lahonton and Colorado Deserts	6.4

When one realizes that most of the extensive agricultural areas of the state, which provide a considerable proportion of the nation's fresh fruits and vegetables, are located in the Central Valley and Central Coastal areas, the magnitude of this problem becomes clearer.

---

*An acre-foot is the amount of water necessary to cover one acre of land—roughly one football field—to a depth of one foot.

FIGURE 1

Hydrologic Study Areas
of California

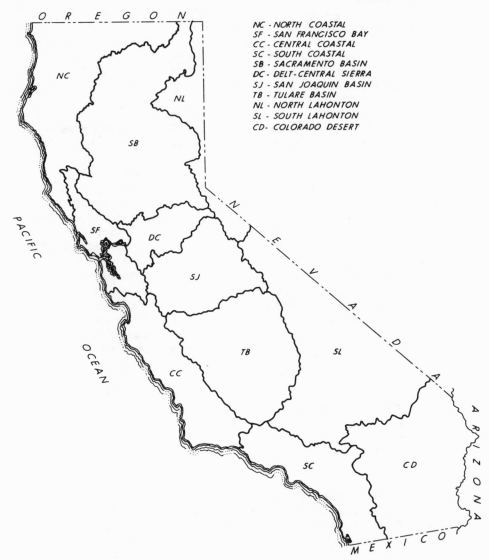

NC - NORTH COASTAL
SF - SAN FRANCISCO BAY
CC - CENTRAL COASTAL
SC - SOUTH COASTAL
SB - SACRAMENTO BASIN
DC - DELT-CENTRAL SIERRA
SJ - SAN JOAQUIN BASIN
TB - TULARE BASIN
NL - NORTH LAHONTON
SL - SOUTH LAHONTON
CD - COLORADO DESERT

Source: State of California, The Resources Agency, Department
of Water Resources, Adapted from Bulletin 160-70.

The areas that have developed the greatest need for water are those with the least available usable surface water. About 75 percent of the surface runoff occurs north of the Sacramento-San Joaquin Delta, but about 75 percent of the water demand occurs south of this delta. This imbalance between supply and demand, which is in part a function of population distribution, has led the residents of deficient areas to expend ever-increasing amounts of money to obtain adequate water supplies. As would be expected, political and legal battles over water resources within the state have been extensive and frequently very bitter.

During the early years of California's history, around the Gold Rush days, water was considered an often unavailable but basically inexhaustable resource. There was plenty of water; it need only be brought from where it existed to where it was needed. Planning tended to be short-range, and development of water projects tended to be geographically localized. This attitude continued to some extent into the early years of the twentieth century, but the increased demand for water forced a change in outlook. Water supply was becoming an expensive business, requiring a large bankroll and careful planning.

As the need for water put greater pressure on the existing usable supply, the idea of inexhaustible water resources gave way to the idea that water needed to be conserved. In 1916 the legislature sponsored a Conference on State Water Problems. This conference was followed in 1921 by an authorization for a comprehensive state-wide water resources investigation, which extended from 1921 to 1929. The results were published from time to time in twelve bulletins of the State Division of Water Resources. The planning concept developed during this time was to impound water that was "wasting" to the sea and conserve it behind man-made dams for controlled distribution to human uses through systems of aqueducts and ditches. This philosophy of water management has dominated the thinking of decision-makers to this day.

The culmination of the investigations authorized by the legislature in 1921 was Bulletin 25 of the State Division of Water Resources, published in 1930 and submitted to the legislature in 1931 as the State Water Plan. Bulletin 25 called for the full development of the Central Valley's surface waters, primarily for irrigation, at a cost of about $158 million. After more than a year of studying the proposal, the legislature submitted a referendum to the voters for a $170 million bond issue to finance the Central Valley Project and the voters approved the sale of the bonds.

The 1935 Central Valley Project

Due to the depression that hit America in the 1930s, California's Central Valley Project bonds did not sell. The state then tried to get

a loan from the federal government to build the project. When this
loan was rejected, the state acquiesced to a federal takeover of the
project. In 1935 President Roosevelt approved the Bureau of Reclamation's feasibility report for building and managing the huge Central
Valley Project.

Central Valley Project water was first delivered to San Joaquin
Valley farmers in 1944. This event was welcomed by most farmers,
but with mixed emotions. For along with federal water went federal
regulation, including a reclamation law provision known as the excess
land law, which limits each landowner to enough water to irrigate
160 acres of land. This limitation can be circumvented by various
means and has never been stringently enforced, but its very existence
made the predominantly large Central Valley agricultural interests
extremely unhappy. These interests saw the federal law not as a
measure to prevent federal subsidy through cheap water that would
unjustly enrich large landowners but as an invidious and even
"Communist-inspired" work.

Agriculture is California's number one industry even today, and
in the 1940s and early 1950s the dominant power—both economic and
political—was in the hands of large agricultural interests. Furthermore, the large agricultural and business interests in the state were
one and the same. Many of them, including the Southern Pacific
Railroad, United Fruit Company, and large banking institutions, never
gave up the notion that the Central Valley Project was basically a
state project taken over by the federal government during hard times.
Thus, when the economic outlook began to brighten in California in
the 1940s, Central Valley and business interests began to assert their
power to escape the 160-acre limitation by having the state retake
control of the Central Valley Project. Plans for the federal Bureau
of Reclamation to give the project back to California or for California
to buy the project back from the federal government were supported
by the State Chamber of Commerce, Farm Bureau, and Irrigation
Districts, and championed by State Engineer A. D. Edmonston, but
proved unworkable. An end run around the 160-acre limit was attempted by having the Corps of Engineers, which before 1944 was not
subject to the 160-acre provision, build "flood control projects" and
then deliver the water to the farmers. But the Corps of Engineers
would not be coopted, so this scheme also proved unsuccessful.
Congress plugged the loophole in 1944 by making the reclamation
laws applicable to irrigation water developed by projects of the
Corps of Engineers subject to the acreage limitation. However, the
movement to have California control its own water destiny was strong
and continued on many fronts.

In 1948 the legislature passed the Water Resources Act, putting
the state in the role of planning and managing water resources statewide.

The planning function was put in the hands of a newly-created State
Water Resources Board. In 1947 the legislature directed the State
Water Resources Board to inventory California's water resources
and needs. The results of these investigations were published in
bulletins released in 1951, 1955, and 1957.

A special report on a portion of these investigations was
financed by the California Central Flood Control Association. State
Engineer Edmonston analyzed flood control on the Feather River and
went on to describe the possibilities for using the harnessed water of
the Feather River. This work might have been prosaic. But Edmonston
had a dream to see the state take over water development in California
and he spelled out his dream in this flood control report. The report,
released in 1951, was called "Report on Feasibility of Feather River
Project and Sacramento-San Joaquin Delta Diversion Projects Proposed
as Features of the California Water Plan."

The Feather River Project

Edmonston's report had special significance because the Feather
River Project had become the latest vehicle by which California was
to escape from the clutches of the Bureau of Reclamation. State
planning was important because the bureau at the same time was sur-
veying the possibilities for further developing the northern California
waters for irrigation and delivery to southern California. The legislature authorized the project in 1951 without appropriating money
for construction. In 1955 Edmonston issued a follow-up report entitled
"Program for Financing and Constructing the Feather River Project
as the Initial Unit of the California Water Plan." The legislature
selected the Bechtel Corporation to analyze Edmonston's findings.
Bechtel reported back that the engineering was sound but that:

> The Feather River Project . . . [is] not financially feasible
> on the basis of revenue derived from water charges and
> the sale of electric power at the rates assumed in the
> report unless the federal and state governments con-
> tribute to the cost of the project funds in substantial
> amounts on the basis of statewide concern.[18]

The legislature then reauthorized the project.

From the time Edmonston's first report appeared in 1951 until
1959, the legislature moved slowly on the Feather River Project.
During this time approximately $100 million was appropriated for
studies, right-of-way acquisition, and railway and highway relocation.
However, the legislature could not pass an act to provide funding for

the project because northern and southern representatives were
deadlocked over what guarantees a project enabling act should contain
for each area.

In 1956 the State Water Resources Board passed into history as
the legislature enacted statutes creating the State Department of
Water Resources along with the California Water Commission and
the Water Rights Board. Harvey O. Banks became the first director
of the Department of Water Resources. In 1957 Bulletin No. 3 was
published by the State Department of Water Resources with the recommendation that the California Water Plan it outlined, including the
Feather River Project, be adopted as the general plan for water
development in California. The legislature did not act on the recommendations but instead called for reviews and explanations of the
proposed California Water Plan. The north-south deadlock over the
Feather River Project could not be broken.

The Burns-Porter Act

Governor Edmund G. Brown came into office with a vow to
break that deadlock. He had taken an interest in California's water
dilemma while he was state attorney general, working with and learning
from a state attorney named B. Abbott Goldberg (now a Superior Court
judge in Sacramento County). During his campaign for governor,
Brown promised that the Feather River Project would be implemented.
So important to Brown was the implementation of the Feather River
Project that he virtually staked his political life on its success.

Governor Brown made Ralph Brody, an attorney, deputy director
of the Department of Water Resources and special counsel to the
governor on water matters, and put him to work rewriting the
stymied project enabling act and formulating the strategy for getting
it through the legislature.

The governor's office also asked Harvey Banks, as head of the
Department of Water Resources, to design a feasible project that
would meet water demands within a reasonable point in time. Banks
and his department responded with a project that would take care of
projected water needs through 1985 or 1990 at a cost estimated at
$3 billion with inflation, or $2.25 billion without taking inflation into
account. These figures included funds already expended.

Banks and the Department of Water Resources felt this was a
reasonable planning period that would meet crucial water needs and
yet allow enough flexibility for adjustment to changed conditions and
technological developments in water supply to meet needs after 1985
or 1990. The governor felt the public would not pass a bond issue of
over $2 billion, so Ralph Brody designed a financing package of $1.75

billion in general obligation bonds and $500 million composed of funds already expended and miscellaneous revenue, mostly from tidelands oil funds, for a total of $2.25 billion. The governor and his planners considered inflation an insignificant and speculative problem. Financing for the project would be tight, but if everything went according to plan the miscellaneous revenues would make up the difference.

Financing of the project had been a major stumbling block in past legislatures. The north did not want to pay for the south's water. The north also wanted guarantees that the south would not get all of the north's water as Los Angeles had gotten all of the Owens Valley water in 1905. The south was not willing to pay for water unless there were guarantees that the water would be delivered. To both sides this meant constitutional guarantees. Furthermore, the state constitution limited the amount of general obligation bonds that could be issued by the legislature without approval of the electorate. A constitutional amendment had been considered the natural solution to all these problems. However, the two-thirds legislative vote required to submit a constitutional amendment to the people made any such amendment impossible. Ralph Brody sidestepped this hurdle by utilizing a constitutional provision that allowed the legislature, by majority vote, to submit bond proposals in excess of $300,000 to the electorate, which could then pass the bonds by only a majority instead of a two-thirds vote.

To help allay the fears of the northerners, the act specifically made applicable the area of origin and county of origin laws guaranteeing such areas first rights to all waters originating within their borders. For the southerners, certain works that would guarantee a firm water supply were specified, and the legislature was proscribed from tampering with the provisions of contracts between the Department of Water Resources and the buyers of water. The water bond act written by Ralph Brody truly contained something for everybody, an attribute that caused opponents to label it "pork barrel" and "a grab bag." Brody and the others who had worked on the water bond act knew it was not perfect but believed it to be the best plan obtainable given the necessity for compromise. However, they were not relying on the merits of the act alone to bring it through the state Senate and Assembly.

Governor Brown knew that neither the bill's provisions alone nor the "honeymoon period" traditional for new governors would bring the bill through. Nothing could be left to chance, or the water project would be killed for another year. So to champion the act in the legislature the Governor chose Senator Hugh Burns of Fresno and Assemblyman Carley Porter of Compton. These men together represented the two groups who would benefit most from the act: the San Joaquin farmers and the southern California city dwellers. In addition,

they had seniority and prestige and were masters at the art of legislative politics. Although they had negligible roles in drafting the act
that now bears their names, they were instrumental in winning its
passage.

Allied against Governor Brown's forces were representatives
from the areas of origin and a contingent of legislators from the
southland who joined in the Metropolitan Water District's opposition
to the Feather River Project. The Senate was weighted in favor of
the north and areas of origin while the Assembly was weighted in favor
of the water-short areas in north and south. Thus, the proponents of
the measure were confident that they could win Assembly passage if
they could only get the bill through the Senate.

There were almost as many issues surrounding the Burns-
Porter (B-P) Act as there were legislators. Proponents cited a
desperate need for water in the San Joaquin Valley and southern
California and foretold economic disaster if the project was not
built. They cited increasing overdrafts on the ground water supply
and the resulting shortage of water, land subsidence, and salt water
intrusion into the ground water supply. They pointed out that California
could lose over a million acre-feet of water annually to Arizona as a
result of the Arizona v. California lawsuit over control of Colorado
River water rights then pending before the Supreme Court. In addition
to the economic benefits to central and southern California, the project
would avert a projected water crisis in San Diego and provide flood
control benefits for northern California as well as the economic
benefits that the construction of project units would bring locally.

Opposition to the measure centered around lack of guaranteed
water rights and the huge price tag of the project. Representatives
from water-rich areas were afraid that once their water began going
south it would be lost forever, despite the area and county of origin
laws. Assemblyman Lloyd Lowrey wrote, "Water once put to use in
a foreign environment, from a practical and political viewpoint will
not be withdrawn. Once transported, water is lost to the local area."[19]
Much the same sentiment was expressed by Los Angeles Mayor Norris
Poulson, who was quoted in the Los Angeles Times of June 18, 1959,
as saying:

> I cannot see how any future State legislature could possi-
> bly alter the formula of the new water bill after its 50
> year term expires. Southern California will always be
> the population center of the state and the majority of
> lawmakers and voters alike would not and could not
> make changes damaging to this area.

Furthermore, the price of water would be based upon a "Delta Pool"
charge, computed from the costs for works in and north of the delta,

with any transportation costs added on. The delta charge would be paid by users upstream from the delta as well as users in and down-stream from the delta, and upstream users thought it ridiculous to pay for water they normally would use for nothing. This pricing mechanism prompted Assembly woman Pauline Davis to say that such a method made the area of origin laws meaningless.[20]

Representatives from water-scarce areas claimed that the Burns-Porter Act guaranteed no water rights to any water buyers, that the county and area of origin laws made other rights meaningless. The Metropolitan Water District, led by its chairman, Joe Jensen, opposed any plan that did not provide ironclad guarantees to the south. Time was on their side; economic and political power was shifting from the rural north to the heavily populated south, and in a few more years the south could get whatever it wanted without having to make any compromises for the benefit of anybody else. Several legislators identified closely with this position and opposed the Burns-Porter Act to the end.

Financing of the Feather River Project was another hunting ground for its opponents. The wisdom of building such a huge project seemed questionable when technological advances promised to make water available at less cost by the time the State Water Project was in full operation. Assemblyman Clark Bradley opposed building any conveyance works over the Tehachipi mountains on the ground that waste water reclamation could handle the needs of urban southern California more cheaply. Furthermore, the project appeared to be underfinanced, which meant that the $1.75 billion would not be adequate to complete construction of the system. Opponents contended that more money would be needed later, either from more general obligation bonds or from some other source. In the meantime, voters would be deceived into thinking that the $1.75 billion was full payment and not just a down payment on the Feather River Project.

The governor and his appointees would have final authority to authorize projects and spend the bond revenues, and many legislators felt this would be tantamount to giving the governor a blank check with no meaningful controls. Some also felt that such power would usurp the legislative function and give the governor complete control over California water development.

The 160-acre limitation, or lack thereof, played a supporting role in the battle. Some legislators felt that the Feather River Project was designed as a subsidy for large agricultural interests in the San Joaquin Valley, and they called for measures to benefit the small farmer, at least by giving him cheaper water. The chief advocates of such limitations were Assemblyman Lloyd Lowrey and Senator Virgil O'Sullivan. Interwoven with these arguments was an element of preference for federal construction of water projects.

Another point of contention was use of the Sacramento River as a "free" transportation canal at the expense of contiguous land owners. Problems were expected to arise from erosion and seepage damage occasioned by construction and operation of water projects. Assembly-man Lowrey authored legislation to make water projects responsible for any such damage.

Governor Brown's strategy was to attack the opposition in its Senate stronghold. If he could get the Feather River Project through the Senate, he felt confident of victory in the southern-dominated Assembly. Battle was first joined in the Senate when the California Water Resources Development Bond Act was introduced, as Senate Bill 1106 on March 31, 1959. The bill was introduced at the request of the governor by Hugh Burns, and 26 other senators representing counties from Humboldt to Imperial, and it looked very different from the measure that eventually won approval. In three pages SB 1106 authorized $960 million in general obligation bonds to finance con-struction and operation of units of the Central Valley Project. The bill was referred to committee where it lay until May 5, when Burns took the floor to urge the adoption of several amendments. Out went the reference to the Central Valley Project; the authorized bonds were increased to $1.75 billion; specific works were spelled out, as were the basic repayment provisions. A provision relating to the earlier "Davis-Grunsky Act" (see Stats. 1957, c. 2052, Water Code sections 12880-12893) for Assemblywoman Pauline Davis and Senator Donald Grunsky, reserving $130 million of the $1.75 billion for con-struction of local projects primarily in northern California, was inserted. The amendments were adopted and the bill went back to committee.

An interesting side note is the part that the executive branch played in the floor debates and committee discussions of SB 1106. Since neither Hugh Burns nor Carley Porter was intimately familiar with the bond act's complicated provisions, they were accompanied by Ralph Brody and Harvey Banks during the debates. Brody and Banks went right into the committees with Burns and Porter and onto the floors of both houses where they fielded questions on the Bill.

After its amendment on May 5, SB 1106 remained in committee until May 15 when it returned to the Senate floor for amendments recommended by the Water Resources Committee. The important parts of these amendments allowed money to be spent on facilities of either the Central Valley Project or the California Water Plan and guaranteed the sanctity of existing water rights legislation and vested water rights. Further amendments were adopted on May 20, May 26, and May 28, including one introduced May 28 by Senator George Miller, Jr., of Contra Costa County which deemed the Sacramento-San

Joaquin Delta a part of the Sacramento River watershed. This important amendment made the delta an "area of origin" for Sacramento
River water. It also provoked opposition to the bill from water-short
areas that were afraid delta interests would have the power to shut
off water exports if the water were ever needed within the delta. That
same day, other amendments intended to favor either north or south
were defeated, often by only two votes. On May 29 an attempt by
Senator Virgil O'Sullivan to put in a 160-acre limitation failed. But
the balance remained dead even. At this crucial moment, Governor
Brown finally persuaded one of his closest friends, Senator Eugene
McAteer of San Francisco, to vote for the bill. This vote broke the
deadlock and enabled the governor to get a few more votes. Shortly
thereafter, the Senate voted 25-12 in favor of approving SB 1106. Not
all the northern senators voted against the bill, but all who did were
northerners from water supply areas—Hugh Burns called them "mountain men" and "river rats."

Carley Porter was expected to have an easier time in the
Assembly than Hugh Burns had in the Senate, and Porter is credited
with doing a masterful job of managing the bill. It was critical that
the bill get out of the Assembly unamended so that the Senate would
not have another shot at it. This seemingly impossible task was
accomplished, with a whole spate of amendments voted down on June
17, the same day the final vote on the bill was taken. However, the
final margin of 50-30 does not reveal the spirited and often bitter
floor fight in the Assembly. Old-time northerners like Assemblyman
Lloyd Lowrey led the fight against the governor's forces, joined by
Pauline Davis, who did not like SB 1106 even with the Davis-Grunsky
provisions, and Bruce Allen, who had supported SB 1106 until it was
amended to make the delta an area of origin for the Sacramento
River. The final vote on a bill is not always a true assessment of
the fight that has gone before, because once the outcome is clear
legislators often will cast or switch their votes to come out on the
winning side. Reportedly, this is what happened with SB 1106 in the
Assembly. Commentators have attributed the 50-30 vote to a more
favorable balance for the south, masterful managing by Carley Porter,
and pressure by the governor. There are indications that the governor's
pressure may have been crucial.

With the session running well into June, the legislators were
anxious to finish up their business and adjourn. However, many
assemblymen were in favor of holding out for amendments to the
Burns-Porter Act spelling out the policy for spending the bond
revenues. The governor and proponents of the measure urged
adoption of the Burns-Porter Act as it was and promised a special
session in the fall for the specific purpose of amending it. Although
the special session was never called, this promise by the governor

during the press to adjourn may have swayed one or two skeptical
assemblymen.

According to Assemblyman Lowrey, the key factor in turning
potential victory for the opposition into victory for SB 1106 was the
timely promise of an appointment to a municipal judgeship made by
Governor Brown to George Crawford, the Republican southern California assemblyman. By Assemblyman Lowrey's account, the governor
stood to lose his bill in the Assembly. The opposition needed four
additional votes to kill SB 1106, and the key to those four votes was
George Crawford, who had indicated opposition to the bill. During
the maneuvering, Crawford told Lowrey he had been offered a judgeship in return for his support of SB 1106 and that he would support
the bill. Assemblyman Crawford's support of SB 1106 caused the
three other "swing" votes to go for the bill. The bandwagon effect
was good for six more votes to produce the final 20-vote margin.[21]

Judge Crawford takes exception to Lowrey's account and recounts
his own role in the struggle as follows:

> I consider that the success of Senate Bill 1106 was due to
> the efforts of then Assemblyman Jack Schrade and myself
> organizing votes on the floor of the Assembly. We did
> this in opposition to the attitude of the Metropolitan
> Water Authority, who had indicated that we in San Diego
> would never receive an adequate supply of water if they
> had their way. I was in favor of Senate Bill 1106 from
> the very beginning and gathered support which caused
> the success of this Bill. It is my opinion that if it had
> not been for Assemblyman Jack Schrade and myself,
> Senate Bill 1106 would have failed.[22]

Governor Brown emphatically denies that he ever offered a
judgeship on any subject in the legislature. He says, "Some assemblymen may have thought I had and I did put pressure on the legislature
of a legitimate kind."[23]

Whatever the ultimate factors were, the governor's overall
strategy paid off. SB 1106 passed by substantial, but less than two-
thirds, majorities in both houses and was signed into law by Governor
Brown on July 10, 1959. The Burns-Porter Act was ready for the
people.

Proposition 1

A provision in the Burns-Porter Act called for its submission
to the electorate in the November 1960 general election. As Proposition 1 on the ballot, the Burns-Porter Act hit the campaign trail. To

completely defuse a possible partisan campaign by the opposition, Governor Brown selected two prominent Republicans as his statewide and southern chairmen for Proposition 1. Statewide, Thomas J. Mellon, a former campaign chairman for U.S. Senator Thomas Kuchel, and in the south, Los Angeles Mayor Norris Poulson, helped map the strategy to put Proposition 1 over.

Throughout 1960 the battle over Proposition 1 was waged. Proponents of the measure predicted a million-vote margin, but realistically they must have expected a much closer fight. The press divided on the issue. Many smaller papers in the urban coastal and southern areas supported the project. The San Francisco Chronicle staged an acrimonious opposition, while the San Francisco Examiner, Sacramento Bee, and Los Angeles Times were staunchly behind the governor's water plan. Although Governor Brown still stings from the Chronicle's attacks, Thomas Mellon was pleased with the overall press support for Proposition 1.

Support also came from a wide variety of business and civic groups, including the California Savings and Loan League, Irrigation Districts Association, League of Women Voters, Farm Bureau, League of California Cities, State Chamber of Commerce, and numerous local chambers of commerce. Many city councils and county boards of supervisors, including the supervisors of San Francisco and Santa Clara counties, rallied behind Proposition 1. Labor support came from construction unions and from the powerful Teamsters.

But the opposition was formidable. The Metropolitan Water District of Los Angeles opposed the bonds until just a few days before the election. The California Federation of Labor, AFL-CIO, threw its weight against the measure. The prestigious Commonwealth Club of San Francisco and the San Francisco Chamber of Commerce came out against Proposition 1. The state's small farmers voiced their opposition through the Grange. Few doubted the scientific data collected by the Department of Water Resources on the amount of water available in California, but many doubted the department's estimate of California's water needs. Many taxpayers feared the huge bond issue, at that time the largest of its kind in the nation's history, would increase their taxes, despite assurances to the contrary by the governor. The Grange wanted no part of a project designed expressly to circumvent the 160-acre limitation. The California Federation of Labor, with the exception of some of its construction elements, saw the Feather River Project as a giveaway to landed interests in the Central Valley and opposed anything to aid those who fought against unionizing farm workers.

The campaign aroused almost as much interest as the presidential campaign between John F. Kennedy and Richard Nixon. It also was one of the most expensive campaigns on behalf of a ballot measure

in the state's history to that time. And, with all the side issues and
technical data being thrown around, it was confusing. The San Francisco Chronicle wrote on April 29, "People Face Blind Vote on Water."
A field poll taken in July revealed that voters favoring the proposition
were most concerned about the need to meet the demand for more
water while those opposed thought the water supply was adequate and
were afraid the Feather River Project would raise taxes.[24]

The confusion was compounded when the reports of two independent consultant firms, Dillon, Read and Co. of New York and Charles
T. Main of Boston, hired by the governor to review the Feather River
Project, were released simultaneously on October 27. Both found the
engineering of the Feather River Project sound, but both questioned
the financial integrity of the project. They suggested delaying certain
capital expenditures—in particular the Oroville Dam—for up to twenty
years. The Los Angeles Times reported, "Feather River Project
Gets Sound Rating in Two Reports." The San Francisco Chronicle
wrote, "State Water Plan Called Impossible." During the campaign
Harvey Banks submitted his resignation as director of the Department
of Water Resources, effective January 1961. A few days before the
election, 53 economists, engineers, and professors from leading California universities issued a ten-point warning about the engineering
and financial shortcomings of the project. Only six days before the
election, the Metropolitan Water District reversed its strong opposition
and voted to support Proposition 1. The average voter must have been
hopelessly confused.

On November 8 the voters made their decision. By a 180,000
vote majority, Proposition 1 carried. The vote was clearly along
north-south lines, indicating that all the sophisticated arguments may
not have meant much in the end. It probably is not too far from the
truth to say that the fear of thirst in the south simply overcame the
fear of the south in the north and carried the Feather River Project
to victory on November 8, 1960.

It may never be possible to tell conclusively whether the legislature and the voters made a wise decision in approving the Burns-
Porter Act, making possible construction of the Feather River Project.
The decision was consistent with California history. However, the
complex environmental and economic issues were never adequately
explored and discussed in the mass media. The voters almost certainly were unaware of the future consequences of their collective
decision.

Without any question the press performed inadequately on nearly
all counts: as watchdog over the political maneuverings in Sacramento,
as adversary to governmental figures, and as analyst and interpreter
of environmental and technical issues pertinent to California's health
and welfare. The California press has yet to present most of the
details in the preceding discussion of the water project.

BUSINESS AND THE MEDIA

The story related above had and continues to have considerable economic impact on California. Press coverage was made difficult not only by the problems inherent in science writing (particularly the long gestation period and the lack of concrete news pegs) but also by difficulty in access to information from the private business community (in this case agribusiness), which stood to benefit from the project. The environmental news writer is as much a business news writer as a science writer or political reporter since the decisions of private business materially affect the quality of the environment.

The business pages of a daily newspaper usually are not among the stronger sections. There is rather general approval of the business reporting by the Wall Street Journal, Barron's, Forbes, and similar specialized publications. But these are national in scope and cannot report the workings of each metropolitan business community. This is a job for the daily, local press.

Because of the increasing number of individual shareholders in the United States, the demand for business news—particularly stock tables and investment news—has increased substantially since 1960, and in many newspapers business news has more than doubled. Readership studies indicate that about half of all male and a quarter of all female newspaper readers at least look at the financial pages. The type of business news they are likely to receive is summed up by Roy M. Fisher, former Chicago Daily News editor and now Dean of the School of Journalism at the University of Missouri: "We profile Chicago companies in depth. We look for rising businessmen and heads of lesser-known companies who have interesting backgrounds. We watch for shifts in management and management policies of local concerns."[25]

Unfortunately, the business page often becomes a dump for material with no other specific spot in the paper. As Don Teverbaugh, business editor of the St. Petersburg Times, points out:

> The so-called business beat is almost never clearly de-
> fined. Not for the publisher, the editor, the city editor
> or the business writer. The business page in small city
> dailies tends to become sort of a Sargasso Sea into which
> drifts all of the news debris which cannot otherwise be
> classified. Real estate, construction, home building,
> deeds, mortgages, bankruptcies, new legal or medical
> practices being set up, scholarships being offered by
> business firms, fund drives led by business leaders,
> the mobile TB unit schedule, shopping center promo-
> tions and sales—you name it.[26]

Part of the reason for this lack of focus is summed up by the editor of a Florida metro paper:

There is an alarming lack of co-operation and understanding of the importance of business news on the part
of regular cityside editors.
Often business stories are thrown into gaps on
page one of the news section with little regard for news
value, and other, seemingly more important, stories from
the business community are relegated to back pages.[27]

As complicated as the business beat is—or could be—little effort has gone into training business reporters. The financial beat (or "fin") is viewed by other reporters with a great deal of scorn. Alexander Auerbach, a young financial reporter for the Boston Globe, writes, "Friends on the general news side of the Globe and other papers would ask me how I liked 'fin' with the inflection of cautious sympathy. To them the fin department was as exciting as the obituary desk, and as desirable."[28] Such attitudes keep the best reporting talent out of business reporting, and the department often is a dead-end for tired hands.

To further complicate matters, it seems that the business reporter is under more pressure from advertisers to write stories from a prescribed viewpoint than are reporters in other departments. In response to a questionnaire mailed to 162 business and financial editors around the country, 22.6 percent of those answering indicated that as a matter of routine "they were compelled to puff up or alter and downgrade business stories at the request of the advertisers." Said one New York state newspaper executive, "One of my biggest problems is finding time to write captions for all the puff photos that are 'must' from the Ad Department." And a New England editor reported that his copy is censored by the advertising department before it goes into the business section.[29]

There is evidence that the average business executive is a difficult, close-mouthed, irascible news source who has little com-prehension of the meaning of a free press in a democratic society and who believes the press can best be dealt with by his public relations men.

Don Teverbaugh notes, "The businessman's only contact with the press, in most cases, has been with the advertising salesman. Here, the businessman gets what he wants simply by buying it. He is frequently stunned to learn this technique doesn't work when it comes to news."[30] R. K. T. Larson, honorary chairman of the Society of American Business Writers, concurs, adding that whenever a reporter asks a probing question of an officer of a big corporation there is a feeling that the information is none of his business—that the press is the enemy.[31]

Clearly, the average business page is not a promising place to seek quality coverage of public utilities, the nuclear power dilemma, land development, water resource, or other environmental problems. The level of reporting often is low; the section is oriented toward investment news, puff (an uncritical story designed to flatter the news source and local promotions, rather than reporting on the hard corporate decisions that shape a community's growth; the pressures are great; and the business community's attitude toward the press is archaic and heavy-handed.

Jerome K. Full, information services director for Eastern Airlines, reflects on these problems and offers a prescription of great importance to improving the relationship between the press and the business community:

> In my judgement, journalism as practiced in this country is sorely deficient in covering the dominant influence in most people's lives: business enterprise, which provides 83 percent of our civilian employment and 77 percent of our products and services.
>
> I readily acknowledge that most media do the requisite job in covering the security markets, the swings in our economy. Newspapers record the promotions, corporate mergers, the plant openings, the commercial births and deaths.
>
> But the news media do not, generally, concern themselves with the public substance of a corporation. They will not offend the most craven or vicious enterprise nor encourage, for fear of committing the heresy of commercialism, the most socially responsive.
>
> Business can provide useful and high quality services and products; create meaningful employment for people long denied opportunity; it can commission great architecture and fine arts; it may support many conservative social activities. Or it may want only to pollute our environment; deny all social responsibilities; alienate its employees and spew out worthless and fraudulent merchandise.
>
> But you'd never know the difference by reading the newspaper, listening to radio, watching tv. The most critical stories about business appear in the journals most dedicated and—one would assume—favorably inclined to business: the Wall Street Journal, Fortune and Business Week. . . .

Business should be covered like local government:
fairly, intelligently, by capable, well educated—and, may
I add, well paid—reporters.[32]

GOALS

In 1947 Robert M. Hutchins, then chancellor of the University
of Chicago, headed the Commission on Freedom of the Press. This
commission, organized by publisher Henry R. Luce and the Encyclo-
paedia Britannica, was composed primarily of academicians. In its
summary report, A Free and Responsible Press, the Hutchins Commission made five demands of the press that are highly relevant to our
discussion regarding science and public affairs:

1. A truthful, comprehensive, and intelligent account
of the day's events in a context that gives them meaning.
2. A forum for the exchange of comment and
criticism.
3. The projection of a representative picture of
the constituent groups in the society.
4. The presentation and clarification of the goals
and values of the society.
5. Full access to the day's intelligence.[33]

We have seen that achieving these goals in scientific and environmental reporting is no easy matter. Robert Drake tried to do it for
Lake Erie but was unsuccessful. Since he frequently lacked news
pegs and flashy headlines, Cleveland editors would not give him the
regular space the issue deserved; not only had Lake Erie's eutrophication been developing for over 30 years but the public had little
interest in such matters in 1959. In California, because of the media's
limited access to information and apparent disinterest or inability to
fully explicate the State Water Project, the public was unable to com-
prehend the statewide impact of such a development, much less
appreciate the goals and values implicit in it.

Throughout this study, the strengths and weaknesses of the
mass media in carrying out the Hutchins Commission's five points,
as applied to environmental reporting, will become clearer. Specific
contexts give events meaning, and this usually requires a set of
standards against which to evaluate the events.

One point that should become evident is the absence of absolute
biological criteria to assess environmental degradation. It is easy
to assess environmental change since this is the only real constant
in the biological world. Degradation, however, is a concept that has

meaning only within the context of human culture and values. Consequently, the ill-prepared reporter will have difficulty in distinguishing
between acceptable environmental change and environmental damage
or in attempting to evaluate the rupture of life support chains or to
recognize incipient health hazards. These problems require more
than the clipped, superficial approach of the deadline-weary reporter;
they require reportorial and editorial insight into the biological sciences.

The point man in environmental news coverage is the reporter.
Any assessment of the quality of coverage must begin with him (or
her). An enthusiastic reporter can overcome newsroom inertia and
help guarantee that certain stories are given priority by editors.
The reporter with a good reputation and familiar byline becomes a
magnet for environmental information in his community and can
stimulate debate on local problems. Such a reporter often can single-
handedly turn around a news organization's performance on this
subject. He often decides which stories to cover, what facts to include,
and which spokesmen to interview. He and his editor are the key
gatekeepers in the transmission of environmental news to the public.

Among our most important tasks, therefore, was an effort to
describe a meta-ethic for Bay Area environmental reporters. Who
are these reporters? What are their backgrounds? How do they
define their environmental beat? How do they rate their own
performance?

Material for this chapter was prepared by Rae Goodell and
Peter M. Sandman. Ms. Goodell, a former Peace Corps volunteer in
Afghanistan, has worked for the Claremont (California) Courier and
intends to become an environmental news writer. She currently is
completing work on her doctorate at the Department of Communication,
Stanford University. Mr. Sandman received his Ph.D. from the Stanford Department of Communication in 1971 and presently is on the
faculty at the University of Michigan where he heads a new program
in environmental communications within the School of Natural Resources. He is a freelance writer and coauthor of an introductory text
on the mass media.

To answer these questions we first surveyed, by mail, selected reporters and editors at every daily newspaper in the nine-county area, every radio and television station with an independent news-gathering operation, and certain weekly and monthly newspapers. The response rate to this survey, following an explanatory cover letter and two questionnaire mailings, was 80 percent.

In additon, to determine what sorts of pressures affect these reporters in their day-to-day work (and to aid our planning of further studies) we interviewed 14 selected environmental reporters in greater detail.

Survey results are presented first. (Survey methodology plus copies of the questionnaires sent to editors and reporters, with marginals filled in, appear in Appendix A.) The reporters' comments on pressures and obstacles to high-quality environmental coverage are presented in the second half of this chapter.

SURVEY OF ENVIRONMENTAL REPORTERS

In the Bay Area there are 40 reporters, representing nearly two-thirds of the daily news media, who regularly devote some of their time to environmental subjects. Slightly less than half of them fall into a "high" group—those who spend 26 percent or more of their time in covering the environment. In general, it is the reporter in this high group who views himself as having an environment beat.

Table 2.1 presents a list of environment reporters in the Bay Area (accurate as of September 10, 1971). It corresponds roughly to the "high" group of reporters. It also includes two separate notations: (1) science reporters who actively cover environment and (2) general assignment reporters who cover environment less than 25 percent of the time but who can nonetheless be considered to have an environment beat by virtue of their attitudes, and their editors' attitudes, toward their jobs.

Broadcasting is poorly represented. There are no radio stations on the main list, and such top-rated radio stations as KNBR, KFRC, KPFA, KSFO, and KGO are missing altogether. Although the commercial VHF television stations all say they have environment reporters, only Peter Giddings of KGO-TV qualifies for the list.

The major metropolitan dailies are all included on the list, and weeklies and monthlies are proportionately well-represented. The medium-sized dailies with circulation of about 30,000 to 50,000 are notably absent. Only one of these papers in the Bay Area, the San Rafael Independent-Journal, has an environment reporter. The Santa Rosa Press-Democrat, San Mateo Times, Richmond Independent, and Hayward Review have no reporter who qualifies.

TABLE 2.1

Environment Reporters in the Bay Area

Reporter	Editor	Organization	Type	Circulation or Ownerships
Selina Bendix	M. H. Segal	Richmond Freedom News	monthly	7,500
Ken Castle	Ralph Fairchild	Fremont Argus	daily	8,413
Al Cline	Gale Cook	San Francisco Examiner	daily	203,026
George Dusheck	Mel Wax	KQED	TV	VHE, educational
Fred Garretson	Roy Grimm	Oakland Tribune	daily	207,609
Peter Giddings	Pat Polillo	KGO	TV	ABC-owned
Harold Gilliam	Richard Demorest	"This World," Sunday Chronicle magazine	weekly	681,730
Tom Harris	Ben Hitt	San Jose Mercury and News	daily	211,552
John Hart	Stephan McNamara	Pacific Sun	weekly	11,533
Bob Jones	Bruce Brugmann	San Francisco Bay Guardian	monthly	20,000
Michael Lucas	Ken Brown	Fairfield Daily Republic	daily	11,442
Paul Peterzell	Bob Strebeigh	San Rafael Independent-Journal	daily	41,002
Justin Roberts	Richard Davis	Contra Costa Times and Green Sheet	daily	27,925
Scott Thurber	Abe Mellinkoff	San Francisco Chronicle	daily	478,704

Science reporters active in covering environment:

Reporter	Editor	Organization	Type	Circulation or Ownerships
David Perlman	Abe Mellinkoff	San Francisco Chronicle	daily	478,704
Ken Rowe	Dennis Anderson	Redwood City Tribune	daily	20,826

General reporters active in covering environment,
  less than 25% of time:

Reporter	Editor	Organization	Type	Circulation or Ownerships
Andy Gollan	John Jordan	San Francisco Progress	twice-weekly	193,923
Peter Laufer	Dave McQueen	KSAN	radio	FM
Luckii Ludwig	John T. Webb	Antioch Ledger	daily	10,009
Bill Lynch	Robert Lynch	Sonoma Index-Tribune	weekly	6,408
Heidi Schulman	Jim Simon	KCBS	radio	CBS-owned, all news
Jay Thorwaldson	Robert Burgess	Palo Alto Times	daily	45,171

The reporters listed in Table 2.1 do not differ statistically from the rest of the respondents (who did not qualify for the list) in their opinions. The one striking difference is that those in the high group tend to have a higher level of education, with a greater proportion having attended graduate school. And, as would be expected, fewer of those in the high group have general assignment beats; they are more likely to be specialists.

Two points stand out about environment reporters as a whole. First, over half were made environmental reporters in the previous year (1970) after it became apparent that environment was a major news issue. This seems to support the newsmen's own feeling that the media follow, rather than lead, public opinion.

Second, almost all the environment reporters came from within; they were not hired from outside specifically for the job. Typically, each of them covered more and more environment stories on his old beat until a new environment beat was established. In almost half the cases, the beat grew out of a political beat—regional, city, or state government—that included meetings of such agencies as the Bay Area Air Pollution Control District.

In few cases has an environment beat developed from a science beat. Only 14 percent of the reporters had covered science beats; only 9 percent had been science majors. George Dusheck of KQED-TV says he flunked physics. Environment reporting seems to have attracted people with an interest in the workings of government and sometimes in the great outdoors but seldom in science and technology per se. As a result, coverage might be expected to emphasize governmental decisions about the environment more than technical and scientific aspects of the problems.

News media without environmental specialists usually imply they do not need one—there are not enough local stories to justify a specialist or the subject can be handled as well by general assignment reporters. They do not feel the environment warrants a separate beat, either because it is not sufficiently important or because it is not a separate specialized topic that lends itself to a single beat. Their lack of a special reporter may reflect a philosophy about specialization, not a lack of commitment to ecology.

The impression that these organizations do not feel a specialist is necessary is strengthened by the fact that two-thirds of them claim they cannot afford one. If a specialist were considered sufficiently important, a way could be found around the budget problem. Almost all the organizations with a specialist simply have added environment to the reporter's load or substituted environment for other beats. The only organization that hired someone from outside specifically for the job is the Pacific Sun, a weekly newspaper in Marin County. (The monthly Richmond Freedom News also acquired someone from outside, but its staff is all volunteer.)

TABLE 2.2

Reporters' Sources of Environmental Information

Source	Number of Times Mentioned
Conservation groups and spokesmen*	24
Newspapers	24
Magazines	24
Own field work*	21
Conservation publications	20
Government agency releases	18
Government spokesmen*	17
Seminars, institutes, and conventions*	16
University news releases	16
University professors	16
Industry spokesmen*	16
Industry news releases	12
Scientific journals*	10
University task force reports	9
Government task force reports	8
Television	8
Industry task force reports	6
Radio	6

Note: A total of 33 reporters responded to the questionnaire.

*Sources mentioned significantly more (p .05) by reporters spending more than 25 percent of their time on environment.

Significantly more of the reporters in the high group are employed by newspapers than by broadcast stations. Although broadcast organizations claim to have as many specialists as newspapers do, the reporters they name as specialists spend less time on the environment than their newspaper counterparts.

As Table 2.2 indicates, environmental reporters seldom use the broadcast media as news sources. Almost three-quarters use newspapers and magazines frequently, but less than one-quarter use TV and radio. The use of newspapers is as high among newspaper reporters as among broadcasters, suggesting not only a dependence of broadcasting on newspaper stories but also a dependence of newspapers on one another. A few reporters point out this "round-robin" effect. The San Jose paper picks up leads from the Oakland paper, according to Oakland Tribune reporter Fred Garretson, San Francisco gets them from San Jose, and the Associated Press picks them up only when they reach San Francisco. If this is true, a few key newspapers are doing most of the gatekeeping for the Bay Area wire services and the media dependent on them.

The environmental reporters in the Bay Area generally are not active conservationists, and sometimes they are proud of this. But many do rely heavily on the conservationists for environmental information. Almost three-quarters of the group use conservation organizations and spokesmen frequently, and nearly two-thirds use such conservation publications as the Sierra Club Bulletin, Cry California, Environment, Conservation News, and the publications of the Audubon Society and the Planning and Conservation League. Although industry public relations men supply newsmen with as much or more material than do conservationists, the reporters apparently give more credence to the conservationists. Reporters give the impression that they tend to ignore news releases, as Table 2.2 suggests.

A number of reporters complain of being deluged with too much information, with George Dusheck specifically castigating the conservationists. He says he is overrun with ecology stories and most go in the wastebasket. Dusheck maintains that ecology action groups are "spurious" because they are concerned with political reform, not with saving the environment. He says, "It is not advertisers or political interests that pressure me, but militant environmentalists trying to sell me their pet project."

In contrast, some newsmen think the persistent propaganda of such groups as the Sierra Club may have had something to do with creating the environment issue in the media, with the conservationists serving as the catalyst in the information explosion. "Conservationists, who had been vocal all along, increased their warning and were joined by large numbers of young people and concerned consumers," says Jim Simon, former KCBS news director.

In contrast to their involvement with conservationists on the job, few of the reporters are active in conservation or ecology groups outside the job. "I am not," declares Tom Harris of the San Jose Mercury and News, "and I feel I would destroy my objectivity by so joining. It is imperative that I, and others, maintain a stance combining interest with independence to guard against prejudicing approaches and stories." Editors sometimes agree. Ralph Fairchild of the Fremont Argus says, "I believe seriously it is poor editorial policy to try to wear two hats—one as editor and one as a participant in an organization. It is pretty damn difficult to castigate your own organization for indifference, incompetence, or anything else when you belong

to it." If an environment reporter or his editor does belong to a
conservation group, it usually is the Sierra Club, Save the Bay,
California Tomorrow, or the Audubon Society.

With so much agreement on background and attitude, do the
environment reporters also agree on just what they are covering—are
they all talking about the same thing? In an article in the August
1970 Quill David Hendin, news editor for Enterprise Science Service,
gave a definition of environment reporting that almost could be a
composite of Bay Area newsmen's definitions. Hendin said:

> When one thinks about it, it's curious phrase. Is there
> any reporting that isn't environmental reporting?
> Politics is part of the environment. Education is part
> of the environment. Sports are part of the environment,
> and the pollution of air and water are certainly parts
> of the environment.
>
> The environment is the world people live in, and
> ecology is the relationship of living things—men, animals
> and plants—with their environment. When one discusses
> environmental reporting, I suspect he really means
> reporting on the deterioration of ecological relation-
> ships, the upsetting of the ever-so-delicate balance of
> nature.

Definitions of the environment by Bay Area newsmen range from
"reporting on physical resources" to "everything." Seven newsmen
restrict their definitions, as Hendin does, to the negative aspects:
threats, pollution, deterioration in the environment. For example,
Andy Gollan of the San Francisco Progress defines environment
reporting as "identifying the politicians, developers, business interests,
union chieftains, and media corporations involved in a destructive
act or practice."

Over a third of the reporters restrict their definitions even
further than Hendin, limiting environmental reporting to coverage
of physical resources—"air, water, land." Nearly half would concentrate on man: threats to man caused by pollution or threats by
man to the environment.

Clearly, there is some confusion about the terms ecology and
environment, with one reporter defining the latter as "stories affecting
the ecology." Even Hendin might better have said that ecology is the
study of the relationship of living things. Two reporters distinguish
between ecology and environmental reporting, calling ecology a
narrower term dealing with interrelationships. Nearly one-fourth
express their definitions in terms of relationships between living
things or between man and nature, without mentioning the word ecology.

TABLE 2.3

Reporters' Definitions of Environment Reporting

Subject	Hypothetical Story	Percentage of Newsmen Considering It Environmental
Smog	Increases in pulmonary disease in the Bay Area are traced to a common element in smog.	97
Airport noise	A citizen group is formed to protest airplane noise from a nearby airport.	97
Sewage disposal	A sewage recycling plant is set up in a neighboring town.	95
Ocean pollution	Scientists report that shellfish are losing their shells in coastal areas with high levels of nitrogen fertilizers.	93
Population	A University of California research team projects smaller increases in population than were previously supposed.	86
Zoning	A city zoning change is proposed on the local ballot such that a large residential area near downtown can be converted to commercial use.	77
Power shortage	Power shortages like the New York "brownouts" are predicted for the Bay Area by next summer.	72
Rapid transit	A section of underground rapid transit is opened for public use.	53
Birth control	An increase in the popularity of IUD birth control devices among American women is reported.	52
Cyclamates	A sugar substitutes similar to cyclamates is linked to cancer in dogs.	35
Tidal wave	A tidal wave is predicted for the Peninsula coast line.	28
Busing	A bill is passed prohibiting busing of school children.	12
Heart transplant	A new heart transplant is performed at Stanford Hospital.	9

A further idea of the range in newsmen's use of the term environmental reporting comes from their responses when asked whether they would consider each of a series of hypothetical news stories to be "environment" stories (see Table 2.3). Noise pollution turns out to be as standard an environment story for the newsmen as water or air pollution. And population ranks almost as high, although birth control does not. That cyclamates, tidal waves, busing, and heart transplants are considered environmental stories by some reporters again shows the wide range of their definitions.

There is a difference of opinion among Bay Area environment reporters as to just what caused the media's increased coverage of environment in recent years. Almost half feel that the media simply were responding to public demand for more environment news. A reporter for one major newspaper says, "The media's increased coverage stems from increased public interest. We follow the crowd, always have. That may not be the way it should be, but that is how it is."

Another quarter of the newsmen attribute the increase to stories about the environment becoming "newsworthy-good copy." They cite statements by President Nixon and other government officials, dramatic events like the Santa Barbara oil spill and campus demonstrations, startling speakers like Paul Ehrlich, and magazine "scare" articles.

In general, the reporters do not view themselves as opinion leaders or watchdogs on environmental issues. Only one-eighth say the media in any sense are leaders in the development of the issue, while another eighth express a togetherness—everyone including newsmen became aware of the pollution threat at once. Table 2.4 shows the frequency with which various causes of the environmental information explosion are mentioned.

The environment issue exploded, according to one reporter, because "our lives depend on it," but he also feels it is a fad. A few others are equally pessimistic. They feel that the issue will continue to be important but that media treatment will die out. Ben Williams of KPIX television says, "This is a crisis-orientated society and unhappily the media are also crisis-oriented." Only one newsman, George Whitesell of the San Mateo Times, would welcome such a decrease in coverage, presumably indicating that in his opinion current attention to the environment is not justified.

A much more common view is that the environment will continue to be an important issue in the media; coverage may be faddish in that this is a sudden, new, exciting subject, but the underlying issues will endure and with them their coverage. In fact, most Bay Area media give the impression that they are settling down to include environment as a permanent part of their news coverage.

TABLE 2.4

Causes of Increased Media Coverage of Environment,
as Seen by Reporters

Cause		Number of Times Mentioned
Response to public demand, reader interest		36
Existence of pollution itself		19
Newsworthy events		19
Speeches by Paul Ehrlich, etc.	8	
Speeches by public officials	3	
Oil spills	2	
Campus activities	2	
Pollution itself made news	4	
Media took the initiative		9
Response to conservationists' demands, activities		6

Thus, there are some striking features of environmental reporting in the Bay Area. For one thing, an impressive number of daily
and weekly newspapers are making a partial or full-time commitment
to covering the subject while a less impressive number of broadcast
journalists are making the environment a regular news beat and
important subject. The only stations making the effort are an educational television station, an underground FM station, and an all-news
station; perhaps it is too much to expect other types of stations to do
the same.

Economics is the major problem in increasing the number of
environment reporters. Almost all of them already were on the
payroll, which means that other areas of coverage are paying for the
environmental information explosion.

Environment reporters rely heavily on the thoughts and writings
of conservationists, a large and active group in the Bay Area. In
fact, a few reporters credit the rise in interest in the environment to
the conservationists' activities and demands.

Only a few reporters think the media took the initiative in covering
environment. They see themselves as largely responding to the
public request for information rather than acting as educators or
shapers of events.

PRESSURES ON ENVIRONMENTAL REPORTERS

At the heart of the American system of mass communications is the advertiser, and advertisers frequently tend to be polluters as well. So it is not surprising to find advertiser pressure cited as one of a dozen or so obstacles to improving the quality of environmental coverage.

A few reporters contributed examples of this sort of pressure on environmental coverage. One environmental reporter on a Bay Area paper recalls that soon after the start of the Chevron F-310 advertising campaign he attended a respiratory disease convention in San Francisco. Several of the participants, including a Riverside County health official, were highly critical of the new gasoline additive. The reporter wrote the story as a sidebar to the convention. He said:

> The city editor at the time held the story for several days. I questioned him about [it] and he finally red-lined [banned] it with the astounding comment: "Oh, hell. This isn't all that pertinent, and the firm has a big advertising campaign with us now. Maybe later." I have done some intensive research on my own on that score and have determined that it was his own second-guessing of management's desires rather than any kind of order from above that prompted his decision.

Sometimes the pressure does come from top management. A news editor of a San Francisco radio station was on the desk when California State Assemblyman Ken Meade introduced a bill prohibiting advertising by public utilities, and the story was run promptly. Shortly thereafter, the editor received a telephone call from the station's general manager who asked whether the editor had attempted to get "the other side of the story" and provided the names of several local utility public relations men. The editor comments, "It is always fair to ask whether both sides of any story have been covered, but I'm pretty sure this is the first time the general manager has called when I've been on the desk."

However, most reporters were peculiarly ambivalent about advertiser-inspired pressure. They admitted the generality of the phenomenon but denied its application to themselves. Peter Giddings of KGO-TV expressed the majority view: "In a free enterprise system, the media have got to make money, especially television. You can't sell Reynolds Aluminum and ecology show dealing with why Reynolds Aluminum doesn't recycle its cans. But nobody tells me to go easy."

Similar comments came from the print media. Paul Peterzell of the San Rafael Independent-Journal said, "I know of no successful pressure by any advertiser on any story in the I-J. . . . My friends on other newspapers tell me, however, that my experience may be unique." Lee Juillerat of the Fremont News-Register added, "Charges that the media often protect their advertisers are well-founded. . . . Actually, however, it does not constitute a serious problem at the News-Register."

Most environment reporters can describe "touchy" stories they wrote that finally were printed or broadcast. What is most interesting about these descriptions, however, is that they do not revolve around the absence of pressure but, rather, pressure successfully withstood. It is difficult to find an example of a "touchy" story that was printed or broadcast without such pressure. One may therefore surmise that many such stories are never written because of the probability that they would be published, if at all, only after intense debate. As David Perlman of the San Francisco Chronicle puts it, "Certainly there is no encouragement from the top to write that kind of story. The result is inertia at the bottom."

The interests of advertisers are central to the stated or unstated policy of every mass medium, but there are other interests to be protected as well. Kenneth J. Rowe of the Redwood City Tribune, for example, notes that his publisher is convinced the future economic viability of the newspaper will depend on circulation in the huge new Redwood Shores subdivision. Rowe himself believes the subdivision is "environmentally indefensible," as do many area conservation groups and government agencies. He says, "The pressure has come from the circulation department, not to run too many stories about what's wrong with the development." He says he is able to withstand the pressure "when there's a hard news peg to hang the story on."

And George Dusheck of noncommercial KQED-TV asks, "Why don't you ask me how we'd handle stories unfavorable to the Ford Foundation? (The Ford Foundation provides funds for KQED's "Newsroom" program on which Dusbeck was a reporter.) My first-order answer is, I'm curious to see that myself."

Pressure from top management and the reporter's expectation of such pressure are important contributors to inadequacies in environmental news coverage. But they are by no means the only factors involved. The availability of information also is an important consideration.

A major source of environmental news is government. Implicit in this fact is the likelihood that only the most extreme cases of environmental irresponsibility will be publicized, and then only after the damage has been done and all attempts at negotiation have failed. This is not inevitable, of course. Some government agencies are more willing to name names and most seem to be steadily improving in this regard. Nonetheless, it seems unlikely that certain kinds of information will be forthcoming from government sources. Comparisons between environmental advertising and environmental reality are one very important example. And Bob Yeager of the Napa Register points out, "I have often noticed the apparent reticence of government agencies to disclose the names of offending corporations."

Academic and conservation groups are more promising sources of indictments of specific businesses. But they are not as promising as might be expected initially. For example, Mary Jefferds of the National Audubon Society claims she is very careful not to name any companies in her press releases, tending to discuss problems and proposals in more general terms. She says a group's bargaining position with industry is adversely affected by the naming of names, citing as evidence "the Sierra Club's difficulty in discussing alternatives with Standard Oil now that they have openly announced their differences about the gasoline additive." Like governments, pressure groups often prefer to negotiate in secret.

Moreover, reporters may tend to distrust and discount the pronouncements of conservationists. Most of them receive huge quantities of material from conservationists, and nearly all read what they receive. But they do not necessarily trust it. Several criticisms of F-310 were available before the Federal Trade Commission announced its opposition to the additive. But according to Rowe, "The FTC is a source. The Friends of the Earth is a rumor." Lists of detergent phosphate content by brand were in circulation as early as September 1969. Perlman remembers receiving such a list: "I showed it around the office and we posted it on the bulletin board. But we didn't print it until the Interior Department released the figures"—eight months later:

Tom Harris of the San Jose Mercury recalls another instance:

> In October the San Francisco Clean Water Association
> came to me with samples of raspberries and copies of
> a lab report from a private Menlo Park firm, stating
> there were considerably heavy concentrations of fluorides
> therein. Knowing the ingrained bias of the people, I
> kept the basket, thanked them for their trouble and began
> an intensive cross-study of the sources myself. Finally,
> I pressured the Department of Agriculture to do a series
> of immediate tests to see if they could either duplicate
> or not similar levels.

When the Department of Agriculture released its findings, Harris was one of many reporters who covered the story. He preferred a government press release to a conservationist scoop.

Justin Roberts of the Contra Costa <u>Sun</u> writes, "The environmental problems are too serious and far-reaching to allow them to be taken over by public relations whiz-boys whose motives are clearly apparent." He is not referring to corporate flacks but to conservation groups.

Critical information about the environmental impact of specific products, services, companies, and advertisements is likely to reach the mass media only through conservation groups. Reporters frequently distrust the groups and therefore discount the information. There is another source available: the media <u>could</u> generate their own information. But there is a third major barrier to effective environmental news: the demand for a hard news peg.

In the survey of Bay Area editors and environment reporters discussed at the beginning of this chapter, the following hypothetical situation was posed: "A canning factory proposes to move into your area, and no one has brought up the possibility that the factory might pollute nearby waters. Would you investigate the pollution possibility?" A total of 73 percent of the reporters and 76 percent of the editors said they would. These are impressive figures, but they are probably wishful thinking on the part of the respondents. Not one of the 14 newsmen contacted by this researcher was able to cite a single instance in which he actually had looked into the pollution potential of a new industry without a public controversy to spur his interest.

And of those who said they would investigate the story, more than a third volunteered the additional information that they probably would not publish their findings as is. Fred Garretson of the Oakland <u>Tribune</u> was one of several reporters who noted that he would "turn it over to the Regional Water Quality Control Board and then do a story that the situation is being investigated." Not only do many reporters prefer a government source to a conservationist source but they also prefer a government source to enterprising reporting.

The need for a hard news peg and the pressure to be kind to advertisers are mutually reinforcing phenomena. Thus, several reporters commented that the facts of a story must be "nailed down" much more completely if the story is likely to embarrass an advertiser. Perlman said, "When the Federal Trade Commission got after Standard Oil and F-310, then I was free to get after them too. Until then, there just wasn't enough to hang the story on."

The F-310 advertising campaign and the hypothetical new factory both are events that require enterprising reporting for adequate coverage. But at least they are events. In order to counter the effects of environmental advertising, a reporter would have to "cover" a large number of non-events. And reporters are extremely reluctant to do this.

Consider, for example, the issue of recycling. The issue is raised by several varieties of advertising: ads that boast of recycling programs, ads that boast of no-deposit no-return containers, and ads (whatever they boast of) for products whose containers are un- recycled or unrecyclable. To correct the environmental misimpres- sions created by these advertisements, a news story should address itself to such questions as the following: How many containers are collected in corporate recycling programs, and how many are left uncollected? Which manufacturers do not recycle their containers, and why not? What kinds of containers cannot be recycled, and what happens to them?

These questions all have one common characteristic: they are not keyed to any news event. Plans for a new factory are announced on a specific day. Advertisements for a new product are introduced on a specific day. Something happens that a reporter with initiative can cover. But how does the reporter cover something that fails to happen or something that has always happened?

He doesn't. Harris puts it this way:

> We are not a feature magazine, or technical trade journal.
> We are a daily source of current news, and even though
> there is more in-depth and interpretive work herein
> now than ever before, you must understand that the
> major emphasis will be on daily-type news. . . . The
> story is about firms that do recycle and why they do,
> where and when they do. . . . We are too busy report-
> ing stories with solid news pegs. We have no time for
> checking into products and processes unless they hit
> us in the nose. . . . We are reporters, not newsmakers
> or initiators. If someone else brings it up, we'll get
> into it.

Harris's treatment of corporate press releases is in keeping with this stance. He says that if the release seems valid and important, then he writes it up; otherwise, he throws it out. In neither case does he investigate and expose it. That would require covering a non-event, newsmaking instead of news reporting.

None of the reporters queried can recall writings a news story about manufacturers who do not recycle their containers. Perlman offered a typical response: "I suspect that if someone intrinsically newsworthy—say Senator Muskie, for example—were to come to town and declare that can recycling is a must and here are the local good companies and the bad guys, we'd certainly use all the names. . . . What I'm getting at is the need for a news peg."

Occasionally a reporter can manufacture a news peg for a story he badly wants to cover. Several newsmen recalled cases where they telephoned conservationists or government officials for comment on an "issue" that had not been raised publicly. However, they expressed some guilt over this tactic and indicated that they rarely resort to it. The more usual procedure is to ignore the story.

Reporters might be more inclined to conduct their own investigations of environmental non-events if they possessed sufficient environmental expertise to evaluate their findings. Most claim no such expertise. They are specialists, but they are not experts.

Peter Giddings claims that, as a trained meteorologist, he is the only competent environment reporter working for a Bay Area broadcast station. He adds, "The number one reason why environment stories are so rare and those naming names are even rarer is that there are few qualified environmental reporters." Harris agrees: "Unmasking ecological baddies calls for far more expertise than is available at any newspaper. . . . our firm doesn't believe in hiring consultants to do such hatchet jobs, and neither do I."

Specialization without expertise may be worse than no specialization at all. Perlman was one of several reporters who noted that his science beat required him to devote most of his time to conventions, meetings, hearings, and major breaking stories. "I have no time left for specific products and factories," he said. "Usually the city editor leaves them for me because I'm the specialist, which means they don't get covered at all. Or he gives them to a general assignment reporter who has even less training than I do."

Reporters repeatedly stress time pressures as an explanation for inadequate environmental news coverage. Two-thirds of the reporters in the mail survey agreed that "too little time to investigate the story properly" was a major problem in environmental coverage. The next most frequently cited problem (finding sources) was mentioned by half as many reporters.

Again and again, reporters asserted that they would happily investigate more "environmental dirt" if only they had the time. On the question of naming manufacturers that fail to recycle their containers, for example, Jay Thorwaldson of the Palo Alto Times commented: "It seems to me that it would take an inordinate amount of time to first find out where the manufacturers are and then call them." Peterzell commented, "I probably would not prepare such a list if the release did not include one, but only because I am too damn busy to do so."

Many of these problems—space, time, expertise—boil down to a question of money. Many newspapers and broadcast stations feel they cannot afford the luxury of even one environmental specialist, much less three or four. And the idea of freeing an expert to spend

days investigating a single company, to produce a long article that
advertisers will find offensive and readers will find boring, must
sound absurd to the average publisher.

Giddings is employed by KGO primarily as a weatherman. He
does environmental stories on his own, almost as a hobby, and is
paid by the story or by the hour. In 1969 he was up to six such stories
a week. But in the face of declining revenues, the station forced him
to cut back to a maximum of two environmental stories a week.

Another difficulty in environmental news coverage is provincialism.
The large metropolitan dailies often do not bother to report events
"out in the boondocks" while the smaller suburban papers seldom
venture into the big city. Both depend heavily on the wire services for
regional as well as national and international coverage. But the wire
services are the least likely of all the media to expose the underside
of corporate environmental activities. They are the most dependent
on hard news pegs. They are the most rushed and the most understaffed. And as one wire reporter puts it, "We are fantastically
afraid of libel suits."

The list of pressures that can affect the quality of environmental
news coverage now totals ten:

1. Advertiser pressure
2. Management policy
3. Unavailability of information
3. Distrust of conservationist
   sources
5. Dependence on hard news
   pegs

6. Lack of expertise
7. Time pressures
8. Space pressures
9. Money pressures
10. Parochialism.

There is an eleventh explanation that is at least as important as any
of the other ten: the reporter's definition of news, specifically of
environmental news.

The newsmen interviewed for this study were unanimous in
their endorsement of objectivity, rather than adversarity, as the
model of good journalism. Without exception, they were proud of their
efforts to "bend over backwards to be fair." Most recognized that
this standard inevitably implies a failure to report abuses too minor,
too borderline, or too subtle to reach public scrutiny without the aid
of the media. They were willing to pay that price. Harris said,
"If I have to go out looking for a problem, then it can't be too much
of a problem."

Moreover, the majority of environmental reporters appear
to view their roles as one of educating the public on broad environmental issues. In the face of limited resources, this role is in competition with the alternative goal of exposing specific abuses. Giddings
eloquently states the case:

My purpose is education, to teach people about technology
and ecology. There's not much time left for consumer
service. It is much more important to teach people what
it means to live in a spaceship than it is to expose the
evils of environmental advertising and corporate public
relations. What's unsafe to buy and who did a no-no
yesterday—these are interesting sidelights. But they
are not the essence of ecology.

Other reporters echo the same sentiment. "We are not primarily
concerned with consumer protection," says Perlman. "We focus on
issues, not products, and let Consumer Reports handle the rest."
At least four newsmen came up with the same phrase to explain their
reluctance to name names: "It's a matter of priorities."

The cause of the reluctance may not be that altruistic. "It is
possible," admits Rowe, "that reporters share some kind of subliminal
reverence for manufacturers. Maybe we unconsciously veer away
from writing anything 'econo-sacrilegious.'" But he doesn't really
think so. "We're not pulling our punches," he claims. "We're just
not the kind of media to do any punching to begin with. That's not
our job."

If environmental news coverage is to be of high quality, massive
structural, procedural, and attitudinal changes will be required.
Conscious and unconscious deference to advertisers and the business
community must be eliminated. New sources of information must
be found, and old sources must be reevaluated. Reporters must learn
to investigate environmental non-events with no hard news peg to
attract their interest. Experts must be employed and freed from the
constraints of time, space, money, and parochialism. Most of all,
the media must decide that corporate environmental hypocrisy is
a story worth covering.

3

THE EVIRONMENTAL
INFORMATION EXPLOSION

From all indications 1969 was the magic year for news of the environmental crisis. For a variety of reasons—the Santa Barbara oil spill, a choking air inversion over New York City, the proselytizing of Paul Ehrlich and Barry Commoner, the discovery by politicians that environmental deterioration was a popular campaign issue— editors and broadcasters recognized a news story of proportions equal to the Cold War in the 1950s and race relations in the 1960s.

The public mood in 1969 was receptive to this novel focus on environmental problems. Millions of newly affluent Americans had fled metropolitan centers in the 1950s and 1960s to stake out a future in garden suburbs. To their dismay they found that pollution and congestion followed them. They formed the nucleus of the audience eager for information about polluters and special interests.

In 1969 The New York Times transformed its Los Angeles bureau chief, Gladwin Hill, into a national environmental writer. Other papers followed the lead and created environmental "beats"

For this chapter, material on the San Francisco Chronicle was prepared by Debbie Majteles; material on the wire services and coverage of governmental agencies was prepared by Leonard Sellers; material on mass circulation magazines was prepared by Charlene Brown. Ms. Majteles has done graduate work in communications at Stanford University and is a freelance writer. Mr. Sellers, a three-time Hearst award winner and SDX outstanding journalism graduate while at San Francisco State University, is completing work on his Ph.D. at the Stanford Department of Communication. Ms. Brown is on the journalism faculty at Indiana University where she is teaching media law while finishing work on her Ph.D.

for reporters who became environmental specialists. By 1970 there
were enough such specialists in California that Tom Harris of the
San Jose Mercury and Fred Garretson of the Oakland Tribune founded
the California Academy of Environmental News Writers.

In 1969 Time and Saturday Review inaugurated regular sections
devoted to the environment. Look and Life compiled entire issues
filled with articles discussing environmental problems.

The broadcast media joined in: the CBS Evening News with
Walter Cronkite began an irregular feature entitled "Can The World
Be Saved?"; ABC's science editor, Jules Bergman, began to appear
more frequently on the evening news and in ecological documentaries.

Trade book publishers contributed to the information explosion
with a glut of ecology books. At least one, Paul Ehrlich's Population
Bomb, turned out to be a best seller.

Madison Avenue also turned its attention to the environment.
Advertisements began to stress what many corporations were doing
to clean up their operations and improve environmental quality. Many
products with little or no environmental import stretched to get under
the ecological umbrella (see Chapter 5 for a study of environmental
advertising). This chapter presents an investigation of the quantity of
environmental coverage in the mass media in the 1960s and early
1970s. Which of the many environmental problems received the most
attention from the media, and which the least? How did the various
media perform?

To answer these questions we content analyzed, over time, the
San Francisco Chronicle, Associated Press and United Press International wire copy originating in San Francisco bureaus, and nine
mass circulation magazines. We coded only for material dealing with
environmental deterioration.

The major difficulty in executing these content analyses was
defining the term "environment" so that it would be operationally
useful. How could the coder reliably decide that a certain newspaper
article or magazine story was about the environment while another
was not? Because the term environment means many things to many
people (see Chapter 1), we had to severely limit the definition to five
areas and let them stand for the whole of environmental content.
These five are air quality, water quality, human population explosion
and control, environmental additives, and the management of energy-
producing resources. Coders in each of the three content analyses
were instructed to code articles within the five categories as either
supporting or refuting the notion that the environment is deteriorating
and the world in unable to support its plant and animal life. The five
problem areas were narrowly defined as follows:

1. Air quality: articles or stories dealing with such problems
as smog, carbon monoxide, sulfur dioxide, and other pollutants from

automobile exhaust, factory emissions, and other stationary sources; their effects on animal health and plant life; their costs to the economic system; and methods of control.

2. Water quality: articles or stories dealing with such problems as factory wastes, sewage disposal, and thermal discharges; their effects on animal health and plant life; their costs to the economic system; and methods of control.

3. Human population explosion and control: articles or stories dealing with the concept of overpopulation and ways to prevent or cope with the increase (for example, an article or story on the legal problems of abortion without reference to abortion as a method of population control would not be coded).

4. Environmental additives: articles or stories about natural or chemical compounds artificially introduced into the ecosystem that concentrate through successive food chain levels or cause upset in the ecosystem through destruction of a species with possible detrimental effects to plant and animal life (for example, DDT and other pesticides, herbicides, mercury, and radiation but not cigarette smoking, fluoride, or cyclamates).

5. Management of energy-producing resources: articles or stories discussing the supply of flowing water, coal, oil, natural gas, steam, or fissionable materials available for the production of electric power, from the perspective of expanding power needs and decreasing resources.

Although hardly complete, the definition covers the more important environmental topics and seems a valid measure of environmental communications content, one that permits replication of these studies.

In addition to the three content analyses, we examined press coverage, again in time perspective, of the meetings of Bay Area governmental agencies that have jurisdiction over environmental matters.

All these studies showed that there has indeed been an environmental information explosion, both nationally and in the San Francisco Bay Area.

THE SAN FRANCISCO CHRONICLE

Selection of the San Francisco Chronicle for this study was logical both because it has the highest circulation of any newspaper in northern California and because its area of readership includes all nine counties. Our aim was to determine whether or not there had been an increase, over time, in environmental news coverage and editorial comment by the Chronicle.

For our analysis we decided to investigate the time period
beginning in January 1965 and ending in December 1970. Throughout
we used only the "four star final" edition. Rather than analyze each
edition during this six-year period, a total of 2,190 issues, we followed
the procedure described by Guido Stempel in Journalism Quarterly,
summer 1952. He found that a randomly selected sample of 12 issues
per year adequately represented the relative yearly proportion of
newspaper content devoted to a specific news area. Accordingly, we
selected one date per month by a random process to arrive at 12
issues per year as shown in Table 3.1.

Of the 72 dates chosen, only 70 issues actually were analyzed
because the January and February 1968 issues fell during a San
Francisco newspaper strike. Because hard news often was mixed
with entertainment news or obituaries, all pages in the Monday
through Saturday issues were analyzed except the following: women's
pages, personal columns, want ads, sports news, financial news,
editorials, and columns appearing on editorial pages (editorials and
columns were analyzed separately).

The same general pattern was followed for the larger Sunday
editions.* Environmental news was coded in all sections except

TABLE 3.1

Issues of San Francisco Chronicle
Randomly Selected for Analysis

Month	Date	1965	1966	1967	1968	1969	1970
Jan.	12	Tues.	Wed.	Thurs.	Fri.	Sun.	Mon.
Feb.	6	Sat.	Sun.	Mon.	Tues.	Thurs.	Fri.
March	10	Wed.	Thurs.	Fri.	Sun.	Mon.	Tues.
April	21	Wed.	Thurs.	Fri.	Sun.	Mon.	Tues.
May	20	Thurs.	Fri.	Sat.	Mon.	Tues.	Wed.
June	22	Tues.	Wed.	Thurs.	Sat.	Sun.	Mon.
July	2	Fri.	Sat.	Sun.	Tues.	Wed.	Thurs.
Aug.	17	Tues.	Wed.	Thurs.	Sat.	Sun.	Mon.
Sept.	12	Sun.	Mon.	Tues.	Thurs.	Fri.	Sat.
Oct.	30	Sat.	Sun.	Mon.	Wed.	Thurs.	Fri.
Nov.	8	Mon.	Tues.	Wed.	Fri.	Sat.	Sun.
Dec.	10	Fri.	Sat.	Sun.	Tues.	Wed.	Thurs.

*In September 1965, as a result of mergers among San Francisco
newspapers, the San Francisco Examiner took over the Sunday field.

the following: women's columns, editorial pages, want ads, real estate pages, financial pages, sports, comics, and the special Sunday magazines and entertainment guides. Travel and hobby pages were included, as were the inside pages of the Chronicle-produced "Sunday Punch" section. The Examiner's Sunday editorials were separately analyzed.

For our analysis, we employed the five-part definition of environment given above. For hard news stories, the environmental subject matter had to be mentioned in the first two or three paragraphs to qualify. For feature-type stories, the principal subject matter had to concern one of the five aspects of the definition.

As is readily evident from Tables 3.2, 3.3, and 3.4 as well as Figure 3.1, there was a significant increase in coverage of environmental issues over the six-year span, with a dramatic increase in 1969 and 1970. In a newspaper that remained the same size, news stories relating to the environment rose from a total of 112.75 column inches in 1965 to 616.0 column inches in 1970, a jump of almost 550 percent. Indeed, regression analysis shows that this increase is exponential and not merely a linear increase. As with other biological and social systems, we would not expect this exponential rise in coverage to continue ad infinitum, but, rather, would expect it to plateau over the next three to five years.

The most marked increase was in category 4, "environmental additives," which went from a low of 0 inches in 1966 to a high of 218.75 inches in 1970. Category 5, "decreasing energy resources," received very little attention throughout. While the total number of column inches in the other categories averaged 352, decreasing energy resources tofaled only 20.5, with 19 of those inches appearing in 1969 and 1970.

As the total amount of coverage increased, so did the number and length of environmental stories. Coders found only 15 articles in 1965, 25 in 1969, and a total of 38 in 1970. The problem of environmental additives may have had the most space, but air and water pollution received more separate stories in 1970 and in most of the years under study.

With the increase in stories and inches came an increase in accompanying photos. Throughout the six years the most common headline size was one- or two-column, with three- and four-column

---

For that reason, ten of eleven Sunday issues coded were Examiners. Since this is the paper that Chronicle subscribers receive on Sunday, the difference in name and management was deemed irrelevant because the factor being studied was the paper's role as an information source for its readers, not the relative performance of one paper or another.

TABLE 3.2

Column Inches Per Year of Environment
News in San Francisco Chronicle, 1965-70

Subject	1965	1966	1967	1968*	1969	1970	Total
Air pollution	28.5	29.25	36.75	52.5	59.5	136.5	343
Water pollution	48.5	15.5	13.5	0.0	103.75	130.5	311.75
Population explosion	26.75	29.0	106.75	21.0	44.0	119.75	347.25
Environmental additives	7.5	0.0	0.0	15.5	165.0	218.75	406.75
Energy resources	1.5	0.0	0.0	0.0	8.5	10.5	20.5
Average per issue	9.4	6.15	11.0	8.9	31.73	51.33	
Total per year	112.75	73.75	157.0	89.0	380.75	616.0	1,429.25

*Includes only ten issues due to the San Francisco newspaper strike, January-February 1968.

TABLE 3.3

Articles Per Year of Environment
News in San Francisco Chronicle, 1965-70

Subject	1965	1966	1967	1968*	1969	1970	Total
Air pollution	4	3	6	4	4	12	33
Water pollution	7	2	1	0	6	12	28
Population explosion	2	3	4	2	4	4	19
Environmental additives	1	0	0	1	10	9	21
Energy resources	1	0	0	0	1	1	3
Average per issue	1.25	0.67	0.92	0.70	2.09	3.17	
Total per year	15	8	1	7	25	38	104

*Includes only ten issues due to the San Francisco newspaper strike, January-February 1968.

TABLE 3.4

Column Inches Per Article of Environment
News in San Francisco Chronicle, 1965-70

Year	Inches Per Article
1965	7.52
1966	9.22
1967	14.27
1968	12.71
1969	15.23
1970	16.21

heads appearing infrequently until the last two years. Before 1970 exactly one headline was wider than four-column; in that year five stories were considered important enough, or long enough, to rate headlines from five to eight columns wide. And environment stories began to creep slowly to the front of the paper and the top of the page.

Two facets of environment reporting did not change. Despite the greatly increased coverage, the number of staff-written articles rose only proportionately to the overall increase. On the whole, the wire services and special services were responsible for almost twice the amount of coverage that was produced by the Chronicle staff. As to sources of information, the government remained the overwhelming leader, with state and local agencies used most often, followed by federal agencies and then legislators on all levels. (In determining the information source, the problem of choosing between different sources was encountered only two or three times. This suggests that almost all of the Chronicle's environmental coverage has consisted of one-source articles rather than multi-source "in-depth" articles.)

Editorials on the subject showed no increase at all. Only seven appeared in the six-year sample, with air pollution, water pollution, and the population explosion receiving about equal mention.

It is clear that the Chronicle is offering its readers vastly increased amounts of information, if not advice or guidance, with the preponderance of that information coming from government sources.

SAN FRANCISCO WIRE SERVICES

The wire services were picked for study because of their pivotal role in coverage. Also of interest was the effect of a psuedo-event (using Daniel Boorstin's term, defined as an event created specifically

FIGURE 2

Change in San Francisco Chronicle Coverage
of Environmental Problems, 1965-70

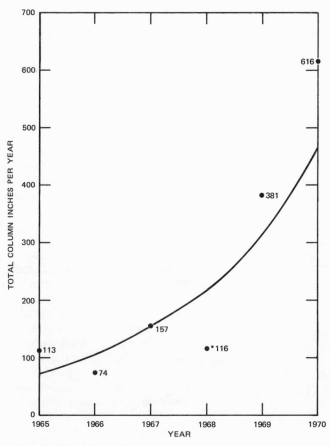

*Corrected value to account for
San Francisco newspaper strike,
January–February, 1968

for publicity) on the kind and amount of environmental copy generated. Earth Day, a nationwide created happening, depended upon the media for its impact. How effective Earth Day was in terms of creating additional copy also was measured by content analysis.

In San Francisco the UPI staff consists of approximately 40 newsmen, photographers, and editors who, with the help of 100 stringers and client newspapers, cover California from the Oregon border to San Luis Obispo. AP has 38 people on news, editorial, and photo, and the bureau chief is uncertain as to the number of stringers employed.

Although the percentage varies from day to day, UPI's copy source is roughly divided among staff, stringers, and pickups from client newspapers. AP did not have any figures available for a breakdown of copy source but said that copy comes "primarily from member papers, then staff, then stringers."

Pickup copy—news copy the wires take from the major local papers, check (most of the time) for accuracy, possibly rewrite, and send out over the wires—comprises approximately a third of all material used.

The pivotal role of the wire services in providing environmental news to Bay Area news media can be understood from the following example of coverage of a Bay Area Air Pollution Control District (BAAPCD) meeting in mid-1971. In the morning session the BAAPCD staff presented the district directors with a report citing a 17 percent reduction in emissions from all sources of air pollution in the district. A Chronicle reporter left during the lunch break and filed his story. After lunch, however, the directors returned and proceeded to take the report apart, item by item. The directors finally concluded that the report could not support its claim of pollution reduction. Other newspaper reporters who covered the afternoon session filed correct accounts of the meeting. But the Chronicle hit the street first, and both AP and UPI picked up its version. The next day radio and television stations and other newspapers in the Bay Area reported that the air was "getting cleaner." Not only was the air not getting cleaner but the Chronicle had managed to muddy the wire services as well.

UPI's copy is sent out over one of three news wires—two are national and one covers the seven western states—and additional material goes over the sports, race, and photo wires. "Audio" copy, rewritten for the ear and mostly worded in the present tense, goes over the radio wire, which serves both radio and television stations. AP has an "A" wire for national and international news; a "California Big Cities" wire limited to California news and primarily serving urban media; and a "Single Circuit California" wire for small newspapers, split into northern and southern California. AP also has sports, photo, and radio wires.

A total of four months' worth of copy sent out over these wires was content analyzed. A word count was used in the analysis, rather than the more common line or inch count, because the two bureaus have different size type on their outgoing teletypes and so this was the only meaningful measurement available.

One month's wire copy in 1966 and 1970 generated by the San Francisco bureau of UPI was analyzed, using the five-part definition of environmental news described earlier. In the four years environmental copy increased some 400 percent, from 830 words in September 1966 to 2,650 words in September 1970. This certainly bore out the belief that there had been an environmental information explosion (see Figure 3.2).

The other half of the survey was to analyze the month around Earth Day to determine the efficacy of a psuedo-event. Associated Press moved 4,685 words in the month around April 22, 1970, as compared with 3,140 in September 1970, an increase of about 50 percent (see Figure 3.2). From this perspective, Earth Day was a striking success. (It should be noted that in addition there was a great deal of copy about Earth Day moved over the wires, but the only stories coded were those that fell within the narrowly drawn categories. Five of the 22 stories coded could be considered spin-offs of the Earth Day bandwagon.)

Environmental wire copy originates from a variety of specific events, handouts, press releases, and staff ideas. An example in the last category was provided by UPI staffer John Lieghty, who got the germ of a feature story by thumbing through a copy of What's New in Research and ended up doing more than 1,500 words on tree-killing smog in southern California.

Environmental features coming out of both bureaus are done by whoever happens to be interested, and in that way they are no different from any other type of feature story. UPI has five staffers who do environmental writing and AP has two. None has any particular qualification other than personal interest.

Environmental copy comes in bunches, according to one UPI reporter. "One story will generate sidebars, reaction pieces, and so on. Conversely, when one type of story has been used, similar stories will be killed until some time has lapsed. Clients do not want continual 'sameness' copy."

The AP bureau has done a variety of environmental features in recent years, such as a survey of proposed skyscrapers in San Francisco—AP considers "Manhattanization" an environmental problem—with interviews of principals involved. AP ran the story with special "before" and "after" pictures of the San Francisco skyline. The bureau also put together a feature on how much smaller San Francisco Bay is now compared to ten years ago. When an AP

FIGURE 3

Wire Service Coverage
of Environmental Problems, 1966-70

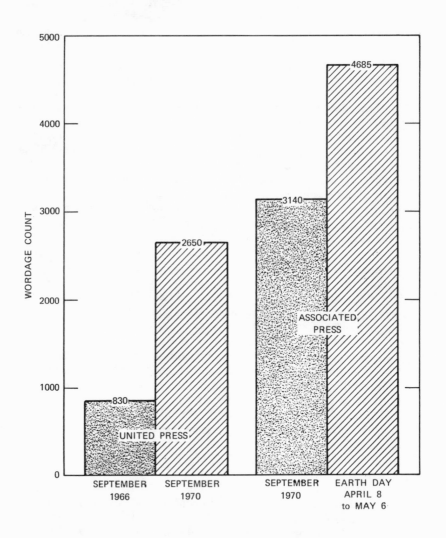

man with an ecology interest was doing a stint in Sacramento, he did
a weekly roundup on environmental bills before the state legislature.
Such efforts do not always pay off, however. At one time two staffers
were doing a monthly roundup of ecology news but according to Paul
Finch AP's bureau chief, "The papers were not using it. Editors
seem to prefer spot news."

UPI's approach to environmental stories is divided between
news value and feature value. News is a spot story, usually with
an average of 300 words on breaking events like a news conference
or a tanker spill. Reaction pieces and sidebars to these events
are done feature style. For instance, UPI ran the full text and a
spot story on a President Nixon environmental speech. The reaction of conservation leaders to that speech was considered feature
material.

The best outlet for feature material at UPI is a service called
"World Horizons." The four divisions send copy to New York, where
the decision on what to run is made, and then from Saturday mid-
night to 8 a.m. Sunday copy is sent on the "A" wire under the "World
Horizons" heading. It is felt in the San Francisco office that environmental feature copy is given better treatment than any other
type. "There is a much greater chance of environmental features
seeing print than any other kind," one reporter claimed. UPI also
has a "Science Today" daily news wire column, provided by staffers
from all bureaus where environmental stories occasionally crop up.

Although the wire services in the Bay Area as yet have not
invested in environmental specialists or created regular environmental beats, the quantity of their environmental coverage rose
dramatically between 1966 and 1970.

MASS CIRCULATION MAGAZINES

The diversity of magazines in the United States, each with a
distinctive personality, made a random selection of magazines un-
suitable for this study. Thus a purposive sampling was made of
circulation leaders in nine of the eleven categories suggested by
Roland E. Wolseley.[1] Selection was based on circulation figures
available for the six months ending June 30, 1970, with the magazine
of highest circulation in each category selected for study. The nine
magazines shown in Table 3.5 were analyzed.

The nine magazines were analyzed for the period January 1,
1961-December 31, 1970. This provides a base of one and a half
years before the publication of Rachel Carson's Silent Spring, an
event many critics believe marked the dawning of the present age

TABLE 3.5

Magazines Analyzed in Study

Category	Magazine	Total Paid Circulation
General Interest	The Reader's Digest (monthly)	17,586,127
Women's	McCall's (monthly)	8,505,221
Men's	Playboy (monthly)	5,290,027
Shelter	Better Homes & Gardens (monthly)	7,859,595
Sports	Sports Illustrated (weekly)	2,043,411
Exploration	National Geographic (monthly)	6,811,745
News	Time (weekly)	4,268,091
Picture	Life (weekly)	8,526,708
Quality	Harper's (monthly)	379,210

of ecological concern. Every issue of the six monthly magazines was examined over the ten-year period. Twelve issues per year of the three weeklies were randomly selected for analysis. Only a portion of the editorial matter in each issue was analyzed, and no advertising was considered. The following types of material were eliminated from the study: fiction, poetry, humor, puzzles; reviews of theater, books, art, dance, film, and music, except when run as news or feature articles; letters to the editor; question-and-answer columns; and such miscellaneous editorial matter as recipes and bridge columns. It was possible to eliminate this material without misrepresenting any magazine's coverage of the environment.

The unit of analysis was the article or story. To be coded as an example of environmental copy, an article had to have one of the five defined subjects as a major theme. Whether discussion of an area constituted a major theme was an issue for the coder's judgment. The only restriction imposed by the coding procedure was the necessary, but not sufficient, condition that to qualify as a major theme the subject had to be noted on the first "page" of copy. This requirement was introduced largely to expedite the analysis. In the discussion of the findings—particularly in the analysis of National Geographic—articles that carry secondary references to environmental issues are noted. While these bits of information were available to the magazine's readers, they do not seem to represent a conscious attempt by the editors to keep their readers informed on environmental issues. By using articles rather than paragraphs or sentences as the unit of measurement, a truer picture is given of the editors' efforts—rather than the writers'—to cover the environment.

In every magazine except Time, the first "page" of copy of each
article was read. One page of copy seemed a reasonable allowance
for the writer to get through his opening anecdote and introduce his
major themes. For the Time format, three paragraphs was considered
an acceptable equivalent. The first "page" was defined as the amount
of copy that would fill one page empty of photographs, artwork, and
headlines—no matter how many real pages one had to turn to get it.
Many magazines lace the first pages of an article with eye-grabbing
photographs. With the reader's attention secured, the photographs
peter out and the copy runs solid, sometimes jumping to the back of
the magazine. Constructing a "first page" provided a comparable
volume of copy from each article. This device insured an internally
consistent analysis for each magazine. Page size, of course, varies
between magazines, but as noted earlier our research was longitudinal,
registering changes in the amount of environmental copy carried by
each magazine. We did not attempt to compare absolute amounts of
copy between magazines.

If one of the five definitional categories was noted on the first
"page" of copy, the entire article was read. The coder, evaluating
treatment of the subject in the entire article, then decided whether
it was handled as a major theme.

Better Homes & Gardens

In Writer's Market '71, potential contributors were warned by
Better Homes & Gardens: "We do not deal with political subjects or
areas not connected with the home, community and family." The
magazine's credo states 2 in part:

> Better Homes & Gardens editorial philosophy is to serve
> husbands and wives who have a serious interest in home
> and family as the focal point of their lives . . . and to
> provide this service in the form of ideas, help, information
> and inspiration to achieve a better home and family.
> Inherent in this philosophy is the editorial responsibility
> to move these husbands and wives to action.[2]

Promoting itself as "the family IDEA magazine," Better Homes
& Gardens overflows with the how-tos: how to entertain; how to cook;
how to garden; how to save money on income taxes, insurance premiums,
and house payments; how to keep your family happy and your kids out
of trouble; how to get on with the business of a middle-class life.
Among the articles published during the 1960s were the following:
"Don't Let Your Youngsters Learn about Communism the Hard Way!"

(September 1961); "We Do Need a Department of Urban Affairs and Housing" (November 1961); "Ten Ways to Overpay the Internal Revenuers—and How to Make Sure You Don't" (March 1962); "Europe— How to Relax and Enjoy It?" (January 1966); "Help Your Child Learn More . . . Better . . . Faster" (September 1967).

Are the issues of pollution, overpopulation, depletion of energy resources, and the dangers from such environmental additives as pesticides not obvious concerns of the home, family, and community? During the 1960s Better Homes & Gardens apparently thought they were not. Perhaps it found these subjects too controversial. From January 1961 to December 1970 it published only one article treating any of the five problem areas. In the May 1966 issue a short article on emphysema discussed polluted air as a suspected cause of the disease.

Several articles that did not fall within the definition of environmental copy are worth noting. In November 1962 Hamilton Mason, Better Homes & Gardens garden editor at the time, responded to the "uproar over the use of chemical insecticides and weed killers" set off by the publication of Rachel Carson's Silent Spring. In a column entitled "Should Gardeners Stop Dusting and Spraying?" Mason accepted Miss Carson's thesis:

> The report is well documented and is disturbing in the most profound sense. It points up tragic carelessness in the large-scale uses of today's chemical killers—on our farms, along our roadsides, in parks, streams, lakes. Strong control laws are already on the books, and strong steps must be taken to enforce them. No editor here believes otherwise.

But Mason would not hold his readers to it:

> We are faced with problems of immediacy. We have invested money in our gardens. We put a lot of work into them. We do not set out ornamental plants deliberately to feed insects. To protect our investment and maintain the beauty we have planned, we must spray or dust.

Mason's advice to his readers amounted to the following: Read the label.*

----

*This article was not coded because there was no explicit discussion of the dangerous properties of pesticides.

During the 1960s and into 1970 Better Homes & Gardens repeatedly encouraged the use of pesticides without informing its readers
that the use of such chemicals was at least controversial and possibly
a serious assault on the environment. In 1961 it advised the following
treatment for roses: "Continue your anti-bug-and-disease spraying
if your goal is plenty of long-stemmed beauties all season long.
Preventive spraying just can't be overemphasized." In October 1964
Better Homes & Gardens responded to a reader's question, "What is
your opinion of the use of ladybugs to control aphids in the garden?"
as follows:

> A commercial rose grower near San Jose, for an experi-
> ment, turned approximately a million ladybugs loose on a
> 12-acre field. For a few days the ladybugs settled down to
> work. They weren't able to clean up all the aphids by a
> long shot. Then, while in the middle of their work, they
> took off for parts unknown. This is why I think sprays
> and dusts are more effective. You can count on chemicals
> to do the job.[3]

Throughout the decade Better Homes & Gardens advised the
use of insecticides, fungicides, and weed killers. Lindane, carbaryl,
tetradifon, malathion, methorychlor, 2, 4-D, and 2, 4, 5-T were among
the chemicals recommended. No note was taken of the relative
persistence of some chemicals in the environment. As late as May
1968 DDT was still suggested as a chemical for control of garden
pests.

In his Magazines for Millions, James L. C. Ford describes the
leading shelter magazines:

> Of editorials there is a void. If opinions are to be ex-
> pressed, it'll not be in these books on any economic,
> political, or controversial subject. They're to supply
> ideas for the environment, the external, not the mind.
> You can't ruffle any reader by what you don't print, but
> the American home and family are seen in this mirror as
> mentally and socially unconscious.[4]

Even if Better Homes & Gardens readers are as mindless
as the contents of the magazine suggest, an instinct for self-
preservation should stimulate their interest in environmental deterioration. In 1963 the magazine ran an article discussing different
kinds of soaps and detergents, but neither then nor at any time during
the period studied did it hint at the threat presented by the use of
phosphate detergents. It featured the joys of having five children

(March 1962) and never warned of the middle-class contribution to overpopulation.

Although a deteriorating environment, defined in our terms, never became an issue for Better Homes & Gardens, 1969-70 did provide meager evidence of a greater social awareness on the part of its editors, sometimes touching on environmental issues. In October 1969 George Bush, eastern editor, discussed population implosion in "The People Squeeze." Air pollution was mentioned as a problem that accompanied the build-up of super-cities. In July 1970 an editorial entitled "Nobody Gives a Damn" again mentioned air pollution. An August 1970 editorial essay, "Will We Bury Ourselves in Trash and Junk?", referred to air pollution from burning leaves.

Better Homes & Gardens is unlikely to be the sole source of information for any family—fortunately for the environment. Given the pervasiveness of the consumer mentality in its pages, perhaps there should be no surprise at its almost total silence on the ecology controversy during the 1960s and in 1970. Continued devotion to an all-is-well-the-problems-aren't-there-if-we-don't-mention-them editorial philosophy would surely make the magazine an anachronism in the 1970s.

McCall's

McCall's, akin to Better Homes & Gardens in its interest in domestic topics, is aimed more exclusively at women. Recipes, handiwork, and child care information fill many of McCall's pages, but it has run such politically committed columnists as Clare Booth Luce, Eleanor Roosevelt, and Senator Eugene McCarthy and it clearly suspects its readers of being interested in political and social topics. Table 3.6 provides the pattern of environmental coverage in McCall's. The trend outlined is irregular at best. Certainly 1970 shows a clear increase over the base year of 1961, but how can 1969 be explained?

McCall's devoted most of its environmental copy to population explosion and control, water quality, and air quality. The general category masks the relevant data: eight stories had population as a major theme (seven discussed only population among our themes, one was a general article discussing population as well as air and water quality); water quality was a major theme in seven articles; and air quality was a major theme in six.

Early in the decade McCall's focused on the dangers from the use and misuse of atomic energy. The pressures of overpopulation and the methods of control were continuing interests. By 1970 air and water quality received more attention as oil covered Santa Barbara beaches and Betty Furness warned McCall's readers of phosphate detergents.

TABLE 3.6

Articles on Environmental Topics
in McCall's, 1961-70

Year	Air	Water	Population	Additives	Resources	General*	Total
1961	0	0	0	0	0	0	0
1962	0	0	0	0	0	0	0
1963	0	0	0	1	0	1	2
1964	0	0	1	0	0	0	1
1965	0	0	2	0	0	1	3
1966	0	0	0	0	0	0	0
1967	0	0	1	0	0	0	1
1968	0	1	2	0	0	2	5
1969	0	0	0	0	0	0	0
1970	1	2	1	0	0	1	5
Total	1	3	7	1	0	5	17

*The categories are not mutually exclusive. Often more than
one of the categories is treated as a major theme in a single article.
Such articles are coded "general."

The coded articles in 1970 do not add up to much of an information
explosion, but in January of that year McCall's made it clear that it
intended to return to the environmental commitment made by Norman
Cousins in 1968. At that time Cousins assumed the editor-in-chief
position for the McCall Corporation, giving him editorial responsibility
for McCall's, Redbook, and Saturday Review. Cousins brought in
James Fixx to edit McCall's, and he initiated a policy of printing at
least one socially relevant article per issue. This policy accounts
for the increase in environmental articles for McCall's in 1968. Late
in 1968, however, Norton Simon, owner of the McCall Corporation,
became queasy about this policy. With little supporting data, he
concluded that it might be causing McCall's to lose subscribers and
advertisers. He relieved Cousins of editorial authority over McCall's
and Redbook and fired James Fixx. McCall's was then under acting
editor Horace Sutton for the 1969 publishing year. Because of Simon's
nervousness and anxieties and Sutton's own inability to deal with such
controversial topics, Sutton did not run any environmental articles
in 1969.
It was not until the 1970 publishing year, with the appointment
of Shana Alexander, a former Life columnist, as McCall's editor,
that environmental coverage resumed. She experimented with her

new magazine, devoting each issue to a specific theme. The theme
for the first issue of the new decade was "The Good Life on Earth."
In "The Earthly Paradise" (January 1970) Josephine W. Johnson wrote
effusively of the beauty of earth and her concern for the destruction of
that beauty. The editors introduced the article and a new series:

> In the three centuries since the first settlers came to
> these shores, we have built a great nation—and we have
> gone far toward destroying the land on which we built it.
> We have slashed the woods, scraped away the topsoil,
> slaughtered the wildlife, dirtied the waters, spewed a
> thousand poisons into the air. The smog hangs over our
> cities, our lakes are dying, oily water laps on our sea-
> shores. It seems appropriate that we should begin a new
> series on these problems in an issue devoted to the good
> life. Every human being has certain inalienable rights.
> The right to pure air. The right to clean water. The right
> to unpoisoned food. The right to the natural, unspoiled
> land. Without these rights, there can be no good life on
> this earth; indeed, there can be no life at all.

A small motif of an uprooted seedling in the palm of an out-
stretched hand identified each article in the series. The series included
such articles as "Diary of a Disaster—the Santa Barbara Oil Spill"
(June 1970), "America's Most Radioactive City" (September 1970),
and articles not within our definition but clearly concerned with the
environment.

In April 1970 Mrs. Alexander devoted her column, "The Feminine
Eye," to her mail and readers' responses to her innovations. The
following letter was her favorite:

Dear Mrs. Alexander:

> Your most recent issue of McCall's depressed me. The
> comforting thing about your type of magazine is that it has
> for the most part ignored the problems that this issue
> deals with. I have always read McCall's and the other, less
> glossy magazines with an eye to being relieved for an hour
> of the responsibilities of being a woman (a person) in this
> spiraling world.
>   Now this is gone forever. . . . When a bright chick
> like yourself agrees to edit a ladies' magazine, one has to
> expect this.
>   Women may have the vote but still act disenfranchised,
> and now, like myself, feel for the first time the clutching
> insecurities of adulthood approaching. The old McCall's

is gone, and the real world is closing in on me. I suppose
now, Mrs. Alexander, I'll just have to grow up.

Even the old McCall's—before Shana Alexander's arrival—had
seen some small changes in the early 1960s. In February 1961
Virginia Taylor Klose, mother of six, wrote of "The Joy of a BIG
Family." By June 1965 Eunice Kennedy Shriver was defending motherhood against attacks motivated by concern for the threatening population
explosion ("An Answer to the Attacks on Motherhood").

Some of the earliest and most relevant information on the environment came in the medical column McCall's ran during most of the ten
years studied. Four items fell within our definition: a March 1962
survey of sources of air pollution; a September 1964 report on the
possible causes of emphysema, with industrial air pollution suspect;
a February 1965 report of a study that did not prove smog endangers
health; and an April 1969 item on population explosion.

In October 1962 McCall's published a brief book review of Rachel
Carson's Silent Spring:

> Silent Spring . . . could well be one of the most important
> books of the year. It is Miss Carson's belief that the
> common crop and household insecticides, such as DDT,
> we now use indiscriminately for pest control are in fact
> killing plants, animals, and, gradually, human beings—
> while the insects they're meant for build up an immunity
> to them. The arguments are perhaps overstated, but Miss
> Carson makes out a convincing and terrifying case.

Unlike the Mason column in Better Homes & Gardens, this review
at least hinted that the magazine's readers might be part of the problem.

Playboy

Playboy's how-to advice and most of its pages are directed to
the bedroom arts, although not limited to the bedroom setting. In
between the nudes and party jokes, the reader can find fiction by first-
rate authors and socially conscious editorial material. According to
historian James P. Wood:

> Playboy is edited for the 18 to 34 year old urban male.
> It tries to appeal specifically to three groups within that
> age limit: those from 18 to 22; those 22 to 29; those 29
> to 34. It hopes to captivate in addition other males under
> 50, but it concentrates on those most susceptible to its
> basic interest. The youngest can skip some of the solid

and sometimes noteworthy editorial material which Playboy offers in increasing amounts.[5]

Table 3.7 provides data on the environmental articles published
by Playboy from 1961 to 1970. The last two years during that period
show a striking increase in interest in environmental topics. (Playboy
prints an average of approximately 20-40 articles per issue, but no
more than an average of 5 or 6 are likely space for "noteworthy
editorial material.")
Overpopulation was a problem that received early attention in
Playboy. In August 1963 the topic was discussed in a Playboy panel
entitled "1984 and Beyond." Two articles by Sir Julian Huxley in
January 1965 and January 1967 raised the issue again. And in addition
to two other articles in 1969 and 1970 treating overpopulation as a
major theme, the ubiquitous Paul Ehrlich was interviewed on population
explosion and a host of environmental topics in August 1970.
Among the articles on water quality were two by ardent conservationist and Supreme Court Justice William O. Douglas: "An
Inquest on Our Lakes and Rivers" (June 1968) and "The Public Be
Damned" (July 1969), a castigation of the U.S. Army Corps of Engineers.
In May 1970 Ken Purdy, writing on "The New Urban Car," offered
the sophisticated playboy an opportunity to cut down on air pollution
without jeopardizing his image.
During the ten years studied Playboy readers hardly were over-
whelmed with information about the environment. If Playboy stimulates
its readers to action, it is not clear that it is the environment that
benefits. Nevertheless, Playboy did run articles questioning the

TABLE 3.7

Articles on Environmental Topics
in Playboy, 1961-70

Year	Air	Water	Population	Additives	Resources	General	Total
1961	0	0	0	0	0	0	0
1962	0	0	0	0	0	0	0
1963	0	0	1	0	0	0	1
1964	0	0	0	1	0	0	1
1965	0	0	1	0	0	0	1
1966	0	1	0	0	0	0	1
1967	0	0	1	0	0	0	1
1968	0	1	0	0	0	0	1
1969	0	1	0	0	0	2	3
1970	2	0	1	0	0	1	4
Total	2	3	4	1	0	3	13

fundamental American belief in the sanctity of science, technology, and progress. In among the breasts and thighs were some warnings about the deterioration of the environment.

One of the problems encountered in this study was finding ten years of unsnipped, unexpurgated Playboys. Few libraries collect the magazine and some librarians are openly hostile to it although it is not clear whether they disapprove of Playboy because they have moral objections to it or because it is obviously difficult to maintain a readable collection. Stanford University library can boast of no more than 18 or so issues from the period 1961-70. Some of those it does have are short a few gorgeous girls and whatever happened to be on the reverse of the pages on which they appeared. This tattered collection is under lock and key.

Sports Illustrated

In its issue on February 2, 1970, Sports Illustrated reprinted from Foreign Affairs a major article on the environment by an eminent British science writer and United Nations science adviser, Lord Ritchie-Calder. In his "Letter from the Publisher" in the same issue, J. Richard Munro highlighted the Ritchie-Calder article:

> It has always been a fundamental concept of this magazine that life should have a quality, a zest, which transcends bare—or even plentiful survival. And we are hardly new-comers to the awareness that, though world inhabitants in general and Americans in particular have more and more, they are getting to enjoy it less and less. Words such as environment and ecology are not, therefore, fresh additions to the vocabularies of our writers. Yet never have we offered a story as encompassing or as definitive of our concern in this direction as . . . "Mortgaging the Old Homestead."

The Ritchie-Calder article qualifies as environmental copy under four of the five categories we defined, yet the article was not counted in our survey because the February 2 issue was not part of the random selection of 12 issues for the year 1970. Sports Illustrated is published weekly by Time, Inc. As was true of the sampling of the other two weeklies in this study, 12 issues were randomly selected from each year from 1961 to 1970. It seems unlikely that a magazine, even one as concerned with environmental issues as Sports Illustrated is reputed to be, will print in a year very many articles with the scope of the Ritchie-Calder piece.

On the average Sports Illustrated printed approximately eight
major articles (plus a few department features that occasionally were
one or more of the major articles) in each issue between 1961 and
1970. The formula of Sports Illustrated is coverage of all sports.
While such sports as fishing and hunting seem naturally linked to
ecology, many sports filling the magazine's pages do not obviously
raise questions related to the environment. Environmental crises
must compete with tennis championships, basketball tournaments,
pennant races, and Saturday, Sunday, and Monday football games.
Sports Illustrated's readers would notice a lapse in timely coverage
of the Super Bowl; they are not likely to miss a piece on the environment.

Nevertheless, James P. Wood favorably describes Sports
Illustrated's interest in the environment:

> Sports Illustrated fights the good fight for conservation
> of the natural resources of the United States. It has
> advocated Congressional establishment of a national
> council of ecological advisers, the establishment of state
> councils, and enlargement of the Department of Interior
> to give it greater powers.[6]

Despite Sports Illustrated's acknowledged contributions to the
debate on the sad state of the environment, this study yielded only
two environmental copy articles for 1970 and a blank for the preceding
nine years. The two 1970 articles discussed polluted water. In the
February 16 issue Robert Boyle chronicled his not very successful
six-year effort as a private citizen to get the government to act
against the Penn Central Railroad's flagrant pollution of the Hudson
River. ("My Struggle to Help the President"). "A Gooey Sickness
Smears the Gulf" was Pat Ryan's report in the March 30 issue on the
oil fire and slick on the Gulf of Mexico.

How can a trend be divined from an increase of two stories over
nothing? We could trust the data and methodology and conclude that
Sports Illustrated did not devote any significant effort between 1961
and 1969 to the environment, discovering water pollution only in 1970.
We could suspect that the sampling procedure consistently betrayed
us or we could question whether a sample of approximately one in
four is adequate for a medium publishing so few articles in each
issue. A fourth alternative we must consider is whether Sports
Illustrated was in fact interested in elements of the environmental
crisis that are not reflected in our definition. The alternatives are
not mutually exclusive.

With the fourth alternative we can concede the creditable job
Sports Illustrated supposedly has done on the environment while

observing that in five areas of great importance to the well-being
of our environment—that is to say, air and water quality, population
explosion and control, environmental additives, and management of
energy-producing resources—Sports Illustrated did not devote sufficient
space, or did not devote space with sufficient frequency, to make
drawing a table worthwhile.

In this study's sample the first issue carrying a "Conservation"
department was July 23, 1962. The department piece for that issue,
Arthur Brawley's "The Fire on New York's Famous Little Island,"
did not fit into any of our categories. Brawley discussed the controversy
surrounding the building of a highway access to the New York resort,
Fire Island.

Evidence of the magazine's interest in conservation appeared
even earlier in the sample. In the issue of May 15, 1961, John O'Reilly
discussed the effects that the proposed Glen Canyon Dam on the
Colorado River would have on the surrounding areas in "Udall at the
Bridge." Again, the article did not fit into any of the study's categories.
Throughout our sample of the 1960s Sports Illustrated ran articles
on endangered species: "Where the Antelope Play: Aches, Pains and
Prizes" (October 12, 1964); "The Golden Shmoo of the Barren Lands"
(July 17, 1967); "Plight of the People Bird" (November 17, 1969). In
this last article, which considered the decline in the pheasant population in North Dakota, one phrase dealt with the danger of pesticides,
but the article was concerned almost exclusively with the problem of
diminishing cover for birds due to modern farming methods.

The issue of November 16, 1964, carried a polemic by Robert
H. Boyle called "America Down the Drain." Boyle wrathfully indicted
"those who despoil his country in the name of progress." (The Boyle
article did discuss water quality at some length, but the topic was not
mentioned on the "first page.")

While it is easy to see Sports Illustrated's interest in the environment, or certain aspects of the environment, in the sample for this
study there were no articles dealing with our five categories in any
significant fashion (with the exception of the 1964 Boyle article
described above) until 1970. And then there were only two.

Within the layout of the 1964 Boyle article was a half-page
response by then Secretary of the Interior Steward Udall. Udall
directed his comments to Sports Illustrated as well as to Boyle:

> One of my concerns is that many of those who could do
> most to help turn the tide—like the editors of Sports
> Illustrated and those who publish other magazines of
> national circulation—will be willing to settle for sporadic
> outbursts of outrage. There is no doubt in my mind that
> we can keep America "a green and pleasant land" if

conservation becomes a constant concern of important
magazines and the daily press. Wrong-headed bureau-
crats, indifferent public officials and shortsighted highway
engineers will put the future uppermost in their planning if
they feel the hot breath of public opinion.

In any event, we can be quite certain of this: our
descendants in the year 2064 will judge us and our civilization far more by other things we did to save the face of
the American continent than by the scores of all our sporting contests or the size of our stadiums. All sensitive men
are haunted by every piece of America that "goes down the
drain," for each of us is lessened by every act that defaces
or diminishes the American earth.

But Sports Illustrated makes its money by providing a score-
board of results and coverage of the sports of the season. In its trade
advertising, Sports Illustrated "stresses its role as a newsweekly,
claiming a leading position among all newsmagazines for readers
with household incomes of $25,000 and over, who hold country club
memberships, own foreign cars, hi-fi's, and color TV." If Sports
Illustrated sneaks some environmental information to this readership
in between the scores, it feels it has made a significant contribution
to the cause of environmentalists. In at least a quarter of the issues
of Sports Illustrated published between 1961 and 1970, there was not
much information passed to anyone about air and water quality,
population problems, environmental additives, or management of
energy-producing resources.

National Geographic

Readers of National Geographic do not pay a subscription fee;
they pay dues, currently $9 per year, to the National Geographic
Society. Their dues fund research and exploration as well as the
magazine. The research and exploration ranges from archeological
investigations to studies of meteorites in Australia, creatures of the
coral reefs off Florida, and insects in Southeast Asia. The information
gathered is reported in the magazine, in National Geographic books,
and, since 1963, on National Geographic television programs.

Gilbert Hovey Grosvenor, editor of National Geographic from
1899 to 1954 and perhaps the most influential editor in the magazine's
development, had a broad conception of the magazine:

I thought of geography in terms of its Greek root:
geographia—a description of the world. It thus becomes

the most catholic of subjects, universal in appeal and
embracing nations, people, plants, animals, birds, fish.[7]

Certainly a short list of some of the titles published in the years
1961-70 illustrates a continuing commitment to Grosvenor's catholic
concept: "The Last Thousand Years Before Christ" (December 1960),
"We Climbed Utah's Skyscraper Rock" (November 1962), "Mobile,
Alabama's City in Motion" (March 1968); "Making Friends with Mountain Gorillas" (January 1970); "Computer Helps Scholars Recreate
an Egyptian Temple" (November 1970). Yet during those ten years
National Geographic published only three articles that had any of the
five subjects of this study as a major theme.

The first of the three was a short—just four pages long—article
printed in November 1962. "Man's Wildlife Heritage Faces Extinction"
was a transcript of remarks delivered by Prince Philip, Duke of
Edinburgh, at a dinner in New York launching the World Wildlife Fund
drive in the United States. Among the threats to wildlife discussed
by Prince Philip was pollution of air, soil, and water.

The other two articles appeared in December 1970 as part of
a trilogy entitled "Our Ecological Crisis." Running more than 40
pages, "Pollution, Threat to Man's Only Home" treated many environmental issues comprehensively, including air and water pollution,
environmental additives, and population control. The author, James P.
Blair, noted that National Geographic had had an early interest in the
problems of pollution, publishing "Pollution of the Potomac River"
in December 1897. Despite that strong start before the turn of the
century, National Geographic did not overwhelm its readers with
articles on any of our five categories between January 1961 and
November 1970, and felt then that such articles "do not meet our
current needs."[8]

The second part of the trilogy was a special map and painting
supplement, "The World and How We Abuse It." It treated in some
detail the problems of population explosion, environmental additives,
air quality, and water quality. The third part, a photographic essay
on "The Fragile Beauty All About Us" by staffer Harry S. C. Yen,
was not counted in the study. The lovely photographs paid tribute to
the world's beauty, not to its problems.

National Geographic printed other articles that fall within a
broader conception of the environment than this study's definition.
In the 1960s it published "Roseate Spoonbills, Radiant Birds of the
Gulf Coast" (February 1962), "Saving the Nene, World's Rarest Goose"
(November 1965), and "Parks, Plans, and People: How South America
Guards Her Green Legacy" (January 1967), among others.

Nevertheless, it seems surprising that a magazine devoted to
describing the environment as comprehensively as Grosvenor prescribed

would carry so few articles alerting its readers to what many see as
some of the most serious symptoms of the deterioration of the
environment.

Grosvenor remarked in 1963:

> Long ago I evolved an editorial policy to govern these
> many and varied contributions. One principle was
> absolute accuracy. Others required that each article
> be of permanent value and avoid partisanship and
> controversy. I also decided that no derogatory material
> would be printed about any country or people. Too often
> in my long lifetime have I seen unfair and erroneous
> statements made about other nations in the name of
> "objective reporting" or "constructive criticism." The
> Geographic has always dealt in facts, not bias, rumor,
> or prejudice.[9]

Is it possible the deterioration of the environment was too
controversial for National Geographic editors to tackle? Denunciation
of pollution was as American as Mom and her apple pie before
December 1970. National Geographic readers did, in fact, get
information about environmental problems in small doses quite early
in the 1960s. In "Cape Cod Where Sea Holds Sway over Man and Land"
(August 1962), everything about Cape Cod was discussed including
research conducted by the Woods Hole Oceanographic Institute on the
ill effects of long-lived radioactive waste dumped in the oceans:

> From deepest sea bottom to surface there is inter-
> communication of creatures and currents. One example
> is the nightly migration of fish and plankton from deep
> water upward—and if this plankton should ever become
> radioactive it might poison the fish that eat it, and the
> fish might then poison man.

The reader was offered this clear assessment of the dangers of
radioactive pollution of the oceans if he stuck with the article for
the first 30 pages. The above quote was 31 pages into a 39-page
story.

In October 1970 National Geographic published "Canada's
Heartland, the Prairie Provinces." Sprinkled throughout the 47-page
article were brief references to the provinces' polluted lakes, a threat
to humans who eat fish caught there. Readers were given clear,
concise information about the danger, but basically the article was
broad description of the Canadian provinces.

A content analysis measuring such secondary references would provide data on whether increasing amounts of environmental information were available in National Geographic, but such an analysis would be extremely time-consuming. The focus in this study has been on what the editors of each magazine decided to give their readers. Editors at National Geographic may have encouraged the author of the article on the Canadian prairie provinces to insert information on the polluted lakes, but apparently they did not see lake pollution as a sufficiently significant symptom of the deterioration of the environment to warrant an entire article on the subject. Not until the end of 1970 did National Geographic editors provide readers with a really substantial body of information on environmental problems, and then they did a thorough job.

In June 1962, in "White Storks, Vanishing Sentinels of the Rooftops," modern civilization was cited as the culprit killing off the storks "at an alarming rate." The article described stork habits and attempts by various people to learn of the bird's habits and migrations through banding. The author noted that some ornithologists suspected, although they had no proof, that many storks were dying of "insecticide poisoning in Africa, where they winter," and that the migrating storks were eating spray-poisoned African locusts. This was no more than an educated guess. Perhaps the guess and the suspicions proved wrong. Seven years later National Geographic ran "Locusts: 'Teeth of the Wind'," which did not even mention the possibility of negative side effects, on storks or anything else, from insecticides used to control the locusts. The average National Geographic reader undoubtedly did not think of the 1962 stork article when he read about the locusts in 1969. It appears National Geographic's editors did not, either. But surely, even without the stork article, if National Geographic's editors were concerned about the dangers of massive pesticide spraying or if they were at least interested in informing their readers that there was doubt about the safety of using pesticide sprays, they would have suggested to Robert Conley, the author of the locust story, that he consider the issue. By 1969 sufficiently sophisticated information about pesticides was available to Conley and the National Geographic. Is it that we do not worry as much about massive spraying in other countries? Pesticides do not respect national boundaries.

Conley asked an African farmer why locusts exist to plague his crops. The farmer, apparently more aware of the principles of ecology than Conley, replied: "To show us that life is not ours alone. It is written that when there are no more locusts, there will be no more world."

Harper's

While Harper's had the largest circulation of any "quality" magazine during the first half of 1970, it had the smallest circulation of the magazines analyzed in this study. For the first half of 1970 it had an average total paid circulation of just under 380,000. Compared with all other magazines, it ranked 104 in average total paid circulation for that same period,[10] a slip from 101, its position in mid-1969. By mid-1971 its circulation had fallen to just over 340,000. But the impact of Harper's is less likely to depend on the size of its circulation than on the quality of its writing and its readers.

In the early 1960s John Fischer, editor of Harper's for the first six and a half years of the period studied and a continuing contributor, described the appeal of Harper's as follows:

The magazine had five major characteristics which represented the aspirations of its editors. It dealt mainly
with ideas, especially those that would make important
news sometime in the future. It gave a highly selective
news coverage by analyzing the events and personalities
that might have a lasting historical significance. It sought
to make an independent evaluation of public issues. It
welcomed controversy. And it provided a medium in which
the literary artist . . . could perform uncramped by conventional forms and formulas.[11]

As was the case for the magazines we already have discussed, Harper's published so.few environmental stories between 1961 and 1970 that looking for trends seems pointless (see Table 3.8).

However, two aspects of the data are worth noting. One is evident from the table. Of the articles Harper's published on any of our five environmental issues, 83 percent were devoted to just two of those issues: water quality and population control. Even more interesting is the fact that almost half of the articles Harper's published in all five categories were written by John Fischer and published in his "Easy Chair" column. Four of the five Harper's articles on population explosion and control were Fischer's, and the 1969 air quality article was his as well.

When Fischer was editor, Harper's printed an average of nine to twelve major articles per issue. When Willie Morris, the young Southerner who brought expensive ideas to his job, took over the editorship in July 1967, the number of major articles dropped to between four and nine per issue. (Morris resigned in 1971 when his generosity—in terms of money as well as his indulgence of long-windedness—to his contributing editors and stellar writers such as Norman Mailer displeased the publisher, John Cowles, Jr.)

TABLE 3.8

Articles on Environmental Topics
in Harper's, 1961-70

Year	Air	Water	Population	Additives	Resources	General	Total
1961	0	1	1	0	0	0	2
1962	0	0	0	0	0	1	1
1963	0	0	1	0	0	0	1
1964	0	1	1	0	0	0	2
1965	0	0	0	0	0	0	0
1966	0	0	0	0	0	0	0
1967	0	1	0	0	0	0	1
1968	0	0	0	0	0	0	0
1969	1	0	1	0	0	0	2
1970	0	2	1	0	0	0	3
Total	1	5	5	0	0	1	12

Despite the change in editors in 1967, Harper's coverage of environment, particularly population control, seems to have been a personal crusade of John Fischer. Fischer's first column on the population problem, "What Women Can Do for Peace" (April 1963), was condensed and reprinted in The Reader's Digest in June 1963. In October 1964 Fischer wrote of India's population problem in "How to Save a Few Million Lives—and Save Money." In November 1969 "Planning the Second America" appeared. In this piece Fischer wrestled with the problems expected to result from the projected doubling of the American population. Just two months earlier in September 1969 Fischer had offered Harper's readers a "prospectus for a really relevant University," which Fischer called Survival U. The piece covered almost all of our topics including population explosion and control.

In April 1970 Fischer explained his conversion and crusade. In "How I Got Radicalized: The Making of an Agitator for Zero", Fischer focused on population explosion and control but also covered the related problems of air and water quality, environmental additives, and diminishing energy resources.*

———————————

*The September 1969 article is coded under air quality and the April 1970 article under population explosion and control because these were the only categories mentioned on the respective "first pages."

Each December Fischer converted his column into a "Christmas List." In 1970 Item 4 on the list was congratulations "to the Campbell Soup Company for devising a highly effective method of preventing water pollution—and making it pay."

The Harper's reader can find departments and articles devoted to books, music, theater, the arts, and the social spectacle, but politics is the real subject for Harper's. From 1961 to 1970 coverage of the environment in Harper's was almost always from a political perspective. In April 1962 Julius Duscha's "The Undercover Fight Over the Wilderness" exposed the battle between three government bureaucracies—the Department of Agriculture, Department of the Interior, and the Army Corps of Engineers—over the development of national forests and parks. In March 1963 Paul Brooks wrote of "how one stubborn man, entrenched in a powerful committee chairmanship can defy the will of Congress and jeopardize a national asset of incalculable value" in "Congressman Aspinall vs. The People of the United States." These two articles did not deal with any of our five topics, but in February 1964 Harper's printed a story by Polly Redford on water quality.

In "Small Rebellion in Miami" Redford described the fight she and her friends were waging against the location of an oil refinery and petrochemical industries on Biscayne Bay. They felt pollution of the bay seemed the inevitable outcome of any intrusion by these industries. Two years later in a follow up report on their "Victory in Miami" (August 1966), Polly Redford wrote:

> Providentially, . . . [the 1964] article appeared a week before local elections. Copies of the magazine became campaign literature [and] in spite of all-out opposition by the hitherto unbeatable Miami Herald, three conservationists were elected to the County Commission, an upset which had a profound effect on local, and ultimately state, politics.

Was Harper's an influential factor in the outcome of that election or did it merely join the winning side? The incident might have made an interesting case study of the comparative influence of a national magazine and a local newspaper on a local issue. How influential are various media for different functions: for conveying environmental information, for establishing desired attitudes toward environmental problems, for modifying irresponsible (in the eyes of the prospective communicator) attitudes? John Fischer's essay "What Women Can Do for Peace" surely was read by more people when it was reprinted in The Reader's Digest (June 1963) than when it first appeared in Harper's (April 1963). But reaching more readers may not be as good as reaching the right readers with a particular message.

The Reader's Digest

If ecology crusaders see a need for indoctrination of the grass-roots American population, The Reader's Digest is the obvious vehicle in the magazine world for their message. The Digest's current circulation in the United States alone is over 18 million. Printed in 13 languages and selling more than 29 million copies a month throughout the world, it is the one really international magazine. (The Digest does not necessarily publish the same articles in its American and overseas editions; some articles appear only in one edition while others appear in different editions in different months.)

The Digest's influence is not dependent on the size of its circulation alone. It is an institution in American and international life. In the words of James P. Wood:

> The magazine is read, admired, and quoted by people of almost every age and profession, by high school students and teachers, clergymen, public officials, housewives, mechanics, and circus performers. . . . Digest pieces have provoked social reforms, legislative changes, and wrought emotional and spiritual change in the lives of countless individuals. . . .
> Its multi-millions of faithful readers look upon the Digest almost as Holy Writ. They read it, believe it, quote it, in some ways live by it. They hardly think of it as a magazine at all. It is the Digest and unique.[12]

Were all the millions of Reader's Digest faithfuls exposed to increasing amounts of environmental information between 1961 and 1970?

The Digest prints an average of 30 to 40 articles a month, not counting such staples of the Digest formula as "Humor in Uniform," "Points to Ponder," "Press Section," "Quotable Quotes," and "Life in these United States". Although—the volume of environmental copy printed in the Digest produces an erratic graph, there was clearly an upsurge of environmental copy published in 1969 and 1970 (see Table 3.9 and Figure 3.3).

During the ten years 1961-70 the Digest provided its readers with frequent articles about air and water quality and population problems. Apparently, the latter was of special interest to the Digest. In addition to a condensed version of the John Fischer piece noted in the section on Harper's, the Digest printed such articles as "Our Population Crisis Is Here and Now" (February 1962, condensed from Look), dealing with the present and coming population boom in the United States and its attendant problems; "Birth Control: The World Problem We Fear to Face" (February 1962, condensed from Look),

TABLE 3.9

Articles on Environmental Topics
in The Reader's Digest, 1961-70

Year	Air	Water	Population	Additives	Resources	General	Total
1961	0	0	0	0	0	0	0
1962	1	1	3	1	0	0	6
1963	1	0	3	0	0	0	4
1964	0	1	1	0	0	0	2
1965	1	1	2	0	1	0	5
1966	0	1	5	0	0	1	7
1967	0	2	1	0	0	0	3
1968	0	0	2	0	0	2	4
1969	2	2	3	2	0	0	9
1970	0	3	3	1	0	6	13
Total	5	11	23	4	1	9	53

discussing the crisis of population increases around the world and the
necessity of birth control; "Birth Control Must Go with Foreign Aid"
(September 1963, condensed from an advertisement in The New York
Times); "How Japan Stopped Its Population Explosion" (March 1966,
first publication); "Toward a World of Wanted Children" (October
1967, first publication); "World Population: Is the Battle Lost?"
by Paul Ehrlich (February 1969, condensed from Stanford Today). Of
the 53 environmental articles the Digest printed in this 10-year period,
47 percent had population as a major theme (23 articles coded as
"population" stories plus 1 coded as "general").

Air and water quality also received substantial attention. Water
quality was a major theme in 38 percent of the environmental articles
counted (11 coded as "water quality" plus 9 coded as "general") and
26 percent had air quality as a major theme (5 coded as "air quality"
plus 9 coded as "general").

In 1922 DeWitt and Lila Wallace set out to condense articles
from the range of periodicals available and present this diverse reading conveniently in The Reader's Digest. The Wallaces realized that
offering a short cut to understanding contemporary problems and
trends would be popular in an upwardly mobile society. In 1933 the
Wallaces modified the formula by placing articles of their own
initiation in other periodicals for first publication. The Digest then
reprinted the articles in its own style and format, with credit to the
outside publication.

FIGURE 4

Articles on Environmental Topics
in The Reader's Digest, 1961-70

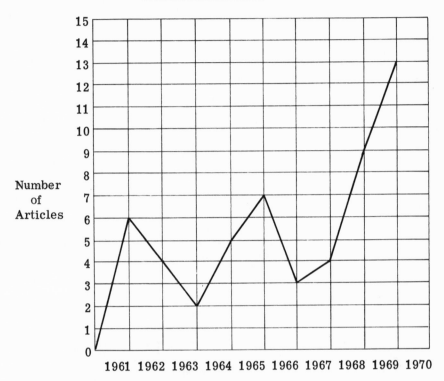

Of the 53 environmental articles published by the Digest between
1961 and 1970, 20 (or 38 percent) had their first publication in the
Digest; the remaining 33 were condensed from such other publications
as Look, Today's Health, House Beautiful, and National Civic Review.
    While the Digest printed nothing in any of our categories in
1961, by the end of 1962 it had published articles in four of the five
categories (energy management was the only one neglected). In addition
to three birth control articles (two are mentioned above), in "What
You Should Know about Fallout" (May 1962, condensed from The
Saturday Evening Post) the Digest told its readers that fallout from
nuclear testing was not worth worrying about, that its effect on humans
was insignificant, and in effect, that it did not harmfully degrade air
quality. Ruth Patrick's work testing the pollution level in rivers was
the subject of "She Takes the River's Pulse" (August 1962, condensed
from National Civic Review).

Also in 1962, in the December issue, the Digest published a
condensed version of Time magazine's report on Rachel Carson's
Silent Spring. Carson's book indicted pesticides as a critical threat
to wildlife and man. Carson had established herself as a competent
scientist and a poetic writer. In Silent Spring she tried to educate
her readers to an awareness of the fundamental ecological inter-
relatedness of all forms of life. Time's report was unsubtly hostile.
The Digest edited most of the hysteria out of the review but left intact
the central thrust that Carson's book was more emotional than scientific.
Time concluded the original piece with this paragraph:

> Many scientists sympathize with Miss Carson's love of
> wildlife, and even with her mystical attachment to the
> balance of nature. But they fear that her emotional and
> inaccurate outburst in Silent Spring may do harm by
> alarming the nontechnical public, while doing no good for
> the things that she loves.

The Digest toned this statement down:

> Many scientists sympathize with Miss Carson's love of
> wildlife, and even with her mystical attachment to the
> balance of nature. But they fear that her emotional
> outburst in Silent Spring may do more harm than good.

In Since Silent Spring Frank Graham, Jr., reported on the response
to Silent Spring including that from the scientific community, government officials responsible for administering pest abatement programs,
the chemical industry, and some of the media. According to Graham,
the editorial response in leading newspapers was generally favorable
to Silent Spring; articles and reviews in national magazines were not.[13]

Graham detailed the Digest's early ambivalence to the pesticide
controversy. In 1948 Rachel Carson learned the Digest was considering
an article on the benefits of aerial spraying of pesticides. She wrote
to DeWitt Wallace, supplying the facts behind her warning. The
article was not published. In June 1959 the Digest published an article
by Roving Editor Robert S. Strother "strongly critical of current
pesticide use called 'Backfire in the War Against Insects.'"

Graham suggests that by the time Silent Spring was published
the Digest had undergone a change of heart. Certainly the review
it chose to publish, even though it did cut the most gratuitously
vituperative phrases, was far from favorable to either Silent Spring
or Carson's message. And in May 1961 the Digest had published a
eulogy for pesticides, recommending many for the home gardener's
use, entitled "Good-By to Garden Pests?: A Reader's Digest Report
to Consumers."

In October 1963 the Digest's account of "The Great Pesticide Controversy" assured readers that everything was all right and there was no real need to worry. (The article is not recorded in Table 3.9 because it did not discuss the specific nature of the pesticide threat). The article provided the general pros and cons of pesticide use, pesticides' successes and disasters, and alternate methods of control.

By November 1969 the Digest was able to erase these aberrations from its institutional memory. Each month the Digest prints a column called "Behind the Lines" in which the editors provide background information on articles in the current issue, follow-up comments to previously published articles, and information about the magazine, its procedures, its circulation, and the like. In the November 1969 "Behind the Lines" the Digest editors sang their own praises as the conservationists' original and influential friends:

> Of course, our concern for the nation's natural resources, for its wildlife and wilderness, is anything by new. . . .
>
> In 1923, less than two years into the life of the Digest, we published an article deploring the destruction by indiscriminate logging, of original American forests. Another article that year urged our readers to cherish and preserve shade trees. A third encouraged protection of the Pacific salmon against plundering salmon-fleet and cannery operators. Some years later, in an article entitled "What You Can Do About Conservation," the Digest's eminent Roving Editor Donald Culross Peattie pretty much summed up how we felt:
>
> "Personal conscience is the beginning of conser- vation. And when conscience moves you to save wildlife, the sheltering trees, the fowl of the air, the waters upon the earth 'and all that in them is,' you are saving America."
>
> The deep-seated conviction that this is the truth has moved us to take sides—to stand up and be counted with the conservationists—not only in the battle for San Francisco Bay, but in other no less vital struggles. . . .
>
> In fact, as technology advances and time runs out, we grow increasingly concerned for our priceless natural heritage. Just last month, the Digest printed "The Alarm- ing Case Against DDT." In it, a biologist-expert told Roving Editor James Nathan Miller how the widely used pesticide threatens extinction of certain birds and fish, and called for an immediate ban on DDT.
>
> Now, in this issue . . . appears Roger Tory Peterson's disturbing "Mystery of the Vanishing Osprey". . . . It, too, points a finger at DDT.

The Digest made a forceful assault on DDT in the closing months of 1969, but the Digest reader surely should question the magazine's silence on the pesticide question between 1963 and 1969 and wonder at the evaporation of the Digest's confidence of the early 1960s in the miraculous pesticides.

To its credit, the Digest was on top of at least one major environmental story—the saving of San Francisco Bay—rather than bringing up the rear guard as it had with pesticides. In the same "Behind the Lines" column in November 1969, Digest editors outlined how important they think a Digest article can be in the cause of conservation:

> Last March, the Digest carried a hard-hitting article entitled "The Battle of San Francisco Bay." In it Roving Editor Earl Selby told the story of the shocking abuse of Bay Area tidelands—how landfill operators, noxious acres of garbage dumps, and poisons of city sewage and industrial wastes were slowly destroying one of the loveliest harbor areas in the world.
>
> The only hope for the preservation of the Bay's natural beauty and splendor lay in the fighting spirit of such organizations as Mrs. Clark Kerr's Save San Francisco Bay Association, in the protests of an aroused public, and in the perpetuation of the San Francisco Bay Conservation and Development Commission (BCDC), which was then scheduled to be phased out of existence.
>
> "The subject," concluded Selby, "is not just real estate, but rather the fate of a great natural resource. . . . Lose that resource now and it is gone forever. The decision is yours, California."
>
> Five months later, California lawmakers yielded to the mounting clamor from Bay lovers not only in California, but in just about every state in the Union. They made BCDC a permanent organization, and gave it full control over tideland development. Save-the-Bay had won.
>
> Certainly major credit is due to millions of conservation-minded Californians. But we're proud that we were on their side, and that, through the Selby article, we may have helped them to victory.

Letters from officers and supporters of BCDC attested to the importance of the Digest article.

The Digest's performance in informing its readers about environmental additives demonstrates that sometimes the information in magazine articles is inaccurate or misleading, either because the state of scientific or journalistic knowledge may have progressed

only halfway to the truth or because the magazine for one reason or
another rejects scientific evidence. Every magazine strives to maintain its credibility. If Digest readers do save articles of long-lasting
value, as the Wallaces suspected, Digest editors should hope these
readers never put Digest pesticide articles of 1959, 1961, and 1969
side by side. The experience might shake readers' belief in the
infallibility of the Digest.

Life

Life devoted its last issue of 1961, an especially thick two-in-
one issue, to the environment. The editor's introduction to the issue
stated:

> This special double issue is about Our Splendid Land—
> America's outdoors—and the living things that share it with
> us. More and more, Americans are beginning to regard the
> delights of the land—its animals, wilderness, seas and lofty
> crags—as a universal heritage. This issue shows how we
> take pleasure in this heritage and how it enchants the
> naturalist, inspires the philosopher and recharges all of
> us. It also shows how we have despoiled it, how threats
> still hang perilously over it and how we are fighting
> everywhere to save the land we love and enjoy.

One article in that December 22, 1961, double issue discussed
water quality, the 14-page "Water: A Land That Has Plenty, But Not
Enough, Feels a Huge Thirst." Life observed that water was a problem
throughout the country either because there was not enough or because,
in areas where water was plentiful, it was polluted.

Life is a weekly that publishes approximately 10 to 15 articles
an issue. A random sample of 12 issues was chosen from each of the
ten years studied (see Table 3.10 for the results). In the sample of
the nine remaining years, 1962-70, no environmental subject of this
study was treated as a major theme in an article until April 14, 1967.
Water quality was again the subject in that issue. "The Oily Flotsam
that Fouled Fair England" was essentially news coverage of the oil
slick caused by the wreck of the ship Torrey Canyon and the resulting
destruction of birds, fish, and beaches.

Despite the dearth of copy on this study's five topics during the
early and mid-1960s, Life did not completely neglect the environment.
The January 11, 1963 issue carried an article on the fight to save
the eagle and the polar bear from destruction. Lady Bird Johnson's
beautification of America program was covered in the July 22, 1966

TABLE 3.10

Articles on Environmental Topics
in Life, 1961-70

Year	Air	Water	Population	Additives	Resources	General	Total
1961	0	1	0	0	0	0	1
1962	0	0	0	0	0	0	0
1963	0	0	0	0	0	0	0
1964	0	0	0	0	0	0	0
1965	0	0	0	0	0	0	0
1966	0	0	0	0	0	0	0
1967	0	1	0	0	0	0	1
1968	0	0	0	0	0	0	0
1969	1	1	0	0	0	1	3
1970	0	1	1	0	0	2	4
Total	1	4	1	0	0	3	9

issue. An editorial on noise pollution appeared in January 27, 1967.
An editorial published on March 3, 1967, discussed abortion but without reference to population problems. An article on the threat of
extinction to the Indian rhinoceros from poachers seeking the supposedly
aphrodisiac horns appeared in the February 7, 1969 issue. There
also were other articles treating issues many or most of us would
say clearly were related to ecological balance. But our sample
suggests there was little if anything on the five topics of this study.

In 1969 Life rediscovered the environment, including the problems
of air and water quality, population, and environmental additives. In
the February 7, 1969 issue Life explored the problem of "Air Pollution" in a "pictorial study of a major threat to human existence."
This was a feature story without a news peg. In the April 18, 1969
issue the news peg was a dead whale. In "Why Did This Whale Die?",
a photo spread in the weekly section "On the News Fronts of the World,"
the story caption related that conservationists were insisting on
examinations of dead whales since the Santa Barbara oil disaster in
January.

In the August 1, 1969 issue—in concert with its sister Time-
Life publication, Time—Life proclaimed its concern for the environment. (The same week Time initiated a continuing "Environment"
department.) In an editorial Life took inventory of what had gone
wrong with the American environment: "The destruction of rivers by
chemicals and detergents, the destruction of wildlife by insecticides,

the destruction of landscape by indiscriminate and ruthless 'development' . . . [and] the shoddy excrescences of bad design, ugly and haphazard travesties of modernity spattered across the landscape in the name of expansion." The editorial was followed by an article showing the threat of spreading civilization and growing population to the wilderness lands. (The editorial was counted in Table 3.10; the article was not counted because it dealt primarily with the disappearance of wilderness through land misuse.) Life promised that it would show the "deterioration of the environment and recommend ways to prevent it."

Life kept its promise in 1969 with such articles as "Last Chance to Save the Everglades (September 5, 1969) and "Rare Elks Lose a Lottery" (November 21, 1969). But only in January 1970 did another article on one of our five topics appear. An interesting range of four environmental articles appeared in the sample during 1970: "Ecology: A Cause Becomes a Mass Movement" (January 30); "The Dirty Dilemma of Oil Spills" (March 6); "The Rhetoric of Ecology", an editorial (March 6); and "Vasectomy: One Man's Answer to Overpopulation" (March 6).

If this does not amount to an explosion of environmental information in 1969 and 1970, Life's own words reveal a new concern for the condition of our deteriorating environment in the late 1960s. If the December 22, 1961 issue on the environment suggests Life had worried over the health of the environment early in the decade, perhaps the August 1, 1969 editorial suggests that there is a need for continuing coverage of our successes and failures in stemming that deterioration. Life seemed to recognize that need in 1969.

In the 1960s civil rights, assassinations, Vietnam, and ghetto riots seemed to dominate Life's pages—problems that are still with us. By now most of the American population is aware of the equally pressing problems of the environment. Unfortunately, by the time the stories about civil rights, Vietnam, or the environment become either "newsworthy" or photogenic, the crises may be of such proportion that solutions are harder, if not impossible, to find. Even though its commitment since 1969 has been most impressive, Life might have done this country a considerable service if it had listened to itself more seriously in late 1961.

Time

In 1969 Time offered a clear example of the environmental information explosion. The conclusion suggested by the statistical data is buttressed by Time's institution on August 1, 1969, of a continuing section on the "Environment." That department, of course,

contributed considerably to the totals for 1969 and 1970. The figures
in Table 3.11 and Figure 3.4 are based on a sample of 12 issues of
the weekly newsmagazine from each year in the study. Time prints
more, and usually shorter, stories than any other magazine studied;
Each issue included 50 to 60 stories in the departments analyzed
(such departments as letters, cinema, music, sport, show business,
and milestones were not included).

Receiving the most attention during the 10-year span was water
quality, a major theme in almost half (27 of 55) the environmental
articles published (19 coded "water quality" and 8 coded "general").
Air quality was a substantial second, a major theme in 38 percent
of the articles (14 coded "air quality" and 7 coded "general"). Population problems were a major theme in 20 percent (9 coded "population" and 2 coded "general"). Environmental additives appeared
as a major theme in only 13 percent (4 coded "environmental additives"
and 3 coded "general"). As in the other magazines studied, management of energy resources received little attention. It was a major
theme in only one article, which was coded "general."

James P. Wood has described Time's style as follows:

> From the beginning . . . [Time] said it would give both
> sides of a story but clearly indicate which side it
> believed to have the strongest position. Its editors have
> reiterated their conviction that it is the duty of the press
> to evaluate as well as to report. Time has never claimed
> to be objective.[14]

TABLE 3.11

Articles on Environmental Topics
in Time, 1961-70

Year	Air	Water	Population	Additives	Resources	General	Total
1961	0	0	3	1	0	0	4
1962	1	0	0	1	0	0	2
1963	0	0	1	0	0	0	1
1964	1	0	0	1	0	1	3
1965	0	3	0	0	0	1	4
1966	0	0	1	0	0	0	1
1967	2	1	1	0	0	0	4
1968	0	1	1	1	0	0	3
1969	4	5	1	0	0	4	14
1970	6	9	1	0	0	3	19
Total	14	19	9	4	0	9	55

FIGURE 5

Articles on Environmental Topics
in Time, 1961-70

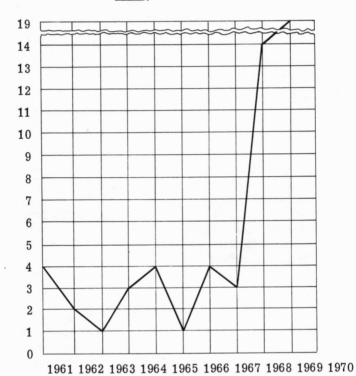

Time's report (September 28, 1962) of the publication of Rachel
Carson's Silent Spring left no doubts on this score. According to
Time, Carson did not have the strongest arguments in the pesticide
debate; Time did. As noted earlier, The Reader's Digest condensed
the article for its own pages in its December 1962 issue. The Digest
version, keeping Time's message, basically rejected Carson's conclusions about the severity of the threat from pesticide spraying.
But the Digest edited out of the original Time piece most of the
phrases that betrayed Time's own unrestrained emotional convictions.

It is difficult to say which article would have most upset Carson's
supporters: the Time version for its vituperation or the Digest version
for its approximation of moderation and rationality. A comparison
of portions of the two versions illustrates Time's stridency on the
pesticide issue in 1962.

From the Digest:

Silent Spring has impact; it is a real shocker. Many
readers will be convinced that the only hope is to stop
using chemical pesticides and let the age-old "balance
of nature" take care of obnoxious insects.

From Time:

There is no doubt about the impact of Silent Spring; it is
a real shocker. Many unwary readers will be firmly
convinced that most of the U.S.—with its animals, plants,
soil, water and people—is already laced with poison that
will soon start taking a dreadful toll, and that the only hope
is to stop using chemical pesticides and let the age-old
"balance of nature" take care of obnoxious insects.

From the Digest:

Scientists, physicians and other technically informed
people recognize Miss Carson's skill in building her
frightening case; but many of them consider that case
unfair, one-sided, and hysterically overemphatic.

From Time:

Scientists, physicians, and other technically informed
people will also be shocked by Silent Spring—but for a
different reason. They recognize Miss Carson's
skill in building her frightening case; but they consider
that case unfair, one-sided, and hysterically overemphatic. Many of the scary generalizations—and there
are lots of them—are patently unsound. "It is not
possible," says Miss Carson, "to add pesticides to
water anywhere without threatening the purity of water
everywhere." It takes only a moment of reflection to
show that this is nonsense. Again she says: "Each
insecticide is used for the simple reason that it is a
deadly poison. It therefore poisons all life with which

it comes in contact." Any housewife who has sprayed
flies with a bug bomb and managed to survive without
poisoning should spot at least part of the error in that
statement.

These few paragraphs convey the strength with which Time
rejected Carson's allegations. In the "Science" department of its
June 19, 1964 issue, Time ran a story entitled "Chemical Controversy"
on a fish kill of 5 million in the Mississippi Delta. The Public Health
Service (PHS) cited chemical pesticides as the cause. Time gave
space to the PHS's arguments, but it gave more space and credence to
critics of the PHS diagnosis. But 1968 Time took a different view:

> In an essay in their May 10, 1968, issue, the editors of
> Time wrote: "DDT is almost certainly to blame for the
> alarming decrease in New England's once flourishing
> peregine falcons, northern red-shouldered hawks and
> black-crowned night herons. . . . One of the prime goals
> in attacking pollution ought to be a vast shrinkage of the
> human impact on other creatures. The war on insects,
> for example, might actually go a lot better without
> chemical pesticides that kill the pests' natural enemies,
> such as birds. One of the best strategies is to nurture
> the enemies so they can attack the pests; more insect-
> resistant crops can also be developed.15

Frank Graham, writing in Since Silent Spring about this change
in Time's attitude, noted that Sports Illustrated, the third Time-Life
publication in this study, had undergone a similar change. Graham
quoted the observation of Roland C. Clement of the National Audubon
Society that Sports Illustrated had taken "hook-line-and-sinker from
one of its lady staff writers" the "hoax of bigger and healthier wildlife
populations, not in spite of pesticides but in many cases because of
them." Almost simultaneously with Time's renunciation of the miracle
of pesticides, "Sports Illustrated repudiated the notion that DDT is
good for wildlife" in several hard-hitting articles.16

On August 1, 1969, in "A Letter from the Publisher" Time
ceremoniously introduced its new "Environment" section. The new
section was explained as follows:

> We plan to clarify and explore man's long-ignored physical
> dependence on the biosphere—earth's thin envelope of air,
> water and soil in which Life exists. Almost every week
> now brings new warnings of impending ecological upsets
> within our planet's infinitely interdependent chain of life

processes: certain birds becoming extinct, hauls of
inedible fish, mysterious animal sickness. Environment
will tackle, for example, the effects of such forms of
pollution as DDT pesticides and radioactive waste, chemical
fertilizers and hot water from nuclear power reactors; it
will explore the cacophony of modern noises that grate on
the nerves and damage living organism.

Time was serious about its commitment, as Table 3.11 illustrates,
and it ran some very serious articles both before and after August
1969. On November 22, 1968, C. P. Snow's "A State of Siege" was
published, discussing the horrors and imminence of overpopulation.
"Tragedy in Oil" (February 14, 1969) and "The Dead Channel" (February
21, 1969) gave coverage in print and photographs to the Santa Barbara
oil spill. The dangers of air and water pollution and urban sprawl
were assessed in "A Matter of Urgency" (June 6, 1969). "Shock at
Sea" (August 15, 1969) was the report by the Norwegian author-
explorer Thor Heyerdahl that large surface areas of the ocean are
visibly polluted by human activity. "The Black Tide" (December 26,
1969) told of ocean pollution from oil tankers. Carbon monoxide as
a threat to pregnant women, victims of bronchitis, emphysema,
chronic heart disease, and the average citizen was the thrust of
"Invisible Killer" (January 26, 1970).

But amid all the gloom, Time—as it always has—was able to
print stories of the kind we all love to pass on to our friends and
family. In the "Money Munchers" (November 2, 1970) Time told how
the burning of worn-out bills by the Treasury Department was
contributing to air pollution. And in "The Mechanical Nose" (October
19, 1970) Time investigated the contributions of the Hopfenmaier
slaughterhouse to gracious living in the nation's capital. According
to Time and some Washington residents, Hopfenmaier's produces an
incredible stench. Washington, D. C., adopted a new air pollution
code outlawing odors injurious to the public welfare. The code was
enforced with the use of the scentometer. The device—unlike most
of the noses consulted—found the air around Hopfenmaier's legally
tolerable.

Observations

Whether or not the increase in magazine articles on environmental subjects in 1969 and 1970 can be termed an explosion, by then the
deteriorating environment was clearly a topic of interest in most of
the nine magazines studied. Conservation had been one of those
soporific topics to which American journalism, except for specialized

publications, gave little attention. By 1969-70 the environment was news worth whole sections and issues of magazines.

However, the participation of the nine magazines in the ecology debate was not uniform. Better Homes & Gardens managed to all but ignore the controversy. Although Harper's published more environmental articles (3) in 1970 than in any other year analyzed, the numbers involved were small and the variations from year to year not great. Sports Illustrated, despite its reputation as a conservation crusader, published only 2 articles in 1970 on the five topics pinpointed by this study. The magazine has had a "Conservation" department since 1962.

Life and Time (sister publications along with Sports Illustrated), in their August 1, 1969 issues expressed editorial alarm over the state of the environment and promised increasing coverage. Time introduced its new "Environment" department. The data indicate that both Time and Life did increase their coverage, although the figures from the Life sample are small and not persuasive.

The Reader's Digest and Playboy also published increasing numbers of environmental articles in 1969 and 1970. Digest editors even called attention to the magazine's efforts on behalf of the environment.

McCall's interest in environmental problems was erratic, although it now seems to be operating with a clearer purpose. National Geographic was surprisingly late in publishing an article on any of the five topics, but its special section on the environmental crisis in December 1970 was substantial and wide-ranging.

Of the five topics, population explosion and control and air and water quality received the most attention. Population problems, particularly, seemed to be recognized earliest. Our definition of "environmental additives" perhaps was excessively narrow and limited the number of articles counted in the study. "Management of energy-producing resources" obviously was not perceived as important. This category was scandalously ignored by all the magazines studied.

None of the publications analyzed gave comprehensive treatment to environmental deterioration before the late 1960s. There were isolated warnings in a number of magazines in the early 1960s, but they did not follow up their own advice and focus unremitting attention on developing problems.

What is the responsibility of a mass circulation magazine? Are they functioning adequately when they give a picture of the advanced deterioration of the environment after neglecting to report or failing to recognize the significance of early symptoms? Magazines, and other media as well, easily can be criticized for inadequate performance, but sometimes they are unjustly criticized for not being

clairvoyant. In Since Silent Spring Frank Graham, Jr., blames the
scientific community for the inadequate communication to the public
of the developing environmental crisis:

> If the pesticide muddle is chiefly the result of a breakdown
> in communications, the bulk of the guilt must lie with the
> academic community. . . .
>   In the face of man's massive intervention in the
> functioning of the natural world, the scientific establish-
> ment simply filed the ominous facts and kept mum. These
> "silent scientists" . . . spoke only to themselves, and
> rarely then. They did not choose to make known the facts
> that vitally concerned the public. They sneered at such
> techniques as "popularization," and recoiled in indignation
> from the suggestion that they cooperate with the mass
> media to put across the story that should have been told.
> For some scientists, Rachel Carson's sin was not only her
> willingness to tell what she knew, but to tell it in such a
> way that it was grasped by the public.17

The media cannot outrun the scientific community in research, but
they can seek to reduce the time lag between scientific discovery and
popular discussion of the findings and implications. The media also
have the unenviable task of separating the scientific Jeremiahs from
the cranks, all the while maintaining their own credibility.
    The argument can be made that Playboy is not the appropriate
magazine for environmental information. Or the magazine in which
to expect environmental information. But if one works from the
premise that environmental deterioration is a serious threat to man's
existence, then there is advantage in seeking intelligent readers where
one finds them. Playboy readers might never be tempted to pick up
a copy of Environment.

MEDIA COVERAGE
OF GOVERNMENTAL AGENCIES

    The approximately 20 governmental agencies in the Bay Area
whose activities directly or indirectly affect issues of environmental
concern range from county transit districts to pollution control boards,
from three-man appointed committees to a dozen elected representatives.
    Because these governmental bodies have decision-making power
that can influence the amount of environmental damage or repair in
the Bay Area, the extent to which their meetings and decisions are

reported by the media is of interest to anyone concerned about environmental deterioration. Such coverage also is an indicator of the media's
commitment to environmental reporting. Because agency meetings
are known in advance, happen with regularity, and follow an agenda,
they are fairly easy to cover.

More than a year before the onset of the environmental information explosion in the Bay Area, Fred Garretson, environmental writer
for the Oakland Tribune, began to keep an informal "scorecard" listing
which newspapers covered which agency meetings and how often.
Garretson's scorecard was compiled before the environment became
a popular issue, and as a rough indication of prior media coverage
it gave researchers a base line measure for determining the amount
of change in media coverage over time.

The four agencies monitored were the San Francisco Bay Con-
servation and Development Commission (BCDC), the San Francisco
Regional Water Quality Control Board, the East Bay Municipal Utility
District (EBMUD), and the Bay Area Air Pollution Control District
(BAAPCD). These agencies were chosen from the many that Garretson
monitored because they deal most directly with environmental issues.

Description of the Agencies

Bay Conservation Development Corporation

The BCDC is a regional agency, originally established in 1964
by the California legislature as the San Francisco Bay Conservation
Study Commission in response to public concern over land developers'
extensive Bay filling projects. Its charge was to ascertain precisely
what the public interest in the Bay should be.

The following year, upon this commission's recommendation,
the legislature established the Bay Conservation and Development
Commission, stating: "It is in the public interest to create a process
by which the San Francisco Bay and its shoreline can be analyzed,
planned, and regulated as a unit. The legislature further finds and
declares that the present uncoordinated, haphazard manner in which
the San Francisco Bay is being filled is inimical to the welfare of
both present and future residenst of the area."

The BCDC's major goal was to prepare, over the next three and
one-half years, a comprehensive and enforceable plan for the conservation of the water of San Francisco Bay and the development of
its shoreline. The BCDC was given jurisdictional authority over
submerged lands, tidelands, and marshlands subject to tidal action.
In order that the Bay remain in existence while this comprehensive
study was being completed, the BCDC also was granted power to

control land fill through a permit system. Much to many developers'
distress, the BCDC adopted a very tough policy toward the awarding
of such permits. By 1969 the BCDC had studied such subjects as
tidal movement, sedimentation, pollution, fish and wildlife, smog and
weather, geology, fill, ports, transportation, recreation, waterfront
industry, ownership, and government. Therefore, the resulting San
Francisco Bay Plan, represented a truly comprehensive study of the
Bay and its uses. In 1969, after a fierce political campaign, the
legislature made the BCDC a permanent regional agency with the
authority to implement its comprehensive plan.

San Francisco Regional Water Quality Control Board

The San Francisco Regional Water Quality Control Board is one
of nine such boards under the parent State Water Resources Control
Board. This statewide system of water resource management was
established in 1967 and its powers expanded in 1969. The state board
formulates state policy for water quality control, administers research
programs, investigates pollution by state agencies, and supervises the
actions of the nine regional boards. The regional boards have considerable authority and are empowered to devise regional water
quality control plans; to prescribe requirements for all waste water
discharges; to require all persons or local agencies that discharge
waste to file reports describing the nature of the discharge; to inspect
facilities involved with waste discharge; and to call for legal action
to stop environmental damage. This last power can be backed by a
$6,000 per day fine. The San Francisco Regional Water Quality Con-
trol Board instituted this fine against the city and county of San
Francisco in 1970 to halt further construction projects until adequate
sewage treatment facilities were built.

Bay Area Air Pollution Control District

The Bay Area Air Pollution Control District (BAAPCD) regulates
air pollution emissions from stationary sources (this does not include
automobile pollution, which is regulated by the State Air Resources
Board). Jurisdiction extends throughout the six counties comprising
most of the Bay Area and portions of the remaining three counties
that complete the Bay perimeter.

East Bay Municipal Utility District

The East Bay Municipal Utility District (EBMUD) and the San
Francisco Water Department are the two largest water purveyors in
the Bay Area. Created in 1921, EBMUD currently provides water for
15 cities in Contra Costa and Alameda counties, with a total population

of 1.16 million. This agency also is responsible for waste water
interception, treatment, and disposal for the cities of Alameda,
Albany, Berkeley, Emeryville, Oakland, and Piedmont.

Reporter attendance at BCDC meetings was monitored for the
meetings of March 4, March 19, April 1, and April 15, 1971. The
San Francisco Regional Water Quality Control Board was monitored
February 24, March 26, and April 22, 1971. BAAPCD was monitored
for February 19, March 3, March 25, April 7, and May 5, 1971. EBMUD
was monitored for February 23, March 10, March 23, April 13, and
April 17, 1971. In all cases the help of the public information officer
or the public relations representative was enlisted. Joseph Bodovitz
of BCDC, William Gingrich of the Regional Water Quality Board, Paul
Fletcher and Bryan McCrea of EBMUD, and Ted McHugh of BAAPCD
all gave valuable assistance.

Media Coverage

Bay Conservation and Development Commission

Before the environmental information explosion BCDC meetings
were staffed regularly by the Oakland Tribune and the San Jose
Mercury. The San Francisco Chronicle and the San Francisco
Examiner, along with United Press International, staffed the meetings
on a drop-in basis, showing up approximately 70 percent of the time.
Associated Press seldom staffed the meetings and only occasionally
printed press releases.

In 1971 the BCDC was covered regularly by the Tribune,
Mercury, Examiner, and Chronicle. The San Rafael Independent-
Journal staffed half of the meetings monitored, and at least one meet-
ing each was staffed by the Fremont Argus, the McGraw-Hill News
Service, television stations KPIX, KTVU, KQED and KGO, radio
stations KCBS, KSFO, and KIOI. Telephone requests for information
were made at least once by the Redwood City Tribune and the Hayward
Daily Review.

San Francisco Regional Water Quality Control Board

Before the information explosion Water Quality Board meetings
were staffed regularly by the Tribune and the Mercury. The Examiner
showed up about 40 percent of the time, and UPI about 10 percent.
The Chronicle and AP did not cover the agency.

In 1971 the Chronicle, Examiner, Mercury, Independent-Journal,
and Tribune all regularly staffed the meetings. Periodic coverage
also was provided by the Contra Costa Times, the monthly Freedom

News, the Fremont Argus, the weekly Pacific Sun, and Peninsula
Newspapers Inc. At one monitored meeting broadcast coverage was
provided by KPIX-TV and KCBS radio. At the same meeting telephone
calls were received from radio stations KFRC, KGO, KSFO, and KYA.

Bay Area Air Pollution Control District

Before the information explosion BAAPCD meetings were covered
approximately 40 percent of the time by the Tribune, Mercury,
Examiner, and Chronicle. UPI staffed the meetings about 10 percent
of the time, and AP did not cover the agency at all.

In 1971 the BAAPCD was covered regularly, either in person or
by telephone, by the Examiner, Mercury, Chronicle, Tribune,
Independent-Journal, and Hayward Daily Review. During the monitoring
period calls were received from the Fairfield-Suisun Daily Republic,
Peninsula Newspapers Inc., the Livermore Herald and News, the
Redwood City Tribune, the San Mateo Times, the Los Angeles Times,
the Pittsburg Post-Dispatch, and the Vallejo Times-Herald. Calls
also were received from radio stations KIOI, KSFO, KNEW, KFRC,
and KEST and from television stations KTVU, KGO, KQED, and
KRON.

East Bay Municipal Utility District

Before the information explosion EBMUD meetings were staffed
regularly by the Oakland Tribune, 30 percent of the time by the
Examiner, and approximately 10 percent of the time by the Chronicle.

In 1971 EBMUD was covered by two papers: the Tribune always
was present and the Hayward Daily Review always called. No other
news media took an interest.

Observations

Obviously media coverage of governmental agencies dealing
with the environment has increased. It is noteworthy that where the
wire services once spasmodically covered these agencies, they now
provide no direct coverage at all. With the increase in local media
coverage, the wires apparently are able to rely on their client newspapers for information.

The increase in coverage by small newspapers is an indication
of the growing awareness of environmental issues and the role governmental agencies play in dealing with those issues. When small papers,
hampered by lean budgets and tiny staffs, find the time to cover
committee meetings and board hearings personally or by telephone,
then the extent of media involvement is large.

The response of the broadcast news media to the increased newsworthiness of such government agencies also is worth noting. Where just a few years ago the broadcast media gave no coverage at all to such meetings, now they are at least periodically checking in when issues are raised or decisions made concerning the environment.

CONCLUSIONS

In assessing changes in media coverage of environmental problems we developed a specific, five-part definition that, while not intended to be all-inclusive, was intended to enable coders to select articles systematically for analysis without relying on each coder's own definition of the environment. We felt that such a definition should serve as a reliable method for showing changes in space devoted to environmental and ecological issues.

As the study progressed there were a few ambiguities with some parts of the definition, notably sections 3 and 4 (population growth and environmental additives). There was confusion about whether all articles referring to birth control should be included or only those articles referring to birth control as a means of curbing population growth. There was uncertainty whether atomic radiation and other radiological pollutants should be included under environmental additives. Consequently these two sections have been reworded.

We offer the following operational definition of the term "environment" for researchers engaged in content analyses of the mass media:

1. Air quality: articles or stories dealing with such problems as smog, carbon monoxide, sulfur dioxide, and other pollutants resulting from automobile exhaust, factory emissions and other stationary sources; their effects on animal health and plant life; their costs to the economic system; and methods of control.

2. Water quality: articles or stories dealing with such problems as factory wastes, sewage disposal, and thermal discharges; their effects on animal health and plant life; their costs to the economic system; and methods of control.

3. Human population explosion and control: articles or stories dealing with the possibility of overpopulation and ways to prevent or cope with the increase, as well as the pressure overpopulation exerts on such life

support systems as living space, food, resources, and
deterioration in the quality of life. Stories related to
birth control or abortion methods should be included
only if these articles refer to birth control or abortion
as a means of curbing population increase.

4. Environmental additives: articles or stories dealing with natural elements or chemical compounds introduced solely by man into the ecosystem, which can be
transmitted through food chains and concentrated at each
successive trophic level or which can alter the dynamic
balance in the ecosystem through destruction of a species
or more subtle methods of articificial selection. Examples
would include DDT and other pesticides, herbicides, mercury, fallout and other radiological pollutants, defoliants,
and crude or refined oil spilled at sea. This would not
include environmental additives that have biological effects
exclusively, or almost exclusively, on man, such as cigarette smoke, fluoride in water supplies, or cyclamates in
food. This also would include methods explicitly offered
to prevent or redress such damage and alternatives to
such chemical elements and compounds.

5. Management of energy-producing resources:
articles or stories discussing the supply of flowing
water, coal, oil, natural gas, steam, or fissionable
materials available for the production of electric power,
from the perspective of expanding power needs and
decreasing resources.

To further refine our definition, there are a large number of
areas that rightly could be considered ecological or environmental
but were not included. For example, we did not code articles dealing with waste recycling, land fill, "Save the Redwoods" campaigns,
or the establishment of the Redwood National Park. Similarly many
stories about the SST were not included since they did not mention
specific environmental effects of the airplane but rather how legislative battles were proceeding in Congress.

While the definition obviously could have been broadened to
include these areas, it is our opinion that it would be preferable not
to for a number of reasons. First, these five areas are very fundamental biological-social issues. Second, they are not parochial but
fully applicable nationally and also internationally, and hence could
be utilized readily by other researchers. Third, this five-part
definition, as revised, was readily comprehended and easily employed
by all of the coders involved in the content analyses.

We found the definition structured in this way to be a reliable and accurate research tool and recommend it for further media studies regarding coverage of environmental issues.

Since 1965 the news media in the San Francisco Bay Area have exponentially increased their coverage of environmental subjects. As expected, the metropolitan daily newspapers and wire services have led the way, but the quantity of coverage in both local dailies and the broadcast media is encouraging. Regular coverage of selected governmental agencies with environmental objectives has increased similarly, with many news media, large and small, at least receiving telephone reports of actions at scheduled meetings.

In addition, as we shall discuss in Chapter 5, the advertising industry and industry as a whole have picked up this scent and begun to slant advertising copy toward the environment. Beginning in 1969 increasing number of articles on the environment have appeared in such national magazines as Life, The Reader's Digest, Time, and Playboy.

While media coverage has increased at an exponential rate, it is most likely performing an alerting function to the general public in the Bay Area: the news media are informing residents daily of major threats to the quality of their life; environmental concern is a steady cantus firmus for the day's events. Although the quantity of coverage has increased, it is legitimate to wonder how useful individuals and professionals in environmental fields have found this environmental reporting and what the quality of that coverage is. The following chapters deal with these questions.

THE PSEUDO-EVENT,
THE ECO-ACTIVIST,
AND THE PUBLIC

"I have this picture of the last great interview: The polar
icecaps are melting. The San Andreas Fault has swallowed
up half of California. Tonga has dropped the big egg on
Mauritius. The cities of the plain are leveled. We switch
from Walter Cronkite in End-of-the-World Central to
Buzz Joplin, who is standing on a piece of rock south of
the Galapagos with the last man on earth, the water rising
now just above their chins. Joplin strains himself on tip-
toe, lifts his microphone out of the water, and, with a last
desperate gallant effort—the culmination of all his years
as a TV newsman—places it in front of the survivor's
mouth. 'How do you feel, sir?' he asks. 'I mean being
the last man on earth and so forth. Would you give us
your personal reaction?'

"The last survivor adopts that helpless vacant look,
the water already beginning to trickle into his mouth.
'Well, Buzz,' he says, gazing wildly into the middle
distance, 'I feel real good.' "

—Michael Arlen, Living-
Room War, pp. 194-95.

If any of the mass media were to survive the "Big Egg," its
explosion would be one of the few "real" events they have reported.
It is not likely that the end-of-the-world story would be broken at

---

Material for this chapter was prepared by Phil Garon. Mr.
Garon, a 1968 graduate of Rice, is teaching news writing and media
law at the University of Maryland, where he is finishing work on his
Ph.D. Until 1972 he was in residence at the Department of Communication, Stanford University.

a news conference or a staged interview, Buzz Joplin notwithstanding, or through a news release or some gimmick hatched in the fertile imagination of a public relations counselor. But who knows?

We are all indebted to Daniel Boorstin and his book The Image for demonstrating the dependence of the contemporary journalist on what he called the pseudo-event: a happening created expressly for the purpose of being reported.1 The world has become sufficiently complex, and the average journalist sufficiently harried and over-worked, that many real events are packaged as pseudo-events for the convenience of the reporter, not to mention the manipulative advantage this affords the packager.

Except in the case of violent crimes, auto accidents, natural disasters, and the like, the reporter rarely unearths an actual event in the making anymore, reporting it breathlessly to his public and shocking the daylights out of the news source. When this does occur, a significant news story is likely to result. Reporters working in the Washington bureau of The New York Times did it in 1968 when they sniffed out, verified, and then wrote in a page one story that Lyndon Johnson was about to send 206,000 more troops to Vietnam in the wake of the disastrous Tet offensive. Unable to manage the announce-ment as he would have liked, Johnson bowed to mounting public criticism, decided not to escalate the war, and dropped out of the Presidential sweepstakes.

The environmental reporter, hobbled by his lack of scientific expertise, the enormity of his beat, the rippling ramifications of everything he reports, and the nonhuman or inanimate nature of most of his news sources, also is a slave to the pseudo-event. Unable to converse with Lake Erie to determine its health, and unable to examine the lake for himself, he is forced to wait for scientists, government officials, academicians, and activist citizens to do the investigation for him and pass on their conclusions at a press conference. By which time, of course, the lake probably has died.

So common is this system in the functioning of American jour-nalism that all parties have mastered their roles. In response to cues from our besieged environment and growing public pressure, some special interest group—usually government but often private business or eco-activists—gathers available data, generates new material, and calls it to the attention of the media. The media report it, after their own fashion, to the general public, whose reaction, along with changes in the environment, keeps the system in motion.

It is the performance of the environmental reporter reacting to the pseudo-event that interests us here. To study this part of the model we observed the press at a full-blown news conference in which a report on Bay Area air pollution was released; we then traced the news play this report received in the print and broadcast media.

The report was a year-long (1970) study of the effectiveness of
the Bay Area Air Pollution Control District (BAAPCD), carried out
by 70 Stanford students under the direction of Ned Groth, now an
advisory member of the BAAPCD. The 380-page report detailed the
sources of air pollution in the Bay Area (naming offensive polluters),
rated the performance of the politicians serving on the board, reported
the results of a public opinion poll on air pollution, and described
how the public could become involved productively. Press performance
in response to this pseudo-event (a valuable one—few are) was not
heroic.

THE PRESS CONFERENCE

As a manipulator, Groth scored one early plus and one minus.
Among the Stanford students he made available for interviews by the
press was a particularly leggy female in a leather micro-miniskirt,
producing a few more pictures than might otherwise have appeared.

On the other hand, Groth dumped the entire report on the media
for the first time as they arrived at the conference, making it rather
difficult for them to ask intelligent questions based on its contents.
After some opening remarks, Groth was asked questions ranging
from the trivial and uninformed to the cosmic. Only two newspaper
reporters (out of a dozen journalists in attendance) were knowledgeable
enough about air pollution to contribute important questions. A television reporter asked Groth to "sum up for the broadcast media in
ten seconds or so what is in the report." Groth somehow did, at
which point the commercial TV crews packed up their lights and
microphones and hustled off to the next press conference for another
ten seconds of wisdom. With the broadcasters gone, the two knowledgeable print journalists engaged Groth and BAAPCD members in the
best exchanges of the day.

To assess the effectiveness of the press conference, however,
one must look at the ensuing press coverage.

NEWSPAPER COVERAGE

Of 28 dailies in the Bay Area, 17 carried at least one story on
the Groth report. Most printed only one, from eight to more than 80
column inches in length. (For a methodological description of this
content analysis, see Appendix B.) Since many papers did not have
reporters at the press conference, they relied on press releases
from Stanford, a wire service story, and rewrites from other papers.
There really was no predicting the diverse coverage that resulted,

so it might be better to intuit a few general rules that seemed to govern the behavior of editors and reporters:

1. "If the Groth report names a specific company in my paper's area of circulation that is polluting up a storm, don't mention it in the story." The San Leandro <u>Morning News</u> lives side by side with the Fry Roofing Company, which has accumulated enough violations from the BAAPCD to paper some of its customers' roofs. Yet the local newspaper ignored the data on this company in the Groth report. Dailies in Contra Costa County excluded mention of the activities of numerous oil refineries in their stories. Only three of the seventeen papers discussed the performance of local industry.

2. "Disregard the evaluations of the performance of the BAAPCD member who represents our area." Again, only three papers presented this information.

3. "Place the story in some obscure position in the paper," such as page 45 of the San Francisco <u>Chronicle</u> opposite the TV log. Only ten of the seventeen papers that carried stories on the report placed them somewhere in the first three pages of the paper or on a special section page.

4. "Stick to generalities and polls." Twelve of the seventeen papers focused on the "ineffectiveness" of the BAAPCD, without naming any names, and ten reported poll results on attitudes toward air pollution. These were by far the favorite themes stressed.

5. "Don't help the public to help itself. Keep the average reader in the dark." Only two of the papers listed some of Groth's suggested activities for the public to improve air quality, and not a single paper told its readers how to obtain a copy of the report.

BROADCAST COVERAGE

Not surprisingly, the best performance here was turned in by the educational television station in San Francisco, KQED, which did a more thorough job with the Groth report than either of San Francisco's daily newspapers. Reporter Marilyn Baker, who attended the news conference for KQED, initially focused on the public opinion poll, displaying charts constructed at the station to facilitate the visualization of opinion preferences. She then described the report's abrasive criticism of certain local industries, singling out the Fry Roofing Company for its excesses. She presented the evaluations of individual BAAPCD directors, and she told viewers how to obtain a copy of the report.

The local all-news radio station, KCBS, carried reports of the press conference for two days, and snippets of Groth's findings turned up on a continuing feature entitled "Ecology Scene." KPIX, the top-rated San Francisco television station, placed the story just ahead of the sports and weather, leading with the public opinion poll. This preceded a film segment in which KPIX Newsman Rollin Post asked Groth's opinion on the effects of proposed state legislation banning automobile engines running on leaded fuel, an illustration of the broadcast media's propensity for focusing on whatever question, however inane, their own man at the scene poses. The remainder of broadcast coverage was below the KPIX standard.

THE PUBLIC AND THE PSEUDO-EVENT

Despite the discouraging nature of the coverage, without the press conference there likely would have been no coverage at all. The pseudo-event is the news peg that is a necessary condition for press coverage, even though it is an inefficient means for the exchange of information. The press conference gives legitimacy to the media's involvement with this story. Had Groth simply mailed his report to the media, it is unlikely anything would have appeared in print or over the air.

It is fair to ask who benefits from this sort of media coverage. Members of a special interest group, such as Groth, initiate the pseudo-events in hopes of capturing public attention and raising the level of consciousness and expertise. They know it is one of the few ways of capturing media attention. The media in turn respond to pseudo-events because it is the easiest way for them to operate. The mass public may or may not pay much attention to the reports, but it is quite clear that the people who are concerned enough about air pollution to organize politically to fight it do not benefit from such superficial coverage. Indeed, special interest groups do not rely on the mass media for the information they need to function, because they cannot. The mass media are too slow, too superficial, and too unreliable. Coverage of the Groth report demonstrates that.

We polled by telephone 301 members of the Sierra Club in northern California on their environmental information-seeking habits. Only 18 percent of these eco-activists said they consult the mass media for ecology information, and better than half named an information source more up to date with environmental information than a daily newspaper or broadcast station. Their most important sources were conservation groups and clubs, knowledgeable friends and other individuals, and the academic community.

The wise public relations man recognizes that the model of special interest group to pseudo-event to mass media to unorganized public is not where the action is. For example, a Pacific Gas and Electric executive who has responsibility for governmental and public relations told us that he was not concerned about the quality or quantity of environmental information in the mass media. He is concerned only with where the eco-activists themselves get their information because their lobbying can affect his company's fortunes. Thus, he follows club publications, special interest magazines, and is himself a member of the Sierra Club.

Of what importance, then, is the environmental information appearing in the mass media as the end-product of the pseudo-event system? First, at its best it can act as an alerting mechanism for the activists, reminding them of upcoming events or problems and forcing them to seek further information. Second, it indicates to politicians the issues their constituents are likely to be discussing. The political system is more willing to face up to the environmental challenge if there is massive, if superficial, press coverage. Third, and most important, mass media stories about environmental deterioration can convert previously inert members of the public into organized eco-activists. As their numbers grow, the likelihood of solving environmental problems increases. This is the main advantage the Sierra Club sees in the increased media attention to environmental deterioration.

News executives who would prefer to transcend the Buzz Joplin image and speak more directly to the special interest groups who make things happen must shed their dependence on the pseudo-event model. They must devote more attention to the political and economic battles being waged over environmental problems. They must approach the environment as a news beat with the same vigor and manpower as they do the local sporting scene. But this is not likely to happen.

To editors of conservation publications and members who work in club offices, the message should be clear. Eco-activists and the better environmental reporters rely heavily on the clubs for information. A high priority of all clubs should be the collection and dissemination of information on local environmental problems for all who request it. If the activists and their organizations do not meet this challenge, the media cannot take up the slack.

ENVIRONMENTAL ADVERTISING
AND SOCIAL RESPONSIBILITY

Early in 1970 Potlatch Forests Inc. began a new national advertising campaign featuring a photograph of breathtaking natural beauty. The accompanying headline of the ad reads, "It cost us a bundle but the Clearwater River still runs clear." According to Newsweek of December 28, 1970, the photo was snapped some 50 miles upstream from the Potlatch pulp and paper plant in Lewiston, Idaho. Newsweek sent its own photographer out to get a picture of the river just downstream from the plant. It looked like a cesspool.

Every day Potlatch dumps up to 40 tons of organic wastes back into the Clearwater River and the nearby Snake River. True, it has announced plans to spend $9.6 million on pollution-abatement equipment for the Lewiston plant. But at the time of the ad campaign these were only plans—formulated after the federal government charged the company with illegally polluting the river. Potlatch also contributes 2.5 million tons of sulfur gases and 1.8 million pounds of particulates to the local atmosphere every year. It has, says Newsweek, the "dubious distinction of being the only industrial mill in the U.S. to have been the subject of separate air- and water-pollution abatement hearings before Federal authorities."

For failing to mention the facts in the above paragraph, the Potlatch ad may be judged misleading. For asserting that the Clearwater River runs clear, it may be judged inaccurate. For backing up the assertion with an inappropriate photograph, it may be judged fraudulent.

––––––––––––

Material for this chapter was prepared by Peter M. Sandman. Please see Chapter 2 for Mr. Sandman's biography.

A significant percentage of the information about the environment that reaches the American public does so through advertisements. The sole purpose of most advertisements is to persuade the public to purchase a specific product, or type of product, or to promote the image of a company in the public mind. The environmental message that accompanies these ads may be an incomplete statement of the truth. It may be inaccurate, misleading, or fraudulent.

Quasi-environmental ads entail corporate claims that their activities, marketable products, or services affect energy consumption, pollution, waste disposal, health, or growth. Frequently they imply that these corporations are "improving" the environment, either from previous industrial damage or as an enhancement on nature. Invariably there is scientifically inaccurate use of such terms as ecology, environment, and natural. Such advertising is misleading and, from a biological standpoint, frequently without any sound basis whatsoever. Since this form of advertising fails to demonstrate concern for genuine environmental stewardship, we prefer to call it eco-pornography, after the term suggested by Thomas Turner. The Potlatch Forests ad is distinctly eco-pornographic.

In this chapter we provide other notable examples of eco-pornography and then discuss where the responsibility lies in policing such advertising. The Federal Trade Commission (FTC), other government agencies, and the courts are concerned with ads that are factually inaccurate. The advertising acceptance standards of newspapers, magazines, and broadcast stations affect advertising quality, and they receive close scrutiny here. Should such ads be accepted by the mass media? Which ads are now rejected, and why? How can socially responsible editors and station managers, who are not environmental experts, decide which ads to exclude? What are their legal obligations on advertising acceptance? The chapter concludes with recommendations for editors and broadcasters on establishing workable acceptance criteria.

THE ENVIRONMENTAL ADVERTISEMENT

The most widely discussed environmental advertising campaign to date is the Standard Oil of California campaign for Chevron gasoline additive F-310, which began on January 1, 1970.

F-310 is a gasoline detergent additive. It helps clean out dirty engines such as those found in very old cars. Since dirty engines emit more unburned hydrocarbons and more carbon monoxide than clean engines, F-310 significantly reduces the output of those pollutants. However, it does so, only on very dirty engines and only for the first few tankfuls. Once an engine is reasonably clean, F-310 is of no further use. Moreover, detergent additives do nothing whatever about ozone, nitrogen oxides, or lead—the three most important automobile components of smog and air pollution. Detergent additives have been added to gasolines customarily for several decades. F-310 may indeed be a new formula, but that fact is disputed. It certainly is not a new kind of formula.

The print and broadcast ads claim otherwise. "NEW," they shout. "The most outstanding development in automotive fuel technology in years." "Now, research scientists at Standard Oil Company of California have achieved the most long-awaited gasoline development in history." The campaign is very dramatic. It features balloons and plastic bags, statistics and testimonials, all orchestrated by former astronaut Scott Carpenter.

Much of the debate on F-310 has centered on whether or not it works. California's Air Resources Board, among others, found that it did not; others have claimed that it does. But unless F-310 is really new, and unless it works considerably better than other detergent additives, the ads must be termed misleading.

Shortly after the F-310 campaign began, the FTC reached the tentative conclusion that the advertisements were misleading to the point of illegality. It proposed that California Standard voluntarily withdraw all ads—which the company refused to do. The case is now being adjudicated.

The FTC's major objection to the F-310 campaign was simply that the additive is neither new nor significantly different from competing additives. But it also charged the company with false advertising on several other grounds:

1. A specially formulated gasoline was used to stimulate a dirty engine and produce black exhaust for comparison with the F-310 exhaust. (A Chevron spokesman later admitted fooling with the gas mixture a bit to give the ad more impact.)

2. The ads were staged outside a building labeled "Standard Oil Company Research Center." The building actually was the Riverside County Courthouse.

3. A local resident who claimed that she watched the commercials being filmed said she saw two large, inflated balloons—one clear, the other jet black. Neither was attached to any car.

4. The "clean" balloon in the televised test actually contained large amounts of invisible pollutants, including even carbon monoxide and hydrocarbons. All it was missing was carbon particulates from the specially contrived dirty engine.

After reviewing the charges and counter-charges, the Wall Street Journal entitled its article on the subject, "Chevron's F-310 Gas: A Lesson in How Not to Promote a Product."[1]

The FTC was concerned that the ads would mislead consumers into buying the product. But the F-310 campaign was misleading in another sense as well. By implying that F-310 was a major break-through in pollution control, the ads also implied that motorists need no longer worry about automotive air pollution. The word "misleading" thus has two different meanings when applied to environmental advertising. An ad may mislead the consumer into a false view of the product, thus violating the FTC's standard of truth. Or it may mis-lead him into a false view of threats to the environment, thus violating the ecologist's standard of environmental responsibility. The F-310 campaign does both.

Pacific Gas and Electric (PG&E) is northern California's largest electric utility. As a government-regulated monopoly, its rates are set by the state, which allows it a fixed percentage of profit over and above costs. Since an advertisement increases costs, every PG&E ad makes money for the company. If an ad also encourages greater use of electric power and less attention to the environmental effects of power plants, it makes all the more money.

On April 21, 1970, PG&E ran a full-page ad in the San Francisco Chronicle. "PG&E and the Environment," the headline read, "A bal-ance of ecology and energy." (Since ecology is the study of the inter-relatedness of organisms and environmental factors, including energy, one can hardly "balance" one against the other.) The ad goes on to assert that a nuclear power plant that heats water by 18 degrees causes "no harmful effect." It adds that the danger from radioactivity is nil and that the company is doing everything it can to put electric lines underground. It concludes that "the use of electricity produces no pollution at all."

The statement about radioactive danger is debatable; the others are demonstrably false. Thermal pollution, for example, is known to affect the metabolism, feeding habits, growth rates, and reproduction patterns of water life. Some fish refuse to cross a warm water "barrier" to get to their spawning grounds; such species die out in the face of thermal pollution. Heated water also affects micro-organisms and plant life, permanently altering an area's ecology. All these facts are well established and presumably well known to PG&E.

Many environmental ads, of course, are entirely unobjectionable. A bookstore that advertises its stock of ecology books is guilty of nothing. Neither is a manufacturer who advertises his pollution-control devices, or a supermarket advertising the availability of low-phosphate detergents. In late 1970 a consortium of steel and aluminum can manufacturers began an advertising campaign urging consumers to return their cans for recycling; some of the ads included a complete list of local recycling centers. Quite probably the cam-paign was designed to fight a possible move to returnable bottles.

Nonetheless, the ads are factually accurate and environmentally responsible.

But others use catch words in an irresponsible manner to cash in on environmental concern; such ads include the "Stop Smogging" slogan of Lark cigarettes and "Eye Pollution" from Murine. Others finesse the major issues in their ads. The Koppers Company, a manufacturer of laminated electric transmission towers, placed an ad in Business Week featuring the photograph of a graceful, modernistic Koppers tower with the headline, "Don't stop progress. Just make it gracefully." The implication is that a few talented engineers and perhaps a sculptor in residence are all that is needed to solve the environmental problems of electric power transmission.

These are but a few of the more prominent examples of environmental advertising. The Ecology Center in Berkeley, California, collected more than 400 such ads in an eight-month period in 1970-71.

The possible undesirable social effects of such advertising could be offset by hard news coverage on the topics in the ads themselves. But it is unreasonable to expect the news media to devote their resources to correcting the misimpressions of their own advertisements. Only when an ad is so misleading as to warrant government sanction is the press likely to "cover" it, and even then such stories are small and inconspicuously located (see Chapter 1 for a discussion of the pressures on the press that lead to this protection for advertisers). Even a vast improvement in news coverage will not solve the problem of misleading ads. Advertising censorship—either by regulatory agencies, legislation, or the media owners themselves—seems the only viable alternative to curbing such ads.

ADVERTISING ACCEPTANCE:
STANDARDS AND PROCEDURES

The reasons why a particular mass medium rejects a particular advertisement often are muddled, unclear, and inexplicit. Nonetheless, the following list of eight prototypic reasons will prove helpful in this chapter's overview of advertising acceptance standards and procedures:

1. Because the advertisement is illegal. The fear of government regulation is ever-present in the minds of broadcasters. Actual government regulations are scrupulously followed by all three media (newspapers, magazines, and broadcast).

2. Because the advertisement is in violation of a professional code to which the medium subscribes. This is the principal reason why local broadcasters reject ads. Although they make use of Better

Business Bureau guidelines, newspapers and magazines have few
professional codes on which to rely.

   3. Because the advertisement is indecent or in poor taste.
Because tasteless ads are thought most likely to produce criticism,
broadcasters are ever-vigilant about matters of taste. Except for
certain product categories (notably movie ads), newspapers and
magazines are less concerned about taste.

   4. Because the advertisement is likely to offend specific
minorities or pressure groups. The thought of offending anyone
frightens broadcasters and influences their advertising policy tremendously. Newspapers and magazines are less concerned about
offensiveness.

   5. Because the advertisement is dishonest, inconsistent, fraudulent, or otherwise misleading. Newspapers tend to be extremely
scrupulous about ads that are misleading on their face. Magazines
and broadcasting are considerably laxer.

   6. Because the advertisement fails to give an accurate or
complete impression of the product or service advertised. Except
for certain magazines, none of the three media requires itself to
investigate the validity of claims. But all (especially newspapers
and broadcasting) make exceptions for product categories that have
caused problems in the past.

   7. Because the advertisement is inconsistent with the function,
intent, or image of the medium. Magazines reject ads primarily for
this reason; newspapers and broadcasting seldom consider it.

   8. Because the advertisement is socially undesirable. Newspapers consider this standard primarily for political ads. Broadcasting considers it when required to do so by government or public
pressure. Magazines seldom consider it at all.

   These patterns of advertising acceptance, it should be stressed,
reflect inherent characteristics of the media as well as historical
developments. Broadcasting is super-sensitive to offensive ads
because it is the only medium required by law to serve the public
interest. Magazines reject ads that contradict their image because
they are the only medium that depends for survival on the allegiance
of a specialized audience. Newspapers concern themselves primarily
with misleading ads because they are the only medium that is supported
almost entirely by local (retail) advertising.

   How do these patterns influence the acceptability of environmental advertising? Once again, it will help to run through the eight
criteria in order.

   First, environmental ads are legal. To the best of this researcher's knowledge, there is no law or local ordinance currently
in force that speaks directly to the environmental impact of advertising.

Second, environmental ads do not violate professional codes. The only National Association of Broadcasters Code interpretation that deals even remotely with the environment is the one entitled "Insecticides." It is devoted entirely to questions of health, especially the health of children and pets.

Third, environmental ads are in good taste. Despite our label of eco-pornography, not a single ad discussed at the beginning of this chapter could be called tasteless in the usual sense of the word.

Fourth, environmental ads are not offensive to any pressure group powerful enough to effect a change in media standards.

Fifth, environmental ads are seldom dishonest or misleading on their face. Because environmental issues are technically complex, the validity of environmental claims rarely can be assessed merely by examining the ads themselves.

Sixth, environmental ads are likely to fail to give an accurate impression of the product or service advertised, especially of the environmental impact of that product or service. However, they do not constitute a category that the media customarily investigate for accuracy.*

Seventh, environmental ads are not inconsistent with the public image or self-image of any of the mass media, with the exception of a small number of environment-oriented magazines.

Eighth, environmental ads are (in our opinion) socially undesirable in many cases. However, the media show no signs of agreement, at least not to the extent of assigning environmental ads to this seldom-used category.

There are, in short, two potential reasons for rejecting environmental advertisements: inaccuracy and social desirability. The media seem disinclined to use either one. A look at local standards and procedures may help to explain why.

_____

*In 1970 the Alyeska Pipeline Service Company ran a series of newspaper and magazine ads defending the Alaska pipeline on environmental grounds and offering to send proof on request. The "proof," to those who requested it, turned out to be a series of proposals for yet-to-be-done (at that time) experiments. Only The New York Times questioned these ads, and not one newspaper or magazine asked to see the proof before running the ads. Similarly, the Standard Oil Company of California received no requests from the media for substantiation of claims until after the Federal Trade Commission accused its F-310 ads of being false and misleading. Even after the FTC complaint, most of the media continued to run the ads; only a small minority asked for documentation or demanded changes.

The advertising or continuity acceptance departments of 36 newspapers and 16 broadcast stations in the San Francisco Bay Area were queried and respondents were asked for a copy of their advertising acceptance standards. In the vast majority of cases where no such written document existed, respondents were asked to describe briefly, in their own words, their acceptance standards and procedures. All interviews were conducted in June and July 1971.

The responses were remarkably homogeneous. Newspaper respondents indicated that questionable ads were referred to the advertising manager who, sometimes with the aid of a committee, made the final decision. Although misleading ads were the principal source of difficulty, few papers had specific policies to deal with them; as a rule the advertising managers based their judgments entirely on common sense and experience. Papers were far more likely to have policies in the areas of erotic and suggestive advertising (14 papers) and political advertising (11 papers). In addition, two respondents mentioned special policies on palm-readers and spiritualists; two mentioned cigarettes; and one each mentioned alcohol, land developments, hemorrhoid remedies, and gambling.

Of the 16 broadcast respondents, 12 indicated that their advertising acceptance standards were more or less identical with those of the National Association of Broadcasters (NAB) Codes. Policies were likely to be stricter or more detailed than the Codes only in the areas of erotic advertising (six stations), tasteless advertising (five stations), political advertising (three stations), and advertising volume (three stations). In addition, two respondents commented that they took special care with drug advertising and one each mentioned the following categories: alcohol, land deals, lotteries, news simulation, and misleading advertising. In all cases a continuity director was in charge of previewing the ads, with questionable ones often referred to the general manager for final disposition.*

Several other points of interest emerged from this informal survey:

1. Reliance on sources of information aside from the ads themselves was minimal. Only one respondent specifically mentioned the

---

*In the three-year period 1968-70 the Federal Communications Commission received 422 listener complaints about Bay Area radio stations. Of the 87 complaints that dealt with advertising, the majority commented generally on taste or volume. Only 19 complaints referred to specific ads. Of these, five concerned social effects (drugs, gambling, cigarettes); four concerned offensiveness (sex, racial and religious slurs); four concerned misleading ads (land development, retail); and six were miscellaneous complaints.

Better Business Bureau, while several volunteered that "common sense" was their only guide. Respondents cheerfully admitted their willingness to carry ads for products whose dangers or defects were exposed in their news columns or even their editorials.

2. Distrust of the government was widespread. Many respondents indicated their opposition to government regulation of advertising, although predicting its increase. Several volunteered their disinclination to use government opposition to an ad (as in the case of F-310) as even a contributing factor in their acceptance decision.

3. Economic considerations were paramount. Several small newspapers and radio stations admitted that they accepted ads they would prefer to reject because they needed the revenue. Alcohol was the most frequently mentioned example.

4. Advertising rejection was confined almost entirely to local ads. Several newspapers indicated that any ad acceptable to their national ad agency was acceptable to them. Broadcast stations left the acceptance of national advertising to the Code Authority, the network, the chain, or the agency.

5. Political advertising produced the greatest diversity (and specificity) of standards. Policies ranged from outright bans through timing and labeling requirements to total acceptance. Many respondents referred all political ads to their legal departments.

Only two respondents mentioned environmental advertising during the interviews. Television station KRON indicated that as a result of government scrutiny it now pays careful attention to oil company claims for gasoline additives, although as yet no ads have been rejected on these grounds. And the Contra Costa Times & Green Sheet boasted that it was the only newspaper in the country with a special environmental editor whose job it was to solicit, write, and censor environmental advertisements. His goal, he said, is to "help local companies present their environmental message in a way that will be effective and credible to the public." With his help, the Times & Green Sheet published a 68-page environmental supplement on June 27, 1971.

In an effort to gain greater insight into advertising acceptance policies, procedures, and philosophies, representatives of five local media were interviewed in depth.

The San Francisco Examiner

Charles L. Gould, publisher of the San Francisco Examiner, is also the newspaper's principal advertising censor. In the early 1960s the Examiner had a full-time ad acceptance person but the job disappeared when the paper organized a joint operating agreement with

the morning San Francisco Chronicle. Today the San Francisco
Newspaper Printing Company solicits ads for both papers and refers
questionable ones directly to the two publishers.

The Examiner is well-known locally for its strict censorship
of "pornographic" entertainment and movie ads. In 1965 the paper
began evolving a complex code for movie copy and illustrations. "We
dry-cleaned the ads until they were acceptable," explains Gould.
"But I began to worry that this was a form of entrapment. The ads
were clean, so readers attended the movies, which were by no means
clean." Therefore, in 1970 the paper revamped its strategy. Certain
movie theaters were identified as "wholesale grind houses," and all
advertisements from those theaters were rejected, regardless of the
tastefulness of any particular ad.

Gould is ambivalent about the reasons for that decision. On the
one hand, he stresses that "our readers concur in our judgment of
pornography." On the other hand, he maintains that he would have
rejected the ads in any case. As an Examiner editorial on December
8, 1970, put it:

> [In the past we] grudgingly accepted the decision of the
> Supreme Court that "community standards" should deter-
> mine what is obscene and what is not.
>
> After witnessing the results of this decision, we are
> now convinced that community standards do not deter-
> mine what is pornography. Quite the contrary. We be-
> lieve the results in San Francisco are proof positive that
> proliferating pornography creates debased community
> standards. . . .
>
> We should have thrown this ugliness out of our ad-
> vertising columns long ago.

Yet Gould is reluctant to impose his own standards on his
readers. Although he was willing to do so in the case of pornography,
he points out that "we do accept ads for 'peace' marches even though
they are destructive, divisive, and socially damaging. They have a
right to be heard."

Aside from pornography, the Examiner flatly rejects or carefully screens the following ad categories: dating bureaus, massage
parlors, political ads, help-wanted ads for models or waitresses,
hypnotists, homosexual groups, lonely hearts clubs, and guns. Because the Examiner has no time to investigate individual advertisers,
most of these restrictions are categorical. They are designed to
protect readers from danger, entrapment, and bad taste.

Like most newspapers, the Examiner also is concerned about
misleading advertising. It is especially careful about land developments

investment ads, and mail-order ads, all of which are routinely checked
out with the Better Business Bureau and other sources. Employment
agencies and home rental agencies also are carefully watched because
the paper has had trouble with them in the past. Retail ads that seem
misleading on their face often are referred to Gould, who may demand
alterations. He cites as a typical case a camera advertisement that
featured three expensive lenses in a photograph although the copy
admitted the lenses were not included in the sale price.

The only environment-related ad that Gould can recall rejecting
was a "Save the Seals" appeal that he believed (on the advice of the
police department) to be a swindle. To the best of his memory, Gould
has never rejected any ad on environmental grounds.

This is in part a reflection of Gould's own untroubled environmental attitudes. He claims he has never seen, in any publication,
an ad he thought environmentally irresponsible. But it also is a
reflection of Examiner procedures. The San Francisco Newspaper
Printing Company rejects an average of six ads a week on standing
instructions from Gould. It refers to him an additional one to five
ads a week. A few of these are misleading on their face; most are
in categories that have been flagged for special attention because
of potential fraud or offensiveness. An ad that is superficially honest
and not in a special category has no chance whatever of reaching
Gould's desk prior to publication.

The Examiner, Gould maintains, "has refused hundreds of
thousands of dollars in questionable advertising." But many questions,
including all those that are the subject of this chapter, are never
asked.

The Palo Alto Times

Advertising censorship at the Palo Alto Times is divided into
three parts. Certain ad classifications are forbidden or restricted
as a matter of management policy. Questions of taste in advertising
are adjudicated by the editor. And matters of business ethics are
decided by the display advertising director, Howard Schonberger.

Ads that are rejected by the Times "policy book" include
alcoholic beverages; fortune tellers, astrologers, hypnotists, and the
like; race tracks and other gambling ads; last-minute election ads;
and anonymous ads. These categories are rejected simply because
the founders and principal owners of the newspaper consider them
socially detrimental. In the case of alcohol, the only big-money
rejection, their disapproval is supported by the proximity of Stanford
University and the municipal ordinance barring liquor stores.

Schonberger diligently enforces these restrictions, but he does not agree with them. "The media shouldn't make moral decisions for the public," he says. "If a product is bad, then the government should outlaw it. If it's legal, we shouldn't censor any commodity." If he were to reject any category of ads, Schonberger maintains, he would not pick liquor since both cigarettes and automobiles (this may be facetious) are more harmful to society. For philosophical reasons, Schonberger himself does not ban any product category although he has the authority to do so.

Taste and offensiveness are relatively minor issues at the Times, whose readership tends to be fairly permissive. But some movie ads have been censored, as was a water bed advertisement that contained sexual allusions.

Schonberger tends to find business-related reasons for rejecting ads that other papers might question on grounds of taste or propriety. An ad for a topless bar, for example, was rejected on the ground that the waitresses wore "pasties" and therefore the ad was misleading. Similarly, when an anti-war group wanted to run a list of local merchants who had refused to put anti-war posters in their windows, Schonberger turned down the ad because the implication that the merchants favored the war was misleading. He says he would have accepted a list of merchants who did put up the posters.

Schonberger's principal concern is misleading advertising, and in this area he depends heavily on his salesmen. "Every salesman is trained in the legal and ethical aspects of advertising," he explains. "If an advertiser wants to run something misleading, the salesman suggests that an honest ad might be more effective—and he helps the advertiser write an effective, honest ad. If necessary, he refuses the dishonest one. The only ads that get to me are the borderline cases."

When necessary, Schonberger is very hard on misleading advertisers. He lobbied the city to pass a law banning "closing out sales" from stores that are not actually going out of business. When a reader calls with a complaint that Schonberger thinks is justified, he may well take it to the district attorney; he did so a few years ago and caused the failure of a local Dodge dealership. Investment ads, in particular, are carefully investigated and cleared through the Better Business Bureau. But these are rare events. Because of the scrupulousness of his salesmen, Schonberger himself looks at no more than two or three ads a week.

Although the Times adheres religiously to legal and Better Business Bureau standards for ad presentation, it rarely checks into the validity of advertising claims, except for investment ads. "There's a big difference," says Schonberger, "between the scientific judgment of a product and flat-out deception in an ad. A newspaper

shouldn't print deceptive ads, but it should not judge products either.
We're not equipped to make that judgment in any case."

Because of these principles, Schonberger has never censored
an ad on environmental grounds and suspects that he never will.
He agrees that "cigarettes and DDT are unhealthy, and F-310 is
probably next to useless." But none of that has been proved, he says.
"It's enough that we print the charges and complaints in our news
columns. People aren't idiots. They know what the charges are.
And charges aren't proof."

Schonberger himself is not insensitive to environmental considerations. "If I had a DDT ad, I would try to persuade the advertiser to advertise something else instead." But if persuasion
proved ineffective, the ad would run.

Sunset Magazine

In the middle of the advertising department of Sunset's Menlo
Park office is a three-drawer filing cabinet labeled "Rejected Ad-
vertisements." Some 500 files are located there. Labels in the
"A" section read (in chronological order): Arthur's Books, Acme
Manufacturing Company, Acorn Press, Age-Less Cosmetics, All-
American School, Alii Land, Ralph Allum Company, Alva Tranquil
Corporation, Amaz-on, Abbott Laboratories, American Petroleum
Institute, and 21 others.

According to Richard R. Kitson, Sunset advertising service
manager, every one of these ads was rejected "because it did not
fit the Sunset image." Kitson says, "Sunset is a travel, building,
food, and gardening magazine. We try to confine our ads to those
four areas. Anything that does not complement the editorial product
is rejected."

What sort of ads fail under this standard? Liquor ads for one,
although not wine ads, which are "a part of Western living." Also
tobacco ads (for more than 25 years), feminine hygiene products,
money-making schemes, gambling ads, and controversial books.
Also underwear ads and anything that pictures the undraped female.
Also investment trusts, mutual funds, and stock offerings. Also
political advertising. Also (with some exceptions) health foods,
internal and external medicines, real estate promotions, and contests. Also, Kitson says, any advertisement "that makes claims
Sunset is unable to substantiate." In all, 25 percent of national magazine advertising volume consists of ads that are unacceptable to
Sunset.

Kitson reads every advertisement before it goes into the magazine. If the ad is one of those forbidden in Sunset's extensive "Policy

Book," he rejects it. If the ad is tasteless, offensive, suggestive, or strident, he rejects it. If the ad includes product claims, he checks them out; if he cannot verify the claims, he rejects the ad. Even if the ad is perfectly innocent but "just doesn't sound like a Sunset kind of ad," he rejects it. When in doubt, Kitson may appeal to a committee including the publisher, the assistant publisher, the advertising director, himself, and his assistant. But, usually, when in doubt about an ad, he rejects it.

Not every magazine can afford such stringent advertising acceptance standards, as Kitson himself readily admits. Certainly, he says, most newspapers and broadcast stations cannot. "But Sunset is very well off, and we can afford to be picky. And it is in our long-range best interests to make sure that every ad we publish is consistent with our image as a home and family informational magazine."

In 1969 Sunset's gardening emphasis began to involve the magazine in environmental issues. It editorialized against DDT and certain other chlorinated hydrocarbons, and immediately announced that it would no longer carry advertisements for products containing such substances. Kitson then began referring all pesticide ads to the gardening editor for comment. The following was a typical response:

> I cannot state any official [i.e., as defined publicly in Sunset] objections to the ad. But, from the position of Sunset's integrity, I would object if we would run any of these ads. Many of the products . . . contain chlorinated hydrocarbon ingredients which we know from common sense and experience are just as capable of causing death of non-target organisms as DDT was. We just don't have the final scientific evidence yet to indict these ingredients.

The ad was rejected.

Sunset now rejects a considerable number of ads on environmental grounds. Kitson maintains a file on the environmental impact of various products and industries, together with his files of BBB and FTC reports. He is familiar with many of the environmental ads discussed in this chapter and maintains he would have rejected most of them.

Moreover, Kitson says, "We are beginning to move from the simple question of accuracy to the much harder question of environmental effects. Last year we took a PG&E ad on nuclear power plants and a Shell ad on how clean its Richmond plant was, because our research showed that both ads had a strong base in scientific data. Today, we might well reject them anyhow. One of the items we have on the back-burner now is to look into the environmental

effects of dyed paper products." And Sunset has announced a policy
of rejecting ads for trail bikes and snowmobiles because of their
environmental impact.

According to Kitson, Sunset's strong stand on the environment
is partly a result of the environmental commitment of its publisher
and many of its editors. "But the big reason is that so much of our
editorial content deals with the environment, and so many of our
readers are concerned about the environment. We try very hard to
be consistent. I wouldn't expect other publications with other kinds
of content to go along."

KPIX Television

KPIX is an affiliate of the CBS network and a member of the
Westinghouse chain. It is not a subscriber to the NAB Code (because
Westinghouse considers the Code too lax in a number of areas), but
it does obey nearly all Code provisions. Thus, depending on its
origins, a commercial on KPIX may have to satisfy several censors:
the Code, Westinghouse, CBS, and KPIX Film and Traffic Supervisor
A. Dean Lucas.

National ads begin with the Code Authority. From there, they
go to CBS, which is a little stricter than the Code in a few areas,
and then to Westinghouse, which is a lot stricter than the Code in
many areas. It is a matter of tremendous inconvenience to everyone—
from the accountants to the engineers—for a local station to yank an
ad off the network feed and substitute its own. But for several years
all Westinghouse stations did precisely that to every cigarette ad
and every Frito Bandito ad (which offended some Mexican-Americans).
They are now doing the same thing to every feminine deodorant ad.

Lucas is not sure why Westinghouse is so much stricter than
the rest of the broadcast industry. "In part it's because we disagree
as to what the public will tolerate," he says. "We believe that it is
in our long-range best interests to avoid commercials that might
antagonize our viewers. But our rules are also a reflection of corporate personality. I think our top management really believes cigarettes are harmful and feminine deodorants are in bad taste."

In theory, KPIX, not CBS or Westinghouse, is responsible even
for national ads. But Lucas says that neither he nor General Manager
William Osterhaus has ever rejected one. "I don't even see the network ads until they are broadcast," he says.

However, Lucas does see every local spot before broadcast,
and censoring these ads is the major part of his job. But even here
he is not on his own. "Most of the time I just enforce the Code and
Westinghouse policy. If there's a spot I don't like that doesn't seem

to be covered by those, I take it to the general manager." What sorts
of ads get rejected in this fashion?

    1. <u>Illegal ads</u>. Lucas has a lot of trouble with lotteries and
contests that border on lotteries. He also is very attuned to the truth-
in-lending laws and has rejected several ads that violated them. His
files of government regulations are enormous.

    2. <u>Offensive ads</u>. Movie trailers and foundation garment ads
are carefully screened. Lucas recently rejected a commercial for
Kangaroo Shorts because the outline of the model's genitals was
visible to the viewer.

    3. <u>Socially undesirable ads</u>. In this category Lucas puts ads
that disparage competitors, mention gambling, or stress violence
or fear (Lucas has rejected a burglar alarm ad because it was likely
to frighten children). By order of the general manager, military recruiting ads also are banned, although Lucas is not sure why.

    Lucas is most on his own in the area of misleading advertising.
If an ad is misleading on its face, he rejects it, but Lucas says this
happens very seldom. For the most part, his concern for misleading
ads is limited to product categories covered by government regulations,
such as truth-in-lending. In addition to these, he pays careful attention
to land development ads and will check out any product claim he personally finds difficult to believe. A book ad that implied an American
Medical Association endorsement, for example, was referred to the
AMA, while a Memorex commercial claiming its tape recorder could
shatter glass was cleared with the Westinghouse office in New York.
But very few ads are checked so closely. "We're not about to set
up testing labs to make sure that the paint really lasts seven years,"
Lucas says.

    Environmental advertising is not one of the categories that
gets special attention from Lucas. Corporate image ads are passed
on by the network and the chain, neither of which has any policies
dealing with environmental impact. As for product claims, Lucas
is familiar with the environmental arguments against such products
as Ecolo-G (his example), but he maintains that they are not proved
and so he carries the ads.

    When the Chevron F-310 campaign first began, Lucas accepted
the commercials without question. Only after a variety of government
agencies had criticized the ads did Lucas take action. He requested
further information from the company and eventually demanded (and
received) several changes in the ads themselves. "It's not my job
to worry about the social or environmental effects of commercials,"
Lucas explains. "That's up to Westinghouse or the NAB. I wouldn't
reject an environmental ad on my own initiative unless I thought it
was misleading in the classic sense."

KSFO Radio

Jack W. Riaska, continuity director for KSFO Radio, does not believe in rejecting commercials unless he has to. "We aren't trying to turn business down," he explains. "We're trying to get as much business as we possibly can. That's what capitalism is all about."

What sorts of commercials does Riaska feel he must reject? "Anything that might endanger our license," he says. "That includes illegal ads, of course, and also ads that violate the Code. We also reject anything that's likely to get our listeners up in arms, such as pornography."

Riaska maintains that his standards are more stringent than those of most local radio stations. He says, "Agencies submit the ads to us first. They know that if KSFO takes it, everyone will take it." Yet he averages only four or five rejected ads a year.

Riaska himself listens to every taped commercial before it is broadcast and reads all ad copy before it goes to the disc jockeys. If he finds an ad that might be illegal (most often a lottery), he refers it to the sales manager, who may take it up with the station's attorneys. If necessary, the agency is informed that the ad is unacceptable. Clearcut violations of the NAB Code (such as liquor ads) are returned to the advertiser immediately with an explanation as to why they cannot be accepted. More subtle Code violations (suggestive ads, for instance) also go to the sales manager, and sometimes the station manager, for final disposition.

Riaska has only one other standard to enforce aside from illegal ads and Code violations. As a matter of station policy, all commercials for pornographic movies are rejected. This is a recent policy. Riaska comments, "We got into a lot of trouble about 'The Stewardesses.' The ads were clean but the movie was filthy, and a lot of listeners objected. So now we use the movie ratings and just don't take ads for the dirty ones."

Riaska says he is always on the lookout for misleading advertising although he seldom runs across any. For example, he recently previewed a spot for Automotive Engineering offering brake overhalls at a bargain price of $40. The commercial began by stating that one could overhall one's "Ford or Chevy" for this price. Later it referred to "all models." Riaska objects to this ad on the ground that it falsely implies that $40 will cover a brake job even on a heavier automobile. He intends to refer the ad to the sales manager and expects that some sort of alteration will be required.

Although careful about ads that are misleading on their face, Riaska says he almost never checks product claims. "We don't have the information to do that," he says. "And even if we did, that's not our job. Misleading ads are against the law. That's why we reject

them. We're in business as a commercial venture, and we don't have
to restrict ourseleves to only best buys. As long as a commercial
is legal and in good taste, it's okay."

Accepting all ads that can be safely and legally accepted is more
than just a matter of economics for Riaska. It is a matter of principle:
"I don't feel any of us has a right to say this is good for society and
this is not good for society. That's authoritarian, not democratic. I
run things by the book. What I personally think of the ads is irrelevant."

KSFO has carried commercials for Shell's No-Pest Strip, the
Alaska pipeline, and Ecolo-G. Riaska says he is unaware of the environmental objections to these three, but "it wouldn't matter if I
knew." He continues to accept advertising for F-310 without question.
"That hasn't been settled yet. It's still a matter of opinion, so we take
the ads," he says.

Riaska understands his job, and he believes in it. "Some other
stations, maybe, turn down ads because they disapprove of them. At
KSFO, we turn down ads only because the government or our listeners
disapprove of them, and we'd be in trouble if we ran them. That is
how it should be in a democratic, capitalist society."

Observations

Environmental advertising is deserving of censorship on two
grounds: (1) that the ads give an inaccurate impression of the products or services advertised (by ignoring or misrepresenting their
environmental impact) and (2) that the ads are socially undesirable.
Neither reason is employed by the mass media very frequently in
the development and administration of advertising acceptance standards.

To the extent that the media reject advertisements only for
self-interested reasons, they are unlikely to begin rejecting environmental advertisements unless public pressure or government
regulation forces them to do so. Nearly all newspapers, magazines,
and broadcast stations will turn down any ad that a significant percentage of their audience finds offensive. Nearly all will turn down
any ad that has been declared illegal or is in serious danger of being
declared illegal. Perhaps it is inevitable that the media will follow
the public and the government in this matter instead of leading the
former and remaining independent of the latter.

Undoubtedly there are many publishers and broadcasters for
whom this is true. Undoubtedly there are many who would be unwilling to reject any ad they felt they could safely accept, even if

convinced the ad deserved rejection. For these individuals, public
pressure and government regulation are the only answers.

But there is reason to suspect—or at least to hope—that the
media's failure to reject environmental advertising is not entirely
on self-interested grounds.

On the procedural level, it is far easier to check an ad for
internal consistency or consistency with common sense than for
consistency with reality. Many magazines go to tremendous expense
to evaluate products and substantiate product claims; in certain
product categories, so do a number of newspapers and broadcast
stations. Many more might be inclined to do so if it were rendered
less difficult and less expensive.

On the philosophical level, some publishers and broadcasters
may well have conscientious objections to imposing on their audience
their own judgments of the value of advertised products and the
effects of advertisements. The "common carrier" view of the media
holds that only in the most extreme cases should any message be
denied access. Many of the most responsible media executives ear-
nestly subscribe to this view, especially in their advertising policy.

Moreover, most publishers and broadcasters simply are not
accustomed to thinking of advertisements in terms of social desirability. Ads that are misleading, offensive, or illegal are rejected
as a matter of course, for these are labels with which all the media
are familiar. But only the representative from Sunset magazine
was at all familiar with the concept of a socially undesirable advertisement. Only after considerable explanation did the others
recognize—apparently for the first time—that an ad could be accurate,
tasteful, and legal but nonetheless damaging in its social effects. It
was hardly surprising that they had no policies for coping with such
ads.

Publishers and broadcasters, in short, do not permit themselves or have not trained themselves to think in terms of an advertisement's social effects. They may reject some ads simply because
they disapprove of them, but almost invariably they find another
justification for the decision. And where no such justification exists,
as in the case of environmental advertising, they feel compelled to
accept the ads.

There is no doubt that the media have failed to establish sufficiently stringent acceptance standards for environmental advertising.
To the extent that this failure is the result of self-interest, it is
subject only to pressure, not to persuasion. But to the extent that it
is motivated by procedural and philosophical considerations, it is
not immutable. New procedures and new philosophies can be suggested.

ENVIRONMENTAL ADVERTISING AND THE LAW

In 1968 radio station KBAY in San Jose received a listener complaint about a possibly misleading booklet on the profit potential of land investments. In his reply to the complaint, KBAY Station Manager R.C. Hollingsworth dealt briefly with his reasons for accepting the ad:

> Remember, it is their business to sell real estate, which is still a good investment in this state. And, remember too, <u>we in the advertising business are obligated to accept advertising as long as the copy meets the code of the National Association of Broadcasters.</u> [Emphasis added.]

Hollingsworth is not alone in this belief. Nearly all of the media personnel questioned by this researcher expressed some uncertainty about their right to reject advertising. Most felt reasonably confident with respect to ads that fell into some traditional category of advertising acceptance: misleading ads, tasteless ads, NAB Code violations, and the like. But when faced with an ad they wished to question for less conventional reasons, the majority were fearful of the legal implications of rejection.

The Right of Rejection

Although apparently very common, this fear is entirely unjustified. With the exception of a single early case,[2] the courts have agreed unanimously that the media are free to reject any advertisement they wish as long as the rejection is not the result of an illegal conspiracy in restraint of trade. At least 15 appellate courts have reached this conclusion.

A leading case in this area is <u>Shuck v. Carroll Daily Herald,</u> decided by the Iowa Supreme Court in 1933. Shuck, who operated a cleaning and dyeing service, claimed that in rejecting his advertisements the <u>Herald</u> was discriminating between him and his competitors. The court ruled that such discrimination was entirely legal:

> The newspaper business is an ordinary business. It is a business essentially private in nature—as private as that of the baker, grocer, or milkman, all of which perform a service on which, to a greater or less extent, the communities depend, but which bears no such relation to the public as to warrant its inclusion in the category of businesses charged

with public use. . . . Thus, as a newspaper is a strictly
private enterprise the publishers thereof have a right
to publish whatever advertisements they desire and to
refuse to publish whatever advertisements they do not
wish to publish.[3]

More recently, the owner of a local movie theater sued the
Battle Creek, Michigan, Inquirer and News after both papers refused
to print his ads for an "adult" movie. Citing the Shuck decision and
a number of other precedents, the court decided in favor of the publisher:

The First Amendment to the Federal Constitution
declares and safeguards the sanctity of freedom of the
press. Our founding fathers recognized that well-informed
citizens are essential for the preservation of democratic
institutions, and toward this end, an independent press is
indispensable. The public interest, therefore . . . demands that the press shall remain independent, unfettered
by governmental regulations regardless of whether that
regulation stems from legislative enactments or judicial
decisions.[4]

The comparison of these two decisions is instructive. On the
one hand, the media are declared free to reject whatever advertising
they please on grounds of freedom of contract, the right of any business to choose its customers. On the other hand, they are accorded
the same freedom on grounds of the First Amendment, the Constitutional reluctance of the courts to regulate the press. The two rationales
are not entirely consistent, but both lead to the same conclusion.
Whether viewed as an ordinary business or as a special entity, the
mass media are entitled to reject whatever advertising they wish.
   On either or both of these grounds, other courts have ruled
that the media may reject not only general advertising but also
classifieds and even legal notices. Political advertising also may be
rejected. The reasons for the decisions are immaterial, even if
based on caprice, prejudice, or malice. Also immaterial is the fact
that a newspaper has sufficient advertising space available or that
it willingly accepts advertising from other businesses of the same
sort. Deciding what ads to reject is, in short, entirely at the discretion of the media themselves.[5]
   There are only three exceptions to this principle. First, the
media are obligated to accept advertising if they have contracted to
do so. For this reason, nearly all ad contracts contain a clause
explicitly reserving the right of rejection of any grounds whatever.

Second, the decision to reject an advertisement is illegal if it is a restraint of trade. Thus, for example, several media may not conspire together to force an advertiser out of business by rejecting his ads. And the dominant medium in a community may not condition its acceptance of advertising on a pledge not to advertise in competing media. However, mere ownership of a de facto monopoly does not in itself constitute a restraint of trade. Monopoly media also may reject whatever ads they wish, as long as the rejection is not calculated to preserve the monopoly.[6]

Third, government-owned media may not discriminate among advertisers on ideological grounds; to do so is a violation of the First Amendment. This is a recently established principle, based primarily on two cases: (1) a Wisconsin decision requiring the student newspaper at a state college to accept all political advertising if it accepts any and (2) a federal decision requiring the New York City Transit Authority to accept a billboard from the Students for a Democratic Society. Neither case, of course, applies to privately owned media.

The right to reject advertising even on the most egregiously irresponsible grounds has been consistently upheld by the courts. In 1969 four Chicago newspapers turned down an ad from the Amalgated Clothing Workers of America. The ad urged readers not to buy imported clothes and specifically named Marshall Field & Company as the largest single importer of men's apparel in the Chicago area. The four papers apparently decided to reject the ad because it might be offensive to Marshall Field, a major advertiser who also happens to own two of the newspapers involved.

The union took the case to Federal District Court, which decided in favor of the papers. The judge said, "Political advertisements are constitutionally protected to no greater and no lesser extent than other forms of speech, and interference by state action with such expression is prohibited." He added that there was no validity to the argument "that those who can pay for political advertisements are constitutionally entitled to have them published by private businesses."[7] The union promptly appealed the case to the Federal Circuit Court, which affirmed the lower court's decision.

The leading judicial decisions on the right to reject advertising all stem from the print media, newspapers and magazines. Broadcast complaints customarily are taken not to the courts but to the Federal Communications Commission (FCC). On several occasions (notably in the case of cigarette commercials), the FCC has held that the acceptance of controversial advertising obligates broadcasters to pay adequate attention to competing viewpoints, either through more advertising or through other means. But the FCC has never restricted the right of broadcasters to reject any particular commercial on any ground whatever.[8]

In fact, the FCC traditionally has imposed on broadcasters an affirmative obligation to reject certain categories of advertising. In its early years the FCC often commented during license hearings on the qualitative merits of certain ads, notably harmful medical advertising, liquor commercials, and ads for contraceptive devices. In addition, the FCC has long held that it is the responsibility of each broadcaster to "assure that no material is broadcast which will deceive or mislead the public."[9]

In 1954, for example, radio station WMPS applied for a television channel in Memphis in competition with station WREC. The former's application was turned down because the station was known to have accepted "bait and switch" advertising. As the FCC put it:

> Acceptance in good faith of all advertising offered un-
> accompanied by an investigation into the practices of the
> advertiser is an avoidance of the proper responsibility
> of the broadcaster. . . . Had more care been exercised
> by the WMPS management it would have been informed
> of the undesirability of such advertising and have eli-
> minated it from its programs.[10]

A distinction must be drawn here between FCC standards for broadcast responsibility on the one hand and criminal and civil liability on the other. The latter is administered by the Federal Trade Commission and the courts, not by the FCC. Traditionally, publishers and broadcasters have been held liable for actionable advertisements only under four very special circumstances: (1) if the ad is patently illegal; (2) if the medium itself is a sponsor of the ad; (3) if the medium voluntarily prepares the ad on behalf of its sponsor; or (4) if the medium endorses the ad with a seal of approval or some other explicit guarantee.[11]

It occasionally has been suggested that media liability for actionable advertising should be extended beyond these limits. In a 1927 right-to-reject case, for example, a New York court commented that not only was a newspaper entitled to turn down a misleading advertisement but it was legally obligated to do so.[12] More recently, several "consumer protection" bills have been introduced in Congress to subject the media to suit on grounds of false advertising even if they were unaware of the deception. However, current legislative and common law limits media liability for advertising to the four circumstances listed above.

It is ironic that the only appellate law case dealing with the right or obligation to reject an environmental advertisement concerned an ad from a conservation group. The ad protested the construction of an animal byproducts rendering plant in Denver on the ground that it would pollute the surrounding countryside. Two Denver newspapers, the Post and the Rocky Mountain News, refused to print the ad because it urged consumers to boycott the manufacturer. When the boycott copy was eliminated, the newspapers again rejected the ad, this time because it still named the manufacturer and his product line. Following the established precedent, a Federal District Court ruled that the papers were not obligated to carry the ad. The Circuit Court of Appeals upheld the decision.

Thus, the current law governing advertising acceptance may be summarized in four principles:

1. The government may through legislation declare certain categories of ads illegal.

2. The media are liable for actionable ads only if the ads are illegal or if the media have sponsored, written, or endorsed them.

3. Broadcasters may be required to air responses to an ad under the Fairness Doctrine, and their advertising acceptance policies may be considered as a factor in license renewal.

4. Under no circumstances are any of the media required to accept a particular advertisement; they may reject any ad they choose except as limited by contract and anti-trust provisions.

To the extent that the media are reluctant to censor environmental advertising for legal reasons, their reluctance is unjustified.

The Right of Access

Nonetheless, there is a much-discussed philosophy that might preclude such censorship. It is both a legal theory and a journalistic one, and it has been most eloquently expressed by Jerome A. Barron:

> The changing nature of the communications process has made it imperative that the law show concern for the public interest in effective utilization of media for the expression of diverse points of view. Confrontation of ideas, a topic of eloquent affection in contemporary decisions, demands some recognition of a right to be heard as a constitutional principle. It is the writer's position that it is open to the courts to fashion a remedy for a right of access.[13]

The legal ramifications of Barron's "right of access" are far-reaching and complex; since the courts have not yet accepted the doctrine, those ramifications also are beyond the scope of this chapter.

What must be considered here is the normative concept of access, the notion that, even if the media have the right to reject advertising as they please, they should not exercise that right.

The extreme version of this argument—that the media should accept any advertisement whatever—is seldom advanced seriously. Nearly all observers agree, for example, that the media should retain the right (if not the obligation) to refuse misleading and grossly offensive ads.

Barron himself would limit the right of access to political advertising. After reviewing the major right-to-reject precedents, he comments:

> But the broad holding of these commercial advertising cases need not be authoritative for political advertisement. Indeed, it has long been held that commercial advertising is not the type of speech protected by the first amendment, and hence even an abandonment of the romantic view of the first amendment and adoption of a purposive approach would not entitle an individual to require publication of commercial material.[14]

Similarly, William A. Resneck points out that "presently, newspapers have the right to reject both political and commercial advertisements. To espouse abolition of discretion as to the former practice is not to challenge the latter."[15]

The distinction between political and commercial advertising is much more complex than Barron and Resneck appear to believe. Both authors imply that political advertising is more or less the same thing as ideological advertising. But many commercial ads contain ideological content, either explicitly or implicitly. An ad for a book arguing against the Vietnam war, for example, is clearly ideological although it is also clearly commercial. So is a liquor ad that advocates (or even implies) the social benefits of drinking. So is an ad for a contraceptive device or one urging readers to fight recession by purchasing an automobile.

Advocates of the right of access presumably would dispute the media's moral (and legal) right to reject such advertisements. The following are additional examples in point:

1. The Los Angeles Times refused to print an ad for a commission-free house-buying service because it competed with profitable classifieds from conventional real estate brokers.

2. Four Chicago newspapers, also under pressure from the real estate business, refused to allow an agency to advertise itself as "an equal opportunity broker."

3. Again because of advertiser pressure, newspapers around
the country have from time to time refused to accept ads for Consumer
Reports magazine. All three of these ads are strictly commercial,
yet all three clearly are of ideological import. A theory of access
that excludes these three ads is a weak theory indeed.

The issue is further complicated by the fact that many ideological advertisements, including some noncommercial ones, are
desperately in need of censorship. Toward the end of the 1970 election
campaign, a group called the Committee for a Responsible Congress
attempted to place a series of ads accusing Democratic candidates
of being the tools of radicals and extremists. The Columbia Journalism
Review, usually a staunch supporter of access, notes with approval
that "several conscientious papers . . . rejected the ad."[16]

Similarly, many observers have attacked the magazine industry
for encouraging a massive increase in cigarette advertising in the
wake of the 1971 ban on broadcast cigarette commercials. Yet the
decision to restrict cigarette ads is clearly an ideological one, based
on the opinion that cigarettes are harmful to society and the judgment
that harmful products should not be entitled to advertising space.

In a different context, Mark E. Watkins has commented that
"having applied the fairness doctrine to cigarette advertising on the
theory that the commercials impliedly state a position on a controversial issue, the FCC cannot very well argue that advertising does
not involve some element of speech protected by the first amendment."[17]

Watkins' point is as applicable to the media as it is to the FCC,
and as applicable to other ideological advertising as it is to cigarette
commercials. If an ad is sufficiently damaging to society to require
censorship or regulation, it is very likely to express (at least by
implication) some viewpoint on an issue of public importance. The
ads most desperately in need of censorship or regulation are so
considered precisely because of the ideology they express and the
accuracy or tastefulness with which they express it.

Certainly this is true of environmental advertising. The vast
majority of the ads discussed at the beginning of this chapter are
objectionable because of the environmental attitudes or opinions they
state or imply. The argument that these ads should be rejected is
based explicitly on two propositions: (1) that the environment is an
issue of public importance and (2) that the ads promulgate irresponsible
attitudes about that issue. An access doctrine that prohibits censorship of any advertisement with ideological content effectively protects
those ads most in need of censorship, including the overwhelming
majority of environmental advertisements.

Thus, as a normative guide for media acceptance standards,
the distinction between "political" advertising and "commercial"
advertising is not helpful. If the definition of a political ad is

interpreted strictly, then the genuine problem of access to the media is not significantly alleviated; too many "deserving" ads are not political. But if the definition of a political ad is extended to include all ads with ideological content, then the ads most in need of censorship become uncensorable. At that point the only ads left to the discretion of the media are strictly commercial price messages, which raise few serious censorship issues to begin with.

In lieu of the distinction between political and commercial advertising, a typology of reasons for rejecting advertisements may prove more useful. Thus, most critics would agree that the media should never reject an ad purely for self-serving reasons, such as pressure from competitors. Even the media themselves would accept this statement, although they do not always abide by it.

Similarly, all but the most devoted adherents to the right of access would agree that the media ought to reject advertisements they know to be misleading. Whether political, ideological, or strictly commercial, an ad that is misleading on its face does not deserve to be published or broadcast.* Once again, the media would endorse this assessment overwhelmingly although they do not always adhere to it.

In the area of misrepresentation also, consensus is possible. A demonstrably false advertising claim, whether for a product, an opinion, or a political candidate, is not entitled to publication in the mass media. The frequent failure of the media to eliminate such claims results from procedural considerations, not philosophical ones.

The same may be said, with somewhat less certainty, for offensive advertising. Nearly all offensive ads contain some ideological content; the very fact that much of the public is offended by them renders them controversial and ideological by definition. Nonetheless, even access-oriented critics often agree that it is appropriate for the media to enforce some standards of taste and propriety.

The consensus violently explodes when one reaches the standard of social desirability. A publisher or broadcaster who rejects an ad because it is misleading, false, or offensive is on reasonably safe and familiar terrain. But a publisher or broadcaster who rejects an ad because he personally believes it is likely to influence the public in socially undesirable ways is in deep water indeed. It is with respect to the social desirability standard that access advocates are most adamant and media executives most hesitant.

---

*However, it is currently illegal for broadcasters to censor the contents of political (election-related) commercials even if they are false, misleading, unfair, or libelous.

No one denies that there are in fact advertisements whose social effects are unfortunate. And no one denies that many such ads are neither illegal nor offensive nor false nor misleading. However, no one agrees precisely which ads these are. The media do not have the option of rejecting socially undesirable advertisements. Their option is to reject advertisements they believe to be socially undesirable. They inevitably will disagree with their audiences, their critics, and each other.

In late 1970 the San Francisco Examiner announced its decision to refuse to print ads for "pornographic" movies. It could easily have based this decision on the offensiveness of the ads themselves, but instead it reached the independent judgment that the movies, and therefore the ads, were having an evil effect on society. In response, the San Francisco Chronicle editorialized:

> After these advertisements have been flatly censored out of its columns, we wonder what the Examiner will turn to next?
>
> Will it delete automobile advertising because large numbers of people are killed by motor vehicles every day?
>
> Will it then refuse advertisements from political candidates with whom the Examiner disagrees or whom the Examiner does not intend to support?
>
> Will it next delete advertisements for those churches at whose altars the Examiner editors do not worship?[18]

However exaggerated, these questions are certainly relevant. If the Examiner feels free to reject ads for pornographic movies because the publisher believes them to be evil, although he knows that many disagree, it presumably would feel free to reject ads for any product, service, or ideology about which the publisher had similar convictions. There is no reason why this principle should not extend to automobiles, political candidates, and churches.

At this point the central question is no longer one of legal theory but rather of journalistic ethics. Does the "social responsibility" theory of press performance require the media to accept even those advertisements they believe to be socially undesirable? Or does the social responsibility theory require the media to reject such advertisements?

The leading authority on social responsibility theory is of course the Commission on Freedom of the Press (Hutchins Commission), whose conclusions and recommendations were published in 1947. It is likely that the Hutchins Commission never considered the question of advertising acceptance standards; certainly none of

its documents considers the problem. But the Hutchins Commission
report does include several brief references to advertising, some
of which are relevant.

In discussing editorial bias, for example, the Hutchins Commission observes that "the individual whose views are not represented
on an editorial page may reach an audience through a public statement
reported as news, through a letter to the editor, through a statement
printed in advertising space, or through a magazine article."19 (Emphasis added.)

The Hutchins Commission's concern for access derives from
the recommendation that the media serve as a forum for the exchange
of comment and criticism. Theodore Peterson notes that "this requirement means that the great agencies of mass communications
should regard themselves as common carriers of public discussion,
although it does not mean that laws should compel them to accept all
applicants for space . . . or even that one can demand, as a right,
that the media disseminate his ideas."20

This is not a literal common carrier concept at all. It is not
the case that the media are to publish whatever they encounter.
Rather, they are to publish whatever they consider socially desirable
to publish, bearing in mind the great social desirability of access for
conflicting and minority viewpoints.

The validity of this interpretation with respect to access to
the news is undeniable. Even the Hutchins Commission does not
argue that the media should publish all the news they receive. The
bulk of the commission's report, in fact, is an effort to guide the
media in their selection of news.

A case can be made (although the Hutchins Commission does
not make it) for a more literal common carrier view of advertising.
The ads, after all, are one of the last resorts available to a viewpoint
that has not survived the process of news selection. Certainly the
selection criteria for advertising ought to be less stringent than those
for news. For example, a publisher might justly reject a frivolous
news story on the ground that it is a waste of space, but frivolity is
hardly sufficient justification for rejecting an advertisement.

But to argue that he should reject no advertisements whatever,
a publisher first would have to demonstrate that society would gain
more from completely open advertising columns than it would lose
from the most objectionable ads published in those columns. This
judgment makes more sense for postal and telephone communications
than for the mass media, and even the postal and telephone systems
make exceptions for obscenity and the like.

A WORKABLE POLICY OF ADVERTISING ACCEPTANCE

All of the media allow for certain exceptions to advertising access. According to social responsibility theory, they must do so whenever they believe society is better served by the denial of access than by a particular advertisement—and under no other circumstances. Thus, a publisher is both entitled and obligated to reject an untruthful ad because of his conviction that society loses more than it gains from exposure to lies. He is similarly entitled and obligated to reject a truthful ad if similarly convinced that its publication will do society more harm than good.

This is not to say that the media should reject every ad with which they disagree. There is a vast difference between disagreeing with an ad and believing that its harmful social effects outweigh the substantial social advantages of access. Thus, publisher Charles L. Gould of the San Francisco Examiner turns down ads for pornographic movies but does not reject ads for political candidates whom he opposes. Nor does Gould refuse to print advertisements for anti-war demonstrations, although he editorially opposes the demonstrators. "The ads are bad for the country," Gould says, "but not to let them into the paper would be worse for the country."

It is in weighing the harmful effects of an ad against the beneficial effects of access that the ideological content of the ad becomes relevant. It is generally true that a viewpoint tends to deserve a hearing in proportion to its coherence and its applicability to some identifiable worldview—in other words, its ideological content. In the environmental area, for example, an ad that urges the audience to purchase a DDT-containing pesticide has a reasonably strong access claim if it explicitly argues that killing insects is more important than protecting against the known environmental hazards. It is much less deserving of a hearing if it finesses the environmental issue and pitches itself to the petty annoyance of mosquitoes on picnics. And its access claims are weaker still if it ignores the environment entirely and fails even to mention that the product contains DDT.

In general, then, ideological content tends to increase an advertisement's right of access. An ideological ad must be judged more socially undesirable than a non-ideological ad to justify its rejection. But there still are many non-ideological ads that deserve a hearing, and some ideological ads that do not deserve a hearing.

Similarly, the informational content of an ad also tends to be proportional to its right of access. An ad that says a given product is available at a given place at a given price is strictly informational. If it goes on to say why one might want to buy that product, and does so intelligently and factually, it is even richer in information. By contrast, many ads urge the audience to purchase a product for reasons that have little to do with the nature of the product, or for no reasons at all. Such ads are low in information value and thus have a weaker case in demanding access to the media. But there are non-informational ads that nevertheless deserve a hearing, and informational ads that do not.

Thus, the social responsibility theory requires every media owner to decide with respect to every item—news and advertising alike—whether the public will best be served by carrying or by omitting the item. The desirability of access is one of the criteria to be considered in reaching this decision. It is a criterion that deserves greater weight for advertising than for news, and still greater weight for advertising rich in ideological or informational content. But it still is only one of many criteria. It is always irresponsible to publish or broadcast any advertisement, whatever its nature, without first considering its probable social effects.

There are very few ads that the media are legally obligated to reject, and no ads that they are legally obligated to accept. This is as it should be, given the danger of government control. But on the ethical level, the media are obligated to reject all ads that they believe would do the public more harm than good, and to accept all ads that they believe would do the public more good than harm.[21] This is the true meaning of the social responsibility theory as applied to advertising.

Once the philosophical doubts of publishers and broadcasters have been laid to rest, more practical doubts are likely to surface. These center on two questions: Can I afford to reject all ads I believe are socially undesirable, and how do I go about finding out which ads these are?

The economics of advertising acceptance are not overly complicated. Every rejected ad reduces the gross income of the medium that rejects it by roughly the price of the ad. No doubt there are marginal media in the country today that already are in grave danger of failure and for which even a few additional rejected ads are likely to turn the danger into a reality. These marginal media cannot be expected to revise their advertising acceptance standards in the direction of greater stringency. Perhaps they should not do so in any case. Survival is clearly one of the most important functions of the media; in a period of dangerous consolidation and monopolization, it may be more important than advertising responsibility.

But it is evident that the vast majority of newspapers, magazines, and broadcast stations can reject a great many additional ads without the slightest danger of economic collapse.

Moreover, a significant percentage—perhaps a majority—of the advertisements likely to be rejected on grounds of social undesirability

are salvageable. Only occasionally will the media feel compelled
to reject an entire ad category, such as the Examiner's rejection of
pornographic movie ads. Many, perhaps most, unacceptable advertisements can be revised to make them acceptable.

Of course it is always possible that an advertiser will refuse
to revise his ad to suit a particular newspaper, magazine, or broadcast station. This is most likely when the medium's standards are
so restrictive that the advertiser stands to gain little or nothing
from the revised ad. The New York Times, for example, currently
requires cigarette advertisements to include the surgeon general's
health warning; since the requirement was instituted, cigarette
advertising linage in the Times has declined precipitously.

But whenever it is possible for an advertiser to redesign his
ad in such a way that it will satisfy the medium and still attract
customers, he is likely to do so, even if he greatly prefers the original
version. It is a media truism (one often forgotten by media owners)
that advertising boycotts are rarely successful. Advertisers need
the media at least as much as the media need advertisers. A metropolitan newspaper, for example, can survive without a particular
supermarket but the supermarket very possibly cannot survive without the newspaper. A shampoo manufacturer depends more heavily
on network television than the networks depend on shampoo manufacturers. Even when an advertiser is offended by unfavorable news
coverage, his boycott threat seldom materializes. As one newsman
put it: "They come back within a few weeks. You can't sell without
advertising."[22]

The overwhelming experience of all the media indicates that
advertisers do not quit advertising when ordered to revise their
ads; they revise the ads. The economic cost of stringent advertising
acceptance standards is thus considerably lower than the total price
of the rejected advertisements.

The procedural misgivings of publishers and broadcasters
also stem from economic considerations: it costs money to investigate
the accuracy of advertising claims.* There is no doubt that this is
true—that few of the media could improve their investigative policies
significantly without first employing additional staff.

But the cost should not be prohibitive. Several strategies are
available to the media at minimal expense:

1. The media can make a practice of routinely requiring advertisers to substantiate their claims at the same time they submit

---

*Time is also a consideration, especially for newspapers, but
it is seldom the major factor. Most ads are or can be submitted well
in advance, and often they run for months without change.

their ads. The New York Times does this already, with considerable
success.

2. The media can encourage competitors to point out the flaws
in each other's advertising, with suitable substantiation where possible.

3. The media can solicit complaints from readers, listeners,
and viewers, and from interested civic (and pressure) groups in the
community.

4. The media can arrange to share information on advertisers
and advertising claims, perhaps instructing their professional associations to set up data banks of evidence and complaints.

5. The media can make greater use of government information
sources, expanding the list of ad categories that are routinely checked
with government agencies.

In the long run, the last item may have the greatest potential
for significant change at insignificant expense. In June 1971 the
Federal Trade Commission announced a new policy of routinely
requiring advertisers to submit evidence in support of advertising
claims. The information was to be used by the FTC in the preparation
of formal complaints against false advertisers. But it also was to be
made available to the public and to the media.

According to William Arbitman of the FTC San Francisco office,
the new policy is not a major breakthrough in government regulation
of advertising. "It doesn't alter the criteria for formal complaints,"
he explains. "It just provides the Commission with a backlog of information to refer to when a possible complaint comes up." But the
wholesale scope of the policy and its provision for public exposure
are revolutionary indeed.

Access to an up-to-date FTC data bank on advertising claims,
of course, would greatly reduce the cost to the media of verifying
those claims. Publishers and broadcasters would remain free to
reach different conclusions from those reached by the FTC, and even
to employ different criteria. But the work of collecting documentation
would be done by the government at public expense.

It is inevitable, at least in the short run, that the more advertisements a medium rejects, the smaller its profits will be. The cost
of investigating the ads cannot be reduced to zero; the price of every
ad cannot be recouped through a replacement. But the loss easily
can be held to an acceptable level, a level that in no way endangers
a medium's economic viability.

Publishers and broadcasters who wish to maximize profits
at all costs will be disinclined to accept even a minimal loss. These
individuals must be written off; only public pressure or government
regulation will force them to upgrade their advertising acceptance
standards.

Responsible publishers and broadcasters, on the other hand, may find the following a persuasive syllogism: Environmental advertising often is harmful to society, even in the face of news coverage that tries to counteract it. Social responsibility theory requires the media to reject advertisements they believe harmful to society. Therefore, the media should reject much of the environmental advertising they currently accept.

RECOMMENDATIONS

It is not the purpose of this chapter to tell the media what advertisements to censor and how to censor them. The fundamental premise is that each publisher and broadcaster must decide for himself what ads are harmful to society and how they can be made acceptable. There is merit in the likelihood that each will decide differently; diversity is the lifeblood of the mass media.

But in deciding what ads ought to be rejected, the media should make use of the widest possible range of information sources: government, industry, civic and pressure groups, readers and viewers. The objections to environmental advertising already have been outlined. It is now appropriate to state explicitly how those objections might be translated into advertising acceptance standards.

Advertisements that violate the "truth" criterion should of course be rejected without fail. This category includes ads that are misleading on their face and ads that are fraudulently staged, both of which the media already feel obliged to reject. It also includes ads that are factually inaccurate. The media currently accept a theoretical obligation to censor these ads as well, but they have not yet evolved procedures for checking the truth of environmental advertising claims. They should do so.

Even publishers and broadcasters with no special concern for the environment should wish to reject untruthful environmental advertisements. Violations of the "environmental responsibility" criterion, on the other hand, are objectionable only to those who agree that the environment is an issue that demands responsibility.

Particularly repugnant to those who share this view are direct affronts to the environment, ads that seem to go out of their way to be environmentally irresponsible. A paper diaper manufacturer who boasts of "the disposable environment" should be instructed to find another pitch. The only ads of this sort that may deserve acceptance are those that tackle the issue head-on, explicitly arguing that a given environmental issue is an unimportant red herring. Because of its ideological content, this viewpoint has a strong claim to the right of access. But casual anti-environment references have no

such claim; a publisher or broadcaster sympathetic to the environmental crisis should feel obliged to reject them.

Advertisements that suggest corporate environmental responsibility are environmentally misleading if the responsibility
suggested is greater than the responsibility exercised. That is not
a question of truth but one of judgment and perspective.

Consider the advertising claim, "We spent $6 million to clean
up our Richmond plant." Assuming the statement is true, an environmentally acute (and suspicious) media owner might still ask
three questions: (1) How does that $6 million compare with the cost
of this ad campaign or with last year's net profits? (2) Did the government require or threaten to require the clean-up? (3) How many
plants aside from the Richmond one still have to be cleaned up? If
the answers to these questions seem to shed new light on the ad, the
advertiser might legitimately be required to include them. In short,
the environmentally concerned media should endeavor to insure that
their advertising content does not paint an overly optimistic picture
of corporate environmental responsibility.

Environmentally irrelevant ads are misleading in that they steer
the public in the wrong environmental direction. To catch ads that
suggest inappropriate solutions to environmental problems, the
media must develop their own expertise or rely on the expertise of
others.

Is unsightly litter really the big problem with unrecycled cans,
or is it mineral shortage and waste disposal? Is sudsing the big
problem with detergents, or is it eutrophication? Are hydrocarbons
the big problem with automotive air pollution, or is it nitrogen oxides?
If the media do not know the answers to these questions, they should
find them out. And ads that suggest incorrect answers should be
appropriately modified.

The largest category of environmental advertising is made up
of ads that have no environmental content whatever although they
concern products or services with significant environmental implications. These are perhaps the most difficult ads to deal with. Although the ads themselves ignore the environment, the environmentally
concerned media cannot afford to ignore the ads because their environmental irrelevance is itself misleading.

Some environmentalists have suggested, quite seriously, that
all ads for environmentally detrimental products and services be
banned from the media. Unfortunately, such a broad prohibition
would wreak more havoc than the media or the manufacturers could
accommodate. Moreover, such products as automobiles, detergents,
and real estate developments are established facets of American
society. Although they are environmentally detrimental, their manufacturers have a right to advertise and their users have a right to be
exposed to the ads.

Lesser restrictions are more feasible. Adman Jerry Mander, for example, has recommended that automobile advertising be limited to strictly informational ads such as "We have the following second-hand Fords available today." Ads would not be permitted if they encouraged new cars, unnecessary trips, pointless accessories, or increased production.[23]

Or we might develop a restriction based on ideological rather than informational content. According to this standard, anyone who wished to advertise a product or service with clearly detrimental environmental effects would be required to deal explicitly with the environmental issue. He might content himself with a simple warning: "Caution: This product may be hazardous to the environment." Or he might go on to defend the product on environmental grounds. Either way, he would not be permitted to advertise the product on extraneous grounds without first coming to grips with the environmental question. All quasi-environmental advertisements would be required to become environmental advertisements.

This proposal is not without precedent. The federal government now requires advertisements for cigarettes and cyclamate products to carry an explicit health warning. Where appropriate, the media should require an "environmental health" warning as well.

Another precedent of interest is the 1969 National Environmental Policy Act. According to this legislation, every agency of the federal government must publish an environmental impact statement concerning every proposed government action that has been attacked on environmental grounds or that is otherwise deemed environmentally controversial. The media might require a similar environmental impact statement from every environmentally controversial advertiser, and require it in every ad.

Something very close to this requirement has been proposed for detergent advertising. In January 1971 the Federal Trade Commission announced that it would seek legislation requiring the following warning in all detergent ads and commercials:

> Warning: Each recommended use level of this product contains [number] grams of phosphorous which contributes to water pollution. Do not use in excess. In soft water areas, the use of phosphorous [phosphates] is not necessary.[24]

Naturally, the detergent industry opposes such a regulation.

But the federal government should not have the primary responsibility for forcing advertisers to deal explicitly and accurately with environmental problems. That responsibility properly belongs to the media, which must learn to exercise it.

ACCESS TO ENVIRONMENTAL
INFORMATION: ORCHESTRATED
CONFUSION IN ATOMIC ENERGY

In 1913 Woodrow Wilson wrote in his book The New Freedom, "The business of many of those corporations which we call public service corporations and which are indispensable to our daily lives and serve us with transportation and light and water and power . . . their business, for instance, is clearly public business; and therefore, we can and must penetrate their affairs by the light of examination and discussion."[1]

Wilson identified a problem of serious consequence for environmental news writers in the 1970s: How can one gain access to information in the private business community where many decisions directly affecting environmental quality are made?

Of course, information is not so easily obtained from government bodies or academicians, either. The security classification system, the doctrine of executive privilege, the executive session, and the bureaucratic labyrinth all serve to obscure the public's business. But the freedom of information movement, the adversary relationship between press and government, and the internalization by government officials of the "public's right to know" help unlock some of the doors. In addition, numerous members of the academic community have made their findings and opinions available to the press and public despite pressure from colleagues to avoid popularization.

But the attitude of the business community toward the public's right to know lags far behind. Eileen Shanahan, the experienced business reporter for The New York Times, has described the problem as follows: "The average businessman has nothing but

---

Material for this chapter was prepared by David M. Rubin.
Please see the "About the Authors" section for Mr. Rubin's biography.

contempt for the individual reporter, and the average businessman
has almost no understanding of the role of the press in a free society.
This I think is why he refuses to talk to us and expects the press
agent to handle us."[2] The press is the enemy to many corporate
officials. What occurs behind the corporate wall is considered none
of the public's business.

This chapter focuses in detail on the secrecy surrounding a
decision with environmental consequences made by the business
community: the siting and construction of nuclear power plants in
California. The electric power industry was selected for study because,
as a public utility with monopoly status and a regulated return, it is
closest to government in structure among private corporations. One
might therefore expect that its activities are more open to public
scrutiny.

The environmental aspects of nuclear power plants have been
detailed at length.[3] Utility siting and construction plans are of great
importance to groups studying thermal pollution, radiation leaks, air
quality, and a host of other concerns.

Among the problems addressed in this chapter are the following:
How much information does the utility make available? How early
in the siting procedure is information made public? How useful are
public hearings in affecting utility decision-making and in gaining
press coverage? Are such government regulatory agencies as the
Atomic Energy Commission important sources of information for
the press and public? How useful are California's open meeting and
open record laws, and the Federal Freedom of Information Act, in
opening utility files and meetings, either directly or indirectly
through government regulatory bodies?

The chapter concludes with a discussion of the effects of this
information policy on actual press coverage of nuclear power plant
sitings in northern California. In addition, the results of a national
poll of editors, utility executives, and environmentalists provide a
broader data base for conclusions and recommendations.

FREEDOM OF INFORMATION

The move to open by statute the meetings and records of
governmental bodies at the municipal, state, and federal levels is
largely a post-World War II phenomenon. Most of the important state
access legislation has been passed since 1940, and the key federal
legislation on open records did not come until 1966. Growing population and the increased size of government at all levels have made it
more and more difficult for the individual to participate in the
governing process. With the increased size of government comes

the temptation for public officials to operate beyond public scrutiny so as to better protect the reputations of decision-makers and more easily bury mistakes. Access legislation is one method of making the "public's right to know" possible in the face of a large and powerful government.

California's Ralph M. Brown Act is one of the strongest open meeting laws in the country, and it is regarded as something of a model for right-to-know legislation.[4] Introduced in January 1953 by Assemblyman Ralph M. Brown (D.-Modesto), it was signed into law by Governor Earl Warren on July 2, 1953. The act's widely quoted preamble is an excellent summation of the philosophy behind it:

> In enacting this chapter, the Legislature finds and declares that the public commissions, boards and councils and the other public agencies in this state exist to aid in the conduct of the people's business. It is the intent of the law that their actions be taken openly and that their deliberations be conducted openly.
>
> The people of this state do not yield their sovereignty to agencies which serve them. The people, in delegating authority, do not give their public servants the right to decide what is good for the people to know and what is not good for them to know. The people insist on remaining informed so that they may retain control over the instruments they have created.[5]

The original act provides that "all meetings of the legislative body of a local agency shall be open and public, and all persons shall be permitted to attend any meeting of the legislative body of a local agency."[6] The term "local agency" was defined as follows:

> a county, city, whether general law or chartered, city and county, town, school district, municipal corporation, district, political subdivision, or any board, commission or agency thereof, or other local public agency.[7]

A "legislative body" was defined in the following way:

> the governing board, commission, directors or body of a local agency, or any board or commission thereof, and shall include any board, commission, or other body on which officers of a local agency serve in their official capacity as members and which is supported in whole or in part by funds provided by such agency, whether such board, commission, committee or other body is

organized and operated by such local agency or by a
private corporation.[8]

Beginning in 1955 the legislature periodically amended the act
in an effort to balance the public's right to know against the needs of
government officials to conduct public business without undue harassment. This has required statutory definitions of what constitutes a
meeting, under what circumstances a legislative body can hold
executive session, and how the act applies to meetings that are ad-
journed or continued. In 1961 the legislature provided that meetings
held in violation of the Brown Act would make each member of the
legislative body guilty of a misdemeanor and authorized any person
to stop or prevent such a violation by mandamus or injunction.

Assemblyman Brown had intended that the original act cover
state agencies as well as local agencies, but pressures from various
state agencies forced a change. Beginning in 1957, in piecemeal
fashion, he began to bring state agencies under open meeting requirements applying to local agencies with a series of separate bills.
Finally in 1967 a bill was enacted providing uniform open meeting
requirements for state agencies.[9]

The intent of the bills is to afford the public access to meetings
at which public servants are deliberating or acting upon public policy.
(Of course, it would be impossible to draft a piece of legislation
covering social conversation between two public officials during which
some public policy is discussed.) Access legislation is valuable
because it requires that public servants

> make a conscious effort to air viewpoints on each issue so
> that the community can understand on which premises
> decisions are based. . . . This does not mean that all
> discussion must be in public. For example, political
> horsetrading is a necessary fact of viable government.
> Much of this must be in private for it to be effective. Yet
> when secret horsetrading becomes the only means of
> contesting political viewpoints, the community is left out
> of the decision process. A method must be found to
> accommodate the needs of the legislative body with the
> needs of the public.[10]

The Brown Act is designed to encourage public officials to act openly
and to remind them of their public responsibility.

Whether or not discussions of land acquisition by local and state
agencies are to be open to the public is a question we shall meet
again. The Brown Act does not exempt such meetings from public
scrutiny. Although secrecy might give an agency greater flexibility

in the negotiations and lead to a lower purchase price, the agency still must pay a fair market price for the land and it always may resort to the power of eminent domain. In 1965 the California legislature turned down an Assembly bill that would have allowed school boards to consider acquisition of real property in closed session. However, a Harvard Law Review article of April 1962 outlines a model open meeting statute permitting closed sessions for discussion of land acquisition because an open meeting might benefit a party whose interests are adverse to those of the general community. Many public officials favor this position and believe that the Brown Act is detrimental to the public good because publicity drives up land prices.[11]

Access to the documents and records upon which public decisions are based is as important for freedom of information as access to public meetings. To facilitate inspection of public records, the California legislature in 1968 passed the California Public Records Act, which stipulates that "public records are open to inspection at all times during the office hours of the state or local agency and every citizen has a right to inspect any public record, except as hereafter provided."[12] This act covers roughly the same state and local agencies covered by the Brown Act, including, at the local level, "municipal corporations."[13] Public records are defined as follows:

> all papers, maps, magnetic or paper tapes, photographic
> films and prints, magnetic or punched cards, discs,
> drums, and other documents containing information
> relating to the conduct of the public's business prepared,
> owned, used, or retained by any state or local agency
> regardless of physical form or characteristics.[14]

The act specifically excludes from public inspection thirteen classes of documents, three of which are of particular interest here:

1. "Preliminary drafts, notes, or interagency or intra-agency memoranda which are not retained by the public agency in the ordinary course of business, provided that the public interest in withholding such records clearly outweighs the public interest in disclosure."

2. "Geological and geophysical data, plant production data, and similar information relating to utility systems development, or market or crop reports, which are obtained in confidence from any person."

3. "The contents of real estate appraisals, engineering or feasibility estimates and evaluations made for or by the state or local agency relative to the acquisition of property, or to prospective public supply and construction contracts, until such time as all the property has been acquired or all of the contract agreement obtained, or provided however, the law of eminent domain shall not be affected by this provision."[15]

An agency must justify withholding a document from the public either under provisions of the act or by showing in a particular case that the public interest would not be served by disclosure. Any person may enforce his right to inspect by instituting proceedings in any court of competent jurisdiction.

Neither the open meeting nor the open record laws seem to apply directly to private investor-owned utility (IOU) such as Pacific Gas and Electric (PG&E), the largest electric utility in northern California. As a municipal corporation, the Sacramento Municipal Utility District (SMUD), which provides power for the city of Sacramento, does seem to fall within the scope of local agency as defined in the acts, although the exemptions in the Public Records Act listed above also seem to provide the utility with a number of grounds for withholding information. In the absence of court test or an advisory opinion by the state attorney general, such conclusions are open to debate.

Although a detailed examination of freedom of information legislation in other states was not made, a preliminary reading indicates that other state laws provide no greater access to the meetings and records of IOUs. Private corporations simply are not covered by such legislation as it exists today.

The public's legal right to know is not entirely thwarted in the case of IOUs, however. As private companies with public utility status, they are regulated by a state commission (Public Utilities Commission of the State of California, or PUC), and that commission has spelled out in some detail which meetings and records are open to the public. Section 306 of the Public Utilities Code states that "Except for the commission's [PUC] deliberative conferences, the sessions and meetings of the commission shall be open to the public and all persons shall be permitted to attend." What constitutes a deliberative conference is not defined, and the general order issued by the commission specifying the business that may be conducted in a deliberative conference could be applied to most business before the commission.16 The PUC's position favors secret meetings. Although not a judicial tribunal in the strict sense, its deliberative conferences (at which it considers and issues decisions and orders) are comparable to the conferences of Supreme Court justices and therefore should be closed to the public. Only the formal public hearings would be open.17

Access to utility records filed with the PUC also is tightly controlled. Section 583 of the Public Utilities Code provides:

No information furnished to the Commission by a public utility, except such matters as are specifically required to be open to public inspection by the provisions of this

part, shall be open to public inspection or made public
except on order of the commission [PUC], or by the
commission or a commissioner in the course of a
hearing or proceeding. Any officer or employee of the
commission who divulges any such information is guilty
of a misdemeanor.

Records that are expressly open to the public include the annual
reports and general orders of the commission, annual reports filed
by the utilities, all pleadings, briefs, exhibits, and transcripts in
formal proceedings, and materials filed in compliance with PUC
decisions.[18] Although the Public Records Act places the burden of
proof for maintaining secret records on the agency, the PUC may
keep secret all records not expressly named in its General Order
No. 66-A. This puts the public somewhat at a disadvantage. Thus,
some basic information about the utility is available through the
PUC, and this also is true in other states with regulatory commissions.

At the federal level, the Atomic Energy Commission (AEC) and
the Federal Power Commission (FPC) have the strongest regulatory
authority over both IOU and municipally-owned utilities, particularly
the AEC as regards nuclear power plant siting. The Freedom of
Information Act, passed in 1966 and amended in 1967, is similar to
the California Public Records Act in that it puts the burden of proof
on the agency for keeping information secret.[19] As Attorney General
Ramsey Clark points out in his memorandum to the act,

the decision to withhold or disclose particular records
cannot be controlled by any detailed classification of all
official records, but has to be effected through countless
ad hoc judgments of agency officials, each intimately
familiar with the particular segments of official records
committed to his responsibility. Those executive judgments
must still be made, for Congress did not attempt to
provide in the revised section a complete, self-executing
verbal formula which might automatically determine all
public information questions.[20]

The act makes clear that it is the intent of Congress that the
public's right to know be honored by the executive agencies, but it
is often left to the interested citizen, newspaper reporter, or the
watchdog House Subcommittee on Foreign Operations and Government
Information to bring the enforcement machinery of the act to life.

Over the years, the AEC has proven unwilling to make public
its activities in the area of weapons technology but it has been much

more open with information on the "Atoms for Peace" program. The
Freedom of Information Act lists nine categories of information
exempt from its provisions, the first of which concerns matters
"specifically required by Executive order to be kept secret in the
interest of the national defense or foreign policy." Atomic weapons
information has long been considered vital to the national defense,
and according to one critic the AEC is "at liberty to classify and
withhold information at its own discretion."[21] Even Senator Clinton
P. Anderson of New Mexico, when he was chairman of the Joint
Committee on Atomic Energy, to which the AEC is responsible,
claimed that he was not fully informed of AEC activities.[22] Sub-
chapter XI, "Control of Information," Atomic Energy Act of 1954 in
United States Codes, Title 42, makes clear how broad the AEC's
powers of secrecy are.

The FPC, while not directly concerned with nuclear power plant
siting, has an unimpressive record of disclosing information it has
gathered about utilities. In 1963, for example, the FPC proposed
and asked for comment on regulations that would have required IOUs
to reveal their contributions to charitable organizations and their
expenditures to influence public opinion. A number of newspaper
editors submitted their views, all them opposed to the disclosure
requirement. Editors felt it would inhibit utility advertising, gag
private utilities, and be "another step toward the ultimate socializa-
tion of the utility industry." The FPC finally ruled that contributions
exceeding $1,000 had to be itemized, but most IOUs ignore the rule
and the FPC is too understaffed to enforce it.[23]

In sum, the most that can be said about access to records and
meetings of IOUs and municipally-owned utilities is that the picture
is slightly brighter for municipals than IOUs. Such municipal utilities
as SMUD seem to be covered by California's public record and open
meeting laws. Such IOUs as PG&E are not, but some of their records
are made public by the PUC, which can decide which PG&E meetings
and records are to be made public. Some information about both
types of utilities is available from the AEC or the FPC, particularly
the former. As is usual in questions involving the public's right to
know, right of access cannot be determined in general. One must
deal with specific records or meetings, and then a formal request
or court challenge may be required of those seeking access.

We now turn to the specific case of nuclear power plant siting
in California for a look at the manipulation of information by the
business community.

THE SITING PROCEDURE

The scramble for access to information about the siting of nuclear power plants is prompted by figures from The Energy Policy Staff of the Office of Science and Technology which predict that by 1990 electric utilities across the nation will have to find 255 new thermal generating plant sites of 500-megawatt capacity or larger; of this number, 164 will be nuclear. Ten new sites will be needed in California, six in northern California.[24] The total number of thermal generating plants in the United States will more than double in just the years 1970-90. The implications of these figures are just beginning to hit home to the environmentally-conscious public, prompting the curiosity that now surrounds the siting procedure.

Before examining this procedure as it now exists in California (and the role of the public and its access to information in that procedure), it is necessary to understand some of the basic assumptions held by utility and government planners and to examine the framework within which siting decisions currently are made.

Although the brownouts in New York City have been burdensome for its residents, they also serve a positive propaganda value to utility and AEC spokesmen around the country. The brownouts play an important role in the industry's predictions of what will happen if more power plants are not built, and fast.

No one doubts the definite power crisis facing some sections of the country. But the brownout psychosis has succeeded in limiting the scope of the power debate nationally to the location of future plants and the type of fuel to be used. Foreclosed are discussions of the overall relationship of population increase, population density, and electric power; alternate solutions to the power shortage other than the construction of more generating stations; and how critical the power shortage really is. The urgency with which the utilities and the AEC argue also has precluded serious research toward developing methods other than the use of fossil or nuclear fuels in the generation of electricity. Because the nation may be close to a general brownout, the industry must push ahead in the advancement of nuclear power technology at the expense of research into other technologies. It is perhaps in the nature of a bureaucracy that such philosophic and policy questions are difficult to bring into everyday decision-making, but it is significant that the public siting struggle being waged today is almost totally bereft of this larger vision.

In California, utility officials, elected state officials, and planners within the Resources Agency, the PUC, and the AEC (the four important power blocs in the siting procedure) all are committed to the rapid facilitation of utility plans for more power plants and to the notion that these plants be nuclear. In authorizing the

preparation of the report Siting Thermal Power Plants in California
(February 15, 1970), the California State Assembly noted:

> WHEREAS, The continued growth of California and the
> welfare of its people are vitally dependent upon the
> reliable availability of electric power; and
> WHEREAS, California electric power demands are
> doubling every eight years, and by the year 2000 will
> approximate the 1968 power consumption of the entire
> United States; and
> WHEREAS, Most of the new plants will be nuclear,
> preventing air pollution and maintaining low power costs,
> but further limiting the choice of acceptable sites; and
> WHEREAS, There will be an increasing problem in
> establishing, on a timely basis, power plant sites suitable
> for their purpose and acceptable to the public, so that
> California can avoid the power shortages which have
> occurred from time to time in other parts of the country;
> and
> WHEREAS, It is desirable for the public, the electric
> utilities, and the state to have a basis for future plans and
> commitments relating to power plant sites; now, there-
> fore, be it RESOLVED. . . .

The report that resulted from this resolution states: "It is also
the policy of the State of California to encourage the use of nuclear
energy, recognizing that such use has the potential of providing direct
economic benefit to the public, thus helping to conserve limited fossil
fuel resources and promoting air cleanliness." The State Air
Resources Board is on record as favoring nuclear over fossil fuel
plants because of the less objectionable nature of the air pollutants.
The AEC has promoted construction of nuclear plants and aids the
utilities in research and in procuring fissionable materials. And the
PUC is concerned primarily with guaranteeing to Californians the
most power at the least cost.

In short, within the power planning and regulatory establishment
there is not a single important anti-nuclear power plant spokesman,
nor is there anyone advocating solution of power shortages by any
means other than the rapid construction of nuclear power plants.
The only serious question is where to put them. Opponents are largely
outside the planning structure.

The goals of the utilities' legislative efforts in Sacramento and
Washington, D.C., are to cut down the time required to license and
begin operation of a new plant (either fossil fuel or nuclear) and to
limit regulatory power to a state siting committee and the AEC.

At present a utility must budget six to nine years from inception of a plant to actual operation. Some nuclear plants have been completed but are being held out of operation through court action at an estimated cost of $50,000 to $100,000 a day to the utilities involved. In writing such legislation as AB 818, introduced in 1970 and 1971 in Sacramento by Assemblyman John Briggs (R.-Orange County), the California private utilities are trying to eliminate all local control over siting. They would grant to a state siting committee the power to decide on a site's environmental suitability, leaving radiologic safety questions to the AEC. The Nixon administration has proposed a bill to stream-line the siting procedure by establishing two levels of effective regulation: a state siting committee to decide on environmental matters and the AEC to handle nuclear safety. This is known as the "one-stop shopping" concept, and it was narrowly defeated in 1970 and 1971 in Sacramento at the state level through the efforts of the Sierra Club.

The siting procedure in California has many overlapping layers of authority and provisions for public participation (or at least harassment). Many local, state, and federal agencies are involved, and while they are all of the same mind, enough procedural delays are built into the system to provide some checks and balances.

Under the present system and in all projected siting procedures for California, the authority for developing a plan showing future power needs and designating sites on which to build plants to meet those needs rests solely with the individual utilities. Local and state agencies and the AEC are in a reactive position: they can say "yes" or "no" to a particular site but they cannot plan with the utility at the outset. The state of New York has authorized its Atomic and Space Development Authority to select and in some cases acquire sites for plants and then sell them to the utilities, but there is little enthusiasm for such a plan in California. The usual argument is that the state should not be in the siting business and that planning is a utility function and responsibility best performed by experts.

Because the regulatory agencies rarely disapprove a utility-selected site, these early decisions are the most important in the siting procedure but they are made with the least public knowledge—behind closed utility doors without supervision by state or federal officials and without input from conservation organizations and the public.

Not only does the siting initiative rest with the utilities but so does the major responsibility for gathering environmental information about the proposed site before construction begins, as well as for monitoring the effects of the plant on the environment. No local or state government agency has the money or manpower to conduct the enormous geologic, hydrologic, meteorologic, or other studies necessary to determine the suitability of a site, and so the utilities take this over by default. A number of men within the Resources Agency in Sacramento are well-qualified to assess the information brought to them by utility engineers or their paid consultants, but again they are in a reactive position. All the agencies that in theory must independently pass on the environmental suitability of a site are relying on the State Resources Agency people, who in turn are relying on the utilities. Although no one even implies that the utilities are playing fast and loose with the data they collect, it is nonetheless a risky regulatory scheme in which the business being regulated provides most of the basic data.

These prefatory remarks should help the reader understand the detailed siting procedure and the motivations behind it. In siting, the utility usually will work from local government agencies up, so the material has been organized along those lines.

The Utility

Despite the bitter opposition of some of California's conservationist groups, the electric utilities in general have enjoyed the faith and trust of the people of the state. A 1967 public opinion poll, commissioned by six major California utilities and two reactor systems manufacturers, showed that over 70 percent of the public believed that a utility would not build a nuclear power plant where there would be any danger to the public. In addition, 73 percent believed the plants "are necessary to supply additional electricity for California's growth and progress" and 51 percent felt that "providing a new source of electricity is more important to the community than keeping the land and wildlife the way they are."[25] Thus, a most important advantage to the utility in the siting procedure is that it starts with the confidence and sympathy of a majority of the public.

In a general way in the early 1970s there has been pressure on the utilities to make known their siting plans. In the previously mentioned report to the California State Assembly, Siting Thermal Power Plants in California, the utilities made public their plans through 1990. They outlined how many more sites are likely to be needed, based on population projections and expectations of increased industrialization; why the sites likely will be coastal because of the economies of ocean cooling water and the scarcity of fresh flowing water in California; and what the expected balance between fossil fuel and nuclear plants is to be. Such long-range reports have been institutionalized through AB 1247, passed in 1970, which directs the Resources Agency, in cooperation with the utilities and the PUC, to develop a 20-year plan identifying power plant "locations suitable

from an environmental standpoint." The project is funded with
$150,000 from an environmental fund collected from the selling of
personalized license plates. Also with an eye on the environmental
movement, the PUC, in its General Order No. 131 of July 1, 1970,
ordered the utilities to submit each year a 10-year forecast of loads
and resources as well as a description of the generating and transmission facilities that will be required to meet those forecasts.
Biennially each utility must submit a 20-year forecast. Such information is available to the public and press from either the Resources
Agency or the PUC.

Specific sites under consideration are another matter. At any
given time Pacific Gas and Electric (PG&E), an investor-owned
utility that serves San Francisco and much of northern California,
may have as many as 130 different sites under consideration, but
until the utility has taken an option to purchase the land it is extremely
reluctant to disclose which sites are receiving special attention. In
1959, for example, PG&E did not officially announce that Bodega Head
in Sonoma County was to be the site of a plant until after a portion of
the land had been purchased. The usual reason given for the utility's
secrecy on specific sites is that a landowner will raise the price if
he learns that PG&E is interested in his land. Both public and private
utilities have condemnation powers, so if the utility and the landowner
cannot reach a settlement satisfactory to both, the sale goes into the
courts where a price is determined by a condemnation jury. The
utility feels that it receives less than a fair shake from these juries,
although there is little evidence to support this claim. A PG&E
spokesman said the utility prefers not to use the condemnation power
because it can be accused of abusing it and this is bad public relations.

There are two other reasons for utility secrecy at this early
stage. First, speed is of the essence and jury proceedings can take
up valuable time, especially considering delays to be expected later.
Second, if the utility has invested a substantial amount of money and
time in preparing a site before public awareness and opposition
develop, a "prior investment" argument may be used to keep the site
alive.

Within PG&E there is some evidence of change on this point.
A few officials recognize that there is a difference in the way PG&E
ought to conduct itself and the way Standard Oil or General Motors,
truly private companies, can make decisions. "We are responsible
to the public in all ways," said former PG&E engineer Gene Blanc,
who is now with the AEC, "and we must do all things in the public
eye. But it may take a generation to change—and we may not have a
generation."

The only role the public now plays at this site-selection stage is through the accumulated pressure of the environmental movement. According to Blanc, there is a tremendous philosophical battle going on at the highest levels of management over how much concern to give the environmental question. After World War II PG&E, partly at the urging of the PUC which wanted the most power at the least cost, began to think of its fossil fuel plants as industrial endeavors. None of the environmental concern that had been evidenced in the siting of hydroelectric plants was carried over into the planning and operation of these plants. Now the consequences of this cavalier attitude toward the environment are being felt. At present a number of otherwise perfect sites for nuclear power plants (such as sites on estuaries) undoubtedly are vetoed immediately because of the predictable public outcry.

At an early stage it does not seem that the siting plans of a municipal utility, such as the Sacramento Municipal Utility District (SMUD), are any more open to public scrutiny than are those of an IOU, such as PG&E. SMUD nominally is run by a five-man board of directors, elected to terms of four years. Their twice-monthly board meetings are open to the public, and any purchase involving more than $4,000 or any policy decision must be approved publicly at these meetings. However, a siting decision probably would not reach the board in public meeting until the end of the option period when the land was to be purchased. At this point both the IOUs and the municipals usually announce the acquisition to the press anyway. A number of utility and state employees point out that the municipal utility in Los Angeles (Department of Water and Power) has been more close-mouthed about its plans than any IOU.

The rights to be balanced are the public's right to know what specific sites are being considered for power plants and the utility's right to negotiate for land in private for the sake of speed and economy (which the utility also feels is in the public interest). At present, the utility's right is preeminent. However, the results of such a policy frequently have left a bad taste. In Santa Cruz there were rumors for months in 1970 that PG&E was considering building a power plant in nearby Davenport. The public learned of it only when a political candidate opposed to the siting announced it in an ad in the local paper. Only then did the utility hold a press conference to reveal its plans. Perhaps as a result of the secrecy, a substantial citizens' group in Santa Cruz is fighting the plant.

At least until an option has been taken on the land under consideration, utility policy follows the old adage, "No news is good news." Only a reporter with intimate knowledge of utility plans and the nose of a private detective could get the story.

Local Government

In some cases, with an option to purchase in hand, the utility approaches the county board of supervisors and requests approval to construct a nuclear power plant from the county planning and zoning departments. But this is not always the procedure. Both PG&E and SMUD assert that county officials have no legal authority over them. SMUD points to Chapter 6, Article 1, Section 12703 of the Municipal Utility District Act, which states that in the proceedings, venue, and trial relative to the exercise of the right of eminent domain, "the district has all the rights, powers and privileges of an incorporated city and all rights, powers, and privileges conferred in this division." PG&E officials have indicated that the PUC now wields absolute authority over its affairs at the local and state level, and if the PUC approves construction on a particular site, the county must acquiesce.

In the 1965-66 siting of its Rancho Seco nuclear power plant in Sacramento County, 25 miles southeast of the city of Sacramento, SMUD did not seek the approval or advice of county planning officials. Earl Fraser, planning director for Sacramento County, says, "We would have appreciated working more closely with SMUD on the siting, since we had just adopted a master plan for the southeast area of the county where the plant is located. They did advise us of their plans, but they did what they wanted to without consulting us." Fraser called it a "poor job of interagency relations" and would like to see all districts and municipalities become more conscious of one another. Vera Stetler, clerk for the County Planning Department, echoed Fraser's feelings and stated that the utility "was too big for us to take on."

PG&E's policy has been more conciliatory. Realizing that most county boards of supervisors are delighted to have a utility build a plant in their area because of increased revenues and growth, PG&E policy is to acquire all customary use permits even though it does not believe it legally needs them. Indeed, in the past PG&E has found local boards most cooperative. Concerning the attempt by the utility to site a plant at Bodega Head from 1958 to 1964, Sonoma County Harbor Commission Chairman Robert M. Harkness stated, "The job of government is to create the proper environment to attract private enterprise." The Sonoma County Board of Supervisors was most cooperative, going so far as to recommend against public hearings on the utility's plans for the site. Similarly, the boards in Mendocino and Solano Counties rapidly approved PG&E plans for nuclear plants at Point Arena and Collinsville.

In Santa Cruz, however, given the different political climate in which the utility must now work, there is some doubt that the county board will approve construction of a nuclear power plant at Davenport. According to Supervisor Phil Harry, the board could split 3-2 either way, depending on the nature of the utility's proposal. What would happen if the utility came to the county and was rebuffed? No one seems to know. Harry asked a PG&E official that question and did not receive an answer. It is doubtful that the utility will risk approaching the county.

At stake is the earliest, official public hearing on the utility's plans. A public hearing must be held by the Santa Cruz Board of Supervisors before zoning can be changed. At this early stage the utility would prefer to avoid such a hearing. It is an excellent news peg for the press, and the resultant publicity could cause the utility to change its plans.

There is heated debate over the degree of control local officials should be afforded in the siting procedure. Recently Southern California Edison applied to the PUC for a certificate of public convenience and necessity to construct a fossil fuel plant at Huntington Beach in Orange County. The PUC gave its approval over the protest of the Orange County Air Pollution Control District, which felt that the lungs of the county's residents could not bear another fossil fuel plant in the area. The PUC argued that it has exclusive control over siting and that the county board cannot overrule it. The case (Orange County Air Pollution Control District v. PUC, S.F. No. 22766) was decided by the California Supreme Court on May 26, 1971. The court found against the PUC and in favor of the local board but did not settle the preemption question beyond this specific case.

In April 1972 the U.S. Supreme Court ruled that the state of Minnesota could not enforce regulations on nuclear power plant radiation leakage that were much stronger than regulations promulgated by the AEC. The authority of the federal body took precedence. This decision also could affect PG&E-Santa Cruz relations.

The utilities prefer to be free of local control. This is the thrust of their one-stop shopping legislation. What they most want to avoid is a local referendum on construction of a nuclear power plant, as occurred in Eugene, Oregon, in May 1970, when citizens voted to stop construction by a municipal utility. The utilities claim, with much justification, that electric power is at least a regional need and deserves state planning. Traditional boundaries do not make sense when applied to the state's power needs.

But local officials feel, also with much justification, that they must live with the patterns of industrial development that a new power plant would occasion. They cannot see the wisdom in permitting state officials, insulated from the voters living near the plant, to make these decisions over local protests. Utility officials have said repeatedly that they would not construct a plant in the face of significant local protest. That remains to be tested.

From the standpoint of access to information, it is clear that
early site hearings at the local level would be valuable. As will be
made clear, the first mandatory public hearing on a site may not
come until many months after the land has been purchased, when the
utility has made a significant investment and is reluctant to back off.
A public hearing before purchase of any land is essential if the
public's right to know is to be satisfied at this important stage.

The State Power Plant Siting Committee

One of the lessons the environmentalists within the State
Resources Agency learned from PG&E's unsuccessful attempt to
construct a plant at Bodega Head in Sonoma County in 1958-64 was
that no one body was responsible for approving sites on environmental grounds. The PUC, wholly without environmental expertise,
was concerned only that the plant really was needed and that it was
being built economically; the AEC was concerned only that the plant
was radiologically safe to operate. But no agency was analyzing the
impact of the plant on the air, water, and land around it, independent
of radiologic considerations. Many state governments still do not
recognize this oversight, and only since 1969 with passage of the
National Environmental Policy Act has the Federal Government
recognized this problem. California was about five years ahead of
the rest of the nation.

Concerned about this problem, Governor Edmund G. Brown
created by executive order, on June 30, 1965, the Power Plant Siting
Committee. The committee's ten members include the heads (or
their delegates) of the following departments within the Resources
Agency: Department of Conservation, Department of Fish and Game,
Department of Navigation and Ocean Resources, Department of Parks
and Recreation, Department of Water Resources, Air Resources
Board, State Water Resources Control Board, Department of Public
Health, and State Lands Commission. The tenth member is Chairman
Paul Clifton, representative of Norman B. Livermore, Jr., secretary
for resources and political appointee of Governor Ronald Reagan.

The State of California Policy on Thermal Power Plants,
adopted June 30, 1965, and revised March 12, 1969, makes clear the
duties of this committee:

> It is the policy of the State of California to ensure that
> the location and operation of thermal power plants will
> enhance the public benefits and protect against or
> minimize adverse effects on the public, on ecology of the
> land and its wildlife, and on the ecology of State waters

and their aquatic life. Also, the public's opportunity to enjoy the material, physical, and aesthetic benefits of these resources shall be preserved to the greatest extent feasible. . . .

To ensure implementation of the State of California policy a committee called the State of California Power Plant Siting Committee has been established. Among its functions is the review of proposed power plant sites throughout the State as to their conformance with this policy. . . .

Individual members of the committee are delegated the authority and responsibility, by their respective department directors or board executive officers, for reviewing proposed power plant sites, for consulting with all concerned parties within their respective departments or boards on each proposed site, for seeking resolution of conflicts at whatever level of management required, for keeping the department director or board executive officer informed of the status of siting actions, and finally, for communicating in writing the comments, conclusions, stipulations and official position of the department or board relative to each proposed site. . . .

It should be clearly understood that a site may be selected and approved long before many of the details of plant design and operation are firmly established. Site approval by the State of California Power Plant Siting Committee need only recognize the necessity of developing said details within the framework of the overall quality and integrity of the natural environment . . . prior to operation of the plant.

Although it is the most important watchdog over the environment in the siting procedure, the Power Plant Siting Committee has no official legal status. The utilities need not approach it for approval of a site, and any contact between utility and committee is strictly voluntary. Nevertheless, all major utilities in the state, with the exception of the Los Angeles Department of Water and Power, do approach the committee to sign an agreement for each site. In the agreement the utility agrees to follow certain procedures in the construction of the plant, to consult with the committee or specific departments about problems as they arise in construction, to undertake certain ecologic studies, to provide recreational facilities for the public at the plant site, and so on. In return, the Resources Agency, through its agent the Power Plant Siting Committee, agrees not to oppose the utility as it seeks other licenses and certificates (from the PUC or AEC, for example) later on in the siting procedure. Although voluntary, the agreement has the legal status of a contract once it has been signed by Livermore and the utility representative, and it puts the state on record as approving a specific site. The utilities have determined that this arrangement is important from a public relations and tactical perspective, and it has become the first important step in the siting procedure.

From 6 to 18 months of research and negotiation between members of the committee and utility engineers and consultants goes into an agreement. Each committee member requests different materials from the utility on which to base his decision on the suitability of the site and the terms to be written into the agreement. The State Lands Commission, for example, concerned with the use made of tide and submerged lands adjacent to the site, requests information on the effects of construction on the boundary between the uplands owned by the utility and the publicly owned tidelands and submerged lands. The State Water Resources Control Board will ask the utility for a reconnaissance study of the water around the plant. All such studies are paid for and executed by the utility or its consultants. At present the state does not have the money or manpower to do them independently. Members of the State Power Plant Siting Committee expressed varying opinions on the depth, quality, and suitability of this research.

Once the initial data are in and the individual departments have formulated positions on the site, negotiations begin with the utility in which dissenting agencies are heard and a general accord reached. There are no public hearings in which interested parties or conservation groups can express their views to the committee before the agreement is signed. Committee Chairman Paul Clifton believes the utilities would oppose public hearings because they would slow up what they feel is already a slow procedure. He maintains that the utility-committee meetings at which the agreement is hammered out are open to the public, but such meetings are not announced in advance and thus the public is never present. According to the provisions of the Brown Act, such meetings need not be open to the public as long as the Power Plant Siting Committee is an unofficial body. One former committee member, James Trout of the State Lands Commission, likes the flexible, private nature of the meetings and feels that if the public were present many agency representatives would be afraid to speak their minds honestly about a site.

Although the committee holds no public hearings or open meetings, it was the unanimous opinion of its members that any information received from the utility on which an agreement is based is open to the public. This puts the burden on the public to determine when negotiations on an agreement have begun (there is no announcement of this) and who should be approached for utility material. Apparently, in the past the public and press have not availed themselves of this opportunity for an early look at the utility studies. It is possible that Clifton and the committee members, under pressure from the utility and the governor, might become less cooperative in opening up this information if an actual demand for it arises; it seems likely that as long as the committee is unofficial and the agreement voluntary, the California Public Records Act probably would not cover the utility reports.

The agreements signed by the Resources Agency and the utility are public, and we had no difficulty obtaining copies of all those in existence. But the degree to which the signing of these agreements is cloaked in secrecy, despite the public nature of the documents, was revealed in late October 1971. At that time the Sierra Club became actively involved in opposition to a plant proposed by PG&E for Mendocino County. An agreement for that site was signed in 1968. Sierra Club spokesmen charged that the document had been suppressed for three years by the utility and that it was "illegal." The entire agreement procedure was called into question.

If one of the supposedly public activities in the siting procedure causes bitter debate because of its secrecy, then it is clear how difficult it is for the press to penetrate those affairs which the utility admits are secret. Agreements have been available to press and public as a matter of course, but they were buried in the files of a fairly obscure agency—obscure before the interest in the environment developed—in Sacramento. Certainly the press and public, and perhaps the utility and Resources Agency, are to blame for the ignorance surrounding this issue.

The thrust of the utility bills and the Nixon legislation is to make official the role of the State Power Plant Siting Committee or some similar body with a few public members (although the utilities are opposed to public members on ground that the state officials represent the public interest). It is likely that such a committee will have official status by the mid-1970s. The trade-off will be removal of all siting authority at the local level. A mandatory public hearing on environmental matters probably will be a part of the new scheme. These steps may help the public and press follow utility plans more closely than at present.

Current procedures are not in the public interest because they involve an unofficial committee in political fealty to a governor sympathetic to utility interests. The committee has a small staff and little money for independent investigation of the utilities' environmental claims. It holds neither public hearings nor open meetings, yet it has the power to sign an agreement binding the Resources Agency not to oppose the utility on environmental grounds.

The substitute should be a Power Plant Siting Committee with provision for public members, which conducts a site review with public hearings and open meetings before the utility has made any land purchases. Such a committee must have adequate staff and money to conduct independent investigations and the power to accept or refuse a utility's request for a specific site.

The present committee has yet to deny an agreement on a site for a nuclear facility to a utility. Important decisions of environmental consequence are being made with little public access or participation.

The Public Utilities Commission

The California Public Utilities Commission is, in theory, the public's most significant point of access to the utility decision-making process. Before an investor-owned utility can build a plant or lay transmission lines, it must secure from the PUC a certificate of public convenience and necessity. This requires the utility to submit detailed information about the plant to the PUC, with all the information available to the public, and it demands a hearing in which the public may play a significant role. Furthermore, the 1911 act that created the PUC states that it must act in the public interest, giving the commissioners broad powers to consider whatever information they feel is important and in the public interest in determining the disposition of the utility application. A PG&E spokesman has called the PUC "the protector of the public . . . with responsibility to make sure the public is represented in all its viewpoints."

Although the PUC could investigate the environmental impact of proposed plants and transmission lines, it has left such matters to the State Power Plant Siting Committee, depending heavily on the committee's agreement with the utility. At the present time the PUC does not have the scientific expertise to evaluate environmental impact, and its budget is being constricted rather than expanded. According to Walter Cavagnaro, PUC utilities division engineer, "The Commission basically determines if the plant is really needed, based on projected power needs, and whether the proposed location of the plant is adequate to those needs. Occasionally some questions of radiologic safety are considered, but those are really the province of the AEC." The PUC has no environmental specialist on its staff and is essentially an aggregation of engineers and attorneys. Its major concern is with the dollar-costs of power.

After the utility has signed an agreement with the Power Plant Siting Committee, it approaches the PUC for pre-filing meetings. Through these hearings, the utility learns what it must provide the

PUC staff in its certificate application. These informal exchanges
help both sides prepare their cases and make sure that the public
record is thorough. As staff-level meetings, they are not open to the
public by provisions of the Brown Act. The regular deliberative
sessions of the commissioners also are closed to the public because
they are considered in the same light as judges meeting in chambers.

At least 12 months before a decision is required from the PUC,
the utility must file its application for the certificate of public convenience and necessity. It must include a statement of why the
proposed facility is necessary; safety and reliability information;
estimated cost information; a schedule showing the program for
design, material acquisition, construction and testing, and operating
dates; available site information, such as geological, ecological,
seismic, water supply, and population data; a description of the
provisions for the mitigation of air and water pollution problems; and
a list of the governmental agencies from which various approvals
already have been obtained. Public notice of the filing of the application must be made within ten days through publication of a notice in
a general circulation newspaper in the county in which the proposed
facility will be located.

The entire application is open to the public, but the PUC has
neither the manpower nor the inclination to provide assistance in
understanding it. To illustrate this point, former PUC Commissioner
A. W. Gatov recalled that, when he was a federal maritime commissioner, columnist Drew Pearson was looking into a ship sale
scandal and asked to see all the minutes of Federal Maritime Commission meetings from 1945 to 1950. Pearson sent one of his
researchers to do the work and Gatov provided the minutes, stacked
up in piles in a conference room. He soon received a call from
Pearson, who complained that he only wanted the minutes pertaining
to ship sale scandals. Gatov told him that it was his job to weed out
the useful material. The public is in the same position with regard
to the utility applications.

Unrelated to the application but apropos of utilities and access
to information, many state commissions themselves cannot get much
basic data, such as how much the utility earns for each share of
stock outstanding, interest costs on long-term debt, a detailed
breakdown of how funds collected from ratepayers are spent, and
ownership. Senator Lee Metcalf of Montana has regularly introduced
legislation that would compel utilities to provide state commissions
with this information, but thus far it has been defeated by the utility
lobby.[26]

The public hearing on the application is held as near to the plant
site as possible, although if the hearing is particularly long a portion
of it may be held in San Francisco, seat of the PUC. The hearing is

run by an examiner whose job it is to develop a full record. He
writes a decision based on the testimony, which is submitted to the
presiding commissioner. Three of the five commissioners must
assent to the examiner's decision for it to become final. At present,
any member of the public may contribute testimony or cross-examine
a witness during the proceedings. The PUC provides a team of staff
people who assist individuals in making statements for the record.
A person need only show up at the hearing and fill out an appearance
form to participate. The impact of the testimony, of course, depends
on the logic and expertise of the presentation. But former Commissioner Gatov notes that a real public outcry at a hearing has
impact because that is the only way the commissioners "can judge
what is going on in a community."

In general the utility must allow a year to obtain the certificate
for a new site, six months for permission to add a second or third
unit to an already operational site.

The PUC has never turned down a request for a certificate of
public convenience and necessity for a nuclear power plant. Part
of the reason is in the nature of American regulatory commissions:
the PUC is as much a creature of the utilities it must regulate as the
Federal Communications Commission is of the broadcast industry.
The PUC's Cavagnaro admits that for a utility to suffer a reversal
at this stage of the siting procedure "would be a great shock."

For the press and public, the PUC represents a point at which
to gain access to some detailed information on the proposed plant
which is available in the utility's application, although it will take an
informed person to sort out the useful from the useless. At present,
the PUC also offers the first major set of public hearings on the site
so that private citizens and conservation groups can register their
feelings. It also is a natural news peg for the media to investigate
the plant site and report on the nuclear dilemma. But the likelihood
that the public, the press, or the PUC staff can effect major changes
in utility plans at this stage is as remote as the possibility that the
FCC will take a broadcast license away from a network-affiliated
television station.

The Atomic Energy Commission

By the time the utility has secured the certificate of public
convenience and necessity, a minimum of two years, and probably
closer to three, have passed since the opening of negotiations with
the Power Plant Siting Committee, perhaps four years since the
utility first took an option to buy the property. The final two regulatory
hurdles of consequence, the construction permit and the operating

license, come from the AEC and they add at least another three
years to the siting procedure. (This time factor is the reason utility
officials chafe as an "obstructionist" public seeks further delays.)

Before the federal government passed the 1969 National Environmental Policy Act, the AEC's responsibility was uncomplicated: it
was to review the design specifications of the nuclear plant and insure
that it would operate safely. This is still the AEC's most important
function. Until recently the AEC was both promoter and regulator
of nuclear power as well as an advocate for the electric power
industry. Its responsibilities to the public were somewhat less clear.
With the appointment of James R. Schlesinger as chairman in October
1971, the AEC seems to be changing its attitude. Shortly after his
appointment, Schlesinger told a group of uncomfortable utility executives, "You should not expect the AEC to fight the industry's political,
social and commercial battles. The AEC exists to serve the public
interest."[27] Two months later, the AEC was dramatically reorganized
to give increased emphasis to civilian-oriented programs, with
creation of a new position of assistant general manager for environmental and safety affairs. How this change will affect the procedure
detailed below remains to be seen. In October 1972, however,
environmentalists praised an AEC decision which asked the Consolidated Edison Company to add an expensive cooling system to the
Indian Point No. 2 nuclear plant to protect fish life in the Hudson
River. This is the first time the AEC has asked a utility to modify
its cooling system to protect the environment.[28]

In applying for the construction permit, the utility submits a
massive Preliminary Safety Analysis Report or PSAR (SMUD's
PSAR for the Rancho Seco site was five volumes, each three inches
thick) that describes and analyzes the characteristics of the site and
explains the technical and design features of the plant and their
relation to safety. The AEC regulatory staff probes for potential
problem areas, asks for additional information, raises questions about
the design, and tests the assumptions about safety. After the AEC
staff review, the PSAR is reviewed by the independent Advisory
Committee on Reactor Safeguards, which also must approve the
safety of the plant. These two groups do not always agree; the design
for the Bodega Head plant was approved by one and found unsafe in
case of earthquake by the other, and PG&E withdrew the application
as a result.

After these reviews, there is a mandatory public hearing near
the plant site, conducted by an atomic safety and licensing board
consisting of two technical members and a lawyer. At the hearing
the utility applicant presents evidence summarizing its application.
The AEC regulatory staff presents expert testimony on its safety
evaluation of the proposed plant. Members of the public whose

interests are affected (and who are granted "intervenor" status by
the AEC) can call witnesses and cross-examine in order to develop
the record more fully on the safety of the plant. Those members of
the public who are not intervenors still may participate in the hearing
on a "limited appearances" basis, allowing them to express their
views on the plant to the atomic safety and licensing board.

Only after these reviews will the AEC issue the construction
license. Because of the evolving nature of nuclear power plant
technology, the AEC is likely to permit a utility to solve some problems
in construction. This has been a sore point with many AEC and
power plant critics, who believe such "provisional" construction
permits give the utility license to solve serious safety problems as
it sees fit. However, the AEC review does seem to be comprehensive.

To receive an operating license, the utility must go through
essentially the same procedure as for the construction permit, with
the AEC staff and the Advisory Committee on Reactor Safeguards
examining a Final Safety Analysis Report. At this stage the AEC
will hold a public hearing only if an outside group can show good
cause why such a hearing is necessary—for example, if new safety
problems have arisen in light of additional research since the
beginning of construction. At this point the AEC and the utility are
least tolerant of delay. The plant is ready for operation and, according
to the utility, it is needed to provide power in its area of service.
Delays can mean a cost of $50,000 to $100,000 a day. Nevertheless,
citizen groups have held up operation of the Calvert Cliffs plant near
Baltimore and the Indian Point plant near New York through additional
hearings and a court order. Under pressure from the Scientists'
Institute for Public Information and the Union of Concerned Scientists,
which questioned the reliability of untested emergency cooling
devices, in late 1971 the AEC called a virtual halt to the issuance of
operating licenses for new plants until safety questions could be
answered. In the spring of 1972 the AEC resumed issuance of
operating licenses.

To the AEC's credit, all documents that the utility must submit
for the construction permit and the operating license are public.
The AEC staff evaluation of the plant is public. The entire file is
available both in Washington, D.C., and at a place near the proposed
site. The AEC's assistant director of public relations, Joe Fouchard,
emphasizes that the nuclear program is totally unclassified. He
admits that the AEC was born in secrecy and much secrecy still
surrounds the weapons testing program, but says this is not the case
for nuclear power. In support, Representative John E. Moss of
California, past chairman of the House Subcommittee on Foreign
Operations and Government Information, which acts as the freedom
of information watchdog, states that only one or two complaints about

AEC secrecy come to his attention each year from the public. In this regard he terms it one of the best agencies in Washington, an image at odds with the traditional picture of the AEC, based largely on secrecy in weapons technology.

The only conflict over access to information that has arisen at this stage of the siting procedure concerns the AEC's compliance inspection reports. These are reports filed by AEC investigators stating what they found wrong with the safety of the proposed plant through their independent research. Potential intervenors at hearings would like access to this information. These reports have not been made available, although enforcement action taken on the basis of the reports has been made public. Officials feel that these reports are internal to the AEC and that making them public could hurt the AEC's inspection function. Fouchard contends that the AEC is changing its position on the compliance inspection reports and that, with some excisions (at the behest of equipment manufacturers who are concerned about competition and a bad public image), they will become available. Such reports could be valuable to the public. Indeed, they probably are more valuable to a plant's opponents and to the press than to the utility's own PSAR.

This was the limit of the AEC's responsibility before the environment became a political issue. Since passage of the 1969 National Environmental Policy Act, every federal agency issuing a permit, license, or funds for a project must make a preliminary assessment to determine whether the project will have an impact on the environment. If the determination is positive, the agency must draft an Environmental Impact Report (known as a "102 statement," in reference to the section of the act requiring it) that discusses the following points:

1. The environmental impact of the proposed action.

2. Any adverse environmental effects which cannot be avoided should the proposal be implemented.

3. Alternatives to the proposed action.

4. The relationship between local short-term uses of man's environment and the maintenance and enhancement of long-term productivity.

5. Any irreversible and irretrievable commitments on resources which would be involved in the proposed action should it be implemented.

In licensing nuclear power plants, the AEC does not bother with a preliminary assessment. It must issue a 102 statement for each plant.

The AEC requests from the utility a document entitled "Applicant's Environmental Report—Construction Permit Stage." Originally, the AEC wanted to circulate this report to the various federal, state,

and local agencies with environmental expertise for comment, but
the President's Council on Environmental Quality prevailed on the
AEC to write its own draft statement based on the report. Agencies
that receive copies of the draft are given a fixed period in which to
comment and then the AEC must write a final draft 102 statement in
which it incorporates the comments and states its own view on the
plant's environmental impact. Before the construction permit can
be issued, this final statement is circulated to other agencies, most
importantly the Council on Environmental Quality which, if it disagrees
with the AEC assessment, might recommend presidential interven-
tion. The AEC must issue both draft and final 102 statements at the
construction permit and operating license stages.

The purpose of all this is to force all federal agencies to consider
environmental impact in all their decisions. The goal of the Council
on Environmental Quality is that this procedure become internalized
in each agency so that it will not have to police the federal government
on environmental matters forever. And the best way to internalize
the environmental ethic is to require these written statements. The
AEC has hired new personnel to evaluate the utility environmental
reports and prepare the 102 statements. (But, as is true throughout
the siting procedure, the major burden of providing environmental
information rests with the utility.)

At first the AEC was unwilling to make both the draft and final
102 statements public, but under pressure from the Council on
Environmental Quality the AEC has agreed to do so. The entire file
of utility reports, agency comments, and AEC 102 statements is
public.

It now takes at least 18 months for the AEC to act on the construction permit application and two years to grant the operating license.
More and more hearings are being contested.

As a result, the AEC is pressing for legislation that would call
for an early site hearing, to be held by either the AEC or a state
power plant siting committee, at which all environmental matters
would be considered. If the site were approved at this stage, the
AEC would not have to consider environmental matters at the
construction permit stage. Furthermore, the public hearing at the
construction permit stage, at which environmental matters now can
be introduced, would be limited to questions of radiologic safety and
there would be no public hearing at the operating license stage. This
clearly would streamline the procedure and speed up the licensing
process, but it would be a blow to the groups battling the siting of
nuclear power plants. It would limit further the public's participation
in the decision-making process and reduce the amount of information
on environmental impact available to the press.

Under utility pressure to get into operation nuclear plants that are ready but stalled in the courts, the AEC and the Nixon administration asked Congress, in March 1972, for legislation to permit licensing of these plants even though they have not satisfied all provisions of the National Environmental Policy Act. If Congress acquiesces, this would be a severe blow to public participation in the siting procedure.

The AEC's public hearings, 102 statements, and compliance inspection reports are valuable resources for the press and public. The AEC and the utilities feel that perhaps there is too much participation and potential for harassment at this stage. However, it must be recognized that, if utility plans have proceeded to the construction permit stage, it is most likely that the plant eventually will be built and operated. The public can only become involved negatively at this stage. The time for positive action was two or three years earlier.

Observations

1. The volume of information available to the public about the suitability of the proposed power plant site and the safety of the design specifications is substantial. It includes, to name only the most important, the agreement between the PUC and the utility; the application filed with the PUC for the certificate of public convenience and necessity; the applications to the AEC for the construction permit and operating license; the AEC's compliance inspections reports; and the draft and final Environmental Impact Reports. But it takes a knowledgeable member of the public or press with time and motivation to get at this material and interpret it.

2. On actions of an IOU, the public will receive a minimum of three public hearings, and more likely six or seven. On actions of a municipal utility, the public will receive one hearing less since the municipal utility need not apply to the PUC for a certificate of public convenience and necessity.

3. For both types of utilities, the public hearings and the availability of information come late in the siting procedure, after the utility has invested two or three years and hundreds of thousands of dollars in preparing a site for a plant. By the time the public is given access to the decision-making process, the utility is committed to a site by prior investment and the public can act in a negative, delaying fashion only. There is little or no cooperation between the utility and the public in deciding basic power and siting questions. Nor does there seem to be a willingness on the part of the utility to include the public in a positive way. Utility secrecy until such time as the site has been purchased is testimony to that fact.

4. The lateness of public involvement also is reflected in the stance of the State Power Plant Siting Committee, the PUC, and the AEC, all of which must react to the sites chosen by the utility. Government does not now share siting responsibility with the utility, nor does it plan to. It is also obvious, but worth emphasizing, that there is no ombudsman-like governmental agency independent of the utility to protect the public interest in this matter. The state agencies must depend on the utility for much basic information about the site, and the key state officials involved are under political pressure from a pro-utility administration and cannot act as free agents. The PUC is not independent of the utilities it regulates, and the position of the AEC as both promoter and regulator of the uses of atomic power makes it ineligible for the role of ombudsman. By default, this role falls to the press.

5. The public hearings, the "official" points of entry for the public to the decision-making process, are too few and too late. A municipal utility can avoid a public hearing of consequence until it approaches the AEC for a construction permit. An IOU participates in a public hearing a bit earlier, at the PUC stage. The public should be heard on the suitability of the site before the utility has purchased any land and before it has made any investment in time or money. In any case, an interested and potentially activist public without information is a public crippled in a hearing procedure. Without accurate information, a public challenge is more likely to be emotional and frivolous.

6. It seems that all levels of government impinging on the siting procedure have internalized the goals of the Brown Act, the California Public Records Act, and the Federal Freedom of Information Act. They show a regard for the public's right to know on this issue and are willing to make information available to anyone who knows what questions to ask and when. The problem is that these agencies do not receive adequate information from the utilities at the start of the siting procedure.

7. Generalizing from the PG&E and SMUD experiences, it seems that the utilities have not internalized the notion of the public's right to know. Since freedom of information laws do not apply directly to IOUs, at least, it is debatable whether they should be expected to open their files and meeting rooms. Yet improved press coverage of their activities and a more informed public may depend on it.

COVERAGE OF NUCLEAR POWER PLANT SITING

Given this control over information by the utility, how has the problem of access to information affected actual press coverage of

nuclear power plant sitings in northern California and across the
nation?

To answer this question we first content-analyzed daily newspaper coverage of three plant sitings from 1958 to 1971. In each
case we studied coverage in the local newspaper nearest the site
(always rural) and the nearest metropolitan paper. Because each of
the sitings was prolonged for many months and years, we were forced
to sample among press coverage. We resorted to a "critical incident"
content analysis. For each siting we compiled a list of critical
incidents, such as public hearings, land purchases by the utility,
PUC decisions, and the filing of applications. We analyzed newspaper
coverage in both the week preceding and the week following the
critical incident, or 14 issues in all. Our assumption was that, if
the newspaper was motivated to report the nuclear power debate at
all, stories were more likely to appear at the time of such incidents.
We also wanted to determine whether any advance notice of these
critical events was given to the public.

The following power plant sitings and newspapers were selected
for study:

1. Bodega Head site: San Francisco Chronicle and Santa Rosa
Press-Democrat . This site was sought by PG&E over the years
1958-64, challenged by a citizens group, and terminated by the utility
after the AEC expressed reservations on the safety of the plant in
case of earthquake.

2. Rancho Seco site: Sacramento Bee and Lodi News-Sentinel.
SMUD has been seeking this site from 1965 to the present; it is
unchallenged and scheduled to start operation shortly.

3. Davenport site: San Jose Mercury and Santa Cruz Sentinel.
PG&E has been seeking this site from 1970 to the present; it is
challenged by a citizens group and is still in the early stages of
development.

In all, some 632 issues of the six newspapers were analyzed
over a 13-year period. A total of 156 issues each were coded for
the Chronicle and Press-Democrat; 100 issues each of the Bee
and News-Sentinel; and 60 issues each of the Mercury and Sentinel.

The complete content analysis coding sheet appears in Appendix
C. Briefly, coders were instructed to analyze news articles,
editorials, columns, and advertisements containing any of the following
words or expressions: nuclear power plant; atomic power plant;
radiation standard; radiation level; radiation threshold; electrical
brownout or blackout; and the supply, demand, production, or consumption of electric power. Length of the article, location, dateline, and
similar quantitative data were noted. In addition, to assess the
quality of coverage, a list of 20 "adversary items" was devised based

on the standard arguments in the nuclear power debate. Coders were to note whenever one of these adversary items was mentioned in the news story, column, editorial, or ad.

We found that the quantity of coverage was much greater for the two challenged plant sitings than the unchallenged siting and that the local papers devoted more space to the subject than their metropolitan counterparts. Rancho Seco, the unchallenged plant, was totally ignored by the Lodi paper and only briefly mentioned by the otherwise respectable Bee. Table 6.1 presents a paper-by-paper breakdown of the total number of articles appearing on the nuclear power debate, column inches, and adversary items. The "per 14-issue" figures have been computed by dividing the totals by the number of issues analyzed (see page 180) and multiplying by 14 to make them comparable, since the total number of issues analyzed was different for each pair of papers.

When quantity of coverage is examined for each critical incident, we find that coverage began relatively late, as we would expect from our discussion of the siting procedure. In the case of Bodega Head, the press did not pick up the story in any detail until the first public hearing, held by the Army Corps of Engineers on granting PG&E permission to construct an access road to the site. This hearing came nearly four years after PG&E first announced its intention to construct a plant in Sonoma County and five months after the utility filed for the certificate of public convenience and necessity with the PUC.

TABLE 6.1

Coverage of Three Plant Sitings in Six Newspapers:
Number of Stories, Column Inches,
and Adversary Items

Paper	Number of Stories		Number of Column Inches		Number of Adversary Items	
	Total	per 14 issues	Total	per 14 issues	Total	per 14 issues
Press-Democrat	82	7.4	1,618	145.7	155	13.9
Chronicle	39	3.5	673	60.6	60	5.4
Sentinel	43	10.0	673	156.5	82	19.1
Mercury	22	5.1	347	80.7	46	10.7
News-Sentinel	0	0	0	0	0	0
Bee	18	2.5	249	35.1	17	2.4

The only critical incident the Sacramento Bee covered in any detail for the Rancho Seco plant was the AEC-run public hearing on granting a construction permit to SMUD. The paper virtually ignored land purchases by SMUD, the filing of the construction permit application, and SMUD's initial announcement of its plans for Rancho Seco. The Lodi paper did not cover Rancho Seco at all. By the time the general public, dependent on the mass media, received substantial information on either the Bodega Head or Rancho Seco siting, the utilities were too deeply involved to change course.

Coverage of Davenport started earlier in the siting procedure, before land actually was purchased by PG&E, because the siting had become a political football, much to the utility's consternation. Phil Harry, a candidate for the Santa Cruz County Board of Supervisors, first revealed PG&E's plans in an advertisement in the Sentinel, accusing his political opponent of smoothing the way for the plant. Thus, the siting story became entwined with a local political race. In addition, the Santa Cruz County Board of Supervisors, not as enamoured with the plant as other boards in other times, scheduled two unofficial public forums at which the pros and cons of nuclear power were discussed. Both the San Jose and Santa Cruz papers gave much space to these forums.

We also noted whether the six newspapers mentioned the impending critical incident in the seven editions prior to the event itself. Their records on providing advance notice to the public were uniformly dismal. Of 11 critical incidents for Bodega Head, the Santa Rose Press-Democrat mentioned three and the San Francisco Chronicle only one. Of seven incidents for Rancho Seco, the Lodi News-Sentinel mentioned none and the Sacramento Bee but one. For Davenport, the Santa Cruz Sentinel provided advance notice for two out of four incidents while the San Jose Mercury mentioned only one.

For any individual or group organizing to contest the utility, the lack of advance notice is a great handicap. Interviews with plant opponents in California indicate that it is impossible to get this information from the utility. With proper contacts, it is available in a general way through the government agencies involved, but often these agencies do not know utility plans in advance, either.

Among the more serious omissions was the Chronicle's neglect of the Army Corps of Engineers hearings and both sets of PUC hearings (which were held in San Francisco), and the Mercury's neglect of the second public forum in Santa Cruz.

On the dimensions of overall quantity of coverage providing advance notice, the two local dailies covering IOUs in challenged situations provided more comprehensive coverage than did the metropolitan papers as a group or the two papers covering the unchallenged situation in Sacramento.

Table 6.1 established the ratio between column inches published and the number of adversary items discussed. As we would expect, papers that printed more stories and column inches also touched on more adversary items. But these numbers do not indicate which adversary questions were raised or with what frequency. The 20 adversary items coded were as follows:

A. The effects of radiation on plant and animal life

B. The adequacy of radiation protection standards

C. The possibility of plant accident

D. The adequacy of insurance in case of plant accident

E. The potential impact of thermal discharge on marine life

F. Cooling methods employed

G. The adequacy of methods for the transport and/or disposal of radioactive wastes apart from plant discharges

H. Aesthetic arguments on the plant siting

I. Costs to the consumer of the electric power produced by the plant

J. The future availability of nuclear and/or fossil fuels

K. The economic impact of the nuclear plant on the site community, such as change in land values, availability of jobs, and increased tax revenue

L. A non-evaluative description of the siting procedure

M. Attacks or defenses of the siting procedure

N. Points at which the public can, or has, become involved in the siting procedure

O. The demand for more electric power in California or the United States

P. The effects of increased power consumption for California or the United States

Q. The effects of decreased power consumption for California or the United States

R. The possibility of developing technologies other than nuclear power to produce electricity

S. The necessity for a speed-up in the siting procedure for nuclear power plants

T. The necessity for a slow-down or moratorium in the siting of nuclear power plants.

Figure 6.1 shows the number of times each of these 20 adversary items was discussed in a newspaper article, (with a maximum of one mention coded for a single category per article). The design-coded bar graph presents the data separated into five categories: (1) the scientific pros and cons of nuclear power; (2) esthetic arguments; (3) descriptions and critiques of the siting procedure; (4) economic data on the production of electricity with nuclear fuel; and (5) planning/overview data on present and future power needs.

FIGURE 6

Adversary Topics Raised by the Press
in Coverage of Plant Siting

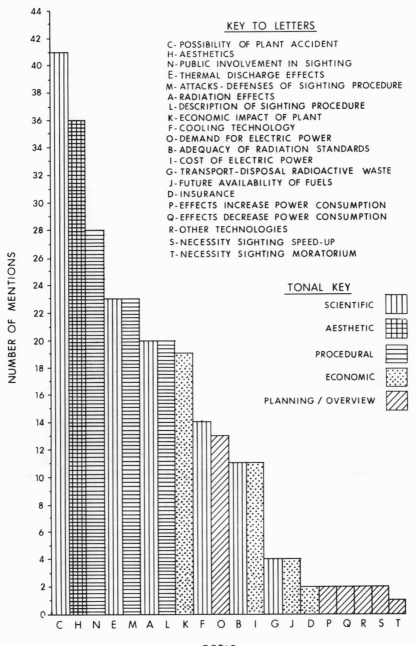

KEY TO LETTERS

C- POSSIBILITY OF PLANT ACCIDENT
H- AESTHETICS
N- PUBLIC INVOLVEMENT IN SIGHTING
E- THERMAL DISCHARGE EFFECTS
M- ATTACKS - DEFENSES OF SIGHTING PROCEDURE
A- RADIATION EFFECTS
L- DESCRIPTION OF SIGHTING PROCEDURE
K- ECONOMIC IMPACT OF PLANT
F- COOLING TECHNOLOGY
O- DEMAND FOR ELECTRIC POWER
B- ADEQUACY OF RADIATION STANDARDS
I- COST OF ELECTRIC POWER
G- TRANSPORT-DISPOSAL RADIOACTIVE WASTE
J- FUTURE AVAILABILITY OF FUELS
D- INSURANCE
P- EFFECTS INCREASE POWER CONSUMPTION
Q- EFFECTS DECREASE POWER CONSUMPTION
R- OTHER TECHNOLOGIES
S- NECESSITY SIGHTING SPEED-UP
T- NECESSITY SIGHTING MORATORIUM

TONAL KEY

SCIENTIFIC

AESTHETIC

PROCEDURAL

ECONOMIC

PLANNING / OVERVIEW

NUMBER OF MENTIONS

TOPIC

What seems most significant is the paucity of information in the economic and planning categories.* The other three categories received most of the newspaper attention. Why?

One possible explanation is access to information. For the three categories receiving the preponderance of attention there are information sources outside and independent of the utilities. Information on the siting procedure, for example, is not the monopoly of the utilities. Many scientists have presented data on the scientific pros and cons of nuclear power. And esthetic criticism is everyone's prerogative.

But the utilities hold all the cards in the economic and planning areas. The utilities alone have the experience and manpower to estimate what the use of various fuels in plants of differing design with different cooling methods will mean to the average customer. They and their colleagues in the oil industry are virtually alone in the ability to estimate the future availability of various types of fuels. They are best equipped to estimate the full economic impact of a new plant on a given community. Similarly, planning information is jealously guarded by the utilities, as we have seen. The utilities initiate; all other groups react.

Clearly, one of the most crucial variables determining the quality of coverage in these three cases was active citizen opposition. Press coverage and opposition fed on one another, the opposition

---

*It should be noted that it is impossible to insure that the conceptual sizes of these adversary categories are equal; that is, it is possible that the category "esthetics" (H) is in some sense "bigger" than the category "insurance in case of plant accident" (D). If it were possible to explicate and measure the conceptual size of a category, then some adjustment could be made in Figure 6.1, such as weighting, to take this into consideration. Since this does not seem possible, the reader should bear in mind that some categories may be more wide-ranging than others, although all of them are rather broad. Since only gross manipulations are made with the figures, the author does not consider this a serious problem.

The data in Figure 6.1 is accurate over time, as well. The author graphed similar charts for each of the three case studies to determine if adversary categories being discussed at Davenport in 1970 were being discussed at Bodega in 1960. (Figure 6.1 is, of course, a composite for all three case studies.) Throughout the 13 years, approximately the same adversary categories were discussed, or ignored, by the press.

providing additional news pegs for stories and the press acting as a
forum in which the fight could be waged. Given that the preponderance
of coverage was event-pegged (to such events as public meetings,
hearings, press conferences, and statements), it is essential that some
recognized opposition group be formed to head off utility control of
the information channels. This is what was lacking at Rancho Seco.
Both the Sacramento Bee and the Lodi News-Sentinel supported the
plant and neither felt impelled to present the nuclear debate without
a community controversy (a traditional and accepted journalism
ethic), so the coverage was one-sided and thin.

Distance of the paper from the plant site is a second important
variable. In the Bodega and Davenport cases the paper at the scene
did the most thorough reporting job. But local papers do not have
the resources metropolitan papers can command and thus are at a
handicap in reporting such complex stories. The question "Whose
story is it?" is an important one.

Utility domination of the siting procedure and news about it is
the norm. The press begins coverage relatively late in the game,
has difficulty reporting (in a balanced fashion) advance planning and
the economics of a site, can provide only advance notice of public
events without a great deal of investigative work into private utility
plans, and generally is at the mercy of the utilities and plant opponents
for information. The utilities, acting like any other private businesses,
only release and publicize information that will aid in realization of
their plans, and they have skilled public relations staffs to accomplish
what secrecy and news management cannot.

THE NATIONAL PICTURE

To supplement the content analysis and gain a broader view of
national coverage of nuclear power plant siting, we queried 244
individuals who had written about, participated in, or opposed the
siting of a nuclear power plant. We sent questionnaires to editors,
utility executives, and plant opponents (where names were available)
at every site at which a nuclear power plant had been constructed
or proposed as of June 1971. The respondents answered questions
on press-utility relationships and access to utility information.
Parallel forms of the questionnaire were used for each of the three
groups. The overall response rate was 54.9 percent with only a
single mailing. (Copies of each of the questionnaires—to editors,
utility executives, and plant opponents—appear with marginals in
Appendix C.)

When editors were asked to indicate how important they felt
nuclear power was as a story for their community, 71.6 percent

answered that it was "very important, meriting large news play" while another 25.4 percent stated it was "of above-average importance, meriting moderate news play." Utility executives concurred: 62.2 percent stated it was a very important story and 32.4 percent felt it was of above-average importance.

Editors were asked to enclose clips of articles on nuclear power from their papers, and the clips received indicate that in many parts of the country the subject is receiving a thorough airing. The Cincinnati Enquirer ran a special 12-page section (with no advertisements) on nuclear power, the product of ten months of research. The Portland Oregonian ran a 26,000-word series on nuclear power and the environment, for which it received the Atomic Industrial Forum Award. The Milwaukee Journal presented a "Power to the People" series of non-news peg stories detailing the debate. The Providence Bulletin devoted 65 articles to the Rome Point plant in parts of 1970-71 alone, and the Huntsville Times, which maintains that it broke the story of the Tennessee Valley Authority's nuclear plans for Alabama, ran a six-part series on atomic power.

Nor has activity been limited to the metropolitan papers. The Pottstown (Pennsylvania) Mercury ran a special section on the Philadelphia Electric Company's Limerick plant. And perhaps the most famous of all newspaper treatments of the issue to date was done by a small paper, the Eugene (Oregon) Register-Guard. That paper's investigative reporter, the late Gene Bryerton, detailed the nuclear plans of the Eugene Water and Electric Board (a public utility) in a series of articles that were under the title Nuclear Dilemma.[29] In a May 1970 referendum on whether or not the plant should be constructed, the citizens of Eugene voted a three-year moratorium. A utility spokesman in Oregon credits the Bryerton series in the Register-Guard with helping bring about defeat of the plant.

The environmental information explosion that began in 1969 probably also has influenced the amount of coverage. Many citizen challenges to plants have come since 1969, and as they have created the news pegs and the demand for information, the press has responded.

The most important and interesting variable affecting the responses of the editors was whether or not the plant was challenged. Of the editors, 73 percent said they experienced no trouble getting information from the electric utility in their area. However, editors in challenged situations were more likely to have experienced trouble $(p < .10)$ and editors who reported trouble were more likely to have assigned a specialist, such as a science or environmental news writer, to the story $(p < .05)$. Editor dissatisfaction with utility information policies may vary positively with better press

performance. A reporter first must ask probing questions to find
out that answers are not forthcoming.

A majority of editors, 59.7 percent, stated that extension of
open meeting and open record laws to cover electric utilities would
be of use to their reporters, and 73.1 percent said they would support
such a legislative effort in their states.

Among plant opponents, 83 percent said they experienced difficulty
in getting information from utilities in their area. Jesse Waller, who
is opposing the Duke Power Company's William B. McGuire Nuclear
Station, wrote,

> All questions on safety, experience, radioactivity, and
> thermal discharges received PR answers. "Clean, safer
> than fossil fueled plants, etc." We wrote to EPA
> [Environmental Protection Agency in Washington, D.C.]
> in desperation on this matter. EPA referred the letter to
> their office in Virginia, who referred us to the Duke Power
> Company for any questions.

The experience of opponents is best put by Alfred Eipper of the
Department of Conservation, Cornell University. Eipper was one of
many faculty members concerned about the effects on Lake Cayuga
of a nuclear plant planned by the New York State Electric and Gas
Company. He wrote of his experience in Science magazine of July
3, 1970:

> The utility company's actions in the Cayuga Lake case
> seem to illustrate a behavior pattern fairly common in
> controversies of this general type. The strategy was to
> announce the proposal after plans for implementing it
> were already well under way, and to keep things moving
> rapidly thereafter. The substance of the company's
> numerous publicity releases was that the plant would
> benefit the community in many ways, and that the company
> would never allow the plant to "harm" the lake, and was
> conducting contract research projects which, it said, were
> expected to demonstrate that its operations would not
> damage the lake. . . .
> Company spokesmen tended to be close-mouthed,
> unwilling to debate issues or to discuss alternatives, and
> generally confined themselves to rather standardized
> publicity releases and announcements. They were
> challenged on their lack of receptiveness to the idea of
> using already available technological safeguards that would
> eliminate virtually all hazard of thermal and radiological

pollution to Cayuga Lake. . . . Their public posture still
seems to be that the only feasible way to operate the
plant is by the relatively unique method that they have
proposed from the outset.

The Company proved to have been less than frank in
some instances, and indeed appeared cynical. For example,
it developed that the company already(1) invested some
$5 million or more in site preparation and (2) contracted
to sell half to three-fourths of its power to Consolidated
Edison, in New York City, while research to assure that
the lake would not be harmed was under way and before
even one year's data were available for analysis.

Neither metropolitan nor rural editors across the country were
willing to concede that the siting story was properly one for some
other medium to cover, yet the difficulties for both groups were
apparent. The editor of one southeastern metropolitan paper
commented as follows about his efforts to cover siting of an unchallenged plant in a small town about 150 miles away: "We tried in
this instance to develop some interest. We approached its people,
both officials and citizens, and found no opposition. We pointed out
what had arisen in other areas and questioned the cooling method
selected, as well as the radiation safety measures. We got nowhere."

The editor of the Gloucester (Massachusetts) Daily Times
speaks for a number of concerned editors of small papers:

We have attempted to report the status of the proposal here
and the study by the city manager. [The plant is planned
by a group of small public utilities.] We are attempting to
get and print an in-depth report on nuclear plants in
general done by the League of Women Voters. To do a
report of this depth ourselves would mean pulling one of
three city reporters off his regular beat for weeks perhaps.
Papers our size (10,000 circulation) can't do that very
often. We are trying to counter this weakness generally
by plugging into the many citizens groups which do report
and study . . . and often then don't know how or where to
get their message across to the public.

The frustration of a news editor trying to deal with emotional
plant opponents, close-mouthed utility executives, and government
agencies, and still come up with a comprehensive report on nuclear
power for his community is summed up by a Newsday (Long Island)
executive in discussing his paper's coverage of the siting of the
Shoreham Nuclear Power Station of Long Island Lighting, an IOU.
The Newsday executive said:

Covering the Shoreham debate turned out to be an arduous
assignment, requiring long hours for minimal stories,
requiring great expertise in order to write the simplest
of statements with perception, understanding and accuracy. The opponents were trying to use Newsday as a
forum for a media war against the AEC—and the utility—
with its legion of public relations men—did likewise.
We endured what has become the longest continuing
construction permit hearing, but not without this writer's
beginning to question the entire hearing process. I do not
yet know of what value the latter stages of our coverage
was to those members of the reading public who had
missed out on the early stages of the hearings themselves.
A certain amount of background was a necessity for the
readers and I'm not sure they got it. I am not sure that a
daily newspaper can cover such hearings intelligently. I
do know that the AEC procedures are an absurdity. I do
know that the issue of nuclear power plants is not being
discussed adequately anywhere in this nation. We have
said these things editorially. What we haven't said
editorially is this: The opponents of the Shoreham project,
who handled their case very poorly, did succeed in casting
reasonable doubt upon whether or not such an installation
would be safe. . . . The AEC procedures are such that the
project will go ahead in spite of this. I find this enormously
frustrating and depressing, and this is what I do not find
well covered in the media.

CONCLUSIONS AND RECOMMENDATIONS

In recent years the work of John Kenneth Galbraith, Morton
Mintz and Jerry Cohen, Ralph Nader, Senator Lee Metcalf, and others
has demonstrated that private business in America has equaled
government in its day-to-day power and influence over American
life. But conventions to facilitate newsgathering in the business
community have not kept pace with this realization. Freedom of
information laws do not extend to private companies or to privately-
owned public utilities, which are close to government in organization
and function. Business leaders do not recognize the public's right
to know and do not appreciate the value of an adversary relationship
with newsmen. Hostility is often an accurate description of their
relations with the press. As major supporters of our system of
mass communications, they sometimes feel they can purchase or
demand the type of image they desire in the press. As a result.

press coverage of private business in America lags well behind coverage of government in satisfying the public's right to know.

The findings outlined in this chapter indicate why the press-business relationship must be redefined if press coverage of environmental deterioration is to improve. Thus far it seems that only the challenges of a few environmental activists have forced the press into providing coverage of the nuclear debate, coverage that has been slow in coming and largely reactive to the pseudo-events of both utility executives and plant opponents. The public is not being provided with the information about the business community necessary for intelligent decisions in purchases and life-style or informed public participation in decision-making by private business. The adversary relationship, which is in part responsible for the often excellent coverage of government by the American press, does not now exist between newsmen and business executives.

Although the content analysis and study of siting procedures were limited to California, it seems sensible to generalize nationally from these findings. The newspapers in California have not been found significantly poorer than those in other parts of the nation, and if anything the siting procedure is more open to the public in California than in other states. Thus the problems raised in this chapter are likely to be just as serious elsewhere in the nation.

This study suggests that legislators consider extending access legislation to cover public utilities (and eventually all business enterprises colored with the public interest), both for the psychological effect it might have on the business community and for the legal tools it would afford the working press and the public.

The definition of "news" should be reworked so that regional problems receive the same attention from major papers as local problems. The press must recognize its obligation to report fully the activities of the business community in this age that is so vulnerable to new technologies. The newspaper editor must recognize that his medium is the public's major source of science and business news, and probably its only source of news about the activities of local utilities.

At the heart of the change must be a redefinition of the press-business relationship and a recognition of the value of information sources outside traditional government and business channels.

7

THE PRESS AND THE GROWTH ESTABLISHMENT: A CASE STUDY OF SAN JOSE

The vast majority of mass media are dependent on either advertising or subscription revenue (or some combination of the two) to survive. We have shown in previous chapters how advertiser pressure can influence media content and lower the quality of environmental news coverage. This is a well-known and often demonstrated problem. Advertiser control affects the quality of all sorts of media content, not just news. This is inescapable.

Receiving much less attention, but undoubtedly more significant, is the affect on environmental coverage of a news medium's legitimate efforts to improve its economic position: to attract more advertisers and build a larger circulation. It should be obvious that as the community in which the medium is located grows, and as more companies are attracted and shopping centers built, the medium must benefit economically.

It probably is unreasonable to expect a newspaper or broadcast station to remain neutral in this process of expansion, simply reporting objectively the growth of the community. Too much is at stake financially. Often we can expect media owners to boost their own communities and, in the process, assume the characteristics of the local chamber of commerce members. Once a community reaches the take-off point in its development, and if the local media become involved, can news coverage of such "progress" remain balanced

---

Material for this chapter was prepared by David W. Jones, Jr. Mr. Jones is a specialist in urban problems and a political adviser to numerous candidates in northern California. A Yale graduate, he is completing work for his Ph.D. at the Department of Communication, Stanford University. He has published his own monthly newspaper and currently is studying communication substitutes for transportation.

and objective? Or must news be manipulated for the greater good of
the community and the medium? What are the consequences for news
coverage of such local issues as crowding, open space, planning, and
noise pollution?

The city of San Jose and its two chain-owned daily newspapers—
the Mercury and the News (owned by the Ridder family)—provide an
excellent laboratory for study of the press and the growth establishment. San Jose grew faster than any other California city in the
1960s, and the now wealthy Mercury and News have played a major
role, through both the activities of their executives and the quality
of their news coverage.

Some of the problems of too-rapid, unplanned growth are now
burdening the residents of San Jose: smog, lack of open space,
crowded highways, poor schools, and a depressed inner city. The
citizenry and newspaper staffers are beginning to question the growth
ethic and the role of the press in advancing that ethic.

To study this relationship we conducted telephone polls of
chamber of commerce members, realtors, and environmentalists in
San Jose, querying them on their attitudes toward two key problems
for the community: mass transit development and airport expansion.
We also asked each group to evaluate coverage of the two subjects
in San Jose newspapers. We content-analyzed newspaper editorials
and hard news copy on these issues from 1968 to 1970 and interviewed
reporters and executives at the papers involved.

The resulting study exposes an area too long ignored by journalism researchers, one that is at the very heart of press coverage of
environmental problems. What is the relationship of a newspaper
and a growing community?

THE NEWSPAPER AND ECONOMIC GROWTH

Behind the blush of First Amendment freedom, objective reporting,
and social responsibility, the newspaper is a business. On the average,
two-thirds of newspaper operating revenue is derived from advertising.
In an era of rising taxes, personnel costs, and newsprint rates, growth
in advertising sales is critical for sustaining newspaper profitability.

The lifeline of the newspaper is the health of the local economy;
it is dependent not simply on a virile local economy but on one of a
particular shape and form. The big-city paper is as healthy as its
potential advertisers with regional or total-city markets—markets
as heterogeneous as the paper's circulation.

In this sense, the newspaper has a direct stake in the growth
patterns, transportation accessibility, and customer appeal of the
city's regional shopping outlets. In a healthy city it is these

advertisers that are most stable and predictable, and far less likely to transfer their messages to direct mail, subcommunity weeklies, or shoppers.

The nature of the boomer and booster projects that gloss a newspaper's prestige, power, and economic interest, insert it squarely in the activity of the "mixed economy." These projects coincide with the effort to stem the flood of middle- and upper-income residents to suburban homes and neighborhood buying habits and to displace low-income families from the central business district.

The simple act of servicing advertisers gives the newspaper a vital role to play on behalf of the growth establishment. The possibility of a leadership role must be more tempting still.

Presuming that newspapers do desire to operate in their economic self-interest, two behaviors that would serve these interests can be projected. The first would be to promote growth: the plain and simple proliferation of people in a concentrated area who can act as customers and subscribers. A newspaper's economic benefit from growth is suggested by our research, which made the following findings among 11 California evening dailies:

1. Of the variance in the rate of increase in ad lineage from newspaper to newspaper, 44.5 percent can be accounted for by the rate of growth of population in the ABC zone. The results were significant at the 0.05 level.

2. Of the variance in the rate of circulation growth from newspaper to newspaper, 51.5 percent can be accounted for by the rate of growth of population in the ABC zone. The results were significant at the 0.01 level.

The results take on special interest in light of the large number of variables that can account for the remainder of the variance. But everything from the aggressiveness of the advertising department to the state of the national economy pales beside the impact of population growth.

The second behavior would be the promotion of public and private policies that lead to the continuing vitality of regional marketplaces. As Morris Janowitz points out, too great dispersion of population growth lends itself to the proliferation of subcommunity weeklies: "In a demographic sense, the growth of the community newspaper was as dependent on the dispersion of the population from the center of the city to outlying areas as it was on increases in total population."[1]

Thus, in terms of competition, the metropolitan newspaper would be wise to promote urban population and economic growth policies that increase the characteristics of concentration and ease of circulation. The economic interests of the metropolitan press encourage a role in the determination of the public policy and subsidy decisions of the mixed economy, especially those relating to the

rate, concentration, and location of transportation facilities, urban
redevelopment, and urban growth.

With the added inducement of economies of scale in the newspaper's manufacturing operation—such as lower limit costs of
newsprint, press runs, salaries, news and wire services—the print
media have a distinct interest in concentrated bigness, both corporate
and urban.

If the newspaper pursued its interests, it is obvious that its actions
would coincide with those of the growth interests of the community
and most often collide with those of environmentalists, minorities,
and the poor. How fair, balanced, and probing the press is and can
be in this setting is the concern of this chapter.

Like any complex social organization, the newspaper has many
interfaces with the community. The average citizen has contact only
with the newspaper's printed product. He may complete a loop in
the sense that he patronizes advertisers with the want ads or sale
pages in hand, but his contact with the newspaper is distant, passive,
and non-interactive.

For the purposes of this discussion, the most important interfaces between the newspaper and the community are those that are
interactive: the relationship between newsman and news source,
between newspaper executive and community influential, between
marketing director and community association.

At the risk of gross oversimplification, some possible typologies
of relationships between newspaper personnel and community influentials may be suggested. These typologies have the advantage describing
a dynamic relation rather than a static situation. They have the
disadvantage of overlap. The possible typologies are as follows:

1. Active newspaper roles

    Prestige seeking: the newspaper or its personnel makes
    a commitment to a course of action with the intent of
    creating the acclaim, satisfaction, or prestige of accom-
    plishment.

    Profit seeking: the newspaper or its personnel makes
    a commitment to a course of action with the intent of
    keeping or realizing economic advantage.

    Information seeking: the newspaper or its personnel
    makes a commitment to gathering information of neutral,
    advocacy, or adversary value.

    Acceptance seeking: the newspaper or its personnel
    makes a commitment to action with the intent of gaining

    or keeping the friendship, membership, or acceptance
    of valued others.

2. Passive newspaper roles
    Accommodation: the newspaper accepts outside direction
    for action, defining or suppressing goals in terms of
    significant others.

    Withdrawal or noninvolvement: the newspaper remains
    or becomes inactive out of choice or the inability to
    effect goals of action.

  The conceptualization places economic interest in the perspective
of a wider constellation of interacting motivations. It further suggests
the very real likelihood of conflict between the news providing and
other goal-realizing activities of the newspaper.[2]
  The conflict between even-handed news and goal-seeking would
occur where the agenda for public policy is undecided or contested
or where divergent conceptions of the public good divide the community.
This, of course, is likely in a city of metropolitan size where public
needs and private prerogatives differ among persons of different
income and belief. In this setting of conflict, the newspaper's goals
would be expected to coincide with those of the commercial and
financial elite since they are most capable of articulating the goals
and providing the rewards we have described.
  The conflict between the goal-seeking roles and the provision
of fair, balanced, and probing news has been underlined in studies of
newspaper performance in Chicago and Atlanta. The studies suggest
the diversity of motives and commonality of goals that unite newspaper
management with the community influentials of the central business
district.

Prestige and Profit-Seeking: The Chicago Tribune
and the Lakefront Exhibition Hall

  The etched marble lobby of the Chicago Tribune carries the
solemn motto, "The newspaper is an institution developed by modern
civilization to present the news of the day, to foster commerce and
industry, to inform and lead public opinion and to furnish that check
upon government which no constitution has ever been able to provide."
  The staunchly Republican Tribune historically has taken at
least one part of that motto very seriously: the fostering of commerce
and industry. Part of that effort was to secure convention and exhibition facilities for Chicago in the immediate postwar era. The

Chicago lakefront seemed an ideal location for such facilities: past fairs in semipermanent structures had prospered, the location offered easy access to Loop hotels, freeway access was ideal, the location was one of natural beauty and provided a magnificent vista of Chicago's "golden age architecture" rising above the shores of Lake Michigan. And a Tribune reporter told the author in 1967, without a convention center "the colored people" would crowd out everybody else on the shorelines.

A permanent convention center on the lake was the "baby" of the Tribune's owner, Colonel Robert R. McCormick. He had put $50,000 into a lakefront fair and raised another $950,000 from downtown businesses. A permanent facility would be a feather in the Tribune's cap and a boost to urban growth.

With help from the Chicago Convention Bureau, Marshall Field, and the Bismarck Hotel, the Tribune pushed through tax and enabling legislation in Springfield.

With lobbying effort from Tribune reporter George Tagge, race track bets were taxed and the revenue placed in a trust fund for convention facility development. Edward Banfield describes it as follows:

> The race-track owners, fearing the additional tax would hurt their business, opposed the bill vigorously. Nevertheless the bill passed, largely because of the efforts of a Tribune reporter to see it through. Tagge had covered the legislature for fifteen years, and he knew more about its inside workings than did most of its members. Many legislators were his friends of long standing. Others wanted to get on his good side or stay there.
>
> Governor Stevenson was inclined to veto the bill. He was opposed to state aid for fairs of any kind and he was under pressure from a Chicago publisher, John S. Knight of the Daily News, who had had an interest in a race track. However at the urging of Richard J. Daley, who had been his director of revenue and had since been elected Cook County clerk, and of Joel Boldblatt, a Chicago merchant, he let the bill become law without his signature.[3]

Tagge's influence was such that Colonel McCormick's brain-child was profaned as "Tagge's Temple" by Springfield pundits.

Further enabling legislation passed over the opposition of the Chicago Real Estate Board and the Association of Commerce and Industry, groups that hoped convention activities would be located even closer to the Loop. In this effort, W. Don Maxwell, then Tribune managing editor, met almost weekly with the newly elected Republican governor. As Banfield puts it, Governor Stratton "owed the Tribune a great deal and was on close terms with it."[4]

Conservationists provided the last-gasp opposition to the convention hall site. They viewed lakefront siting as both a crass desecration of natural beauty and a first-step effort at development of the entire lakefront shoreline. The opposition of planners and conservationists was "not shared by the newspapers, the civic associations and the politicians. They took it for granted that publicity and dollars made cities great."[5]

A conservationist lawsuit failed—as both a delaying effort and a legal one. The exhibition hall was built and dedicated to the memory of the Tribune publisher: "McCormick Place."

Maxwell, elevated to publisher after Colonel McCormick's death, described the Tribune's interest in the ten-year effort:

> Why did we put so much time into this? Because it's good for the city. But partly from selfish motives too. We want to build a bigger Chicago and a bigger Tribune. We want more circulation and more advertising. We want to keep growing, and we want the city to keep growing so that we can keep growing.
>
> We think the community respects a newspaper that can do things like that. People will go by the hall and say, "See that? The Tribune did that singlehanded." That's good for us to have them say that.
>
> If it hadn't come off—if those lawsuits had turned out wrong—it would not have been good. It's good that people should think that their newspaper is powerful. It's good that it be powerful.[6]

It is clear from the willingness of public officials to play dead if not overtly boost the construction project, as well as from the Tribune's news pages, that news coverage was the primary instrument of the Tribune's potency. One example will suffice. Banfield describes what happened when the conservationist forces issued a press release opposing the lakefront site:

> Following her usual practice, the conservationist's public relations manager issued the release in the names of several persons of whose support she had been assured. She did not, however, check with each of them as carefully as she might before the release went out. Tagge of the Tribune called them and found that about half did not know exactly what had been said in their names and had not specifically authorized it. This, of course, was front-page news.[7]

The Tribune leadership felt few qualms. They were, after all,
fighting for their city and its best interests. That's the role of a
crusading newspaper and Maxwell liked the role. He said:

> You want to see your city continue to grow rather than to
> die. We have nowadays—what do they call it?—"urban
> movement" or something like that. The core of the city is
> being gutted. There are great investments at stake. You
> can't stand by and let it die. We thought we could prevent
> it from dying by bringing conventions here, on the front
> porch of the city.[8]

Accommodation: Floyd Hunter's Atlanta

Floyd Hunter's study of Atlanta popularized the notion of a
"power structure" manipulated by "power leaders."[9] Hunter describes
the power structure, composed of leading industrialists and financial
leaders, as "a dominant policy-making group using the machinery of
government as a bureaucracy for the attainment of certain goals
coordinate with the interests of the policy-making group."[10]

While it can be argued that Hunter's power structure can operate
only in a setting of mutual threat (the insurgence of the black community) and "value agreement" (the pervadingly conservative ideology
of the South), the role he ascribes to the press is worth examining.

Political influence, Hunter maintains, allows the elite to prescribe
personal invisibility in the press. Errand runners in the form of
elected officials, lower-level management men on the make, and
professionals receive press coverage only after policy matters have
reached the implementation stage. At the formulation stage, media
accommodation guarantees the elites' desired level of anonymity.
Controversy is scrupulously avoided by the elite, and subsequently
by the media coverage of elite projects:

> "Don't rock the boat," describes the general theme of the
> propaganda which issues forth on the radio and is dis-
> seminated through the columns of the press in Regional
> City [Atlanta]. The stories are not new, and they fit into
> the stereotype given to us by R. A. Brady in describing
> the propaganda put forth by the National Association of
> Manufacturers for the edification of the citizenry. . . .
> "All economic issues are transmuted [by the NAM] into
> terms of social and cultural issues, increasingly, as the
> political implications and military possibilities of cumu-
> lative economic power are realized."[11]

In other instances, where "the initiators" wished to "activate the under-structure of power," the newspapers would create the appropriate build-up. Two examples suffice:

> When the Plan of Development project [a highway project] was to be officially launched, [one of the power elite] was asked to take the presidency of one of the more powerful civic associations for a year to "swing that group into line." He was given an impressive build-up by the newspapers for his broad civic interests and for a year he devoted a great deal of time to getting the Plan of Development underway.[12]

Similarly timed propaganda was used in floating an International Trade Council. The newspapers did not release the story until funding, a board of directors, and tacit approval of the elite had been secured. As one member of the Atlanta elite put it:

> The public doesn't know anything about the project until it reaches the stage I've been talking about. After the matter is financially sound, then we go to the newspapers and say there is a proposal for consideration. Of course, it is not news to a lot of people by then, but the Chamber committees and other civic organizations are brought in on the idea. They all think it's a good idea. They help to get the Council located and established. That's about all there is to it.[13]

In the Atlanta case, the elite requires the obscurity of non-coverage to defuse the controversy of issues and establish consensus before they reach the public agenda. One elite member mentioned these components of continuing elite influence: "the newspapers that print only that which is 'fit to be read'" and the newsreels that show no news, only horse races, beauty contests, train wrecks and screwballs."[14] And Hunter describes the elite as follows:

> They know full well that the manipulation of various factors in the community—such as the departments of government, the labor force, and the press—is to their advantage. The relation with these parts of the community is not one of deceit, in the main, but one of value agreement. If the little fellow comes out on the short end of affairs, or if he is "not in the know," as the popular expression goes, it is for reasons other than fraud.[15]

GROWTH AND DETERIORATION IN SAN JOSE

In what may have been a moment of weakness, the publisher and owner of the San Jose Mercury and News told an interviewer from San Francisco magazine, "Trees don't read newspapers." The comment typified the Mercury's celebration of growth, both urban and corporate.

The strategy, of course, paid off: the Mercury and News are members of the million-line advertising club (in 1969 the News ranked second nationally among afternoon papers in ad linage and the Mercury ranked fifth in the morning field); they have a proud new newspaper plant, the world's largest on one floor; they share with other Ridder papers on the West Coast the only true Washington correspondent for the Bay Area press; and their combined Sunday edition is more than 200 pages.

With 80 percent coverage of the greater San Jose area, the Mercury and News have tapped the growth curve of Santa Clara County. In its explosive annual growth, the San Jose metropolitan area was topped only by Orange County. Its annual growth rate between 1960 and 1968 was 5.3 percent. Fast-growing San Diego and San Bernardino counties in the southland recorded only 2 percent and 3.6 percent, respectively.

The Mercury did not just sit back and let the dollars roll in. It has the most active promotion and marketing department in the Bay Area. It aided in the recruitment of industrial and commercial clients to the county. It made a cause célèbre of convention and sports facilities for San Jose. And it applauded the annexation and growth policies of City Manager Dutch Hamann.

In most details, San Jose is a microcosm of the process of urban growth, central city deterioration, and suburban sprawl. Most distinctive is the rapidity with which the cycle of growth and deterioration, and now revitalization, are proceeding in San Jose.

In 1920 San Jose was a sleepy rancho settlement of 39,600 in an area of 6.5 square miles. By 1940 its population had increased to 68,500 in an area of 10.9 square miles. The postwar growth of the defense, aerospace, and electronics industries led to a decade of explosive growth in the 1950s. From a 1950 figure of 95,000 people in 17 square miles, San Jose mushroomed to a population of 202,600 in 1960 while the city's boundaries leapfrogged on radial spokes to encompass 92.5 square miles. In 1961 the city projected a population of over a million for the year 1980 within municipal lines bounding more than 200 square miles.

San Jose's growth is the product of an aggressive promotion and annexation policy that eagerly sought development. A study by the Stanford Environmental Law Society describes the process:

The tremendous expansion which San Jose experienced during the 1950s was masterminded by City Manager (A.P.) "Dutch" Hamann. The carefully managed annexation program which he instituted in the early 1950s caused the city to double in size by 1960 and again by 1970. Dutch Hamann's goal was to make San Jose, in his words, the "Los Angeles of the North." Hamann worked for and looked forward to the day when San Jose would be the biggest city in northern California.

San Jose was able to carry on its aggressive annexation policy by providing much needed sewage and drainage systems to the Santa Clara valley. With the county unable to provide adequate service, San Jose could offer sewage lines to subdividers in return for annexation of the subdivision to the city. Deals of this type were easily accomplished under a state law that permits an unpopulated area to be annexed by petition of the property owners.[16]

The attitudinal setting for San Jose's growth ethic is suggested by former City Manager Hamann's introduction to the Capital Needs plan for the 1970s:

San Jose was a town of 92,000 population and 17 square miles just 20 years ago. Today San Jose is a City with an area of more than 135 square miles, a population of 450,000 and is just beginning to find its pace. There is no question in my mind that San Jose will be the dominant City of Northern California before the next 20 years have passed. The growth which lies before the City will dwarf all that has gone before. . . .

It has become fashionable in recent years to run down the community and government, whether national, state or municipal. San Jose has been called a sprawl, a conglomeration, an "ugly" City. It seems to me the people who say this must never have driven through the major cities of the West, driven up and down their residential, business, and industrial streets, good and bad. Surely they have never passed through Chicago, St. Louis, Philadelphia, New York, Baltimore or any other of the Midwest and Eastern cities.

There's an old saying—if you can't stand the heat, get out of the kitchen. Well, I've never minded the heat and I don't mind the criticism—as long as people don't start believing it, and don't give up on their City and quit trying.

The fact is that San Jose, whatever its faults, is a fine city
and a beautiful one. It's going to be a great one.[17]

The aggressive and promotional aspects of San Jose's expansion
are masked in the language of laissez faire. This apologia appears
in the discussion draft of the city's master plan of 1964:

> Within the City of San Jose no attempt has ever been made
> to phase urban development to rationally balance the input
> and output costs and benefits that the public-at-large
> shares. One of the most pointed criticisms directed to-
> ward the city relates to policies that encourage and con-
> done uncontrolled and undirected growth. It is thought
> that the results of such policies are wasted land resources,
> burdensome taxes, inefficient public services and costly
> utilities. To truly satisfy the goal stated relative to resi-
> dential development would necessitate the phasing of urban
> development. No precise legal tools exist for this purpose.
> Exclusionary zoning has generally failed as a development
> control. Public ownership of undeveloped land other than
> Natural Reserves, forests, monuments, etc. is not feasible
> under our democratic system. The only controls that have
> been used with some degree of success are annexation
> controls and restrictions on the provision of storm, sani-
> tary, street and highway facilities.
>   These devices could be used in San Jose to phase
> development in a manner to achieve the highest benefit
> at the lowest cost to the greatest number of people, if
> such a goal is conceded to be community-wide in accep-
> tance. So far, action at the local level by the electorate
> has not stressed such a goal, no matter how hard profes-
> sional planners may press for such an objective.[18]

The results of such a policy are appallingly predictable.

The Stanford Environmental Law Society concludes that "due to
its growth and its orientation toward development," urban dislocation
problems are exaggerated in San Jose. These problems include lack
of unique identity, high cost of service provision, sprawl suburban
development, haphazard land use and destruction of open space, highway strangulation, lack of usable open space, hodgepodge zoning
patterns, air pollution, and water pollution.[19]

The Environmental Law Society notes that San Jose's scatterization, sprawl, and disorganization are the product of an ethic that
embraces "growth for its own sake." A more convincing analysis of
the growth ethic—one that is dynamic rather than static—is offered

by the county planning department. The county suggests that the growth patterns are the interaction of permissive government and an aggressive private sector: growth for profit's sake. The county's transportation planning study puts it this way: "Programs and policies appear to be based on the implied assumptions that the private sector, alone, is responsible for deciding the broad distribution and kinds of land uses and that government's job (rather than planning, ordering, or staging development), at most, is to help this development occur."[20]

In the "mixed economy," the modern entrepreneur seeks to maximize profit by manipulating government subsidy. The flow of profits and the investment of capital is most secure where government's purposes coincide with those of developers or where government is controlled by the electoral investments and political influence of growth interests. In San Jose the developer's needs for zoning variances and for public subsidy in the form of streets, utilities, and schools have been accommodated—in advance. Where the developer's ethic has been so completely accepted by government, it is difficult to tell which dog is wagging which tail.

San Jose defends its land use policies on the ground that it is organizing land that will see eventual urbanization under a governmental umbrella capable of effectively delivering urban services. They maintain such a role is suitable for the regional headquarters city of the South Bay, a city that can have a central focus and a sense of urban identity. At the same time, official San Jose contends that it is developing the potential for balanced development and a balanced tax base. Critical to the argument is the ability of a large city to attract industrial land users, an effort that has been largely disappointing to date.

In the process of expanding its periphery through annexation, San Jose has lost much of the vitality of its central business district (CBD). The decline mirrors the national picture, but again the rate of change has been swifter. In the mid-1950s, such large retailers as Sears moved from locations in the CBD. They were followed by car dealers and such heavy middle-income employers as the city and county office centers and the Mercury-News. Similarly, finance and office center executives with high incomes shifted their consumer activity to regional shopping centers on the periphery. The result was a drastic shift in clientele for central city retailers: to low-income, elderly, minority, or student consumers.

In a multiplier effect, many service agencies followed car dealers and retailers to less centralized locations. The flight was aggravated by the inconvenience of parking facilities, congestion, and the deteriorating physical plant of downtown buildings.

Census tract figures for 1967 show that in seven of the ten tracts contiguous to the CBD, the proportion of Mexican-American citizens

was greater than 20 percent; in half the census tracts the proportion
of Mexican-Americans was greater than 30 percent. These figures
compare with a countywide average of less than 10 percent. In all
but one of the ten census tracts surrounding the CBD, unemployment
was above 5 percent; in seven of the ten it was higher than 9 percent.
These figures compare with a 1967 countywide unemployment figure
of less than 4 percent.

In the same year all the census tracts surrounding the CBD
displayed a high percentage of households with an income of less than
$4,000. In all tracts the percentage was above 25 percent; in seven
it was above 35 percent. The figures are a graphic indication of the
concentration of students (primarily in one tract), poor, elderly, and
minority groups on the CBD periphery.

Its blighted surroundings sapped the vitality of the CBD's retail
market. A declining range of merchandise compounded by rising tax
rates and suburban shopping alternatives led to a loss of middle- and
upper-income customers. The same customers sought entertainment
beyond the CBD where shopping could be paired with night life and
easy access.

The business leadership of the CBD responded by engineering
the creation of the San Jose Redevelopment Agency. In two redevelopment projects, Park Center and San Antonio Plaza, it has replaced
blighted areas with high-rise office headquarters for the Bank of
America, Wells Fargo Bank, a motel-convention center, and several
other financial institutions. Commercial development has been paired
with a community theater. Park and parking development also have
been high priorities in San Jose's efforts at urban regeneration, as
has freeway development.

The emphasis on the economic well-being of the CBD where it
conflicts with the needs of residents of peripheral neighborhoods is
suggested by the inverted semantics of the Master Plan:

> Single persons, childless couples and retired persons
> desiring the amenities and services of close-in living
> can appreciably contribute to the well-being of the Central
> Business District. These persons can provide an impor-
> tant night time population to an area now partially dried
> up by the exodus of its daytime office population.[21]

The ultimate goal for the revitalization of San Jose's CBD is
to create a real estate climate and prestige ambience that will attract
corporations to locate their regional headquarters in what will soon
be the largest city in northern California. According to the 1964
master plan draft, specific objectives for the San Jose Central Business
District are as follows:

1. Unification of the CBD architecturally and visually.

2. Improvement of site characteristics through the provision of new relationships between the elements comprising the core, retail stores, offices, hotels, motels, parking, pedestrians, motorists, trucks, and cultural and residential complexes.

3. Elimination of blight, deterioration, and obsolescence.

4. Provision of new amenities.

5. Joint action for cohesive management.

Principles to be used in the development of the CBD are as follows:

1. Compactness of elements for pedestrian movement.

2. Convenient and easy accessibility to the Central Business District.

3. Circumferential routes to remove through traffic.

4. Functional internal circulation in the core to aid and maximize accessibility of elements.

5. Off-street parking properly located and of sufficient quality to overcome objections to core conditions.

6. Transportation terminals coordinated as impetus to mass transit.

7. Peripheral development of nature to best enhance the Central Business District.

8. Appearance of highest possible order for visual enhancement.[22]

The optimistic program for redevelopment is based on projections that San Jose's population will double in 15 years. Redevelopment on a more massive scale is occurring under the auspices of the federal Model Cities program. The demonstration project, in its early planning stages, encompasses an area just west of the CBD that includes 10 percent of the city's population. Of the people in the project area, 38 percent are Mexican-American. The federal government supplies 60 percent of the funding under Title 1 of the 1966 Demonstration Cities and Metropolitan Act.

Thus it is apparent that in San Jose, as nationally, urban redevelopment and the revitalization of the central business district are tapping the resources of the mixed economy: the interface between public subsidy and private profit.

THE ECONOMIC IMPORTANCE OF TRANSPORTATION

One of the most significant inputs to the mixed economy is public subsidy for transportation: highway, transit, and airport. The siting and routing decisions of publicly funded transportation facilities affect the real estate, business, and financial futures of an area. In the case of transit routing, John Meyer notes:

Historically, the creation of high property values in downtown areas has occurred because such sites are at the
point where major transport networks, both inter-city and
intra-city, converge. Many owners of central business
properties have therefore looked on expansion of the transport system—in particular, increasing the extent to which
the transit network is centered on their properties—as a
means of producing an increase, or a greater increase, in
property values. This is especially true if the cost of
providing such transport improvements does not fall upon
the owners of central properties. Then they can hardly
lose. Such owners naturally become strong advocates of
government subsidies to improve downtown transportation
facilities, particularly when the tax base used to supply
such subsidies is statewide or nationwide. However, if
urban property values today are less dependent on public
transit service than they were under more primitive technological conditions, then it is not clear that improved
transit access will confer major benefits upon centrally
located properties. . . .

Stated another way, the availability of high-
performance public transit may relocate or concentrate
dense activities but there is no evidence that it creates a
new demand for such density.[23]

Although the amount of demand that is concentrated may be small
in terms of the scale of the city, there is a considerable multiplier
effect. Night life, convention activity, retail sales, hotel facilities,
regional office centers, and high-income apartment concentrations
tend to develop interactively. This is the strategy in San Jose, one
that includes both bus and Bay Area Rapid Transit (BART) transit.
According to a 1967 planning department bulletin:

Reduced to a simple statement, our problem now is to
choose between a restrictive provincialism on one hand,
or a significant share of the Bay Area's economic potential as a regional center. BART is already stimulating
economic growth in its service area. The pattern of
regional economic development will soon be set; San Jose
and Santa Clara county can participate if we act deci-
sively. . . .

In addition to relieving traffic congestion, rapid
transit has a major impact on construction rates of office
and commercial facilities. In the low-density city of
Toronto, transit-generated construction alone has raised

the assessed valuation $1 billion per year over the last ten
years, equalling two-thirds of the total city increase of 40%
during the decade. In the Bay Area, the Bank of America
and Pacific Telephone and Telegraph cite BARTD as a
major stimulant of downtown development in San Francisco,
Oakland and Berkeley. In Berkeley, a 50% increase in
downtown office space is being constructed or planned,
located in three buildings within one block of the BARTD
station.24

The San Jose Master Plan calls for study of transit feasibility
but boasts that a downtown terminal "could considerably enlarge the
trade area of the CBD and tap a vast employee pool ranging throughout the Bay Area."25

Predictably, the Association of Metropolitan San Jose, now
called the Chamber of Commerce, in 1970 supported County Ballot
Measure A, which would have established a countywide transit district.
A poll taken for this study found that of 41 members of Chamber of
Commerce action councils, 38 approved some form of high-speed
public transit, 2 disapproved and 1 was undecided. Nine of the
members mentioned growth or the economy as reasons for transit
development, 31 mentioned congestion or the inefficiency of the private
car, and 11 mentioned environmental advantages for mass transit.
(A further description of this poll and the polling procedure is included
in Appendix D.)

In a sample of 42 members of San Jose Board of Realty issue
committees, 37 supported some form of high-speed public transit
and five opposed it. Eleven realtors reached their position on the
basis of economic or growth arguments; 5 on environmental grounds;
and 33 because of congestion.

Clearly, the growth establishment of San Jose supports some
form of rapid transit. Among environmentalists, a distinctly different
pattern emerges. Members of the Save Our Valley Action Committee
favored transit 45 to one. Environmental reasons were mentioned
by 20; congestion and freeway inadequacy by 32; and economic arguments by only four. The content of environmentalists' economic
arguments also differed: the emphasis was on financial feasibility
rather than the effect on the county's economy.

In summary, the growth establishment sees transit planning as
an instrument of the mixed economy that could relieve congestion
and realize economic growth potentials. But a majority of both San
Jose and county voters opposed Measure A.

Airport planning is a similar instrument in the mixed economy.
A Bay Conservation and Development Commission report indicates
the effects of air transportation:

There have been no definitive studies of the effects of air
transportation on the Bay Area economy, but enough is
known to indicate that the benefits are substantial. The
benefits are realized first in the direct employment and
purchases by airports, airlines, commercial aviation
service operators, military aviation and other public and
private suppliers of air transport services. Employment
at the 34 Bay Area airports is estimated at 35,000 exclud-
ing military personnel. Aggregate outlays for salaries and
wages and purchases of materials and supplies of these
airports amounts to billions of dollars annually.

Of even greater importance, however, is the higher
level of economic activity made possible in the Bay Area
by the availability of good air transportation. . . .

Not only does air transportation affect regional economic growth, airports are major determinants of local
land use and traffic patterns. Proximity to airports is
and will continue to be a major factor influencing many
business and industrial location decisions. An airport
acts as a "magnet" or stimulus for development in much
the same way as a freeway interchange or rapid transit
station, although on a larger scale. The industrial development on the San Francisco Peninsula would not have occurred as intensively or as quickly but for the presence of
San Francisco Airport.

On the other hand, airports have a negative effect on
some land uses. Within metropolitan areas, airports are
competing for scarce land which may be desirable for
housing and recreational uses. The presence of an airport,
particularly a large one, will usually repel such uses from
occupying nearby sites while attracting more business-
oriented activities. However, the degree of "repulsion"
depends on the supply of land in the general area. In-
compatible uses can and often do locate near airports
when no other sites are available, usually to the detriment
of all concerned.

To summarize, an airport can be used to direct,
focus, guide and create a business and employment center
and to stimulate area development and commerce. In a
real sense an airport can be used as a tool in regional
planning. Decisions to alter the pattern of air carrier
service, to expand existing facilities or build new ones
can have important implications for Bay Area regional
development and should not be taken without considering
these effects.[26]

The economic potentials of airport expansion in San Jose are
clearly recognized. In 1970 the Chamber of Commerce transmitted
a report to San Jose's city council which warned:

> With the tremendous economic forces stimulating the
> community, any action by the council to severely limit
> the development of the Airport will undoubtedly have a
> profound influence on the economic growth of the Metro-
> politan San Jose area. . . .
>   During the last ten years, 653 new industries located
> in Santa Clara County. It would certainly seem safe to
> assume that an equal or a greater number of industries
> will locate in the County by 1980. One thing is certain,
> that many of these new plants will be branch operations
> of firms located in other parts of California and the United
> States which will be counting on convenient air transpor-
> tation. . . .
>   San Jose, until the last two years, has been dormant
> in terms of any significant development which would iden-
> tify it as a major city in California and the Nation. Now
> we suddenly see millions of dollars being invested in the
> development of the Core Area, industrial parks, and office
> parks. The San Jose Municipal Airport was the key factor
> which influenced the decision of Dillingham Corporation to
> move ahead with its Gateway Center Project and Allied
> Properties to develop their land. The establishment of
> San Jose's first major industrial park by Boise Cascade
> was influenced by the San Jose Municipal Airport which
> will also be an important factor in the future industrial
> park development. . . .
>   It is also important to consider the City's positive
> role in the redevelopment of the Core Area and its desire
> to see San Jose become a major regional headquarters
> center. In order to succeed, San Jose is going to have to
> influence many firms to locate office facilities to absorb
> the millions of square feet of office space that will be con-
> structed. The availability of convenient air passenger
> service will be a major factor in their decision whether
> or not to locate in San Jose.[27]

The economic advantage of airport location also was underlined
in testimony before the county planning policy committee's subcommittee on airport location.

In this context, it was no surprise that poll results of Chamber
of Commerce members found 28 supporting airport development,

5 opposing it, 6 desiring development with relocation, and 2 undecided.
Among realtors, 23 favored development, 8 opposed it, 8 opted for
airport relocation, and 5 were undecided. (See Appendix D for methodology for the telephone poll.)

Among Save Our Valley environmentalists, 5 favored expansion
at the present location, 36 opposed development, 5 favored development at another location, and 1 was undecided. Among Sierra Club
members with homes in the flight path of the airport, 7 favored
development, 26 opposed it, 5 favored relocation, and 4 were undecided.
Among Sierra Club members with foothill homes located well beyond
the noise nuisance of the airport, 14 favored development at the
present site, 21 opposed it, 6 favored relocated development, and 2
were undecided.

Growth or economics was mentioned as persuasive by 25 of 41
Chamber of Commerce members and 17 of 44 realtors but only 21 of
122 conservationists. Opposition to the airport on environmental
grounds was mentioned by 8 Chamber of Commerce members, 8
realtors, and 87 conservationists. In all, 11 realtors and 11 Chamber
of Commerce members mentioned environmental issues in their
poll responses on the airport issue.

Predictably, members of the growth establishment downgrade
environmental issues in their positions on this mixed economy development proposal. However, the mention of environmental issues
by over 25 percent of Chamber of Commerce members is indicative
of a growing awareness of the environmental implications and hazards
of the growth economy. This new awareness is even reflected in the
1971 promotional brochure of the Chamber of Commerce:

> The Economic Development Council [an action council of
> the Chamber] will dedicate itself to the creation of ad-
> ditional jobs for those people who have been displaced as
> the result of the recent shift in employment. Toward
> achieving this goal, the Council will vigorously recruit
> new selective payrolls to the area, keeping in mind that
> compatibility between industry and environment is neces-
> sary.

In other words, more companies as long as they don't pollute! The
outcome of these policy decisions will have a dramatic effect on the
environment of Santa Clara Valley: its land use, population, size,
and density; its levels of air and noise pollution; and the well-being
of its ethnic minorities and other underprivileged groups. These
decisions also will have a significant impact on the financial ledger
of news media in the Santa Clara Valley.

THE INVOLVEMENT OF THE SAN JOSE
MERCURY-NEWS

The vaulting enthusiasm that the Mercury and News have for growth is revealed in their editorial pages: "When San Jose is twice its present size, ideally it should have pleasant residential areas, extensive commercial and industrial centers to provide jobs and tax revenues, a major park system and first rate educational, entertainment, cultural and sports facilities. San Jose can have all these things and more." The tone sounds almost anachronistic for 1969; ironically, it is anachronism in the name of "progress."

However, there are hints of a changing attitude behind the boosterism of Mercury and News editorials. Even in the inverted semantic priorities of their 1969 New Year's day editorial, a new caution is evident: "Growth will continue to challenge the framework of government and society to meet its needs." Or in an August 1969 editorial quoting the Bank of America: "This area, in short, can anticipate a busy, bustling and prosperous future. Accordingly, it can anticipate also having the resources necessary to cope with the problems that continued growth is bound to bring." Even core-city redevelopment is described as an antidote as well as an elixir: "A focal point—to give a sense of unity to a growing, sprawling community."

The Mercury's involvement in the growth establishment of San Jose does not end with its editorial page. Mercury management is deeply committed to membership in the associations and organizations that seek to promote growth through manipulation of the mixed economy. Membership, per se, cannot be considered an indictment of the Mercury or News performance in presenting a fair, balanced, and probing picture of public policy debate in San Jose. However, it cannot help creating professional awkwardness for reporters who must cover not only the activities of government officials but also those of newspaper management itself.

Mort Levine, publisher of the weekly San Jose Sun, described the Mercury's interest in growth acidly but accurately. Speaking of airport development, he said:

> The Mercury's interest in the airport issue goes back to
> their concept of what kind of Valley this ought to be, what
> kind of trade area they ought to develop. They have a
> very aggressive policy of shaping their own market.
> Major metropolitan newspapers are playing a game for
> big stakes. They are playing a game with numbers and
> very sophisticated demographic analyses in order to con-
> vince Madison Avenue that this is where the big dollars
> ought to be put. The more you can improve on those

demographics—the income level, the mobility factor, the
more jet-set types—the more it will redound to their
national advertising benefit. I think this has been their
goal.

And there's another factor too. Most major metropolitan newspapers feel as threatened as any establishment
institution by unrest and dissent and all this. As a result
they would like nothing better than to see 99.9 percent of
the population in this Valley white collar, employed by an
electronics industry, with three cars, and nice kids who
are all going to have short hair: people who take long
vacations and have two houses and are consumers and
spenders and have high education levels. All this helps
them make a better case to the [national advertising]
agencies.

I think that their concern has been to change or at
least embroider the image of the valley from some place
out in the fruitpicker country between Fresno and Coalinga
that somebody thinks about back in New York—that's the
image San Jose has back there.

I think there is one more concern in the airport
issue. There is still an atmosphere of old-fashioned
boosterism that still lingers in San Jose. It's kind of red-
blooded. We want to be the biggest and best of everything.
If you can beat out San Francisco airport in terms of any
kind of statistic, let's do it. If we can build a big stadium
to steal the 49'ers—oh boy, what a coup this would be.
Well, this is the whole growth syndrome which most of
the leadership in San Jose has been happy to embrace
because it's good for business.28

The most visible example is the Mercury and News membership
in the growth establishment of the community. It should be noted
that membership offers as much potential for promoting environmental and social responsibility as for promoting unbridled growth.
The Mercury and News have interfaces with the growth elite in the
following settings:

1. Al Stahl, editor of the yearly "Progress Issue," a supplement
that records the growth and economic vitality of the past year in
glowing language, arranges for the use of the edition in recruiting
industrial and commercial clients for San Jose.

2. Marketing Director Gerald Zarwell is a member of the
metropolitan core subcommittee of the San Jose Goals Committee.
The subcommittee pushed for a commitment to urban renewal and
redevelopment. As a member of its steering committee, Zarwell
arranged for free Goals Committee advertising.

3. P. Anthony Ridder, business manager of the Mercury-News, is a member of the Board of Directors of the Association of Metropolitan San Jose, now renamed the Greater San Jose Chamber of Commerce. Other board members include representatives of PG&E, PT&T, the Bank of America, Citizens Federal Savings, General Electric, Crocker-Citizens Bank, and Security Savings & Loan. Advertising Director Louis E. Heindel was the Chamber's president for two terms.

4. Real Estate Editor Marvin Gallop is chairman of the Greeters Committee of the San Jose Real Estate Board. Its other members are representatives of the major title companies in San Jose.

5. Norman Bowman, the Mercury's business and financial editor, is an honorary member of the Board of Realty.

6. The Mercury's former city hall reporter, James Spaulding, became an administrative assistant to former Mayor Ron James. Until shifting employers, he covered city hall's role in the airport issue.

7. The Mercury has subscribed in the commissioning of studies to determine convention center feasibility and airport needs for San Jose. Ridder's role in the convention center/sports arena effort parallels the enthusiasm of the Tribune's McCormick.

8. Mercury-News General Manager Anton F. Peterson is airport development chairman for the Chamber of Commerce, a trustee of the Metro San Jose Trust Fund, and president of the Western Newspaper Industrial Relations Bureau. His resume reports that he is a member of "numerous special committees for development of San Jose/Santa Clara County."

These are static membership arrangements rather than dynamic influence relations, but one still can ask with considerable justification whether the memberships of Mercury-News management deter probing reporting and promote unbalanced emphasis in the news pages of the Ridder publications.

THE POSITION OF THE SAN JOSE SUN

The Mercury does have "competition" in the San Jose market. The San Jose Sun is the flagship paper of a chain of weekly newspapers with a total staff of 55 and a circulation of 83,000. Less than one-third of combined circulation is paid; the remainder is throwaway. The chain has five neighborhood editions, including the Milpitas Post.

Mort Levine, the Sun publisher, emphasizes personalized stories of neighborhood interest, the school district beat which is largely ignored by the Mercury, and initiative reporting with a strong environmental emphasis. He says initiative reporting will increase in the Sun as urban growth more thoroughly integrates the paper's once

distinct neighborhood areas into the metropolitan whole. Levine says
growth is erasing the distinct character and identity of the suburban
areas his papers serve.

The bulk of Sun advertising, Levine says, comes from neighborhood shopping centers. The Sun is able to attract some regional
retailers but no national advertising accounts. The paper's critical
coverage of zoning decisions, sprawl, and expansion has eliminated
its appeal to developers. According to Levine, the paper has lost
"90 percent of the developer ads we once carried" and he speculates
that downtown influentials may have discouraged advertisers in other
businesses as well. He says the advertising department believes
airline ads are unattainable given the paper's strong opposition to
airport expansion.

The Sun papers are financially viable, as indicated by a paid
reporting staff of 20 and a healthy volume of supermarket ads. The
narrowness of the viability margin is suggested by a sign on the door
of the squat and crowded Spanish-style building that houses the Sun
and the Milpitas Post: "This is NOT a post office."

The Sun, with its stake in neighborhood identity, local advertising
appeal, and Levine's strident environmentalism, is a suitable foil in
studying news coverage in a setting of economic self-interest.

MEDIA COVERAGE OF THE MIXED ECONOMY

The mixed economy is a setting in which the private elements
of the corporate state seek to enter and influence the public policy
process at the point where government subsidy can be translated into
private profit. The public policy role of the private sector forces us
to reexamine the traditional role of the press, our concept of news, and
the orthodox assumption that public policy is shaped singularly by
those who hold public office or titled authority.

In the mixed economy, we will argue, the scrutiny of the press
must extend to the private sector if it is to identify responsibility
for public policy and "the secret springs of political design."

The press as watchdog of democracy is a role enshrined in
constitutional guarantee and American political theory. Theodore
Peterson describes the historical evolution of traditional libertarian-
ism as follows:

> Six tasks came to be ascribed to the press as traditional
> [libertarian] theory evolved: (1) servicing the political
> system by providing information, discussion, and debate
> on public affairs; (2) enlightening the public so as to make
> it capable of self-government; (3) safeguarding the rights

of the individual by serving as the watchdog against
government; (4) servicing the economic system, primarily
by bringing together the buyers and sellers of goods and
services through the medium of advertising; (5) providing
entertainment; (6) maintaining its own financial self-
sufficiency so as to be free from the pressures of special
interests.29

Even without the libertarian faith in the perfectability of man
and the inevitable primacy of "definite and demonstrable" truth through
"free and open encounter" in the "marketplace of ideas," there remains this prescriptive role for the press: that it equip citizens and
their leaders with the information to make reasoned judgments on
matters of public policy; that it assign responsibility for errors of
judgment or action in the public sphere; and that it make understandable the means and ends of the conflicting interests of the democratic
polity.

This study accepts the descriptive and prescriptive notion of
news as political intelligence. We see the role of the press as functioning to service and challenge the political system, to enlighten the
public and guard the liberties of individuals against the incursions of
government while maintaining freedom and integrity from the pressures
of private interests.

These propositions are standards and not operational criteria.
From them, however, we can derive a set of operational criteria
toward which media can strive and against which their performance
may be measured:

1. The media should provide the citizen with information that
makes him aware of policy agendas while they are still in the stages
of formulation and debate.

2. The media should present information that enables the citizen
to understand and assess the likely impact of public policy decisions
before they are made.

3. The media should provide information that enables the citizen
to assess the interest and motivation of actors, both public and private,
in the public policy process.

4. The media should seek out alternatives to policy before its
determination and offer them as an agenda for debate.

5. The media should work to secure open deliberations of policy
bodies and inform citizens with notification and agendas so that they
may observe or participate in the decisions of government councils.

In developing this set of criteria, the problem of news coverage
has not been viewed from the perspective of the publisher, the
reporter, or even the layout man. Instead, the perspective has been
that news is the stuff of public policy deliberations and that it is

both appropriate and essential that the public have access through
its media to political intelligence that equips it to make reasoned
judgments on matters of public policy. Therefore, newspaper ownership is a public trust and subject to judgments of its performance in
the public good.

The origin of the newspaper's immunities and the subject of its
watchdogging traditionally have been government. Today, however,
the concentration of corporate power and its policy-setting role in
the mixed economy have added a new dimension to newspaper responsibility and a new threat to its independence. Its public trust challenges
the press to report the activities of private enterprises with which
it may share economic interests or upon which it depends for advertising.

Three very concrete justifications for critical monitoring of the
private sector will suffice. First, corporate power has reached a
scale and concentration that make it the competitor of elected government in determining the substance and quality of life. Second, the
size of corporations has thrust them into a planning role—organizing
systems of supply and marketing—in which the corrective of market
demand no longer applies. That planning role extends into the manipulation of public policy for institutional goals that may conflict with
the private citizen's conceptions of the public good. Third, no direct
electoral check exists for the exercise of corporate power.

In this situation—which is aggravated by the newspaper's economic interest in a growing population and booming retail activity—
press scrutiny of corporate actions appropriately is circumscribed
to three areas of the mixed economy:

1. Press initiative in the probing and monitoring of corporate
activity that involves public subsidy or public contracts.

2. Press initiative in the probing and monitoring of corporate
activity that requires public policy action or public policy change.

3. Press monitoring in response to citizen initiative in questioning corporate activity in the community that is causing public debate
but is not subsumed by the areas of public subsidy, contract, or policy
action.

This framework for press coverage of corporate activities
underlies the following analysis of Mercury-News coverage of two
environmental problems closely tied to urban growth and redevelopment: public transit and airport development.

TRANSIT: ITS ENVIRONMENTAL IMPACT

Public transit in its several forms has two primary environmental impacts. First, it can serve to replace the private automobile

with its pollution-generating internal combustion engine. Second, it can serve to concentrate land use in corridors and hubs and reduce the sprawl of auto-related land use patterns.

Between 1965 and 1970 the number of cars and trucks in the Bay Area increased faster than the population. The San Jose Planning Department projects at least one million more cars in Santa Clara County by 1980 than there are today. Such a massive proliferation of internal combustion engines obviously threatens to aggravate pollution. Even with new pollution control equipment, the most optimistic predictions are for staying even with the decline in air quality after 1990.

The Bay Area Air Pollution Control District estimates that four tons of air pollution is generated by 40 cars (an average cross-section of those on the road) traveling 1,000 miles each. The rapidity of auto proliferation in a concentrated area and the vagaries of the weather in a bay basin mandate a transportation substitute for the private car.

Furthermore, the private automobile generates the highest volume of emissions at the speeds associated with the start-and-stop driving of rush-hour congestion. Mass transit is most capable of relieving these periods of congestion because of the concentration of job locations in certain hubs and corridors where routing would be most feasible.

In this setting, the ecologically damaging aspects of urbanization are magnified: the diffusion of population and development threaten particularly vulnerable ecological habitats—the marshlands (80 percent of which already have been filled baywide), the estuaries, and, in chain reaction, the bay, with temperature- and oxygen-control implications for the entire valley. Tom Harvey, a San Jose State ecologist, has expressed his professional opinion that urbanization in the Santa Clara Valley has already exceeded "the carrying capacity of its environment."[30]

Mass transit would stem some of the demand for street and freeway proliferation, concentrating urban activity more densely near its routes. The concentration of activity in already urbanized land would lessen the rate of increase of environmental stress. This point becomes critical when considered with interaction of environmental stresses from many sources: pollution, temperature change, removal of greenery, and biotic extermination. The removal of environmental stress at several interfaces of the ecosystem becomes significant given the interactivity of biological systems.

Transit, however, as noted earlier, can be used as a device to raise property values and to force undesirable population elements—the poor, minorities, and the aged—from the central city through either its condemnation and routing decisions or its effect on housing costs. Planners must be cautious that public policy puts high priority

on the housing and relocation of the disadvantaged. In a very real
sense, the housing and living conditions of people are the most pressing
environmental priority.

AIRPORT DEVELOPMENT: ITS ENVIRONMENTAL
IMPACT

The 1970 Federal Airport Development Act (P.L. 91-258) applies
strict environmental standards to airport expansion or development
using federal revenues. A Santa Clara County planning official commented, "This act may mean that no more urban airports are built
in the United States."31 The act requires that federally funded airport
development seek siting alternatives that minimize the following:
(1) adverse effect upon fish and wildlife; (2) adverse effect upon
natural scenic and recreational assets; (3) adverse effect upon water
and air quality; and (4) inconsistency with the plans of planning agencies for development of the area. The federal law further requires
consultation with and agreement from surrounding communities. The
federal legislation offers only a glimpse of the environmental hazards
of airport development. A more expanded list also would include the
following: (1) noise pollution; (2) displacement of other land uses and
pressure upon remaining open space; (3) disruption of flood plain,
drainage, and run off through grading adding to water pollution and
erosion; and (4) extensive topographical alteration.
    The seriousness of environmental effects of airport development
depend on the frequency and type of aircraft operations. Jet operations,
particularly long-distance jet flights with large aircraft, add significantly to the level of noise and air pollution in urban areas. The
practice of dumping excess fuels immediately after take-off adds
unburned jet fuel to the already polluted air of the metropolitan
environment.
    The problem of noise pollution is not so easily solved. The
present design of jet aircraft engines makes noise control at the
source virtually prohibitive; a new breed of jet engine, not simply
modification of present types, is required. Development lag time is
estimated at 20 years.
    Furthermore, airports are incompatible with all but heavy
industrial land uses in the immediate vicinity. The removal of urban
land from both usefulness and the tax rolls creates greater pressure
for the development of peripheral green-belt areas.
    The environmental hazards of airports fly in the face of the
rapidly increasing demand for air travel. In the decade 1953-63
domestic airline flights originating in California increased 217 percent while population in California grew only 45 percent. Nationally,

air cargo tonnage is increasing 20 percent each year. The increase in air traffic is so rapid that the Bay Area will run out of air space for safe operation long before passenger and freight demand is exhausted.[32]

In light of the environmental impact of transportation services, how did San Jose newspapers cover transit and airport planning in Santa Clara County?

NEWSPAPER PERFORMANCE IN SAN JOSE: THE ASSESSMENT OF CONSERVATIONISTS AND THE GROWTH ESTABLISHMENT

It has been argued that the newspaper's public trust is to provide information that will enable citizens to make intelligent judgments on matters of public policy. The importance of newspaper quality is magnified in the complex urban setting in which massive and specialized information cannot be widely diffused by word of mouth or direct inquiry.

In the context of its public trust, public assessment of media performance is a critical measure of news quality. It is easy for the academic—his hands unstained by printers ink, his performance undaunted by payrolls or press deadlines—to arrive at arbitrary and unreachable quality standards for news performance. More critical for the publisher, certainly, is the extent to which his readers feel confident that their news needs are being met on a day-to-day basis.

Working in this framework, reader assessments of the news performance of the San Jose Mercury-News become important. A purposive sample of relevant publics was sought. Because of the implications of the transit and airport issues for growth and the environment, the likely poles of the conservation and development spectrum were surveyed: realtors, Sierra Club members, Chamber of Commerce members, and members of the militantly conservationist Save Our Valley Action Committee (SOVAC). These were publics who were likely to be concerned, informed, and vehement in their opposing opinions.

We obtained the following official membership lists:

1. The names of 147 members of the San Jose Chamber of Commerce Board of Directors and six of its action councils (those on industrial parks, research, parking and traffic, streets and highways, transportation, and aviation)

2. The names of 193 officers and committee members of the San Jose Real Estate Board

3. The names of 52 SOVAC members with homes in San Jose

4. The names of 92 Sierra Club members from the 95120 zip

code, a hillside area identified as having the smallest percentage of
signers of a petition against downtown airport expansion

5. The names of 242 members of the Sierra Club with home
addresses in zip code 91525, the zip code area nearest the airport
flight patterns and noise hazard (one-third of those with telephone
listings were randomly selected for interview).

Only persons with home telephone numbers listed in the directory
were called to avoid the unreliability and awkwardness of seeking
opinions in the workplace environment. Persons were dropped from
the sample when no home listing was available or after there was no
response to four calls, no more than two of which were placed on a
single evening.

The completed survey includes 41 members of the Chamber of
Commerce, 44 members of the Board of Realty, 47 members of
SOVAC 43 Sierra Club members from the 95125 zip code area, and
42 members of the Sierra Club from the 95120 Zip Code area.

Telephone interviews were conducted during a two-week period
that did not involve airport or transit news or attacks on the press by
the Vice President. The interviews were conducted before the
"Selling of the Pentagon" controversy. No mention of student violence
was made by any of the respondents, nor did the refusal rate climb
during the militancy at Stanford University, which occurred midway
through the polling.

The results of the purposive sampling obviously cannot be
generalized to the population of San Jose. The sample is uniformly
skewed toward upper-income respondents. It has a miniscule number
of Spanish-surnamed respondents compared to a San Jose average of
close to 20 percent. It overwhelmingly supported mass transit (209
to 13), whereas the voters of San Jose rejected the transit district
ballot measure in 1970. However, with some confidence it can be
argued that this represents a fair sampling of publics that are highly
curious and/or powerful with regard to airport and transit plans.

Each respondent was asked to identify the local newspaper read
most regularly. In reporting the results, the assessment of the
Mercury and News was combined because the papers produce a combined Sunday edition, their staff and news are virtually interchange-
able, their editorial pages reflect their common ownership, and there
was no difference in assessment of balance or completeness from
paper to paper. Thus, the assessments will be reported for the
Mercury-News, the name of the Sunday edition.

The sample was not large enough to secure a reasonable number
of respondents for analysis of the weekly San Jose Sun.

To plumb our respondents' assessment of news coverage with
a uniform definition of completeness and balance, they were asked:
"Would you say that (your newspaper's) news about airport/transit

plans has been balanced in the sense that their news reports don't try to sway the reader to take one viewpoint over another?" and "Has their news on airport expansion/transit been complete in the sense that you feel they give an adequate understanding of the pros and cons of airport/transit plans?"

The results will be examined for two concurrent interests: (1) the direct results of polling the different memberships and (2) significantly different results between the assessments of the different memberships and different opinion holders.

Given the census approach to each membership, the reader can be confident that the statistics are more representative than would be the case if such small numbers had been sampled from a large and heterogeneous population. The differences between populations will be tested by the chi square test of significance. The results of the poll are shown in Table 7.1.

Perhaps the most interesting and telling result revealed is the high level of discontent with news performance. Only in the Chamber of Commerce sample did more than 50 percent of the respondents think the Mercury-News was balanced and complete in coverage of either issue.

Chi Square tests of statistical significance detected significant differences in the assessment of airport news balance and airport news completeness between SOVAC and Chamber of Commerce members ($p < 0.02$) and realtors ($p < 0.1$). There also was a significant difference between Chamber of Commerce members and hillside conservationists in their assessment of the completeness of airport coverage ($p < 0.05$). The differences between SOVAC members and both realtors and Chamber of Commerce members combined remain significant among those who described themselves as "very concerned" ($p < 0.1$). Cell sizes were too small to test this with hillside conservationists.

The differences in assessment of the balance of airport coverage between realtors, Chamber of Commerce members, and Sierra Club members were not statistically significant.

In examining the airport positions of the entire sample population, it was found that opposing the airport predicted a greater likelihood of finding coverage unbalanced ($p < 0.05$). The statistical analysis was performed with collapsed categories, but the total survey breakdown is offered in Table 7.2. Position on the airport was not found to predict the assessment of the completeness of newspaper coverage.

Differences in the information-seeking behavior of those who favor the airport compared to those who oppose it suggest an explanation for their varying opinions on press coverage. Respondents who identified conservation organizations and the League of Women Voters as their most reliable source of airport information were

TABLE 7.1

Results of Poll on Balance and Completeness of
San Jose Mercury-News Coverage
of Airport and Transit News

Question and Sample Population	Yes	No	No Opinion/ Can't Say
Was airport coverage complete?			
Chamber of Commerce	18(43.9%)	14(34.1%)	9(22.0%)
Realtors	15(36.6%)	13(31.7%)	13(31.7%)
SOVAC	6(15.4%)	21(53.8%)	12(30.8%)
Sierra Club—zip 91525	9(25.0%)	13(36.1%)	14(38.9%)
Sierra Club—zip 91520	8(18.6%)	18(41.9%)	17(39.5%)
Was airport news balanced?			
Chamber of Commerce	23(56.0%)	11(26.8%)	7(17.2%)
Realtors	19(48.7%)	18(46.2%)	2(5.1%)
SOVAC	11(28.2%)	21(53.8%)	7(18.0%)
Sierra Club—zip 91525	16(43.2%)	9(24.3%)	12(32.5%)
Sierra Club—zip 91520	20(47.6%)	14(33.3%)	8(19.1%)
Was transit coverage complete?			
Chamber of Commerce	24(60.0%)	11(27.5%)	5(12.5%)
Realtors	19(48.7%)	18(46.2%)	2(5.1%)
SOVAC	11(28.2%)	21(53.8%)	7(18.0%)
Sierra Club—both zips	32(43.2%)	25(33.8%)	17(23.0%)
Was transit news balanced?			
Chamber of Commerce	22(56.4%)	11(28.2%)	6(15.4%)
Realtors	19(50.0%)	15(39.5%)	4(10.5%)
SOVAC	12(30.8%)	18(46.2%)	9(23.0%)
Sierra Club—zips	31(41.3%)	27(36.0%)	17(22.7%)

most likely to find news coverage incomplete (p < .05). Although not
as clear-cut, the same pattern appears in the assessment of balance
among those who consult conservation organizations and publications
(p < .15).

Thus, it appears that people who are privy to environmental
organizations and value them as their most reliable sources feel
the Mercury-News coverage does not fully probe the environmental
cons of airport plans and that its coverage, on balance, leans toward
a pro-development stance although there is not a feeling that the
environmental hazards of airport planning are systematically short-
changed in news coverage. The substance of SOVAC interviews

TABLE 7.2

Relation Between Respondents' Position on
Airport Location and Assessment of Coverage
by San Jose Mercury-News

Position on Airport	Assessment of News Coverage		
	Balanced	Not Balanced	No Opinion/ Can't Say
Favor airport development in present location	34(45.9%)	26(35.1%)	14(19.0%)
Oppose airport development in present location	31(35.2%)	32(36.4%)	25(28.4%)
Favor relocation	12(48.0%)	5(20.0%)	8(32.0%)
Don't know	6(46.2%)	2(15.4%)	5(38.4%)

supports this interpretation. There was a suspicion that the Mercury-News favors the growth ethic, building in a growth orientation but not leaving out environmental concerns.

On the transit issue, there were significant differences in the assessment of balance and completeness between members of SOVAC and the Chamber of Commerce ($p < .05$). In this case, assessments by SOVAC members tended to include the apology that the Mercury-News coverage favored their pro-transit position.

Because of the small number of respondents who opposed transit development in Santa Clara County, it was impossible to test for a relationship between transit position and news assessment. Further, no significant differences appeared in the assessment of news coverage between respondents who mentioned environmental, economic, or transportation/congestion arguments for their positions. Nor were there any differences in skew.

In comparing the data for transit and airport coverage, we must conclude that the respondents felt that the depth of environmental coverage was greater for the transit issue than for the airport. For those respondents who mentioned environmental issues as persuasive in arriving at their positions on the two issues, the poll revealed the following assessment of the completeness of coverage:

	Complete	Not Complete	No Opinion/Can't Say
Airport	25(25.3%)	46(46.5%)	28(28.2%)
Transit	28(41.8%)	26(38.8%)	13(19.4%) $p < 0.1$

The results obviously are not so clear in the assessment of balance:

	Balanced	Not Balanced	No Opinion/Can't Say
Airport	35(35.0%)	36(36.0%)	29(29.0%)
Transit	23(33.8%)	28(41.2%)	17(25.0%)

In summary, environmentalists were most likely to find the Mercury-News coverage lacking in completeness on the airport issue and leaning toward their pro-environment stance on transit. However, there was sufficient negative assessment from realtors and Chamber of Commerce members that it cannot be concluded that the Mercury-News systematically excludes news of interest to the conservationist community. Rather, imbalance and incompleteness are perceived from both ends of the growth and development spectrum—from both environmentalists and the growth establishment. The differences in assessment that do exist seem to be accounted for by a combination of issue position, level of concern, and the membership-oriented information-seeking patterns of conservationists rather than by a perception of the omission of news content of particular interest to conservationists.

EDITORIAL COMMENT ON THE AIRPORT CONTROVERSY IN THE MERCURY AND THE SUN

The editorial page traditionally has been conceived of as the vehicle of ownership's opinion. Here management is expected to make its brief on the issues of the day, expressing its opinion on the conflicts and directions of public policy. Increasingly, the editorial also has become a means of offering context and perspective on matters of controversy. A tension between the two functions of the editorial arises from presenting management opinion while simultaneously offering a fair perspective on the conflicting goals, values, and facts argued by the opponents of management opinion.

In this setting, it can be expected at minimum that the editorial page offer a cogent and persuasive declaration of the newspaper's opinion and the merits of its case. The editorial page also should offer the following: (1) a presentation of both the pros and cons of policy, as well as the values that undergird them; (2) a presentation of alternatives to policy, particularly when the paper opposes a policy; and (3) an understanding of who is involved in the policy-making process.

In May 1968 the Stanford Research Institute (SRI) reported the results of a "Survey of Airline Passengers Departing the San Francisco Bay Area." The survey showed that "Santa Clara County now has more residents using commercial air services than does any other Bay Area county, with 25.4 percent of the total residents surveyed."[33]

The survey was jointly commissioned and funded by the city of San Jose and the San Jose Mercury-News. The SRI report praised the city and paper for "recognizing the potential planning value of current local origin and destination data." The report certainly did that: it documented the furiously growing demand for air travel in Santa Clara County and the county's rapidly increasing percentage of travelers. In 1950 Santa Clara County accounted for only 9.2 percent of domestic flight passengers, but by 1968 it had leaped to 25.4 percent. During the same period San Francisco's share of domestic air travel passengers declined from 45.1 to 18.3 percent.

Mercury-News executives said they had joined in commissioning the study to determine airport planning needs. However, a second benefit was correctly anticipated. The SRI study resulted in a massive shift in airline advertising from San Francisco papers to the Mercury with its saturation of Santa Clara County. Airline ad budgets were realigned to more accurately reflect the readership patterns of disembarking passengers. News Managing Editor Paul Conroy explained that the passenger data helped the Ridder papers capture 70 percent of the San Francisco Chronicle's airline ad budget.

With this cash register success, tourism beckoning, and Business Manager P. A. Ridder promoting a sports arena-convention center complex for downtown San Jose, it is no wonder that the Mercury editorially supported airport development in Santa Clara County. There were new airlines and new routes to be secured—with new ad budgets. There were a potential 25 to 30 million passengers to serve by 1993—no reason, after all, why the spin-off revenue from conventions and visiting firemen should go to San Francisco. And there is more than a little civic pride in having modern—and big—airport facilities.

Thus, it is not surprising that in 1968 the Mercury printed 17 editorials plumping for expansion of the municipal airport and pressing for development of a twin facility stretching toward the bay in the Alviso mudflats.

What is surprising is an eerie silence during the year 1969, a year of substantial public outcry on the environmental hazards of airport development. From December 28, 1968 to February 2, 1970 the Mercury did not editorialize on the subject of airport expansion or improvement. On April 27, 1970 the Mercury tacked back and advised that "The San Jose City Council should, however reluctantly, abandon plans for a mammoth international airport on the Alviso-Milpitas mudflats and concentrate instead on expansion of San Jose Municipal Airport."

Why was the Mercury's editorial page silent for more than a year? The answer, from Mercury-News Editor Paul Conroy, was that a lot of planning elements—funding, location, political support, airspace—had to be worked out. That kind of planning, he said, requires privacy. He acknowledged that the Mercury's silence was giving airport planners the "low profile" that it takes to work up a development package and put the political pieces together. Conroy said the strategy was developed after a conference with Airport Manager James Nissen.

As a development strategy, the Mercury's self-imposed editorial silence cannot be faulted. For example, urban renewal experts Jewell Bellush and Maurray Hausknecht point out that urban redevelopment has "successfully" replaced old structures with new ones where negotiations with developers and the federal government were nearly complete before either the public itself or local politicos were let in on the projects. "There seems to be a possible correlation between 'success' and 'secrecy,'" Bellush and Hausknecht concluded.[34]

In this case, however, the more serious question is the appropriateness of secrecy as a publication's strategy for realizing editorial goals. Development, of course, is an appropriate policy for the paper to support editorially. It is an arguable, if sometimes self-interested, judgment of the public good. However, promoting development through silence rather than supportive argument is not in the best interest of the public. Nor is it in the long-run best interest of a newspaper that wishes to retain the confidence of its readers.

In this situation, it is appropriate to examine how persuasively the Mercury made its public case for airport expansion in 1968: how successful was the Mercury in arguing for the location of a regional airport in San Jose in the language of public interest?

First, the content analysis examined the Mercury's defense of airport development in the light of environmental hazards (see Appendix D for methodology of the content analysis). Environmental themes were examined in the broad brush of vague references to "environment," "ecology," and "conservation," and in more specific discussions of the impact on air pollution, noise pollution, water pollution, land use, and population growth treated as an environmental stress. In only one editorial was an "environmental" issue raised: the urgency of purchasing land before it is committed to industrial use. In the strictest sense, the Mercury did not treat land competition as an environmental issue. However, competition for the use of urban land in short supply invariably has environmental implications—for open space, biotic stress, pollution levels, and urban amenity.

Not once in 1968 did Mercury editorials address the problems of noise pollution or air pollution. Nor did they critically assess the environmental effects of population and economic growth associated with the airport's expanding operations.

In resuming editorial comment in 1970 the Mercury made passing mention of airport noise problems in one editorial. In supporting

expansion at the present airport site, the Mercury said, "By lengthen-
ing existing runways, even the largest jet transports can be brought
in over downtown San Jose, at a higher altitude than is now the case,
thus reducing engine noise."

This backhand reference was the only mention of jet noise in
the three-year period of analysis. The possibility of reducing jet
noise by altering the approach angle is hotly contested by airplane
pilots; both structural inadequacy in aircraft and passenger discomfort
are cited as adverse safety factors that make the solution questionable.

What then did the Mercury fill its editorials with? There is a
surprising absence of persuasive argument on the economic benefits
of airport development. The Mercury points out that airport revenue
will pay for airport bonds and that centrality of location is critical
for both passengers and shippers. However, there is no discussion
either of direct employment by the facility or of the multiplier effect
of airport development on employment and economic opportunity. The
overweening emphasis is on the inevitability of growth in airline
traffic—and the necessity of planning for it. Thus, the Mercury offers
neither a convincing portrait of the economic benefits nor a defense
of the environmental hazards of airport expansion. It does make
clear the economic viability of the present airport.

Since the Mercury editorials emphasize planning for growth, it
is reasonable to ask whether they pose alternatives to either downtown
airport development or the proposed superport in the Alviso mudflats.
The discussion of alternatives is, after all, central to the planning
process. The Mercury's own argument for careful planning justifies
such a prescriptive approach to editorial content.

Only two alternatives are raised by the Mercury editorials: (1)
commercial aviation at the Navy's nearby Moffett Field and (2) a
single mention of the possibility of a Gilroy location for the superport.
Neither alternative is treated in its environmental aspects. Both are
dismissed: Moffett because the Navy is unwilling and the south county
around Gilroy because of its distance. Transit connection to a site
on the metropolitan periphery is not discussed, although this alternative seems to be favored by the Federal Aviation Agency as the
most reasonable response to the conflicting mandates of airport
congestion, airspace limitations, and environmental impact.

In the context of the close strategy relationship between Mercury
management and the airport commissioner, it was not expected that
editorials would assess the disadvantages of airport proposals. That
was the case. Only in urging the city council to discard the superport
plan and move ahead on municipal airport expansion did the Mercury
editorial page mention opposition to the airport. Even then, the
content of the opposition argument was not discussed.

In summary, it must be concluded that the Mercury's editorial treatment of airport location and development makes an inconclusive argument for its expansion-minded stance. The Mercury editorials exhaustively document the increasing numbers of air passengers in Santa Clara County. However, it cannot be concluded from that documentation that the wisest planning alternative is the location of a regional airport in San Jose. From the standpoint of sound planning, the location decision must weigh the negatives of environmental pollution, limited airspace, the competition for scarce urban land, and the welfare of surrounding communities. These negatives are largely ignored by the Mercury.

The failings of the Mercury's editorial treatment of airport expansion are placed in sharp relief by the articulation and depth of the San Jose Sun's editorial comment.

Like Mercury management, Sun Publisher Morton Levine was actively and personally involved in the airport controversy. Levine was a member of the San Jose Goals Committee that concluded:

> The development of the San Jose Airport at its present location should be restricted because of its inherent limitations and disadvantages—the two major ones now being proximity to the downtown core area which causes building height restrictions as well as noise, and proximity to residential areas which cause noise and other flight and approach problems resulting in physical and mental discomfort to the persons nearby. Curtailment of development of the present airport is not enough. More suitable solutions must be investigated: 1) Either reduce the current airplane handling capacity to size of planes which will not cause limitations on downtown core building or interference with normal activities, or 2) Abandon the current location and relocate the airport in an area which does not have as many physical disadvantages.

The Sun's editorials in 1969 and 1970 make clear that the publisher's involvement did not hinder the editorial page from clarion opposition to airport development plans. One of the Sun's obvious editorial goals was to keep the pot of controversy bubbling. In both position and intent, the Sun's editorial page was at direct odds with the Mercury's.

In the context of the Sun's opposition, the greatest emphasis is put on its performance in delineating alternatives and discussing the impact of airport development on the environment and economy rather than how often the Sun raised arguments challenging the wisdom of airport plans—which obviously follows from their opposition stance.

In 1969 the Sun ran six editorials on airport planning, with an equal number in 1970. Because 1969 and 1970 were the years of greatest public controversy and because there was no editorial silence to account for, 1968 Sun editorials were not examined.

In its 1969 editorials the Sun emphasized environmental arguments against the airport: the problem of competition for urban land, noise and air pollution, and the multiplier effect of airport development in increasing population growth. No mention was made of the positive economic impact of airport development; the competition between airport and industrial land use was emphasized.

In 1970 the Sun continued its environmental attack on airport location plans but broadened its scope to cite the positive economic arguments for airport development. The emphasis remained upon noise and air pollution and the incompatibility of the proposed mudflat site with other land uses—industrial, residential, commercial, ground transportation, and the proposed South Bay Wildlife Refuge.

Lacking in the Sun editorials was a discussion of how noise and air pollution are hazardous to human health or the biota, or the levels at which environmental pollution becomes injurious. In only one editorial were the problems and techniques of noise suppression discussed. The land use compatibility arguments were more conclusive, emphasizing the relationships between planning, balanced development, sprawl, and land scarcity.

Throughout, the Sun advanced alternatives to airport development, including the following: (1) commercial use of Moffett Field, (2) ground transit as a substitute for air service in heavily traveled corridors, (3) improvements in aircraft technology, (4) location of airport facilities on the periphery of the metropolitan population area with a rapid transit connection to San Jose, and (5) the relocation of general aviation aircraft at subsidiary fields.

In one editorial, the Sun charged that the Mercury had released a poll of public opinion on the airport too late to validly represent public opinion. The editorial surmised that the release was timed for political potency at the expense of polling accuracy.

With no stake in airline ad revenues, the Sun attempted to deflate the argument that the pressure of increasing passenger and freight traffic demanded the development of a national-international airport in San Jose. The Sun emphasized alternatives to the San Jose-Los Angeles route, which accounts for 80 percent of San Jose's present air traffic. In response to saturation of airport facilities in Oakland and San Francisco, the Sun urged a regional airport located on the urban periphery. The approach contrasts sharply with the Mercury's San Jose-centered response to new airlines routes typified by this editorial headline: "Today New York; Tomorrow Hong Kong?"

With hindsight, the airspace limitation warnings of the FAA, the environmental protection provisions of the 1970 Airport Revenue and Development Act, and the State Airport Land Use Act seem to have confirmed the wisdom of the Sun's regional-mindedness.

Given hindsight, and in the light of its articulate presentation of planning alternatives and an understanding of the impact of airport plans, it must be concluded that the Sun distinguished itself editorially. However, the absence of a discussion of how pollution endangers health and the biota is an instance of a distressing lack of perspective.

EDITORIAL COMMENT ON PUBLIC TRANSIT IN THE MERCURY AND THE SUN

The Mercury's editorial treatment of transit was both extensive and intensive. In 1969 the paper ran 23 editorials on the subject of public transit needs. In 1970 the number was 29. The volume of editorials peaked prior to elections on November 4, 1970, and September 16, 1969; in both cases voter approval of Proposition A would have established a countywide public transit district. Despite the election peaks, the Mercury gave persistent year-round coverage to transit as a means of reducing air pollution and congestion and to the countywide tax district as a means of bailing out San Jose's privately owned but publicly subsidized bus system.

The Mercury's transit editorials were more than lip service: the paper's parent company made a $3,750 donation to the 1970 election campaign for Proposition A. The list of major donors to the 1970 transit campaign suggests the confluence of interest on the part of what we have called San Jose's "growth establishment":

Mercury-News	$3,750
Chamber of Commerce Trust Fund	$4,000
National City (bus) Lines	$2,000
San Jose Real Estate Board	$ 500
Westgate Shopping Center	$ 250
Eastgate Shopping Center	$ 500
Town & Country Village	$ 500
PG&E	$ 500
General Electric	$1,000
IBM	$1,000
Food Machinery Corporation	$ 500
San Jose Clearinghouse Association	$1,000
Pacific Telephone & Telegram	$ 500
League of Women Voters	$ 100

The San Jose chairman of the transit campaign, Brooks T. Mancini, said that his approach to corporate donors was to emphasize the large amount of land that was unproductively tied up in parking spaces. He said, "Though I personally could not promise, I felt that if the transportation system existed, zoning could be changed to permit more office buildings, factories, or what have you."

Directly in the Mercury's interest would have been the development of transit routes that invigorated both the downtown and regional shopping centers on the periphery. Furthermore, the new district would have relieved property tax pressures in San Jose by shifting the burden of subsidizing San Jose's bus service (National City Lines) to a countywide tax base and federal demonstration project dollars. And, additionally, bus routes focusing on San Jose would have strengthened the city's position as the regional headquarters and service center of the South Bay. All these developments would redound to the advertising, circulation, and tax benefits of the Mercury while creating the kind of downtown cosmopolitan image that allows a paper to garner Madison Avenue national advertising clients.

Support for transit from a confederation of Mexican-American organizations (La Raza Unida), the League of Women Voters, and the militantly environmentalist Save Our Valley Action Committee gave the Proposition A election all the blandishments of a campaign for motherhood and apple pie. Opposition to Proposition A came from United Taxpayers, a taxpayers' revolt organization that drew its leadership from the American Independent Party.

The campaign was waged in the leadership echelons of San Jose; it was lost in the blue- and white-collar precincts of middle-income voters who were unwilling to be taxed for the other guy's apple pie. Mancini blames the defeat of Proposition A on "too much Ph.D."— an overemphasis on the environmental and financing aspects of the transit measure and not enough emphasis on its utility to the average suburban voter with two cars.

If Mancini's assessment is correct, the Mercury's editorial efforts were misplaced for they too placed heavy emphasis on finance, environment, and freeway proliferation, and less on documenting the utility of transit to the average voter that would compensate for his additional tax burden.

Of the Mercury's 23 editorials on transit in 1969, 11 dealt with transit finance; 3 mentioned air pollution; 2 mentioned noise pollution; and 3 mentioned mobility for people now lacking it. Only 2 dealt with savings for people with cars through greater efficiency or lower costs.

In 1970 there were 9 editorials dealing with the financing of the transit district; 12 dealt with the subject of air pollution reductions from transit; one dealt with the land use ramifications of transit service. Savings to the car owner were mentioned by 5 editorials, and 2 mentioned the tension of driving congested freeways, with only one mentioning mobility for people now without transportation.

Rather clearly, Mercury editorials were not dealing with the public's concerns and objections about transit: only twice was the question of whether people would shift from cars to transit raised in 1970 and not at all in 1969; only twice was the likely cost of the transit system specified in 1970 and only once in 1969; only once was the problem of providing realistic and profitable public transit in a scattered, low-density area mentioned in 1970 and never in 1969. And only once, in 1969, was a ban on the internal combustion engine raised as an alternative means of controlling exhaust emissions. Instead the emphasis was placed at the more visceral level of smog and traffic jams.

From a planning perspective, the most serious shortcoming of the Mercury's editorial treatment was the paucity of discussion of the relationship between transportation and land use patterns. The paper noted that buses would facilitate getting to work and shopping centers. The argument is not convincing when people are coming from homes scattered over an extremely low-density land use configuration where present bus service is sporadic and uncomfortable at best. The narrow range of profitable bus routes in a few dense urban corridors deserved more discussion before transit could be presented as a panacea for smog and congestion. The problems deserved more thoughtful discussion and argumentation. This they received in an editorial on January 19, 1970. In the heat of the election campaign this perspective—and its persuasive caution—was lost.

Without shifts in the density of land use, the immediate benefit of improved transit service would accrue to users, employers, and merchants located at the hubs of a few dense corridors. Although public transit would provide mobility in the central city for many now lacking it, it seems unlikely that it would ease very much of the reliance on the private car for reaching scattered destinations on a regular timetable—at least not without massive subsidy. This also deserved discussion and rebuttal. In this context, the frequency of environmental themes in the Mercury's editorials evidences more salesmanship than solution. The comparison with the paucity of environmental themes in airport editorials is perhaps more than just interesting (see Table 7.3).

Its absence of environmental concern on the airport issue and its redundancy at a low level of specificity on the transit issue are not flattering to the Mercury. The environmental hazards of airport development were given wide public airing, including a scathing denunciation of siting and expansion plans by the Santa Clara County Medical Society. The paper hardly could have been unaware of the environmental issues.

TABLE 7.3

Environmental Themes in 1969 and 1970 Editorials
of the San Jose Mercury-News

	Number of Airport Editorials in Which Theme Appears (total of 18 editorials)	Number of Transit Editorials in Which Theme Appears (total of 23 editorials)
Noise pollution	1	2
Air pollution	0	15
Land use considerations	0	1
Population growth treated as an environmental hazard	0	0

More flattering to the Mercury editors was their readiness to take on the highway lobby and the automobile industry. In attacking the values and politics of the car-oriented metropolis, the Mercury evinced a high level of environmental commitment.

The San Jose Sun's editorial page carried seven editorials dealing with transit in 1969 and six in 1970. The configuration of themes in the Sun's editorials was almost identical to that of the Mercury with the exception of a greater emphasis on the utility of transit to drivers faced with the crush of highway taxes, insurance costs, congestion, and gas bills: in effect, the arguments that Transit Campaign Chairman Mancini felt received short shrift in the campaign.

In 1969 four Sun editorials dealt with the costs of transit and three with the means of paying for the costs; three mentioned air pollution; one mentioned the land use costs of freeway proliferation; and two mentioned mobility for people without other means of transportation.

In 1970 the Sun emphasized the economic benefits of transit, such as getting the unemployed to job markets and the savings to car owners from transit (three editorial mentions); three editorials discussed transit finance; two discussed the multiplier effect on the region's economy; three mentioned air pollution; and one mentioned both rising property values and mobility for those now lacking it. Only once each year did the Sun mention the difficulty of adapting either bus or fixed rail transit to a low-density land use configuration. Not once were alternatives to pollution control or population movement mentioned in the context of transit editorials.

TABLE 7.4

Environmental Themes in 1969 and 1970
Editorials of the San Jose Sun

	Number of Airport Editorials in Which Theme Appears (total of 12 editorials)	Number of Transit Editorials in Which Theme Appears (total of 13 editorials)
Noise pollution	9	0
Air pollution	5	6
Land use considerations	5	2
Population growth treated as an environmental hazard	5	0

Thus, the Sun shared in the failure to discuss and rebut the difficult questions of planning and profitability of transit in a low-density urban area. However, serious attention was devoted to changing attitudes toward the use of cars and to informing the public on the massive personal and public investment in the upkeep of the present car-oriented transportation system.

In contrast to the skew away from environmental themes in the Mercury's coverage of the airport issue, the Sun placed greater emphasis on the airport's environmental impact (see Table 7.4).

The Sun's treatment might be considered a crude base line index of the environmental importance of the two issues. As such it is an indication of the significance of the environmental blackout in the Mercury's airport editorials.

The number of editorials in the two papers on each issue in 1969 and 1970 underlines the Mercury's noncoverage of the airport:

	Airport	Transit
Mercury	5	52
Sun	12	13

One Sun editorial is offered here as an example of excellence (see Appendix D for the content themes coded):

TRANSIT PLAN CAN BE A BARGAIN FOR EVERYONE—
How would you like a thousand dollar bill tucked in your pocket?

You'll be offered that real possibility at the November election.

Conservatively careful estimates of the savings to the average family budget are considerably in excess of $1000 if at least one member of the family can use public transportation rather than a private car. Sounds hard to believe? But it's true.

The system, obviously is going to have to be of a quality in terms of timing, accessibility, and safety to make you want to ride it. The goal of the county-wide transit district concept proposed for the November election is exactly that.

Typically, even a work car, will cost well over a $1000 to operate per year.

The transit measure on the ballot would be financed by a half-cent sales tax. Since this doesn't apply to food or shelter, the tax would probably be in the vicinity of $30 per year. With a companion measure now in the state legislative hopper, to allow 5% sales tax on gasoline to go toward transit, the new district would be able to nick each motorist for an additional $12 per year (based on 12,000 miles of driving). With these two sources, as well as the hoped-for federal matching grants, the district could avoid any property tax. The ballot measure specifically eliminates a property tax without coming back to the electorate.

The two largest expenditures government now makes on our behalf are for education and transportation. And economists agree that education and transportation relate directly to the health and growth of any area's economy.

To give you an inkling of what dollars are actually being spent for transportation in this valley right now, take a look at these figures:

$300 million for new and used cars and parts.

$100 million annually for gas and oil.

$70 million in road construction by both local and state agencies this year alone.

When you place against that half-billion dollar figure, the 11 million which would come from the half-cent sales tax to get a public transit system into high gear for the county, you can see that it could be the biggest bargain in transportation ever attained.

There are now 700,000 vehicles registered in Santa Clara county. In a straight line they'd stretch from here to Chicago, bumper to bumper. That image summons up

some of the untabulated kinds of costs no one can measure.
How much economic loss is sustained every year in accidents, in delays caused by congestion, not to mention the
health problems which smog contributes.

First priority of the transit district will be to attack
the home-to-work problem so that the most immediate
benefits can come back to those paying the freight.

But in the ultimate, the district will bring forth
innovative systems of rapid transit coupled with extensive
feeder bus service, so that our sprawled-out county can
be linked together with fast, efficient, low cost travel
options.

The overall benefit to the community can be enormous. And you can accomplish it with the power of your
vote in November.

NEWS COVERAGE OF AIRPORT AND
TRANSIT PLANNING IN SAN JOSE

If newspaper ownership enters the newsroom to manage the
flow of information to the public, it would most likely occur in controversial news stories that affect the economic prospects of the
newspaper as a business enterprise. Both transit and airport policy
qualify as issues in which the newspaper has a direct economic interest. Transportation is the lifeline of an area's economy, the retailer's
ads are the lifeblood of the newspaper industry, and the two go hand
in hand.

With its fortunes tied to the health of the local marketplace, it
is predictable that a metropolitan newspaper would promote public
expenditure for transportation. This we found was the case in the
editorial policy of the San Jose Mercury. A more delicate question
is the impact of the economic interests of the newspaper on its news
coverage, an influence that could subvert notions of balance and
objectivity, discourage probing reportage, and violate the newspaper's
public trust.

Two efforts were made to gauge the existence or extent of management interference in the news gathering process: (1) content analysis
of published news and (2) interviews with reporters whose bylines
were identified during the analysis.

The issues for analysis—coverage of transit and the airport—
were chosen on the basis of their parallelism: both involve the economic interest of the newspaper; both involve visible decisions and
events in the public sector; both involve a similar elite cast from
the private sector. They diverge sharply in their environmental

impact: airport expansion involves increasing levels of environmental stress in the form of noise and air pollution and is a stimulus to growth; transit has the opposite effect of substituting low-polluting transportation for the private car while at the same time imposing an ordering effect on urban growth patterns.

A newspaper that assiduously watchdogs government performance and seeks to shed light on conflict and controversy presumably would give greater play to the environmental aspects of the airport than to transit, as was the case with the Sun's editorials. A metropolitan paper that serves its own interests, on the other hand, predictably would give little play to the environmental hazards of airport location and size; it might find, further, that transit was a "motherhood issue" on which to go all-out environmentalist without danger of offense.

This parallelism between issues appears remarkably neat. In actuality it is considerably murkier. The transit issue came to a public vote; the airport issue did not. Transit coverage had a logical focus and terminal point: Election Day. The airport issue simmered, came to a boil, and was taken off the burner by city council resolution. Parallel periods of analysis are therefore difficult to identify. The difficulty is compounded by the different decision routes in the two controversies: transit was a countywide issue; airport expansion was initiated at the city level.

However, it is possible to identify the crisis point in the airport location controversy: the 4-3 vote by the San Jose City Council to reject the Alviso airport location, which would have conflicted with residential uses and the South Bay wildlife refuge. The events of the previous three months indicate that this was the make or break period for airport plans:

February 11 County Medical Society opposed airport.

February 18 News conference of State Assemblyman Earle P. Crandall and state Senator Alfred E. Alquist, who opposed international airport in north Santa Clara County.

February 24 Neighboring Santa Clara's City Council passed a resolution against San Jose's airport plans.

February 25 San Jose City Council ordered the airport manager to stop promoting airport plans prior to a decision.

March 2 County Parks and Recreation Commission opposed the airport.

March 9 Regional air traffic study released.

March 10 Alameda County supervisors requested San Jose to delay any decision until after regional study.

March 14 Airport opponents and proponents debated at a
          heavily-attended (500 persons present) League
          of Women Voters forum.
March 15 Mercury released a two-month-old poll showing
          voters favored the superport.
March 18 State Senator Clark Bradley opposed the airport.
March 20 Airport Subcommittee of the county Planning
          Policy Committee concluded the fact-finding
          stage of its airport location study.
April 7   Airline Pilots Association petitioned San Jose
          City Council.
April 21 San Jose Airport Commission backed off the
          mudflat site and urged study of other locations.
April 24 Mercury editorially urged retreat from inter-
          national airport.
April 27 San Jose City Council killed the mudflat airport
          site.
April 29 Airport Subcommittee of the Planning Policy
          Committee resolved against both the mudflat
          site and a second north county international
          airport site.

This focus of citizen group and official activity in the March-April
period permits the researcher to pair it with the month before the
transit votes.

Both the Mercury and the Sun were analyzed during the same
period for both issues. A higher incidence of environmental themes
was found in two months of the Mercury's transit coverage than in
two months of airport news. In the Sun, the environmental hazards
of the airport received more frequent attention.

Interviews with bylined Mercury reporters indicated that there
was no effort to manage the news by establishing a policy line or
blue-penciling copy. Reporters were emphatic in stating that their
professional judgment of newsworthiness was the sole criterion of
the coverage of stories on their beats.

Both airport and transit were extremely complex issues. They
involved a diffuse array of government hierarchies, citizens groups,
and influentials from the private sector. They also demanded a
sophisticated understanding of environmental affairs: the interaction
of air pollution, noise pollution, land use, and urban growth patterns.
In both cases, questions of engineering and hardware also are extremely complex.

The complexity of the issues and the diffusion and profusion of
both events and sources logically demanded that the newsroom be
reorganized to cover the stories on a continuing basis. Only

continuity in the reporter's background and expertise would have allowed intelligible reporting on the two controversies. In the case of transit, Mercury reporter Jim Choate was freed to develop a five-part interpretive series and to travel with county planners as they surveyed transit operations in other cities. Choate became an expert and aficionado on the history and hardware of public transit, both bus and rail.

In the case of the airport, the natural entropy of the newsroom was not corrected. Instead, the story bounced from beat to beat, suffering from a fragmented, event-centered reportorial effort that was not equipped to place the issue in perspective or to alert citizens to its increasing momentum in the decision process.

Thus, where the environmental aspects of transit offered a salespoint coinciding with a policy favored by management, reportorial assignment and interpretive freedom insured extensive coverage. Where management's policy line was in the process of change—from favoring the economics of the mudflat airport site to recognizing its political infeasibility—the failure to reorganize the newsroom and correct its tendency to entropy resulted in a low profile for the environmental hazards of the airport site.

During the two-month period March-April 1970 the Mercury ran 11 stories dealing with expansion, siting, or location of airport facilities in San Jose. Three more stories dealt with taxicab service to the airport and a general aviation airport in the foothills. The stories totaled 71 column inches. For comparison with the Sun, which has a different format, a paragraph measure also is used. There were 71 paragraphs of airport news in the Mercury (journalistic style allows a reasonable comparison between numbers of paragraphs). During the same period, the Sun, a weekly, ran 11 stories on the airport issue with a total of 125 paragraphs. The median number of paragraphs per story was four in the Mercury and ten in the Sun. Of the Sun stories, 8 of 11, or 73 percent, ran on page one. The majority of Mercury stories were displayed on the local news page. The Sun appears to have given better play to the airport issue in terms of length and display.

Neither paper offered interpretative or investigative news on the airport during the two-month period; all news was event-pegged. During this period the Sun covered the meetings of five public bodies dealing with the airport issue, the Mercury three. The Mercury covered statements by four public officials (two from its Sacramento bureau); the Sun two. However, in February the Sun offered a lengthy depth piece on the problems of noise pollution: health impact, regulation and control, and means of noise suppression. The distribution of environmental themes in the 11 stories offered in each paper is shown in Table 7.5.

TABLE 7.5

Distribution of Environmental Themes
in Airport Coverage of San Jose Mercury and Sun

Issue	Number of Stories in Mercury	Number of Stories in Sun
Noise pollution	3	4
Air pollution	2	2
Land use questions	1	5
Population growth treated as an environmental hazard	1	2

Differences in the frequency of environmental content between
the Mercury and Sun are perceptible, but both papers offered the
reader some appreciation of the generic environmental hazards involved in airport development. The Sun's coverage offered considerably greater detail: for example, two stories dealt with the effect of
airports as population magnets and four with the incompatibility
between the airport and the use of baylands for parks, recreation,
and wildlife preservation. The Mercury raised these issues in only
one story on page 77; coverage of the same event—the League of
Women Voters forum attended by over 500 persons—received page
one play in the Sun.

The economics of the airport issue were raised in one Sun story—
the coverage of the same League of Women Voters forum. They were
raised once in the Mercury as well, with the same news peg.

Distinctions between Mercury and Sun coverage are greatest
for news content indicating that the newspaper was playing a watchdog
role in relation to the performance of local government. The Sun
topped the Mercury in the presentation of information on possible
adverse effects of the airport, as shown in Table 7.6.

A similar measure sought to determine whether the newspaper's
coverage discussed policy alternatives or gave play to proposals that
countered the accepted wisdom. In this area, too, the Sun offered
more extensive coverage as shown in Table 7.7.

The differences in coverage between the papers are even more
striking because the Sun is published only weekly, its staff size is
minimal compared to the Mercury's, and its news hole for each
edition is about one-tenth that of the Mercury.

Staff and news hole differences would have no significance if
the Mercury had covered all of the available public events in the two-
month period. It did not. Without substituting an outside judgment

TABLE 7.6

Adversity in Airport Coverage
of San Jose Mercury and Sun

Issue	Number of Stories in Which Theme Appeared in Mercury	Number of Stories in Which Theme Appeared in Sun
Adverse effect on wildlife	1	5
Adverse effect on natural, scenic, and recreational assets	1	5
Adverse effect upon water and air quality	2	2

TABLE 7.7

Discussion of Policy Alternatives in Airport Coverage
of San Jose Mercury and Sun

	Number of Stories in Which Theme Appeared in Mercury	Number of Stories in Which Theme Appeared in Sun
Ground transit to existing airports	0	1
Location of airport on the urban periphery away from population concentrations	0	2
Ground transit as a substitute for intrastate air service	1	2

of news value for that of the Mercury editors, the following facts can
be noted:

1. The Airport Commission letter urging the San Jose City
Council to scrap the mudflat site was not covered.

2. Some six meetings of the Planning Policy Committee Subcommittee on Airport Siting were not covered.

3. The Alameda County supervisors resolution urging regional
responsibility was not covered.

Perhaps most interesting, the Mercury published an opinion poll
indicating public support for the mudflat jetport on the day following
the League of Women Voters forum at which airport proponents had
received a drubbing from the heavily environmentalist audience. The
poll ran 12.5 inches on page 35, compared to 39 inches on page 77 for
the forum. The poll, conducted for the Mercury by the Diridon
Research Corporation, was more than two months old, although this
fact was not reported in the Mercury story.

Interviews with three Mercury reporters whose bylines had
appeared on airport stories found unanimous agreement that there
was no "airport line" guiding the stories they filed. Each reporter
insisted he had absolute freedom to report the news on his beat as
he saw it.

All the reporters agreed that their news judgment was likely to
be questioned only on initiative stories, and that then the story was
likely to run. As one of the reporters put it, "The day of the blackout
and arm-twisting is long past." He attributed the failings of Mercury
coverage to the inertia of a large newsroom, noting that stories
received good coverage when they fell to stable beats but got short
shrift when a general assignment reporter had to be specifically
assigned to irregular events. Much environment news, he added,
falls in the general assignment category where reporters without
special expertise or background on the issue must "muddle through."

The Mercury never assigned a reporter to follow through on
the airport issue, and the story bounded among six beats; environment,
county, Sacramento, city hall, general assignment, and aviation. A
reporter from the Fremont Argus noted that the Mercury turned
down an offer from a bylined reporter to take the story on as a unified
whole. The Argus reporter added that "the word went around to other
editors that the Mercury wanted the airport issue kept cool." He
said the Argus, with Fremont located in the jet noise pattern, did no
such thing.

The failure to assign a reporter to cover the complex and controversial airport plan is placed in greater relief by the Mercury's
transit coverage where Choate, the county beat reporter, was freed
to travel with planners to examine transit systems in operation and
to write a highly favorable five-part series on the virtues of public

transit. "County officials pressured the Mercury to have me do the
series," Choate said, "but I was planning to anyway." He said the
series was his own: "I couldn't care less what the edit page says.
On this paper, a reporter has total freedom to do what he wants to
do." He added that the series was "slanted. I personally favor transit
and I felt a duty to slant in favor of anything that could get rid of smog.
It was a motherhood issue."

The Mercury's extensive transit coverage reflected Choate's
enthusiasm. In only 3 of 40 stories in 1970 were transit opponents
quoted or paraphrased.

In the 1969 transit measure election, the Mercury ran 33 stories
with a total of 409 paragraphs and a median of 14 paragraphs per
story. The Sun, in the same month before the transit election, ran
4 stories for a total of 54 paragraphs and a median of 9 paragraphs
per story. The number of stories is a proportional reflection of the
size differences in the papers' news holes.

In the 1970 election; the Mercury's 40 stories totaled 345 paragraphs with a 7-paragraph median. The Sun ran 10 stories for a
total paragraph count of 69 and a 10-paragraph median.

When the volume of airport and transit news in the Mercury and
Sun for two months of airport news and the month of 1970 transit
election coverage are compared, the results are as follows:

	Mercury	Sun
Transit	345 paragraphs,	69 paragraphs,
	7-paragraph median	10-paragraph median
Airport	71 paragraphs,	125 paragraphs,
	4-paragraph median	10-paragraph median

The data argue that the Mercury gave greatest coverage to the
environmental impact of public investment in transportation where
such news would perform a salesmanship role for improved transportation services. When such coverage diverged from the motherhood
issue of clean air to threaten management policy—as was the case
with the airport and the land use implications of transit—coverage
was notably sparser.

The beat orientation of the metropolitan newspaper, which dulls
the ability to give adequate coverage of complex subjects with out-
croppings at many levels of government, was not remedied in the
case of airport coverage: no uniform mechanism for coverage was
developed; reporters were not encouraged to develop interpretive
stories.

The Mercury must be faulted for corporate inertia in failing to
react to a critical environmental story. In comparison to the promotional and aggressive coverage of the transit election—and the

coverage of downtown convention and sports facilities, regional air
pollution problems, and the proposed location of a Swift & Company
slaughterhouse in San Jose—corporate inertia proved greatest in the
airport issue where the economic interests of the paper conflicted
with aggressive environmental news coverage.

In summary, the interview and content analysis data indicate
that the Mercury's coverage of the environmental impact of public
transit service was promotional rather than probing. In the airport
issue, where promotional coverage of environmental impact was
impossible, the Mercury's coverage of environmental themes was
noticeably sparser. Both the airport and transit controversies
involved multiple layers of government and diverse spheres of authority. Both involved complex questions of urban growth, land use impact,
and multiplier effects on the size and density of the urban area.
Neither could be adequately covered without a management commitment
to freeing reportorial time for study, analysis, and diverse spheres
of authority.

CONCLUSIONS AND RECOMMENDATIONS

The metropolitan newspaper's commitment to the health and
vitality of the local economy is appropriate and understandable. Without a healthy economy, public and private expenditure for environmental improvement, much less housing and welfare, are crippled.
However, the most common and accepted wisdom has held that a
healthy economy is synonymous with a rapid growth economy. Newspapers have been slow to discard the boom and booster ethic that
equated growth with progress and the attraction of an industrial tax
base with an improved level of urban amenity. However, the environmental movement has begun to underline the massive diseconomies—
regional in scope—represented by the failure to include air, noise,
water pollution, and the biotic and esthetic damage attendant to sprawl
in the cost-benefit calculus of urban growth.

In this context, competition for growth is a questionable antidote
to inequity in tax base and the inadequacy of dollars for pollution
control, parks, police, education and the myriad welfare services
provided by local government. Urban competition for tax base has
aggravated, rather than solved, these problems by increasing the
number of external diseconomies related to transportation, congestion,
waste, sprawl, pollution, and scale.

What can be done? A few proposals for newspaper management,
reporters, and citizen-environmentalists are appropriate here.

1. Newspaper management: Management must place its downtown focus in perspective. It must recognize the newspaper's

economic interest in the appropriate regional perspective, recognizing
that regional planning rather than municipal growth competition offers
the best possibility for internalizing what economists refer to as
"external diseconomies." With regional planning, urban specialization
within regional diversity can replace municipal competition. In short,
growth and development can be planned and distributed rationally and
regionally while increasing the publisher's net gains after taxes. In
the process, the publisher will be trading political influence for economic benefit and the environmental benefits that accrue to planning.

2. Reporters: Reporters can more forcefully urge, perhaps
through the American Newspaper Guild, that the clumsy mechanisms
of assignment be rationalized to unify coverage according to issue
as well as beat. The reporter can discard the attitude that he "doesn't
know what management is thinking." He should know. He should trust
to his professionalism to prevent being influenced by the management
line. Then, by knowing management's goals, the reporter's professionalism can play the role of a countervailing force to assure that
coverage is not distorted by corporate inertia or economic self-
interest. The reporter can initiate stories before they reach the
public agenda, insuring that private and self-interested parties must
contest with public opinion and glaring publicity in influencing the
public policy of the mixed economy.

3. Citizen-environmentalists: Environmentalists can unlock
the information monopoly of the metropolitan daily and create a
climate of competition by aggressively pursuing the possibilities of
cable television and photo-offset house publications. Citizens might
explore means of establishing person-to-person feedback to newspaper
management on questions of news quality and local coverage. Both
citizens and newspaper management could benefit from the broadening
of perspective and reference groups.

These suggestions are hardly radical, nor are they more than
the bare bones of an agenda for realistic change. Perhaps their virtue
is that they demand very little of man's generosity and expect even
less of his goodness.

EPILOGUE: THE INFLUENCE OF MANAGEMENT
MEMBERSHIP IN THE GROWTH ESTABLISHMENT

The participation of San Jose Mercury-News executives in
associations and organizations seeking more rapid urban growth
raises the following question: Does management's membership in
the growth establishment deter initiative reporting by identifying
policy-makers or policy areas the newsman feels must be treated
with kid gloves ?

To answer this question we surveyed by mail 60 Bay Area reporters from nine daily newspapers. The reporters (49 of whom responded) were asked to rate the likelihood of editor approval for a series of hypothetical, initiative-type stories. The same reporters then were asked to rank their own management's participation in community affairs: Was management perceived as part of the power structure or was management's relationship to community influentials seen as peripheral?

Reporters from the San Jose Mercury, Oakland Tribune, San Francisco Examiner and Chronicle, and San Mateo Times were virtually unanimous in locating their newspaper executives within the power structure. Reporters for the relatively smaller circulation papers—the Palo Alto Times, Redwood City Tribune, Contra Costa Times, and Hayward Review—ranked their executives as peripheral to community influence groups.

Five hypothetical story-line proposals in the questionnaire touched areas that might provoke controversy embarrassing to a community's economic leaders:

1. The role of private sector influentials in lobbying public officials

2. The role of banks and insurance companies in lobbying for pro-growth development policies

3. The role of construction trade unions in lobbying for pro-growth development policies

4. Frequent pollution violations by a local industry

5. Discrimination in housing.

There proved to be no statistically significant difference between the likelihood of story approval expected where reporters perceived their management as peripheral to, as opposed to within, community power groups. Although not significantly different by statistical test, the percentage of reporters who felt the stories would not receive approval is in the predicted direction, as shown in Table 7.8.

A pattern does emerge when we consider why reporters feel stories would fail to win approval. The questionnaire asked reporters to explain their reasons for deciding certain stories would be unlikely to win their editor's approval. Four response categories were offered: (1) not newsworthy, (2) would require too much time or effort, (3) too aggressive or controversial, and (4) other.

Here we do find significant differences between the two groups of newsmen. Reporters who perceived their management as within the power structure were more likely to give "too aggressive or controversial" as the reason for non-approval of story line 1 ($p = 0.04$) and 2 ($p = 0.05$). Reporters from the other group almost universally mentioned the shortage of reportorial time or the problem of obtaining accurate information as the reason for non-approval.

TABLE 7.8

Reporters' Perceptions of Management's Relation
to Power Structure and Likelihood for Non-Approval
of a Potentially Embarrassing Story

Story Line	Non-Approval Where Management Perceived as in Local Power Structure (percentage)	Non-Approval Where Management Perceived as Peripheral to Local Power Structure (percentage)
1. Private sector lobbying	63	25
2. Bank/insurance lobbying	45	25
3. Labor lobbying	35	19
4. Pollution violations	16	6
5. Housing discrimination	43	25

Equally interesting was the finding that reporters who saw their management as influentials felt that bankers would receive more delicate treatment than labor unions involved in the identical lobbying activity (p = 0.01).

On the basis of these results we can tentatively conclude that management activity in the policy-oriented associations and organizations of the private sector elite can be dysfunctional to the operation of journalistic norms in the newsroom. Reporters' comments accompanying the completed questionnaires indicated that some reporters timidly, but resentfully, identify management's community associates as a preferred group who must receive kid glove treatment or anonymity in stories that could provoke public controversy. As one Mercury reporter put it, "Your story-line description fits management and their friends." The newsman rated approval "very unlikely."

Those reporters who feel that approval for hard-hitting, investigative reporting would be refused may be reacting with inappropriate timidity in a situation that is not as threatening as they perceive. Regardless of the reality, the message they perceive is "Don't push and don't probe." In such a situation, it is unlikely that they will be eager to test the proposition.

8

**TOWARD PUBLIC
UNDERSTANDING**

AVAILABILITY OF INFORMATION

The public has essentially four sources from which to obtain information on environmental deterioration. The scientific and academic communities provide the greater part of the data base on which decisions with environmental implications are made by government and business. But too much of their work is unintelligible to the public and available only through professional journals. A few academicians have attempted to communicate more directly with the public, ignoring the strong peer group pressure against such activity. However, information from this sector reaches the public only sporadically.

The other three information sources are government, the private business community, and citizen groups. Although this last source is becoming more and more important, the news media still are wary of information that does not have an "official" look about it. Citizen groups also do not have at their disposal the public relations staffs employed by government and private business. As a result, such groups are not as important a source of information as they might be.

A free flow of information from the remaining two sources is necessary if the public is to be at all informed on threats to environmental quality and efforts at environmental repair. Although the 1966 Federal Freedom of Information Act, amended in 1967, provides a legal tool for access to much government information, hearings in 1972 by the House Subcommittee on Foreign Operations and Government Information showed that the Freedom of Information Act is largely ineffective. Agencies have failed to comply with the spirit of the law, and it is most often invoked by commercial interests for commercial purposes. In addition, the elaborate government classification system and the doctrine of executive privilege can and do effectively hobble the public's right to know.

Passage of the 1969 National Environmental Policy Act (P. L. 91-190, or NEPA) has aided the public in obtaining information on the environmental impact of any project requiring federal license, approval, or funding. Reports detailing the expected environmental impact of proposed projects must be submitted to the appropriate agency before final approval is given, and those statements are public in both draft and final form. Statements dealing with nuclear power plant construction and the proposed pipeline across Alaska have provided important information to the public. Too often, however, NEPA statements fail to treat the impact of federal projects on the rate and form of urban growth; they outline only the most obvious and direct environmental effects in the immediate project area.

Still, the law has contributed materially to the flow of information to the public. At present several bureaucracies, including the Atomic Energy Commission, the Federal Power Commission, and the Department of Transportation, are attempting to have the law amended to cripple the disclosure provision. Such action must be fought vigorously or much information will be plunged into a deep freeze, unavailable for public scrutiny.

The fourth information source, the private business community, remains untouched by the freedom of information movement. The public's right to know the plans and decisions of a private corporation is an amorphous one in a capitalist system. The press and public currently must work through government regulatory agencies to view private documents, and many of these are closed to public scrutiny because they involve trade secrets or other competitive information that generally is held in confidence.

Two aspects of the contemporary American corporation make this state of affairs inimical to an informed public. First, the average corporation can easily affect environmental tolerances by virtue of the enormous resources under its control. The magnitude of the decisions made by a Standard Oil or a Consolidated Edison makes these corporations different in nature from the locally-owned company with a single product line. In their vertical and horizontal integration, such corporations are more analogous to government than to free enterprise.

Second, there is an increasingly blurry line between public and private decision-making. Today some of the most attractive investment opportunities for the entrepreneur lie at the juncture of the public and private sectors of the economy, where the economy becomes "mixed." Land developers, construction firms, and the financiers of urban growth have become adept at manipulating government policy decisions in order to maximize private advantage from the availability of electric power, transportation, water, and tax shelters.

Access to information, leading to an informed public opinion, is one of the few means of controlling the corporate elite that manipulates public policy for private profit.

MEDIA PERFORMANCE

Availability of information is only half the problem in creating an environmentally aware public. The other half is the performance of the mass media in communicating available information. Under the continual prodding of media critics, journalists, academicians, and various scientific and professional societies, plus moral pressure from publishers and broadcast executives who feel a sense of social responsibility, the news media have come to accept the role of watchdog for the public.

Assuming that a broad public knowledge of biological and ecological concepts is at the heart of defining, reclaiming, and maintaining environmental quality, the press should strive to create an awareness of environmental problems and then seek to develop an understanding of principles and issues.

To keep the public informed about the current state of the environment, the news media should act as an "early warning system" to identify environmental hazards before they reach such an advanced state that repair is impractical. The media must inform the public of environmental practices being considered by government or business before they have been adopted. In acting as watchdog of government and business, the news media must cease to merely react to events. They should be particularly alert to instances where laws are being violated, where planning recommendations or policies are being ignored for private profit, and where public opinion on environmental matters is being flouted. In the absence of accepted standards on what is desirable or undesirable environmental change, on occasion the newsman must trust his own instincts on the wisdom of projects with far-reaching environmental effects. Finally, the news media should attempt to synthesize for the public the solutions to environmental problems put forth by government, citizen groups, business, and the academic and scientific communities.

Since mid-1969 the nation's news media have responded with considerable skill and effort in reporting the broad outlines of environmental deterioration in the United States. Although news executives are inclined to downplay their own role as catalyst and attribute the increased coverage to pressure from the public for more information, it is likely the two facets have fed one another and also have been stimulated by the news value of statements from a few crusader-scientists and a number of ecological disasters that have captured public concern.

This environmental information explosion occurred in a receptive atmosphere. Millions of newly affluent Americans had fled metropolitan centers in the 1950s and 1960s to stake out a future in garden suburbs. To their dismay they found that pollution and congestion followed them, turning their suburban dream into a nightmare. They proved a willing audience for stories that put the blame on polluters, special interests, and the cast of political characters that had so deeply disillusioned Americans through the nation's involvement in the Vietnam war.

As a result, numerous mass circulation magazines devoted many editions to the environment. The broadcast networks and the wire services began a more vigilant watch. Many daily newspapers appointed one or more environmental news specialists.

On a national basis, at least, the news media already have achieved the first goal: the public has been made aware of the general scope and consequences of environmental deterioration. Such words as ecology and conservation have taken on a deeper meaning, and substantive writing has replaced some of the gloom and doom rhetoric (although no doubt a certain measure is needed to maintain public interest).

The new interest is manifest in the defeat of legislation to fund construction of the SST; pressure on the auto industry to reduce pollutants from the internal combustion engine; passage of NEPA; concern over construction of an oil pipeline across Alaska; and scores of other incidents.

In the San Francisco Bay Area the amount of environmental news has increased at an exponential rate—more than fivefold since 1965— and environmental stories gradually have crept to the front pages of newspapers and into the hourly headlines of radio stations. There is much evidence that the environment has become a regular news beat; where it is not yet a true beat, at least it is recognized as an area for continuous surveillance. Although environmental reporters almost always have come from within the organization, indicating a lack of financial commitment by news executives, their presence on a news staff is the single most important factor in improved environmental coverage. Once they have established a communitywide reputation, environmental reporters attract public relations materials from citizen groups and industries, often leading to good news stories; they can help change the focus of coverage from a national perspective (provided by the wire services and the networks) to a more local one; they can lobby for increased space and time for environmental news; and they can help overcome the newsroom and management inertia that militates against quality coverage of any non-beat subject.

The marshaling of large numbers of citizens in a community to pressure local government officials and local industrial leaders is another, perhaps more direct and efficient, method of cleaning up the environment. And it is here, on the local level, dealing with specific environmental problems, that the mass media in the Bay Area (and in other metropolitan areas) have much room for improvement in performance.

The disease that permits perceptive coverage of problems in other parts of the country but produces myopia in dealing with similar problems at home is neither new nor unusual in journalism. When caught by editorial writers, this disease is called "Afghanistanism" it is characterized by the presentation of bold editorial solutions for the problems of countries halfway around the globe but only silence for problems at home.

The environment beat is particularly prone to such a malady, as this study has demonstrated. Media in growing communities have a direct financial stake in promoting the growth of population and industry, and they often are blind to alternative land use patterns that may be more beneficial to the community on a long-term basis. The media frequently print stories on what industry is doing to improve environmental quality, but without a hard news peg (preferably one from a government regulatory body) they are unwilling to single out and name companies that violate air and water pollution standards and in other ways refuse to stop polluting. When given the opportunity to print stories naming industrial polluters and rating the performance of elected officials charged with enforcing Bay Area air pollution emission standards, the media failed miserably. Too often regional and national stories have received extensive coverage while the publisher's own backyard goes up in smoke.

THE ROLE OF THE ECO-ACTIVIST

The eco-activists in the Bay Area seem to recognize these serious shortcomings—which tend to preclude meaningful citizen participation—and consequently do not rely on the mass media for the environmental information they need to encourage government regulation and challenge industry. The news media are simply too slow, too timid, too understaffed, and too close to the business community to permit coverage at home that will be of direct benefit to the eco-activist.

Local environmental news may help alert previously inert citizens to certain problems and convert them into environmental activists, and on occasion the media can focus community attention on a single problem, such as proposals to fill San Francisco Bay. But for the day-to-day effort at cleaning up the environment (and all the lobbying at city hall and in Sacramento that effort entails) the news media have proven inadequate. The eco-activist relies instead on his club and trusted colleagues and experts for information. And to a great extent so do environmental reporters, although some regard the eco-activist as an inaccurate propagandist.

Indeed, the news media and the inactive citizen benefit from the work of the eco-activist in two ways. He provides much basic information to reporters, and, through his challenges to corporate and government decision-makers, he creates the necessary news pegs for getting the press involved. It is one thing for the media to report claims and counterclaims from opposing sides, and in the process educate readers and viewers on the subject under debate. It is quite another for the media themselves to research a subject and present the pros and cons. Thus, a community with many eco-activists who challenge decisions, make news, and stage pseudo-events is likely to have better news coverage as a result, and the Bay Area has an active citizenry.

While it is possible for an interested citizen to educate himself on local environmental problems without the mass media, it is time-consuming and expensive. The media should be at the center of this problem locally, and most news executives, cognizant of the special historical obligations of their profession quite apart from economics, want to play a more vital role in solving environmental problems in their own communities.

PRESSURES ON THE MEDIA

Even though media coverage has increased substantially, few would say it is yet satisfactory. The news media suffer many pressures, both internal and external, that blunt their performance.

Among the internal pressures are the following:

1. The news media are so structured that they define and gather news through reaction to specific events or news pegs. Because environmental deterioration often occurs almost invisibly and over a long period of time, it does not offer convenient news pegs and thus is left out of the routine of news gathering. The Santa Barbara oil spill was reported in detail because it conformed to traditional news needs. But stories on energy-producing resources and electric power needs, for example, are rare because there are so few news pegs on which to hang them.

2. The subject is a complicated one cutting across many specialities, and reporters with the requisite skills are hard to find.

3. Editors do not yet perceive the urgency of improving environmental coverage, and they do not afford reporters sufficient time or space to develop and report stories.

4. Editors often are unwilling to print serious and lengthy stories; instead, they push for pieces with more zest, even at the expense of accuracy.

5. Social control by editors and other superiors can lead reporters to slant news according to the values of management, even though this is contrary to their own reportorial instincts.

6. Some editors and reporters believe the interest in the environment is a fad that soon will pass from the scene.

7. Journalists tie themselves to official sources usually government, for most of their environmental information while overlooking many academicians and members of the public with expertise.

8. Environmental stories frequently are regional, and editors often are unwilling to cover stories whose major focus lies beyond their circulation or viewing area.

9. Broadcast journalists force themselves into superficial and inaccurate reportage through self-imposed patterns of behavior and time constraints.

External pressures on the news media with regard to environmental reporting include the following:

1. Relationships between scientist and reporter frequently have been characterized by mutual distrust, the former fearing sensationalism and the latter obscurantism.

2. The vocabulary and intricacies of science frequently have proved strange and virtually incomprehensible to the traditional reporter.

3. The working journalist is on uneasy and unfamiliar terms with the private business community. The socially responsible news medium recognizes that it must serve as an adversary of government. However, the press as a whole has not internalized the adversary relationship toward the business community, and the business executive often has little regard for the public's right to know.

4. Advertiser pressure, direct and indirect, can be brought to bear on a news medium by a company implicated in pollution.

5. Business can educate the public to its perspective through advertising, and it is not unusual for advertising time or space to far outweigh news coverage of an environmental issue.

6. All too often, newspaper and broadcast management finds its economic interests congruent with the growth ethic of the local chamber of commerce, creating in the newsroom an atmosphere that discourages probing, aggressive coverage of the forces behind reckless urban growth.

RECOMMENDATIONS

In order to facilitate communication between environmental news sources and the public, we offer the following suggestions:

1. Those media that have not yet designated a staff member as environmental reporter should do so. He should be afforded as much time as possible for sorting through environmental public relations materials, meeting with local groups, and attending the sessions of government regulatory bodies. Many papers already have done this, even some with circulations under 15,000. With a few notable exceptions, the major network-affiliated radio and television stations are deficient in this regard, and they should attempt to regularize and centralize their environmental coverage.

2. Editors and broadcast executives should seriously consider creating a special environmental news page or a continuing broadcast feature. It might contain news of environmental legislation, public hearings and meetings on environmental matters, and the activities of industry and ecology organizations. Advertisers might be sought from the many companies manufacturing pollution control equipment.

3. The electronic media should aid in the development of a computer-accessed archive system so that the public can make more effective use of the information presented by these media. Until such a retrieval system is developed, broadcast content will continue to remain a mystery.

4. Editors and reporters should make a greater effort to provide specific information the public can use, such as the names of companies with lengthy records of violating anti-pollution laws, the performance of public officials in enforcing those laws, the way to obtain government and academic reports about the environment, and the names of groups lobbying for and against environmental bills. If the news medium itself does not have the time or space to discuss a complex subject, such as nuclear power and electricity, it might offer the audience a list of sources for further reading. This could prove a most valuable service, and in a way it looks forward to the time when the consumer will use the media for reference purposes with a home computer terminal.

5. Advertising acceptance departments should look with a more critical eye at the plethora of environmental advertisments that cross their desks; that is, ads claiming a product or service will improve the quality of the environment. Where feasible, patently fraudulent or misleading ads should be rejected or sent back to the ad agency for modification. Above all, the mass media should not allow themselves to be used by industry in a campaign to lull the American consumer into the belief that corporate America is spending billions on pollution control and is about to solve all environmental problems.

This is not the case, and the public should be put on guard against
such suggestions.

6. Reporters should attempt to extend the adversary relationship they now maintain in covering public officials to reporting on
private industry as well. Historically the business community has
failed to recognize the importance of a free and vigorous press in a
democratic society. Since many pollution problems are centered in
industry, its decisions must be reported as fully as those of government. As a corollary, news executives should press for extension of
open record and open meeting statutes to cover public utilities as a
first step in opening up the secrets of the business community.
Transforming the "puff" of the average business/financial page into
hard-hitting coverage of industry will not be easy, but it must be done
if the private sector is to meet its responsibilities to the environment.

7. News executives should seek to report on the growth of their
communities with all the experience and wisdom about population
increase, unplanned development, and regional growing pains that
recent years have brought. Most news media recognize that the "growth
for growth's sake" ethic is no longer viable; editorial policy and
coverage should reflect that knowledge.

8. Finally, without surrendering balance and fairness in reporting, newsmen should give more attention to nongovernment,
nonindustry news sources. Often citizen groups, scientists, physicians,
and professional societies have useful contributions to make in solving
environmental problems. However, they frequently are ignored
because they do not have the massive public information apparatus of
business and government.

The scientific and medical communities might consider the
following suggestions for improving their lines of communication with
the public:

1. Scientists, and physicians in particular, should assume a
more active role in communicating with the public on issues of
environmental health.

2. The scientific community should appreciate more fully the
problems of science and environmental reporting. Such reporters
are now in a difficult period of readjustment and transition and can
use all the information and assistance scientists can provide.

3. Scientists should adopt a more cooperative attitude toward
the media. More university medical centers and public health agencies
should have technically trained individuals—not public relations
personnel—available to aid in this effort. They would act as an
interface between the media and the scientific-medical community.

4. Private hospitals, clinics, and health maintenance organizations (HMOs), particularly in cities without a university medical
center, should consider hiring a scientific information officer who

would be qualified to discuss with reporters a wide range of environmental issues.

5. Physicians and research scientists have a responsibility to
continue the development of a social consciousness in which actions
and decisions are placed in perspective so that the consequences to
individuals and society are considered.

6. Scientific and county medical societies also should establish
professional committees to investigate environmental health problems.
These committees should plan and produce public education programs,
including a series of articles on topics appropriate for use in newspaper
Sunday supplements; regular radio and television broadcasts on local
stations, which could be sponsored by such agencies as Blue Cross-
Blue Shield or pharmaceutical houses; and advertising campaigns,
when appropriate, such as the widely discussed American Cancer
Society series against cigarette smoking.

7. Scientific and medical organizations should cosponsor with
journalistic organizations seminars for reporters, editors, and
scientists. They should provide both basic background knowledge and
specialized information. Such programs not only can break down
stereotypes and improve communication between scientist and
journalist but also can give scientists a greater understanding of
media problems.

Since 1969 the news media have successfully spread throughout
the United States an ethic and perspective previously appreciated by
only a few. Augmenting that philosophy of environmental protection
to permit insightful understanding and action is difficult. How can a
reporter distinguish between environmental change and environmental
damage, or evaluate the rupture of life support chains, the development of incipient health hazards, or the esthetic loss of clear skies
and natural vistas? What standards can be established as a full
generation matures which does not know the meaning of clean air and
water? Resolution of these questions requires that the reporter have
some of the insight of the biologist.

In his classic book The Forest and the Sea, biologist Marston
Bates poses the following problem:

> People often come to me with some strange animal they
> have found. "What is it?" they ask.
>   Frequently I can't say—sometimes I get a despairing
> feeling of never knowing the answers to questions people
> ask. But at least I know where to look it up; or I know
> someone who is an expert on that kind of animal, so I can
> relay the question to him. And once in a while I know the
> answer.

"Oh," I say brightly, "that is a swallotail butterfly, Papilio cresphontes."

It is curious how happy people are to have a name for something, for an animal or plant, even though they know nothing about it beyond the name. I wonder whether there isn't some lingering element of word magic here, some feeling that knowing the name gives you power over the thing named—the sort of feeling that leads members of some savage tribes to conceal their personal names from all except their intimates. An enemy, learning their name, might be able to use this power for some evil purpose.

But other questions follow, "Where does it live?" and "What does it do?"

I explain that it is a tropical butterfly, common in Florida, which sometimes gets quite far north in the United States. The caterpillar lives on plants of the orange family, and north of Florida the butterfly is usually associated with prickly ash, which is a relative of the orange.

Almost inevitably there will come another question, "What good is it?"

I have never learned how to deal with this question. I am left appalled by the point of view that makes it possible. I don't know where to start explaining the world of nature that the biologist sees, in which, "What good is it?" becomes meaningless. The question is left over from the Middle Ages; from a small, cozy universe in which everything had a purpose in relation to man. The question comes down from the days before Copernicus' theories removed the earth from the center of the solar system, before Newton provided a mechanism for the movements of the stars, before Hutton discovered the immensity of past time, before Darwin's ideas put man into perspective with the rest of the living world.

Faced with astronomical space and geological time, faced with the immense diversity of living forms, how can one ask of one particular kind of butterfly, "What good is it?"

Often my reaction is to ask in turn, "What good are you?"

Science has put man in his place; one among the millions of kinds of living things crawling around on the surface of a minor planet circling a trivial star. We can't really face the implications of this, and perhaps it is just as well—though I think humility is in general improving for the human character. A billion years into the past and a

billion light-years into space remain abstractions that we
can handle glibly, but hardly realize. We remain important, you and I and all mankind. But so is the butterfly—
not because it is good for food or good for making medicine
or bad because it eats our orange trees. It is important
in itself, as a part of the economy of nature.

    The question ought to be, not "What good is it?" but
"What is its role in the economy of nature?"[1]

    This point of view is central to understanding biology and ecology.
As a consequence, human-created environmental changes can only be
judged beneficial or deleterious in terms of human societal values.
From a biological and evolutionary perspective, change is neither
good nor bad. It merely happens. In fact, change constantly occurs
in the biological world and organisms either adapt, migrate, or die.
The changes that confront organisms can occur over thousands of
years, as in the eutrophication of a lake, or can be cataclysmic, as
was the eruption of Krakatoa. Organisms and species that can adapt
survive; those that lack flexibility die. In this way, the evolution of
species continues.

    We commonly hear that eutrophication is an "environmental
problem." Such usage is ambiguous since it does not clearly state for
whom the event is a problem. While eutrophication forces trout,
sturgeon, pike, and walleye to seek other places to live, it poses no
problem for the carp and bream that take their place. Looking at the
situation, a man might say that there is a problem for the trout and
other game fish. He also might consider this a problem for himself
since he likes to eat game fish and can no longer obtain them. He
also might say that man experiences a problem when the lake eutrophies
because the blue-green algae and bacteria, which now thrive there,
produce noxious odors. Such a state of affairs obviously is not a
problem for the microbes; the environment is ideal for their continued
growth and reproduction.

    When someone says there is an environmental problem, he
usually is implying there is a problem for man. Man's position in
nature is unique. Not only does he produce changes in the environment but he also makes value judgments about the changes he produces,
about environmental alterations that other natural events create,
and about the biological adaptations that result. Only man can say
that a specific natural event is good or bad or that a change he has
wrought is beneficial.

    It is important for man to realize that he can produce change
in some areas much more rapidly than would occur without his
influence. He can cause a lake to eutrophy in decades instead of
millenia. A few people might say that this increased rate of change

is good. Others, more oriented to the idea that man is only one
component of the ecosystem, would say that change at the pace man
sets is deleterious. But it is important for those of us who hold this
latter view to realize that we, too, have made a value judgment, for
biologically a eutrophied lake is neither good nor bad. Eutrophication
is merely one stage in the evolution of any lake.

We lack the knowledge to predict accurately the environmental
consequences of many of our acts. This fact is painfully evident
throughout our study, and it is a fact that causes great anguish to
newsmen who must assess the news value of events affecting the
environment.

The consequences of permitting a nuclear power plant to heat
the water it discharges, or of constructing the California Water Project, are difficult to report. It is a challenge to communicate information about such slowly developing areas. But this is a responsibility
the mass media must assume. We must overcome these barriers to
effective communication if we are to have an informed citizenry that
is able to perceive that man is not the center of the ecosystem any
more than the earth is the center of the universe. Biological evolution
and the environment are neutral to man's continued presence. Only
man can really care about his existence on this planet. Whether or
not he is here to enjoy them, time and the river keep on flowing.

THE ENVIRONMENTAL REPORTER

Mail Questionnaire to Bay Area Editors
and Environmental Reporters

As a first step in the environmental project, a mail survey of
Bay Area newsmen was made to determine their standards, or meta-
ethic. The information solicited falls into four categories: (1) a
description of Bay Area environmental reporters; (2) their definitions
of environmental reporting; (3) their views on the quality of Bay Area
environmental coverage; and (4) their standards for handling past,
present, and future environmental stories.

The questionnaires for the survey had a response rate of 80
percent after two mailings. The unusually high response rate may
have resulted from somewhat personalized canvassing methods, as
well as from current interest in the subject.

Each questionnaire was accompanied not only by the usual form
covering letter but also by a personal handwritten note on a separate
piece of stationery. These notes were made possible because the
addressee or someone in his organization had been contacted at least
twice earlier in the process of preparing the questionnaire:

1. David M. Rubin, student leader for the overall project, wrote
to each organization at the beginning of the project describing the
undertaking and asking the editor or news director addressed for his
cooperation and participation. Letters in reply to Rubin's letter could
be answered in the personal notes accompanying the questionnaire.

2. Each organization was telephoned about two months before
the questionnaire was mailed in order to get a list of the environment
reporters in the Bay Area. At the same time, the impending questionnaire was mentioned and the editor's support requested. (A few more
names were added to the list when editors indicated on returned
questionnaires that they had environment reporters who were not
mentioned in the telephone survey.)

In addition, preliminary interviews were conducted with six
Bay Area newsmen, further acquainting their organizations with the
study. George Dusheck of KQED, Fred Garretson of the Oakland
Tribune, Tom Harris of the San Jose Mercury, and Bruce Brugmann
of the Bay Guardian discussed general plans for the study. The

261

questionnaire was pretested in personal interviews with Ken Castle
of the Fremont Argus as a newspaper reporter, Robert Burgess of
the Palo Alto Times as a newspaper (city) editor, Ben Williams of
KPIX-TV as a broadcast reporter, and Chet Casselman of KSFO
radio as a broadcast news director.

Two forms of the questionnaire were developed, one for editors
and news directors and one for environment reporters; there were
several different questions at the beginning of the questionnaire, with
the last four the same in each case. A first mailing was sent on
October 12, 1970, with the follow up on October 26.

The 52 organizations surveyed included all the daily newspapers
in the nine-county Bay Area, "weeklies which have shown an interest
in environmental reporting," and all broadcasting stations with independent (not "rip and read") news operations. The editor form of the
questionnaire was sent to the managing editor or equivalent at each
newspaper and the news director at each broadcast station, usually
someone the project had contacted previously. The reporter form
went to reporters these editors had named: 33 organizations, or 63
percent, had reporters they could call environmental, in a few cases
more than one, for a total of 40 reporters.

In general the questionnaires were filled out more completely,
quickly, and cheerfully than expected. Twelve respondents checked
the option requesting anonymity, although "Don't give a damn" was
another reaction. There was a higher return rate for reporters (83
percent) than for editors (79 percent). The reporters also tended to
make longer and more frequent comments than editors.

A comparison of responses from individual reporters shows a
significant relationship between amount of time the reporter spends
on environment and whether he views himself as having an environment
beat:

		Viewed Self as Having Environment Beat				
			To Some		No	
		Yes	Extent	No	Answer	Total
Time spent	25% or less	2	9	7	0	18
on envi-	26% or more	10	2	1	2	15
ronment	Total	12	11	8	$p < .01$	

The correlation between the editors' and their reporters' estimates
of time spent on environment is $I = .4$, $p < .01$. The correlation is identical between the editor's assessment of whether he has a special reporter and the reporter's view of whether he has an environment beat.

Description of Sample

Statistical results are based on responses received from 33
reporters (45 percent of the sample) and 41 editors (55 percent of the

sample) in 41 organizations. The organizations, staff size, and representation by county are shown in Tables A.1, A.2, and A.3.

TABLE A.1

Organizations in Survey of Bay Area
Environmental Reporters

Organization	Number of Respondents
TV	15
Radio	10
Daily newspapers	39
Weekly newspapers	10
Total	74

TABLE A.2

Staff Size of Organizations in Survey of
Bay Area Environmental Reporters

	Number of People							
	1-4	5-9	10-14	15-19	20-24	25-29	30-34	Over 34
Number of organizations	8	14	8	4	4	1	1	1

TABLE A.3

Representation by County of Organizations in Survey
of Bay Area Environmental Reporters

County	Density	Number of Respondents from Newspapers	Broadcasting
San Francisco	6,930 people/sq. mi.	7	20
Alameda	1,285	10	3
San Mateo	995	3	0
Santa Clara	787	7	2
Contra Costa	696	10	0
Marin	335	3	0
Solano	194	3	0
Sonoma	127	4	0
Napa	102	2	0
Total		49	25

Following are the questionnaires used in the survey, with marginals in percentages (scored) and a breakdown of the sample by type of organization, size of staff, and county.

"The Media & Environment" questionnaire was sent to editors and news directors; "Environment Reporting" was sent to environment reporters. The last four questions are the same on both questionnaires. Editors' and reporters' responses are given in percentages beside each answer.

Questionnaire to Editors

The Media & Environment
percent results

NAME: _____ ORGANIZATION: _____ POSITION: <u>EDITORS</u>

Check here if you wish your answers to remain anonymous. _____
Any comments, qualifications, or elaborations will be appreciated.

1. Approximately what is the size of your reporting staff? (Count reporters, editors, news directors, but not cameramen, copy-editors, etc.)   <u>20%</u> 1-4 people
                                     <u>34%</u> 5-9
   NUMBER OF   <u>19%</u> 10-14
   PEOPLE   <u>10%</u> 15-19
                <u>10%</u> 20-24
                 <u>8%</u> 25 (+)

2. In covering local environmental stories, do you:
   <u>22%</u> (a) give them usually to a special reporter (or reporters) who has an environment beat?
   <u>39%</u> (b) give them usually to a particular reporter (or reporters) although he has no formal environment beat?
   <u>39%</u> (c) spread them throughout the staff in general?

3. IF YOUR ANSWER TO NO. 2 WAS (a) OR (b), that is, if a particular reporter tends to handle environment stories, please answer the following. Otherwise, skip to question no. 4.

   i. On the average, how much of your special reporter's (reporters') time is spent on stories you would consider environmental?
      <u>72%</u> 0-25% of his (their) time   <u>20%</u>   51-75%
       <u>4%</u> 26-50%   <u>4%</u>   76-100%
   ii. How long have you had a special reporter for environmental stories?
      <u>16%</u> 0-6 months   <u>24%</u>   1-3 years
      <u>36%</u> 12 months   <u>20%</u>   over 3 years

iii. Under what circumstances did you acquire a special reporter?
Check as many items as apply.

12% Someone from outside was hired specifically for
the job.

36% Someone already on the staff was assigned to the
job.

32% Someone gradually handled more and more environment stories.

32% Someone covered beats which naturally included
environment, such as regional government, public
affairs, etc.

___ Other:

___ Details:

4. IF YOUR ANSWER TO NO. 2 WAS (c), that is, if you spread environment stories throughout the staff in general, please answer the
following. Otherwise, skip to question no. 5.

i. Check as many items as apply. Environmental stories are not
given to any special reporter because:

25% such subjects can be covered just as well by general
assignment reporters.

6% such subjects can be covered better by general
assignment reporters.

19% we do not have enough local environment stories
to justify a specialist.

63% we cannot afford a specialist.

0% no one on the staff is capable of handling such a beat.

0% we are looking for someone to be a special reporter
now.

___ other:

5. How would you assess the performance of the wire services in
providing your organization with environmental news?
2% excellent 27% good 41% mediocre 10% poor
Comments: 20% had no wire service

6. Do you feel your organization has adequately covered the California
Water Plan?
Comments: 51% Yes   49% No

7. Are you personally active in any conservation or ecology groups
outside of work?
15% Yes   83% No
If yes, in what organizations?

8. The following is a list of hypothetical situations. Please indicate whether your decision would be "yes" or "no" in each case. Comments about the reasons for your decisions would also be appreciated.

    i. You become aware through a reliable source that a local smelting plant is discarding pollutants into the Bay every night, although no organized citizen or government group has yet raised the issue. Would you cover the story?

        95% Yes   2% No

        Comments:

    ii. A canning factory proposed to move into your area, and no one has brought up the possibility that the factory might pollute nearby waters. Would you investigate the pollution possibility?

        76% Yes   17% No

        Comments:

    iii. An oil company which is one of your heavy advertisers has been advertising a new home pesticide. A reliable research team reports that the product is harmful to children and pets.

Would you cover the story?	95% Yes	0% No
Would you need approval from a higher executive level before covering the story?	10% Yes	88% No
Would you need approval of the publisher or station owner before covering the story?	5% Yes	95% No
Would you need to inform the advertising or sales manager if you were covering the story?	2% Yes	93% No
Would you check the research results with other sources to a greater extent than if the oil company were not an advertiser?	12% Yes	85% No

        Comments:

9. There seems to be considerably more information about environmental issues available to the public through the mass media today than there was a few years ago. What do you think might have caused the media's increased coverage of environment as a news story?

54% public demand or interest   30% pollution itself
5% conservationist pressure   23% Ehrlich, Nixon, other
                                      newsworthy stories
15% media leadership

10. Do you think the current attention to environment information is a fad? Or will it continue to be important for some time?

10% fad   78% continuing importance
            7% both

Comments:

11. (a) The following is a list of hypothetical news stories. Please place a check mark beside those which you consider to be "environment" stories.

7% A new heart transplant is performed at Stanford Hospital.

80% A city zoning change is proposed on the local ballot such that a large residential area near downtown can be converted to commercial use.

71% Power shortages like the New York "brownouts" are predicted for the Bay Area by summer 1971.

100% Increases in pulmonary disease in the Bay Area are traced to a common element in smog.

5% A bill is passed prohibiting busing of school children.

100% A citizen group is formed to protest airplane noise from a nearby airport.

29% A sugar substitute similar to cyclamates is linked to cancer in dogs.

83% A University of California research team projects smaller increases in population than were previously supposed.

95% Scientists report that shellfish are losing their shells in coastal areas with high levels of nitrogen fertilizers.

49% A section of underground rapid transit is opened for public use.

27% A tidal wave is predicted for the Peninsula coast line.

56% An increase in the popularity of IUD birth control devices among American women is reported.

95% A sewage recycling plant is set up in a neighboring town.

(b) Please define briefly what the term "environment reporting"
     means to you.
Thank you very much.

Questionnaire to Environmental Reporters

Environment Reporting
percent results

NAME: _____ ORGANIZATION: _____ POSITION: <u>REPORTERS</u>

Check here if you wish your answers to remain anonymous._____
Any comments, qualifications, or elaborations will be appreciated.

1. On the average, what percentage of your working time is spent
    covering stories you would consider environmental?
    <u>55</u>% 1-25%   <u>9</u>% 51-75%
    <u>15</u>% 26-50%   <u>18</u>% 76-100%

2. Do you view yourself as having an
    environment beat?   <u>36</u>% Yes   <u>27</u>% No
                                        <u>33</u>% To some extent

3. Do you hold any other jobs, free-
    lance or part-time?   <u>30</u>% Yes   <u>67</u>% No

4. Are you personally active in any conservation or ecology groups
    outside of work? If yes, in what organizations?
                                        <u>18</u>% Yes   <u>82</u>% No

5. (a) How old are you? ____years <u>18</u>% 20-24 yrs. <u>30</u>% 25-29 yrs.
                                     <u>18</u>% 30-34 yrs. <u>34</u>% 35(+) yrs.

    (b) How many years have you been a newsman? ____years
                                     <u>42</u>% 1-4 yrs.   <u>18</u>% 5-9 yrs.
                                                         <u>12</u>% 10-14 yrs.

    (c) What beats have you covered?
         <u>14</u>% science <u>25</u>% general <u>50</u>% government <u>2</u>% none other

    (d) Did you <u>0</u>   graduate from high school?
                  <u>21</u>%   attend college? Major: _____
                  <u>48</u>   graduate from college? Major: _____
                                                        Degree: _____
                  <u>27</u>   do graduate work? Field: _____
                                                 Degree: _____

6. Would you check the sources of environmental information you
    use frequently:
         <u>30</u>% scientific journals   <u>36</u>% industry news releases
         <u>61</u>% conservation publications <u>48</u>% industry spokesmen

73% conservation groups & spokesmen

18% industry task force reports

48% seminars, institutes, conventions

55% government agency releases

48% university news releases

52% government spokesmen

48% university professors

24% government task force reports

27% university task force reports

64% own field work

other mass media: 73% newspapers   18% radio   24% TV
73% magazines

others: _____

7. What magazines, books, journals, etc. do you read which you find helpful for environmental reporting in general?

30% Sierra Club
39% other conservation publications

15% Time, Newsweek

24% scientific journals
12% none

8. What particular problems do you have covering environment stories? Check as many items as apply.

33% difficulty finding a source which can give me a particular item of information.

27% difficulty translating the jargon of the specialist into the language of my audience

67% too little time to investigate the story properly

15% too little space from editors or air time from directors

0% pressure not to cite companies which are polluting but are advertisers

3% pressure to cover or not to cover stories, pressure from groups such as:

_____

3% "local boosterism": pressure, for instance, not to discourage industry or real estate from coming into the community

18% lack of reader or listener interest

12% difficulty fitting the story into a larger perspective, showing its relationship to general environmental problems

___ others:

9. Are there any environmental issues which your organization is not covering which you feel should be covered? If so, what are they? And why are they not covered?

61% mentioned at least one issue

10. Do you feel your organization has adequately covered the California Water Plan?   51% Yes   45% No

   Comments:

11. The following is a list of hypothetical situations. Please indicate whether your decision would be "yes" or "no" in each case. Comments about the reasons for your decisions would also be appreciated.

   i. You become aware through a reliable source that a local smelting plant is discarding pollutants into the Bay every night, although no organized citizen or government group has yet raised the issue. Would you cover the story?

      90% Yes   9% No
      Comments:

   ii. A canning factory proposes to move into your area, and no one has brought up the possibility that the factory might pollute nearby waters. Would you investigate the pollution possibility?

      73% Yes   27% No
      Comments:

   iii. An oil company which is one of your heavy advertisers has been advertising a new home pesticide. A reliable research team reports that the product is harmful to children and pets.

      Would you cover the story?   97% Yes   0% No
      Would you need approval from
      a higher executive level before
      covering the story?   21% Yes   76% No
      Would you need approval of the
      publisher or station owner before
      covering the story?   9% Yes   88% No
      Would you need to inform the
      advertising or sales manager if
      you were covering the story?   6% Yes   91% No
      Would you check the research
      results with other sources to a
      greater extent than if the oil
      company were not an advertiser?   6% Yes   88% No
      Comments:

12. There seems to be considerably more information about environment issues available to the public through the mass media today than there was a few years ago. What do you think might have

caused the media's increased coverage of environment as a news story?

42% public demand or interest   21% pollution itself
12% conservationist pressure   24% Ehrlich, Nixon, other
                                      newsworthy stories
15% media leadership

13. Do you think the current attention to environment information is a fad? Or will it continue to be important for some time?

6% fad   76% continuing importance
          18% both

Comments:

14. (a) The following is a list of hypothetical news stories. Please place a check mark beside those which you consider to be "environment" stories.

12% A new heart transplant is performed at Stanford Hospital.
73% A city zoning change is proposed on the local ballot such that a large residential area near downtown can be converted to commercial use.
73% Power shortages like the New York "brownouts" are predicted for the Bay Area by summer 1971.
94% Increases in pulmonary disease in the Bay Area are traced to a common element in smog.
21% A bill is passed prohibiting busing of school children.
94% A citizen group is formed to protest airplane noise from a nearby airport.
42% A sugar substitute similar to cyclamates is linked to cancer in dogs.
91% A University of California research team projects smaller increases in population than were previously supposed.
91% Scientists report that shellfish are losing their shells in coastal areas with high levels of nitrogen fertilizers.
58% A section of underground rapid transit is opened for public use.
30% A tidal wave is predicted for the Peninsula coast line.
48% An increase in the popularity of IUD birth control devices among American women is reported.
94% A sewage recycling plant is set up in a neighboring town.

(b) Please define briefly what the term "environment reporting" means to you.

Thank you very much.

THE ENVIRONMENTAL PSEUDO-EVENT

Sampling and Coding of Newspaper Coverage

To analyze newspaper coverage of the Stanford air pollution report, a content analysis of 28 daily papers in nine Bay Area counties was conducted. A "daily" was defined as a newspaper publishing at least five days a week. The week-long sample period began September 9,1970, the day prior to the press conference announcing the Groth report, and concluded September 15. Papers included in the sample, by county, were as follows:

San Francisco:	San Francisco Chronicle
	San Francisco Examiner
San Mateo:	Redwood City Tribune
	San Mateo Times
Santa Clara:	San Jose Mercury
	San Jose News
	Palo Alto Times
Alameda:	Oakland Tribune
	Hayward Review
	Berkeley Gazette
	Fremont News-Register
	San Leandro Morning News
	Alameda Times-Star
	Livermore Herald and News
	Fremont Argus
Marin:	San Rafael Independent-Journal
Solano:	Vallejo Times-Herald
	Vallejo News-Chronicle
	Fairfield-Suisun Daily Republic
Napa:	Napa Register
Sonoma:	Santa Rosa Press-Democrat
	Petaluma Argus-Courier
Contra Costa:	Richmond Independent
	Contra Costa Times
	Concord Daily Transcript
	Antioch Ledger

Pittsburg Post-Dispatch
Martinez Morning News-Gazette

The basic unit of the content analysis was the individual news
story, feature story, or editorial whose predominant subject matter
dealt with the Groth report. (There were no borderline cases regarding subject matter in the data. The individual articles, including
headline and any graphics, constituted both the recording unit and
the context units.) Each article was analyzed according to the following categories:

    1. Space allotted to item: recorded as column-inch length,
rounded off to nearest inch; photos, graphics, and headline space
measured as part of article.
    2. Type of item: recorded as news story, feature story, or
editorial.
    3. Prominence: recorded as page number on which story began.
    4. Authorship: recorded as name of reporter (if bylined), name
of wire service (if given); stories also were compared with the Stanford
News Service press releases to ascertain which sections of media
coverage were paraphrases or verbatim reprints of news release
material.
    5. Thematic issues: ten thematic issues were selected from the
Stanford air pollution report and their presence or absence in newspaper
articles published during the sample period was coded. The presence
or absence of the issues was taken as an index of how completely
individual newspapers informed their readership about the breadth of
topics contained in the Groth report. Two of the issues—(e) and (f)
below—were chosen as indicators of how the individual newspapers
covered the performances of local industries and elected officials,
and another (j) as an indicator of whether the paper prescribed for
its readership specific courses of anti-pollution action, which were
detailed in one section of the Stanford report. The presence of each
issue was coded if even the most general mention of it was made in
the article; i.e., the quantity of coverage given any issue was not
considered in constructing this index (although such information was
noted in a more general outline which was made for the contents of
each story). The following issues were coded:

    a. BAAPCD ineffectiveness in controlling air pollution.
    b. Report's evaluation of BAAPCD Board of Directors (as entire
       group) and/or BAAPCD Advisory Council (as entire group).
    c. Industrial involvement or influence in BAAPCD policy-making.
    d. Attitudes of industries (as entire group) about pollution
       control.

  e. Evaluation of industries located in county where newspaper
     publishes (if applicable).
  f. Evaluation of performance of BAAPCD directors from county
     where newspaper publishes (if applicable).
  g. Environmental impact of automobiles and/or need for
     restructuring transportation systems.
  h. Miscellaneous sources of pollution (other than autos or industry).
  i. Any results from public opinion polls Groth report in.
  j. Suggested activities for general public.

Coding operations were performed solely by the author of this
study. Consequently, no precise statistic can be offered as a measure
of reliability in repeated operations by different coders. The data for
the analysis was quite compact, especially after articles had been
collected from the newspapers. Ironically, this was an instance when
the most revealing feature of the data was the absence of much of it;
i.e., the failure of 11 out of 28 newspapers sampled to provide any
coverage of the Groth report. The newspaper article search and the
coding operations were performed twice (with similar results) to
provide an additional check against error. This information about the
absence of a reliability statistic is intended, then, not as an apology
for any suspected miscalculations in the research but rather for the
benefit of any readers who may be statistical purists.

Study of Broadcast Coverage

To gain perspective on television and radio coverage of the
Stanford air pollution report, transcripts of broadcasts pertaining to
the report were solicited from operations directors of 15 stations.
Television stations included KGO, KPIX, KRON, and KQED, all in
San Francisco; KTVU and KBHK in Oakland; and KNTV in San Jose.
Radio outlets included KCBS, KGO, KSFO, KNBR, KFRC, and KSAN,
all in San Francisco; KNEW in Oakland; and KPFA in Berkeley. These
represented the largest broadcasting outlets with news staffs in the
Bay Area.
Seven stations (5 television, 2 radio) replied to the query. Most
said actual transcripts of coverage were not available; two indicated
they were unaware of the report. (Unlike newspapers, broadcast
stations apparently do not maintain a morgue of their previous coverage
that can easily be accessed by the public or used as background material
for their own reporters.) Some directors offered recollections of
specific coverage of the Groth report, but the accuracy of these comments is, naturally, a matter of speculation. The author of this study
did monitor several stations in the Bay Area (as indicated in the text

of the report), but the observations about their coverage are empirical because the research was not systematic in the manner of the newspaper content analysis. The absence of hard data makes evaluation of the overall quality of broadcast coverage problematical, although the comments on specific stations featured in the report represent factual accounts. The author regrets that the section on broadcast coverage lacks the specificity of that on newspapers, but calls the reader's attention to the disparity.

There are at least two other possible influences on media coverage of the Groth report that our sampling procedures could have obscured. First, the sample, designed to test the initial wave of coverage, extended for only six days following the press conference. A journalist conceivably could have written a feature story dealing in part or entirely with the study and it might have been published more than a week after the press conference. Certainly, the possibility of cutting off a sample too soon besets nearly all research studies utilizing this method. An additional question arises concerning the future use of the Stanford study as an information source for the media. Reporters with an interest in environmental coverage may have filed the report, planning to use it as a reference in future stories dealing with air pollution problems in the Bay Area. In such an instance, the report could have a long-range impact that a one-week sample would not reveal.

ACCESS TO ENVIRONMENTAL INFORMATION

Sample Coding Sheet for Content Analysis of
Newspaper Coverage of Nuclear Power

Paper
Date
Type of Article:　( )　Article with News Peg (check one or more)
　　　　　　　　　　( )　Notice of upcoming decision, public
　　　　　　　　　　　　　hearing, meeting, or conference
　　　　　　　　　　( )　Utility statement made or report of
　　　　　　　　　　　　　action taken
　　　　　　　　　　( )　Government statement made or report
　　　　　　　　　　　　　of action taken
　　　　　　　　　　( )　Citizen or nongovernment scientist
　　　　　　　　　　　　　statement made or report of action
　　　　　　　　　　　　　taken
　　　　　　　　　　( )　Summary of public hearings, public
　　　　　　　　　　　　　meetings, or conferences
　　　　　　　　　　( )　Release and/or summary of a report
　　　　　　　　　　　　　from any source (which is not required
　　　　　　　　　　　　　by the siting procedure)
　　　　　　　　　　( )　Report of a brownout or blackout
　　　　　　　　　　( )　Other news peg
　　　　　　　　( )　Non-News Peg Article: that is, a general in-
　　　　　　　　　　formation story on nuclear power plants,
　　　　　　　　　　radiation standards, electric power, etc.
　　　　　　　　( )　Editorial
　　　　　　　　( )　Column (author)
　　　　　　　　( )　Ad (paid for by)
　　　　　　　　( )　Letter
Length:　( )　1-10 column-inches
　　　　　　　　( )　11-20 column-inches　　( )　Art (columns x depth)
　　　　　　　　( )　21-30 column-inches　　( )　Ad size (columns
　　　　　　　　( )　over 30 column-inches　　　　x depth)
Location (give page)
Head/Kicker
Dateline, if not local

Credit for news article: ( ) Local byline
                                      ( ) Local no byline
                                      ( ) Bureau story byline
                                      ( ) Bureau story no byline
                                      ( ) Wire service
                                      ( ) Special service (identify)

ADVERSARY QUESTIONS COVERED IN CODED ARTICLE

A. ( ) Effects of radiation on plant and animal life
B. ( ) Adequacy of radiation protection standards
C. ( ) Possibility of plant accident
D. ( ) Adequacy of insurance (Price-Anderson Act) in case of plant accident
E. ( ) Potential impact of thermal discharge on marine life
F. ( ) Cooling technology
G. ( ) Adequacy of methods for transport and/or disposal of radioactive wastes apart from radioactive plant discharges
H. ( ) Aesthetic arguments on the plant siting
I. ( ) Costs to consumer of the electric power produced by the nuclear power plant
J. ( ) Future availability of nuclear and/or fossil fuels
K. ( ) Any economic impact of the nuclear power plant on the site community, such as change in land values, availability of jobs, etc.
L. ( ) A non-evaluative description of the siting procedure
M. ( ) Attacks or defenses of the siting procedure (involving the AEC, PUC, State Power Plant Siting Committee, government officials, etc.)
N. ( ) Points at which the public can, or has, become involved in the siting procedure
O. ( ) The demand for more electric power in California/United States
P. ( ) The effects of increased power consumption for California/United States
Q. ( ) The effects of decreased power consumption for California/United States
R. ( ) The possibility of developing technologies other than nuclear power to produce electricity
S. ( ) The necessity for a speed-up in the siting procedure for nuclear power plants
T. ( ) The necessity of a slow-down or moratorium in the siting of nuclear power plants
   ( ) Other issues in the coded article in which adversarity is expressed or implied

In case of editorial, column, or letter, summarize briefly the position taken:

List all individuals, agencies, organizations, businesses, etc., which ar
not already listed above as information sources, along with the context
of the mention, where appropriate (such as a "no comment")

Comments, where coder feels it is appropriate, on the nature of the
non-adversary information in the article or on the general tone and
content of the article

Questionnaire on Nuclear Power Plants and the Press:
Form for Editors*

Editor/Newspaper   Plant name

N = 67

( ) Please check here if you would like a copy of the results of this
     survey.

1. How important a story for your readers do you consider the siting
    and construction of the above-named nuclear power plant?

    71.6% ( ) Very important, meriting large news play
    25.4% ( ) Of above-average importance, meriting moderate news
                 play
    3.0% ( ) Of some importance, meriting small news play
    — ( ) Of slight importance, meriting no news play
    — ( ) Other (please specify)

2. Is it the type of story your paper has the facilities (i.e., time,
    manpower, money, space, etc.) to cover as you would like?

    82.1% ( ) Yes
    17.9% ( ) No   If no, which factors make it difficult to cover?

3. Do you feel that there is another daily in your area better equipped,
    either because of its location or its resources, to cover this
    story?

    18.8% ( ) Yes   If yes, which daily? (N = 69 for this question
    78.2% ( ) No   only.)
    3.0%   No answer

---

*Marginals, in percentage are underscored.

4. Do you feel that it is the type of story that justifies running a
    special series of "in-depth" articles?

    <u>74.6%</u> ( ) Yes   (If your paper ran such a series and it would
    <u>22.4%</u> ( ) No   not be too much trouble, we would be
     <u>3.0%</u>   No answer   most anxious to see some clips.)

5. Were the reporters who covered the story (multiple responses
    permitted):

    <u>76.0%</u> ( ) General assignment writers
    <u>10.4%</u> ( ) Business writers
    <u>22.4%</u> ( ) Science writers
     <u>3.0%</u> ( ) Political writers
    <u>10.4%</u> ( ) Other (please specify)
     <u>9.0%</u> ( ) We did not staff the story ourselves
    <u>14.9%</u> ( ) Environment writer

6. When in the history of the plant did you begin running stories on
    utility plans? (Check one or more.)

    <u>20.9%</u> ( ) Before land had been purchased for the site
    <u>26.8%</u> ( ) As soon as the land had been purchased
    <u>13.2%</u> ( ) When the utility applied for the first permit or license
    <u>44.7%</u> ( ) When the utility first announced its plans to the public
                       (which may coincide with one of the above)
     <u>6.0%</u> ( ) Other (please specify)
     <u>3.0%</u>   No answer

7. Have you or your reporters had difficulty getting complete informa-
    tion from utility officials on siting and construction plans, the
    environmental impact of the plant, or other aspects of nuclear
    power?

    <u>25.4%</u> ( ) Yes   If Yes, please explain:
    <u>73.1%</u> ( ) No
     <u>1.5%</u>   Don't know

8. In covering the affairs of a private, investor-owned utility (as
    opposed to a public, municipally-owned utility), do you feel your
    reporters would be helped by an extension of your state's open
    record and open meeting laws to cover private utilities?

    <u>59.7%</u> ( ) Yes
    <u>31.3%</u> ( ) No
     <u>9.0%</u>   No answer

9. Would you support such extensions of these laws?

73.1% ( ) Yes
9.0% ( ) No
17.9%   No answer

10. Did your paper take an editorial position on the siting and con- struction of the nuclear plant?

47.7% ( ) Yes   If yes, what was that position? Pro   78.2%
47.7% ( ) No   Con   18.7%
4.6%   No answer   No
                                                              answer 3.1%

11. Did your paper receive any letters-to-the-editor on the subject of the plant?

80.6% ( ) Yes   If yes, (a) please estimate the number of
16.5% ( ) No   letters and (b) indicate if this was a large
3.0%   No answer or small number to have received from
                         your community: (a)_____

      (b) **Large number**   ⎱
          Above average number ⎰ 33.3%
          Average number   31.5%
          Below average number ⎱
          Small number   ⎰ 31.5%
          No answer   3.7%

12. Did the utility, plant opponents, or plant supporters use your paper to advertise their feelings on the pros and cons of nuclear power plants?

37.3% ( ) Yes   If yes, which group(s)
55.2% ( ) No   so advertised? Both   24.0%
7.5%   No answer   Utility   44.0%
                                    Opponents 12.0%
                                    No answer 20.0%

13. How do you think <u>utility officials</u> would rate your coverage of the plant?

67.2% ( ) Thorough, fair, and balanced
10.4% ( ) Thin but fair and balanced
  — ( ) Thorough, biased pro-utility
  — ( ) Thin, biased pro-utility
13.4% ( ) Thorough, biased anti-utility
1.5% ( ) Thin, biased anti-utility

3.0% ( ) Other (please specify)
4.5%   No answer

14. How do you think <u>opponents of the plant</u> in your area (if any) would
     rate your coverage?

     50.7% ( ) Thorough, fair, and balanced
     19.4% ( ) Thin but fair and balanced
     13.4% ( ) Thorough, biased pro-utility
      4.5% ( ) Thin, biased pro-utility
       — ( ) Thorough, biased anti-utility
       — ( ) Thin, biased anti-utility
      1.5% ( ) Other (please specify)
      4.5% ( ) There were no opponents of the plan in this area
      6.0%   No answer

15. Do you believe the manner in which you covered this issue had
     any direct or indirect effect on utility plans for the plant?

     26.9% ( ) Yes   If yes, please explain:
     67.1% ( ) No
      6.0%   Don't know

16. What do you think the appropriate role (if any) of one of your
     citizen-readers should be in the decision-making process on
     nuclear plants?

     38.8%   Active
     20.9%   Unclear
     14.9%   Passive
     25.4%   No answer

17. Do you believe a newspaper should develop in its pages the debate
     over nuclear power (once it becomes known that a plant is to
     be built in the area) regardless of whether or not there is an
     organized citizens' effort against it?

     70.1% ( ) Yes   For either reply, please explain:
     17.9% ( ) No
     12.0%   No answer

18. Additional remarks welcome below or on back:

( ) If you wish your answers to remain anonymous, please check
     here.

Questionnaire on Nuclear Power Plants and the Press:
Form For Utility Executives*

Utility   Plant Name

N = 37

( )   Please check here if you would like a copy of the results of this
       survey.

1.   How important a news story for your customers do you feel your
       plans were for the siting and construction of the above-named
       nuclear power plant(s)?

       62.2% ( ) Very important, meriting large news play
       32.4% ( ) Of above-average importance, meriting moderate
                     news play
        5.4% ( ) Of some importance, meriting small news play
         —   ( ) Of slight importance, meriting no news play
         —   ( ) Other (please specify)

2.   Which daily newspaper (if any) do you feel has the responsibility
       of reporting your siting and construction plans (check one or
       more)?

       64.8% ( ) The local daily nearest the site, if one exists
       56.7% ( ) The metropolitan paper nearest the site
       43.2% ( ) The daily in your company's headquarters city
         —   ( ) No paper
       10.8% ( ) Other (please specify)
       13.5%   Weeklies

3.   When in the history of the plant did you make public your plans
       on location, type of fuel to be used, and the cooling procedure?
       (Multiple answers permitted.)

       21.6% ( ) Before land had been purchased for the site
       43.2% ( ) As soon as the land had been purchased
       10.8% ( ) When we applied for the first permit or license
       21.6% ( ) Other (please specify)
        2.7%   No answer

4.   How active has the press been in soliciting information from you
       about the plant and nuclear power?

       _____

       *Marginals, in percentages, are underscored.

56.8% $\left\{\begin{array}{l} (\ ) \ \text{Very active} \\ (\ ) \ \text{Active} \end{array}\right.$

32.4% $\left\{\begin{array}{l} (\ ) \ \text{Somewhat active} \\ (\ ) \ \text{Not very active} \end{array}\right.$

10.8% ( ) Passive; that is, we must take the initiative in supplying them with information

—   ( ) Other (please specify)

5. Have any newspapers in your area done what you feel to be an
    excellent job of coverage?

    67.5% ( ) Yes   If yes, please name the paper and provide a
                         brief description:
    32.5% ( ) No

6. Do you feel existing utility-press relations are adequate to in-
    forming the public of your plans?

    78.4% ( ) Yes
    21.6% ( ) No   If no, please explain:

7. Did you advertise your views on nuclear power in the newspaper?

    35.1% ( ) Yes   If yes, in which paper(s)?
    64.9% ( ) No

8. How would you rate newspaper coverage of the nuclear power plant
    story in your area?

    52.7% ( ) Thorough, fair, and balanced
    23.8% ( ) Thin but fair and balanced
     2.3% ( ) Thorough, biased pro-utility
     2.3% ( ) Thin, biased pro-utility
    14.3% ( ) Thorough, biased anti-utility
     2.3% ( ) Thin, biased anti-utility
     —   ( ) Other (please specify)
     2.3%   No answer

9. Do you believe the manner in which the press covered this issue
    had any direct or indirect effect on your plans for the plant?

    24.3% ( ) Yes If yes, please explain:
    75.7% ( ) No

10. What do you think the appropriate role (if any) of your average
    electricity customer should be in the decision-making process
    on nuclear power plants?

51.4%   None
35.1%   Informed
10.8%   Active
2.7%   No answer

11.   Do you believe that a newspaper should develop in its pages the
       debate over nuclear power (once it becomes known that a
       plant is to be built in an area), regardless of whether or not
       there is an organized citizens' effort against it?

45.9% ( ) Yes   For either reply, please explain:
45.9% ( ) No
8.2%   No answer

12.   Additional remarks welcome below or on back:

( )   If you wish your answers to remain anonymous, please check
       here.

       Questionnaire on Nuclear Power Plants and the Press:
                  Form for Plant Opponents*

Opponent   Plant Name
                          N = 23

( )   Please check here if you would like a copy of the results of this
       survey.

1.   Which daily newspapers in your area do you read regularly?

2.   Which of these papers have run, at fairly regular intervals,
       articles describing the progress in siting, constructing, and
       operating the nuclear power plant mentioned above?

3.   Have any of the papers run an "in-depth" series of articles on
       nuclear power, explaining the pros and cons in the nuclear
       debate?

52.1% ( ) Yes   If yes, which ones?
47.9% ( ) No

───────────

*Marginals, in percentages are underscored.

4. Have the papers provided advance notice of upcoming public
    meetings, public hearings, utility decisions-to-be-made, etc.,
    so that the public can participate if it so chooses?

    73.9% ( ) Yes
    26.1% ( ) No   If no, please state the circumstances of the
                             omission:
    —   ( ) Don't know

5. When in the history of the plant did the press begin running
    stories on utility plans? (Check one or more.)

    13.0% ( ) Before land had been purchased for the site
     8.7% ( ) As soon as land had been purchased for the site
    21.7% ( ) When the utility applied for the first license or permit
    43.4% ( ) When the utility itself first announced its plans (which
                   may coincide with one of the above)
    30.4% ( ) Other (please specify)
    13.0% ( ) Don't know
    13.0%   Hearings

6. Have you or your fellow plant opponents had difficulty getting
    complete information from utility officials on siting and con-
    struction plans, the environmental impact of the plant, or
    other aspects of nuclear power?

    82.6% ( ) Yes   If yes, please explain:
    17.4% ( ) No

7. Has the press sought out you or your group's spokesman for your
    views on the plant and nuclear power?

    56.5% ( ) Yes
    39.1% ( ) No
     4.4%   No answer

8. Has the argument "for" or the argument "against" construction
    of the plant been made more fully in the press in your area?

    52.1% ( ) Argument "for" the plant
     8.7% ( ) Argument "against" the plant
    34.8% ( ) Arguments have been presented about equally
     4.4%   No answer

9. What are the editorial positions on the plant of the papers you
    read?

              Paper: Position:

53.3%   Pro
3.4%   Con
43.3%   Neutral or none

10. Do the papers print letters-to-the-editor about the nuclear power
     plant controversy?

     95.6% ( ) Yes If yes, do they print letters both for and against
                        the plant?
     4.4% ( ) No   If no, which side predominates?
                                        Equal numbers   45.4%
                                        Unequal numbers 31.8%
                                        No answer   22.8%

11. Does the utility advertise its position on nuclear power in the
     press?

     65.2% ( ) Yes
     30.4% ( ) No
     4.4% ( ) Don't know

12. Have plant opponents advertised their position on nuclear power
     in the press?

     30.4% ( ) Yes If yes, as much as the utility? Yes   —
     69.6% ( ) No   If no, why not?   No   71.4%
                                                     No answer 28.6%

13. To your knowledge, has the press ever refused to accept an ad
     expressing opposition to the nuclear power plant, or forced
     changes in the wording of an ad?

     4.4% ( ) Yes   If yes, please state the circumstances:
     56.5% ( ) No
     39.1% ( ) Don't know

14. How would you rate newspaper coverage in your area of the
     nuclear power plant debate?

     8.7% ( ) Thorough, fair, and balanced
     21.7% ( ) Thin but fair and balanced
     17.4% ( ) Thorough, biased pro-utility
     39.1% ( ) Thin, biased pro-utility
     8.7% ( ) Thorough, biased anti-utility
     — ( )   Thin, biased anti-utility
     4.4% ( ) Other (please specify)

15. Do you believe the manner in which the press covered this
    issue has had any direct or indirect effect on utility plans
    for the plant?

    56.5% ( ) Yes   If yes, please explain:
    39.1% ( ) No
    4.4%   Don't know

16. What do you think the appropriate role (if any) of a citizen should
    be in the decision-making process on nuclear power plants?

    26.1%   Referendum
    21.7%   Participate in decision-making
    13.1%   Legal challenges
    30.4%   Informed
    8.7%   No answer

17. Do you believe that a newspaper should develop in its pages the
    debate over nuclear power (once it becomes known that a
    plant is to be built in the area), regardless of whether or not
    there is an organized citizens' effort against it?

    91.2% ( ) Yes   For either reply, please explain:
    8.7% ( ) No

18. In your community, did organized citizen opposition lead to press
    coverage of the nuclear debate, did initial press coverage lead
    to formation of citizens' groups, or were the two not related?

    47.8%   Citizen opposition led to press coverage
    4.4%   Press coverage led to citizen opposition
    30.4%   No relationship
    13.0%   No answer
    4.4%   No local coverage

19. Additional remarks welcome below or on back:

( ) If you wish your answers to remain anonymous, please check
    here.

THE PRESS AND THE GROWTH
ESTABLISHMENT

Method For Telephone Survey on Community
Attitudes Toward Airport Expansion
and Mass Transit

Determination of Sample

The survey was based on a census of four homogenous populations and a one-third sampling of a fifth. The sample populations—
conservationists, realtors, and Chamber of Commerce members—
were selected on the basis of their likely concern over the airport and
transit issues, their likely high level of information, and their likely
position on the poles of the conservation-development spectrum. The
conservationists in the sample included three groups: the membership
list of an organization formed to oppose the expansion of San Jose
Airport, Sierra Club members in the zip code area nearest the airport's noise problem, and Sierra Club members from a zip code area
far beyond the airport's noise hazard. The realtors and Chamber of
Commerce members were drawn from executive committees with
issue orientation.

In the initial design, a sample of manufacturers with plant
locations in San Jose had been planned. Pretest on the sample indicated very little information or concern with the issues. The com-
parably high level of information among our other five populations
and the low number of "no opinion" responses is a validation of our
sampling procedure, one that is reinforced by the contrast with randomly selected manufacturers.[1]

Sampling Frame

In each sample, official membership lists were obtained. Names
from the lists subsequently were checked against telephone book listings. Only those persons with listed telephone numbers were surveyed.
In all but the near-airport Sierra Club list, all persons with listed
numbers were surveyed.

Questionnaire Construction

     The questionnaire was designed to determine the following:

1. The position of the respondents on the airport and transit issues

2. The most persuasive arguments that brought them to their positions

3. Their level of concern

4. The local newspaper read most regularly and their assessment of the balance and completeness of coverage of each issue

5. Sources of information other than the newspaper, and the source deemed "most reliable."

     Census tract data indicated that the respondents would fall largely within the upper- and middle-income brackets. The inclusion of a foothill conservationist sample was another effort to avoid skew in income and education between the conservationist and Chamber of Commerce sample because past research indicates that critical assessment of news performance varies directly with income and education level.[2] Income and education were not directly surveyed in the questionnaire. However, the questionnaire did seek to account for the effect of the level of concern and access to information by the respondents.

     With the exception of "level of concern," the survey questions were open-ended. The approach was mandated by the expected high level of information and concern that would make forced-choice responses restrictive and offensive. The content of the responses indicated that the expectation was warranted, as did the low level of "no opinion" responses.

     The pretest of the questionnaire was conducted on two groups: (1) a small number of public officials with high levels of concern and (2) manufacturers and conservationists living in San Jose's neighboring city, Santa Clara.

Survey Personnel and Training

     The survey personnel included three Stanford undergraduates with journalism training (and thus interview experience) and the author. They were equipped with and memorized a set of dummy responses to familiarize themselves with the issue area. Training proceeded in two forms: (1) role-playing with acting out of cooperative, overcooperative, and hostile respondents and (2) training calls to more Santa Clara respondents using a joint telephone hook-up with rotating interviewers.

     The interviewers were instructed to record verbatim responses to the open-ended questions. Using the joint call as an intercoder reliability test, we found substantively identical results from coder to

coder. They differ only in the length of verbatim quotes that could
be recorded.

Coders were instructed to repeat the exact wording or partial
phrases from the questions but not to substitute wording or explanation when the respondent asked questions. The questionnaires were
administered only to the persons whose names appeared on the
membership lists. Where Sierra Club member lists included both
husband and wife, the survey was administered to the person answering
the telephone or to the parent a child chose to call to the phone.

Each respondent was called twice on each of two evenings before
being dropped from the sample as "not at home." Respondents with
not-in-service telephones were dropped from the sample after the
first call, a call-back to determine that the number had been dialed
correctly, and a directory check.

Survey Analysis

The data were content coded for computer analysis. Issue
position responses were coded on the basis of key words. The key
words were derived from a listing of the responses of ten respondents
from each of the membership populations. The key word approach
allowed coding the "most persuasive arguments" into three categories:
transportation, environment, and growth and economics, categories
implicit in the data.

Coding of the responses on other questions also was accomplished
by the same method of category derivation, but key words proved
unnecessary for this clerical task.

A Q Sort of the responses was considered but discarded for lack
of expert judges.

The data were coded and key-punched onto computer cards in
separate operations to avoid the error involved in combining the two
tasks. Random punching error was checked at the inventory stage:
one extra category was discovered and remedied.

Statistical Analysis

Because of the census approach and the homogeneity of populations, standard error statistics were not applied to the subpopulations
of conservationists, realtors, and manufacturers. The census approach,
proportion of population actually surveyed, and the homogeneity of the
subpopulations give us confidence in the representativeness of the
results.[3] Differences between groups were tested for significance
by the Chi Square Test for two or more independent samples.[4] Probability values for the Chi Square test are reported with the results.
Cell sizes were above the mandatory five for use of the Chi Square

test. In one instance, cell sizes were bolstered by collapsing data into a binary configuration.

Final Survey Questionnaire for Telephone Poll

Group: Call Backs: ( ) ( ) ( ) ( )
Complete ( )   Partial ( )   No Response after four calls ( )

Hello Mr. ------. My name is ------. I am calling for survey being conducted at Stanford University and supported by the National Science Foundation. May we ask about your opinion on two transportation issues affecting people in Santa Clara County?

    1. First, we'd like to ask what is your opinion on the proposal to expand San Jose's Municipal Airport?

    2. What were the most persuasive arguments that brought you to that conclusion?

    3. Now we'd like to ask you to rate how concerned you are about the outcome of the controversy. Would you say you are: (1) very concerned, (2) moderately concerned, or (3) not concerned about this particular issue?

    4. What local newspaper do you read most regularly?

    5. Would you say their news reporting about airport plans has been balanced in the sense that their news reports don't try to sway the reader to take one viewpoint over another?

    6. Has their news on airport expansion been complete in the sense that you feel they give an adequate understanding of the pros and cons of airport plans?

    7. Have you gotten information about airport expansion from any place or anybody besides your newspaper? (If just "yes," ask who or where.)

    8. To what person, organization, or publication would you or do you look for the most reliable information about the airport issue?

    9. Now I'd like to turn to the question of high-speed public transit. What is your position on public transit for Santa Clara County?

    10. What were the most persuasive arguments that brought you to that conclusion?

    11. Would you say you are: (1) very concerned, (2) moderately concerned, or (3) not concerned about the particular issue of transit?

    12. Would you say your newspaper's reporting about transit has been complete in the sense that you feel they give an adequate understanding of the pros and cons of the issue?

    13. Has your newspaper's news been balanced in the sense that their reporting doesn't try to sway a reader to take one viewpoint over another?

14. Have you gotten information about public transit from any place or anybody besides your newspaper?

15. To what person, organization, or publication would you or do you look for the most reliable information on the transit issue?

Method for Content Analysis of Newspaper Coverage of Airport Expansion and Mass Transit

Among the criteria discussed throughout this voulme that might be employed in an operational definition of "newspaper quality" are that the press offer the following:

1. An understanding of the costs and benefits of public policy before policy decisions are made

2. An understanding of the alternatives to any particualr policy

3. An understanding of the weaknesses of any proposed policy

4. Evenhandedness in the presentation of the positions of proponents and opponents of particular policies.

These criteria can be operationalized only in the context of a specific issue. At the same time the researcher must avoid a subjective judgment of what constitutes understanding or of how much or what content fulfills each criterion. Our resolution of this problem— through a twist on the use of expert judges—will become apparent as we describe the operationalized content coding categories for the news and editorial coverage of airport and transit development.

Content Analysis of News and Editorial
Treatment of Airport Siting

The first quality criterion requires that a newspaper offer an understanding of the costs and benefits of airport siting and development. The notion of relevant content was derived from the planning process itself. Airport location and development was the subject of study by the Airport Subcommittee of the Santa Clara County Planning Policy Committee. The subcommittee was commissioned to study the pros and cons of airport plans. Its membership included representatives of the county's cities, a homeowners' association, the Sierra Club, the San Jose Airport Commission, the County Planning Department, and the Chamber of Commerce. Its mandate and membership provided confidence that it thoroughly examined the pros and cons of airport location and development.

Content codes derived from the subcommittee's study categories were used as an inclusive description of news coverage that offers an understanding of the costs and benefits of airport plans. The study categories developed by the subcommittee offer a convenient and

reasonably objective instrument to test for the presence or absence
of themes in news coverage across time. In addition, the modification
permitted an examination of the detail in which themes were presented.
No arbitrary level of sufficiency or excellence was applied. The
presence of content in the theme categories was considered desirable.

Thus the categories sought a descriptive portrait of the presence
and volume of news in the following content areas:

    1. The economic impact of increased air services in Santa
Clara Valley:

        a. Direct employment by the facility

        b. Effect on the growth rate of economy and employment in
           the valley at large

        c. Effect on land and property values

    2. The environmental impact of increased air services in Santa
Clara Valley:

        a. Noise pollution

        b. Air pollution

        c. Water pollution

        d. Population growth treated as an environmental hazard

        e. Land use patterns

The second criterion requires that newspapers offer an understanding of the alternatives to any particular policy. Again the
hearings of the Planning Policy Committee and the positions of planning
experts were drawn on in outlining specific content themes that offer
policy alternatives.

An understanding of alternatives is operationally defined as content in the following theme areas:

    1. Ground transit connection to San Francisco or Oakland airports

    2. Siting of an airport on the periphery of the metropolitan area
beyond population concentration

    3. Introduction of STOL or VTOL or other aircraft technology
to alleviate pressures for airport expansion

    4. Rescheduling to prevent empty-plane flights and peak-hour
congestion

    5. Communication substitutes for air travel such as computer
conferencing or data exchange

    6. Segregation of general aviation (private planes) to alleviate
airport congestion

    7. Civilian and commercial use of the naval air facilities at
Moffett Field.

Once again a descriptive portrait of coverage was sought in
analyzing the data. Although the presence of alternatives is considered
desirable, no arbitrary level of sufficiency was designated.

The third criterion of quality requires that the newspaper offer
information that probes the weaknesses of public policy. In this

instance, content codes were derived from the provisions of the 1970
Federal Airport Development and Revenue Act. The newspaper's
adversary function would be evidenced by offering content indicating
local airport plans would involve actions prohibited by the federal law:

1. Adverse effect upon fish and wildlife
2. Adverse effect upon natural, scenic, and recreational assets
3. Adverse effect upon water and air quality
4. Official expression of adverse effect upon the interest of
communities in or near which the project may be located
5. Undue delay in completion of the project once it is under way
6. Inconsistency with planning agencies' plans for development
of the area
7. Lack of sufficient funds for the portion of the project that
will not be paid by the federal government.

Once again, no arbitrary level of sufficiency is applied.

A fourth criterion of quality requires that the newspaper be
evenhanded and fair in the presentation of the pros and cons of airport
news. Rather than undertake a semantic analysis of questionable
reliability, independent samples of conservationists, realtors, and
Chamber of Commerce members were surveyed—a purposive sample
of the environmental and growth establishments. Researchers asked:
"Has your newspaper's reporting about airport plans been balanced in
the sense that their news reports don't try to sway the reader to take
one viewpoint over another?" and "Has their news on the airport
been complete in the sense that you feel they give an adequate understanding of the pros and cons of airport plans?" It would be concluded
that the newspaper systematically served only certain community
interests if conservationists were more critical of news performance
than realtors or Chamber of Commerce members.

The unlikelihood that a newspaper would realize these quality
standards without probing and initiative reporting is obvious. The
level of political intelligence required of the newspaper simply is
not contained in the direct transmission of the proceedings of public
meetings. Understanding lies in the presentation of the public and
private values, goals, and possibilities, and of the political influences
and the conflicting interests that inform and shape public policy
decisions. These, we maintain, can only be probed and monitored by
a newspaper that frees its staff for initiative and investigative reporting.

On the basis of this belief, researchers recorded the number
and percentage of stories on airport plans that contained no hard
news peg. Once again, no arbitrary level of sufficiency or excellence
was imposed.

Cumulatively, the measures offer a descriptive portrait and
reader assessment of news performance within prescriptive categories.

The first three criteria of quality were applied to editorials as well
as news, offering a descriptive portrait of editorial comment as well
as news content.

Content Analysis of News and Editorial
Treatment of Mass Transit

In developing categories for analysis of transit content, an attempt
was made to maintain parallelism with the content analysis of airport
development. In part, this was impossible. The transit controversy
ended—not permanently but in the study period—with a countywide
public vote; the airport issue was concluded by vote of the San Jose
City Council. Nevertheless, the four quality standards can be adapted
to the transit issue.

The first quality criterion requires that a newspaper offer an
understanding of the costs and benefits of creating a countywide
transit district with bonding and tax powers that would allow it to
operate bus transit and to investigate high-speed, fixed-rail transit.
Parallel to the airport codes and derived from the County Planning
Department Transportation Planning Study of 1969, the content coding
categories sought a portrait of the presence and volume of news and
comment in the following categories:

1. The impact of transit service upon the economy and employment levels of Santa Clara Valley:
   a. Direct employment by the transit system
   b. Multiplier effect of transit service upon rate of growth
      in valley's economy and employment
   c. The costs of developing and operating the system
   d. Effects on land and property values
2. The environmental impact of the development of transit
service in Santa Clara Valley:
   a. Air pollution
   b. Water pollution
   c. Noise pollution
   d. Population growth treated as an environmental hazard
   e. Land use
3. The social impact of transit service in Santa Clara Valley:
   a. Mobility for low-income people
   b. Mobility for youth and aged
   c. Displacement of low-income residents due to condemnation
      or rising property values
   d. Promotion of contact during travel
   e. Lowering of frustration and waste time due to congestion
   f. Creation of a sense of place by development of a pedestrian
      scale in downtown renewal.

Information content in the theme areas was considered desirable, but no level of sufficiency was imposed.

The second criterion of quality requires that the newspaper offer an understanding of alternatives to the development of transit service. Borrowing from the arguments of transit opponents and planning experts, we derived the following categories, which are an operational-ization of "an understanding of alternatives":

1. Development of peripheral or bypass freeway systems
2. Buses with exclusive right-of-ways
3. Public subsidy or other means of improving Southern Pacific commuter system
4. Ban on private autos in downtown area
5. Ban on or massive improvement in internal combustion engine
6. Express laning of freeways
7. Computer control of car-to-car distances, speed, and access to freeways.

In effect, the presentation of alternatives is an adversary function. A second measure of adversarity is incorporated in the third criterion of quality: that the newspaper offer an understanding of the weaknesses of the transit proposition. News and comment were analyzed for the following themes:

1. San Jose has a proportionally small representation on the transit district board compared to its 40 percent share of county population.
2. Low-income families due could be displaced to condemnation, routing, redevelopment, or rising land values.
3. Other land uses could be displaced by condemnation, routing, or right-of-ways.
4. Car owners may not use transit thereby failing to relieve congestion or pollution.
5. Car owners may not use transit thereby creating a large financial burden.
6. Transit would spur density and crowding.
7. Transit would orient the community toward San Francisco, inhibiting the development of local possibilities.
8. Scatterization of population prohibits effective or profitable transit operation.
9. Transit has had financial failures elsewhere.

Once again, no specific level of sufficiency was designated.

The fourth criterion of quality requires that the newspaper be fair and evenhanded in the presentation of the arguments of the pro-ponents and opponents of transit coverage. As in the airport issue, both ends of the conservation and development spectrum were polled to determine their assessment of the balance and completeness of transit coverage.

As in the airport issue, we also determined the proportion of coverage that displayed staff initiative or investigation as opposed to the reporting of event-pegged stories.

The cumulative effect of the coding categories permitted a description of the thoroughness of news coverage and editorial comment. It also provides a description of the presence and volume of content themes that afford the reader the understanding with which to make intelligent (or unintelligent) assessments of public policy decisions. Furthermore, the frequency with which stories and editorials deal with environmental themes, adversary themes, and policy alternatives permits a comparison of the treatment of the transit and airport issues.

1. Mildred Parten, Surveys, Polls, and Samples (New York: Harper & Brothers, 1950), pp. 492ff. Other methodological works used in developing this survey were Sidney Siegel, Nonparametric Statistics for the Behavioral Sciences (New York: McGraw-Hill, 1956); George W. Snecdor and William G. Cochran, Statistical Methods (6th ed.; Ames: Iowa State University Press, 1967).

2. Carter, "Actual and Perceived Distances in the News," Journalism Quarterly, Vol. XXXVIII. Other theoretical works used in developing this survey were Hovland and Sherif, Social Judgment (New Haven: Yale University Press, 1961); Maccoby and Klein, "Newspaper Objectivity in the 1952 Campaign," Journalism Quarterly, Vol. XXXI.

3. Parten, Surveys, Polls, and Samples, p. 294.

4. Siegel, Nonparametric Statistics, p. 104.

CHAPTER 1

    1. Charles E. Swanson, "What They Read in 130 Daily News-
papers," Journalism Quarterly, XXXII, Fall 1955, pp. 411-21.

    2. Survey Research Center, The Public Impact of Science
in the Mass Media, Institute for Social Research, University of
Michigan, 1958, pp. 84-5.

    3. Wilbur Schramm and Serena Wade, Knowledge and the
Public Mind (Stanford, Cal.: Stanford University, Institute for
Communication Research, 1967), p. 83. See also Wilbur Schramm
and Serena Wade, "The Mass Media as Sources of Public Affairs,
Science and Health Knowledge," Public Opinion Quarterly, summer
1969.

    4. James A. Skardon, "The Apollo Story: The Concealed
Patterns" (Part II), Columbia Journalism Review, winter 1967/68,
p. 39.

    5. Quoted in Hillier Krieghbaum, Science and the Mass Media
(New York: New York University Press, 1967), pp. 113-14. Original in National Association of Science Writers Newsletter, December 1963.

    6. Victor Cohn, "Are We Really Telling the People About
Science?" Science, May 7, 1965, pp. 750-53.

    7. Earl Ubell, "Science in the Press: Newspapers vs. Maga-
zines," Journalism Quarterly, summer 1963, p. 293.

    8. James A. Skardon, "Mr. Skardon Comments," Columbia
Journalism Review, spring 1968, p. 62.

    9. Karl Abraham, "NASA and the Press: A Response,"
Columbia Journalism Review, spring 1968, pp. 59-61.

    10. Krieghbaum, Science and the Mass Media, p. 4.

    11. Harvey Wheeler, "Bringing Science Under Law," in The
Establishment and All That (Santa Barbara: The Center for the
Study of Democratic Institutions, 1970), p. 135.

    12. Donald C. Drake, "A Science Writer Looks at the American
Newspaper: Or-What Really Happened in Philadelphia?" AAAS
Bulletin, XVII, 2 (April 1972), pp. 3-4.

    13. Ibid., p. 4.

    14. AAAS Bulletin, XVII, 2 (April 1972), 3.

    15. J. Murray Mitchell, Jr., "Recent Secular Changes in
Global Temperature," Annals of the New York Academy of Science,
Vol. XCV, Art. 1 (October 5, 1961), p. 246.

16. Ibid., p. 248

17. For more detailed discussions of such disease pathogenesis, see M. M. Wintrobe, et al., eds., Harrison's Textbook of Internal Medicine (6th ed.; New York: McGraw-Hill, 1970), pp. 1322-32. For what is perhaps the most graphic description of medical problems produced by a smog disaster, see Burton Roueche, "The Fog," in Eleven Blue Men (New York: Berkeley Medallion Paperbacks, 1953), pp. 194-215.

18. Quoted in George Ballis, An Evaluation: The California Water Plan (Washington, D.C.: Public Affairs Institute, 1960), p. 3.

19. Letter from Lloyd Lowrey, Sr., to Lloyd Lowrey, Jr.

20. Telephone interview with Assemblyman Pauline Davis, January 21, 1971.

21. Personal interview with Lloyd Lowrey, Sr., Rumsey, Cal., September 21, 1970.

22. Letter from George G. Crawford to Lloyd Lowrey, Jr., July 2, 1971.

23. Letter from Edmund G. Brown to Lloyd Lowrey, Jr., March 2, 1971.

24. San Jose Mercury, July 27, 1960.

25. Roy M. Fisher, "The World of Finance Does Not Begin and End on Wall Street," ASNE Bulletin, June 1967, p. 3.

26. Don Teverbaugh, "The Problems Business Writers Face in Smaller Cities," ASNE Bulletin, June 1967, p. 5.

27. Timothy William Hubbard, "The Explosive New Demand for Business News," Journalism Quarterly, Vol. XLIII (1966), p. 706.

28. Alexander Auerbach, "A Young Man Opts for a Career in Business Reporting," ASNE Bulletin, June 1967, p. 5.

29. Hubbard, "The Explosive New Demand," p. 707.

30. Teverbaugh, "The Problems Business Writers Face," p. 5.

31. Eileen Shanahan, et al., "Business Problem: Contempt for the Press," Editor and Publisher, November 5, 1966, p. 19.

32. Jerome K. Full, "Reporting on Business," Editor and Publisher, September 6, 1969, p. 20.

33. Quoted in Theodore Peterson, Fred S. Siebert, and Wilbur Schramm, Four Theories of the Press (Urbana: University of Illinois Press, 1963), pp. 89-91.

CHAPTER 3

1. See Roland E. Wolseley, Understanding Magazines (Ames, Iowa: The Iowa University Press, 1969) p. 9.

2. James L. C. Ford, Magazines for Millions: The Story of Specialized Magazines (Carbondale, Illinois: Southren Illinois University Press , 1969), p. 19.

3. Better Homes and Gardens, October 1964, p. 124B.

4. Ford, Magazines for Millions, pp. 16-17.

5. James Playsted Wood, Magazines in the United States, 3rd edition, (New York: The Ronald Press, 1971), p. 281.

6. Ibid., p. 223.

7. Gilbert Hovey Grosvenor, "The Romance of the Geographic," National Geographic Magazine, October 1963, p. 561.

8. Personal communication with David P. Sachs, 1970.

9. Grosvenor, National Geographic, p. 581.

10. Bernard P. Gallagher, ed., The Gallagher Report, XVIII, 34 (Second Section).

11. Theodore Peterson, Magazines in the Twentieth Centruy (Urbana: University of Illionois Press, 1964), p. 414.

12. Wood, Magazines in the United States, p. 248.

13. Frank Graham, Jr., Since Silent Spring (Boston: Houghton Mifflin, 1970), p. 69.

14. Wood, Magazines in the United States, p. 220

15. Graham, Jr., Since Silent Spring, p. 70.

16. Ibid., p. 70.

17. Ibid., p. 165.

CHAPTER 4

1. Daniel Boorstein, The Image (New York: Harper and Row, 1961).

CHAPTER 5

1. Herbert G. Lawson, "Chevron's F-310 Gas: A Lesson in How Not to Promote a Product," Wall Street Journal, January 7, 1971, pp. 1, 6.

2. Uhlman v. Sherman, 22 Ohio NPNS 225, 31 Ohio Dec 54, 1919. Later decisions in the same jurisdiction explicitly rejected this precedent.

3. Shuck v. Carroll Daily Herald, 215 Ia 1276, 247 NW 813, 1933.

4. Bloss v. Federated Publications Inc. 5 Mich App 74, 145 NW 2d 800, 1966. Affirmed by the Michigan Supreme Court, 380 Mich 485, 1968.

5. For a brief summary of the principal relevant cases, see David C. Hamilton, "Advertising: The Right to Refuse," Freedom of Information Center Report No. 187, School of Journalism, University of Missouri, 1967. See also the legal annotation at 18 ALR 3d 1286.

6. See Daniel J. Baum, "Self-Regulation and Anti-Trust: Suppression of Deceptive Advertising by the Publishing Media," Syracuse Law Review, XII, 3 (spring 1961), pp. 289-304.

7. "Judge Reaffirms Daily's Right to Refuse Ads," Advertising Age, December 29, 1969, p. 4. See also "Papers' Right to Bar Ads Upheld in Court," Editor and Publisher, January 3, 1970, p. 18.

8. Mark E. Watkins, "Implications of the Extension of the Fairness Doctrine to Editorial Expressions Implied in Commercial Advertising," Albany Law Review, Vol. XXXIV (winter 1970), pp. 452-64.

9. "In the Matter of Liaison Between FCC and FTC Relating to False and Misleading Radio and Television Advertising," 22 FCC 1572 (1957). See also Carl R. Ramey, "The Federal Communications Commission and Broadcast Advertising: An Analytical Review," Federal Communications Bar Journal, XX, v 2 (1966), pp. 71-116. See also "In the Matter of Commercial Advertising," 36 FCC 45 (1964); "Licensee Responsibility with Respect to the Broadcast of False, Misleading, or Deceptive Advertising," FCC Public Notice 61-1316, mimeo. No. 11833, November 7, 1961.

10. The case is reported and quoted without citation in Morton J. Simon, The Law for Advertising and Marketing (New York: W. W. Norton, 1956), pp. 349-50. In earlier cases, a number of radio stations lost their licenses because of their willing acceptance of deceptive patent medicine advertising.

11. Leon C. Smith, "Local Station Liability for Deceptive Advertising," Journal of Broadcasting, XV, 1 (winter 1970-71), pp. 107-12. See also Sidney A. Diamond, "Courts Test Whether Publisher Is Responsible for Seal of Approval," Advertising Age, February 9, 1970, pp. 59-60. Additionally, of course, the media are liable for libelous advertisements.

12. Amalgamated Furniture Factories v. Rochester Times-Union, 128 Misc 673, 219 NYS 705 (1927). The comment was obiter dictum and was ignored by later decisions.

13. Jerome A. Barron, "Access to the Press—A New First Amendment Right," Harvard Law Review, Vol. LXXX (1967), p. 1678. See also Jerome A. Barron, "An Emerging First Amendment Right of Access to the Media?", George Washington Law Review, Vol. XXXVII (1969), pp. 487-509.

14. Barron, "Access to the Press," p. 1668.

15. William A. Resneck, "The Duty of Newspapers to Accept Political Advertising—An Attack on Tradition," Indiana Law Journal, Vol. XLIV (1969), p. 232.

16. "Covering the 'Smears,'" Columbia Journalism Review (winter 1970-71), pp. 2-3. The editors also note, with apparently equal approval, that the Washington Post accepted the ad on grounds of access but accompanied it with a discrediting editorial.

17. Watkins, "Implications of the Extension of the Fairness Doctrine," p. 455n.

18. "The Case of the Obscene Cash Register," San Francisco Chronicle, December 10, 1970, p. 60. It has been suggested that this public debate between the two newspapers was little more than a public relations gimmick. The issue is nevertheless a real one.

19. Commission on Freedom of the Press, A Free and Responsible Press (Chicago: University of Chicago Press, 1947), p. 24.

20. Fred S. Siebert, Theodore Peterson, and Wilbur Schramm, Four Theories of the Press (Urbana: University of Illinois Press, 1956), pp. 89-90.

21. In 1960 Federal Trade Commission Chairman Earl W. Kintner put it this way: "In my opinion, the public and moral responsibility of advertisers . . . must in turn be shared by the media. . . . Whether this sharing of public and moral responsibility should also involve a sharing of legal responsibility . . . is another matter, involving serious policy considerations." Quoted in Baum, "Self Regulation and Anti-trust," p. 291.

22. Francis Pollock, "Consumer Reporting: Underdeveloped Region," Columbia Journalism Review, May/June 1971, p. 43.

23. Jerry Mander, "The Media and Environmental Awareness," in Garrett De Bell, ed., The Environmental Handbook (New York: Ballantine, 1970), pp. 256-57.

24. "Warning Sought on Detergents" San Francisco Chronicle, January 26, 1971, p. 3.

CHAPTER 6
1. Woodrow Wilson, The New Freedom (New York: Doubleday, Pages, 1913), p. 125.

2. Eileen Shanahan, et al., "Business Problem: Contempt for Press," Editor and Publisher, November 5, 1966, p. 19.

3. See, for example, the three volumes of hearings, Environmental Effects of Producing Electric Power, Joint Committee on Atomic Energy, October 28-31, and November 4-7, 1969; January 27-30 and February 24-26, 1970.

4. Paul Jeffery, "California's Open Meeting Fight," Freedom of Information Center Report No. 210 (Columbia, Mo., October 1968,), p. 1.

5. California Government Code, Section 54950.

6. California Government Code, Section 54953.

7. California Government Code, Section 54951, as amended in 1959 to include charter cities.

8. California Government Code, Section 54952.

9. California Government Code, Section 11123.

10. Robert Alan Blum, "Access to Government Information," California Law Review, Vol. LIV, p. 1655.

11. Stephen R. Barnett and David M. Wishnick, "Open Meeting Statutes: The Press Fights for the Right to Know," Harvard Law Review, 75, 6 (April 1962), 1199-1221.

12. Statutes of California 1968, Vol. 2, Chapter 3. 5, 6253, p. 2946.

13. Statutes of California 1968, Vol. 2, Chapter 3. 5, 6252 (b), p. 2946.

14. Statutes of California 1968, Vol. 2, Chapter 3. 5, 6252 (d), p. 2946.

15. Statutes of California 1968, Vol. 2, Chapter 3. 5, 6254 (a), (e), and (h), pp. 2946-47.

16. "The Right to Know," Report of Assembly Interim Committee on Government Organization (1965), Vol. 2 of Appendix to Journal of the Assembly, Regular Session, 1965, p. 79.

17. Ibid., p. 100. (Statement of Frederick B. Holoboff, PUC president, in answer to a 1965 questionnaire on PUC open meeting policy circulated by the Assembly Interim Committee on Government Organization.)

18. Ibid., pp. 142-43.

19. See 5 U.S.C. 552 (81 Stat. 54) for the complete act.

20. Attorney General's Memorandum on the Public Information Section of the Administrative Procedure Act, #20402-25¢ (Washington, D.C.: Government Printing Office; reprinted by the Freedom of Information Center, Columbia, Mo.), p. 1.

21. Gene Schrader, "Atomic Doubletalk," The Center Magazine, IV, 1 (January/February 1971), p. 33.

22. Ibid.

23. Lee Metcalf and Vic Reinemer, Overcharge: A Study of the Electric Utility Industry (New York: David McKay, 1967), pp. 135-36.

24. Siting Thermal Power Plants in California, Report prepared for the Joint Committee on Atomic Development and Space, California legislature, February 15, 1970, pp. viii-10.

25. The Electric Utility Industry and the Environment, Report to the Citizens Advisory Committee on Recreation and Natural Beauty (prepared by Electric Utility Industry Task Force on Environment, 1968), pp. 103-4. Reprinted from Electrical World, December 4, 1967.

26. Congressional Record, January 24, 1969. (Statement by Senator Lee Metcalf of Montana.)

27. The New York Times, October 21, 1971, p. 1.

28. The New York Times, October 4, 1972, p. 49.

29. Gene Bryerton, Nuclear Dilemma (New York: Ballantine/ Friends of the Earth, 1970).

CHAPTER 7

    1. Morris Janowitz, The Community Press (Chicago: University of Chicago Press, 1967), p. 29.

    2. A massive literature exists on the conflict between the economic and news-gathering functions of the press. See, for example, Lewis Donohew, "Newspaper Gatekeepers and Forces in the News Channel," Public Opinion Quarterly, spring 1967; Lewis Donohew, "Publishers and Their Influence Groups," Journalism Quarterly, winter 1965; Robert Agger, et al., The Rulers and the Ruled (New York: Wiley & Sons, 1964); William L. Rivers and Wilbur Schramm, Responsibility in Mass Communication (rev. ed.; New York: Harper & Row, 1969); J. Edward Gerald, The Social Responsibility of the Press (University of Minnesota Press, 1964).

    3. Edward C. Banfield, Political Influence (New York: Free Press, 1965), p. 190.

    4. Ibid., p. 193.

    5. Ibid., p. 211.

    6. Ibid., p. 231.

    7. Ibid., p. 217.

    8. Ibid., p. 230.

    9. Floyd Hunter, Community Power Structure (Chapel Hill: University of North Carolina Press, 1953).

    10. Ibid., p. 102.

    11. Ibid., p. 182.

    12. Ibid., p. 99.

    13. Ibid., p. 174.

    14. Ibid., p. 205.

    15. Ibid., p. 180.

    16. Stanford Environmental Law Society, San Jose Land Use Study, unpublished manuscript (preliminary draft), Stanford, Calif., p. 44.

    17. A. P. Hamann, San Jose in the 1970's, report to the City Council of San Jose, November 1969, introductory letter.

    18. San Jose Planning Commission, The Masterplan of San Jose, California, (2nd Rev.; July 1964, mimeo).

    19. Stanford Environmental Law Society, San Jose Land Use Study, Introduction.

    20. Santa Clara County Transportation Planning Study, "Interim Study Report, Governmental Influences on Growth," April 1967, p. 3.

    21. San Jose Planning Commission, The Masterplan of San Jose, California.

    22. Ibid.

    23. John Meyer, "Urban Transportation," in James Q. Wilson, ed., The Metropolitan Enigma (Garden City, N.Y.: Doubleday Anchor, 1970), p. 55.

24. San Jose Planning Department, Planning Communication and Information, Bulletin No. 5 (December 1967), p. 8.

25. San Jose Planning Commission, The Masterplan of San Jose, California.

26. Clifford W. Graves, Air Transportation and San Francisco Bay, consultant's report to the Bay Conservation and Development Commission, 1966, pp. 40ff.

27. Air Facilities Committee, San Jose Chamber of Commerce, "A Report on the San Jose Municipal Airport," (mimeo, 1970), pp. 4ff.

28. Personal interview, July 1971.

29. Fred S. Siebert, Theodore Peterson, and Wilbur Schramm, Four Theories of the Press (Urbana: University of Illinois Press , 1963), p. 74.

30. Thomas Harvey, in testimony before the Airport Subcommittee of the Planning Policy Committee of the Santa Clara County Inter-City Council, 1970. Minutes of the Airport Subcommittee of the Planning Policy Committee of Santa Clara County, mimeo, Santa Clara County Planning Department, mimeo, 1970.

31. Personal interview with Santa Clara County Associate Planner Henry Johnson, July 1971.

32. Frank Happy, representative of the Federal Aviation Agency, in testimony before the Airport Subcommittee of the Santa Clara County Planning Policy Committee.

33. Michael S. Blanding, "Survey of Airline Passengers Departing the San Francisco Bay Area," (Menlo Park: Stanford Research Institute Report, #MC 7568, May 1968.)

34. Jewel Bellush and Maurray Hausknecht, Urban Renewal: People, Politics and Planning (Garden City, N.Y.: Doubleday Anchor, 1967), p. 221.

CHAPTER 8

1. Marston Bates, The Forest and the Sea (New York: Random House, 1960), pp. 3-5.

In creating a bibliography on mass media and the environment, we have focused on research and criticism in eight related fields: press performance, science writing, business writing, access to environmental information, audience, environmental advertising, growth and the press, and ecological medicine. In general, we have included only sources that touch on media performance and responsibility in environmental coverage or on the audience for environmental information. With a few exceptions we have not included the thousands of books and articles about the environment. The emphasis is on mass media channels and the audience for environmental information.

Press Performance in Environmental Coverage

Carlton, John Guy, Jr. "A Quantitative Evaluation of the Current Level of Outdoor News Coverage in the Daily Newspapers of Wisconsin." Unpublished M.S. thesis, University of Wisconsin (Madison), 1960.

Cassidy, Robert. "Stripping Out the Facts," MORE, II, 4 (April 1972), 3-5.

Clausing, Jane. "The Ecological Message of the Outdoor Magazines," The Journal of Environmental Education," II, 4 (summer 1971), 10-12.

Drake, Donald C. "A Science Writer Looks at the American Newspaper: Or—What Really Happened in Philadelphia?" AAAS Bulletin, XVII, 2 (April 1972), 3-4.

Egginton, Hersey. "The Environment Beat: What's Being Done?" New York Press/Publisher, II, 7 (April 1972), 11-13.

Graham, Frank Jr. Since Silent Spring. New York: Houghton Mifflin, 1970.

Hendin, David. "Environmental Reporting," The Quill, August 1970, pp. 15-17.

Kuttner, Bob. "Covering Up in California," MORE, I, 3 (November 1971), 5-7.

Middleton, R. "Fertility Values in American Magazine Fiction, 1916-1956." Public Opinion Quarterly, XXIV, 1 (1960), 139-43.

Moen, Sanford A. "Field and Stream as a Factor in the Development of Outdoor Journalism in America." Unpublished M.S. thesis, University of Wisconsin (Madison), 1955.

Rivers, William L., and David M. Rubin. "Case Study: Regional Organization and the Environmental Crisis." In A Region's Press: Anatomy of Newspapers in the San Francisco Bay Area. Berkeley, Calif.: Institute of Governmental Studies, 1971.

Ross, John E., and Sarah Jenkins. "Newspaper Coverage of Nuclear Power Plant Issues: Lake Michigan, 1966-1969." Mimeo., Institute for Environmental Studies, University of Wisconsin (Madison), 1972.

Rubin, David M., and Stephen Landers. "National Exposure and Local Cover-up: A Case Study," Columbia Journalism Review, VIII, 2 (summer 1969), 17-22.

Shaw, Donald L. "Surveillance vs. Constraint: Press Coverage of a Social Issue," Journalism Quarterly, XLVI, 4 (winter 1969), 707-12.

Stamm, Keith R., and John E. Bowes. "Communication During an Environmental Decision," The Journal of Environmental Education, III, 3 (spring 1972), 49-55.

Urban Journalism Center. "The Pollution Issue: A Survey of Editorial Judgements." Mimeo., The Medill School of Journalism, Northwestern University, 1970.

Witt, William. "Multivariate Analysis of News Flow in a Conservation Issue," Journalism Quarterly, XLIX, 1 (spring 1972), 91-97.

Science Writing

Abraham, Karl. "NASA and the Press: A Response," Columbia Journalism Review, VII, 1 (spring 1968), 59-61.

Burkett, David Warren. Writing Science News for the Mass Media. Houston: Gulf, 1965.

Cohn, Victor. "Are We Really Telling the People About Science?"
    Science, CXLVIII, 3671 (May 7, 1965), 750-53.

Eipper, Alfred W. "Pollution Problems, Resource Policy, and the
    Scientist," Science, CLXIX, 3940 (July 3, 1970), 11-15.

Foster, John, Jr. Science Writer's Guide. New York: Columbia
    University Press, 1963.

Gates, D. M., and J. M. Parker. "Science News Writing: Seminar at
    Colorado State University," Science, CXXXIII, 3447 (January 20,
    1961), 211-14.

Johnson, Kenneth G. "Dimensions of Judgment of Science News Stories,"
    Journalism Quarterly, XL, 3 (summer 1963), 315-22.

Johnson, Lee Z. "Status and Attitudes of Science Writers," Journalism
    Quarterly, XXXIV, 2 (spring 1957), 247-50.

Krieghbaum, Hillier. Science and the Mass Media. New York: New
    York University Press, 1967.

Lear, John. "The Trouble With Science Writing," Columbia Journalism
    Review, IX, 2 (summer 1970), 30-34.

Lessing, L. "Science Journalism: The Coming Age," Bulletin of the
    Atomic Scientists, XIX (December 1963), p. 23.

Light, Israel. "Science Writing: Status and Needs," Journalism
    Quarterly, XXXVII, 1 (winter 1960), 53-60.

Moore, Judith Hoffman. "Defining and Interpreting Ecology," The
    Journal of Environmental Education, III, 1 (fall 1971), 54-57.

National Association of Science Writers (text by Hillier Krieghbaum).
    Science, The News, and the Public. New York: New York
    University Press, 1958.

Robinson, Edward J. "Analyzing the Impact of Science Reporting,"
    Journalism Quarterly, XL, 3 (summer 1963), 306-14.

Sherburne, E. G., Jr. "Science on Television: A Challenge to Crea-
    tivity," Journalism Quarterly, XL, 3 (summer 1963), 300-5.

Skardon, James A. "The Apollo Story: The Concealed Patterns (Part
    II)," Columbia Journalism Review, VI, 4 (winter 1967/68), 34-39.

Snow, C. P. The Two Cultures and the Scientific Revolution. New York: Cambridge University Press, 1963.

Survey Research Center. The Public Impact of Science in the Mass Media: A Report on a Nation-wide Survey for the National Association of Science Writers. Ann Arbor: Institute for Social Research, University of Michigan, 1958.

Tichenor, Phillip J., et al. "Mass Communication Systems and Communication Accuracy in Science News Reporting," Journalism Quarterly, XLVII, 4, (winter 1970), 673-83.

Troan, J. "Science Reporting, Today and Tomorrow," Science, CXXXI, 3408 (April 22, 1960), 1193-96.

Ubell, Earl. "Science in the Press: Newspapers vs. Magazines," Journalism Quarterly, XL, 3 (summer 1963), 293-99.

Business Writing

Allen, J. H. "Business Journalism," Public Relations Journal, XXIII, 1 (January 1967), 19-20.

Auerbach, Alexander. "A Young Man Opts for a Career in Business Reporting," ASNE Bulletin, June 1967, pp. 5-6.

Fisher, Roy M. "The World of Finance Does Not Begin and End on Wall Street," ASNE Bulletin, June 1967, pp. 3-4.

Full, Jerome K. "Reporting on Business," Editor and Publisher, September 6, 1969, p. 20.

Golden, L. L. L. "Three Horror Stories: Corporation Executives Misunderstanding Function of Press," Saturday Review, November 9, 1968, pp. 89-90.

Hubbard, Timothy William. "The Explosive New Demand for Business News," Journalism Quarterly, XLIII, 4 (winter 1966), 703-8.

Kuhn, Ferdinand. "Blighted Areas of Our Press," Columbia Journalism Review, V, 2 (summer 1966), 5-11.

Morgenthaler, Eric. "Some Question Ethics of Putting a Newsman on a Corporate Board," Wall Street Journal, September 4, 1970, pp. 1, 15.

Phillips, Warren. "Is Business News Worth the Bother?" ASNE
Bulletin, May 1967, pp. 7-8.

Shanahan, Eileen, et al. "Business Problem: Contempt for Press,"
Editor and Publisher, November 5, 1966, pp. 19-20.

Teverbaugh, Don. "The Problems Business Writers Face in Smaller
Cities," ASNE Bulletin, June 1967, pp. 4-5.

Access to Environmental Information

Alexander, Louis. "Space Flight News: NASA's Press Relations and
Media Reaction," Journalism Quarterly, XLIII, 4 (winter 1966),
722-28.

Archibald, Samuel J. "The FOI Act Goes to Court," Freedom of Information Center Report No. 280, School of Journalism, University
of Missouri (Columbia), April 1972.

Assembly Interim Committee on Government Organization (1965).
The Right to Know. Journal of the Assembly (California),
Appendix, Volume II, Regular Session, 1965.

Bagdikian, Ben H. The Information Machines. New York: Harper &
Row, 1971.

Baran, Paul. Potential Market Demand for Two-Way Information
Services to the Home, 1970-1990. Menlo Park, Calif.: Institute
for the Future, 1971.

Blanchard, Robert O. "The Freedom of Information Act—Disappoint-
ment and Hope," Columbia Journalism Review, VI, 3 (fall 1967),
16-20.

Blum, Robert Alan. "Access to Government Information," California
Law Review, LIV, pp. 1650-80.

Brady, Edward L., and Lewis M. Branscomb. "Information for a
Changing Society," Science, CLXXV, 4025 (March 3, 1972), 961-66.

Cross, Harold L. The People's Right to Know. New York: Columbia
University Press, 1953.

Jeffery, Paul. "California's Open Meeting Fight." Freedom of Information Center Report No. 210, School of Journalism, University of Missouri (Columbia), October 1968.

Kerbec, Matthew J. Legally Available U.S. Government Information. 2 Vols. Arlington, Va.: Output Systems Corporation, 1971.

Kruger, Helen N. "The Access to Federal Records Law." Freedom of Information Center Report No. 186, School of Journalism, University of Missouri (Columbia), September 1967.

Parker, Edwin B., and Donald A. Dunn. "Information Technology: Its Social Potential," Science, CLXXVI, 4042 (June 30, 1972) 1392-99.

U. S. Department of Justice. Attorney General's Memorandum on the Public Information Section of the Administrative Procedure Act. Washington, D.C.: the Department, 1966.

Wade, Nicholas. "Freedom of Information: Officials Thwart Public Right to Know," Science, CLXXV, 4021 (February 4, 1972), 498-502.

Audience for Environmental Information

Bailey, George Arthur. "The Public, The Media, and the Knowledge Gap," The Journal of Environmental Education, II, 4 (summer 1971), 3-8.

Barker, Mary L. "The Perception of Water Quality as a Factor in Consumer Attitudes and Space Preferences in Outdoor Recreation.' Mimeo., Department of Geography, University of Toronto, 1969.

Catton, William R., Jr. "Wilderness Users—What Do They Think?" American Forests, LXXIV (1968), pp. 28-31, 60-61.

Columbia Broadcasting System. "The CBS News Poll: The National Environment Test." Mimeo., Survey Operations Department, CBS News Election Unit, Series 70, No. 4, Report 1 (June 16, 1970).

DeGrott, Ido. "Trends in Public Attitudes Toward Air Pollution," Journal of Air Pollution Control Association, XVII (1967), pp. 679-81.

Erickson, David L. "Attitudes About Wildlife and Preferences in Television Programs: A Communication Study." Unpublished Ph.D. thesis, Ohio State University, 1969.

Erskine, Hazel. "The Polls: More on the Population Explosion and Birth Control," Public Opinion Quarterly, XXXI, 2 (summer 1967), 303-13.

_____. "The Polls: Pollution and Industry," Public Opinion Quarterly, XXXVI, 2 (summer 1972), 263-80.

_____. "The Polls: Pollution and Its Costs," Public Opinion Quarterly, XXXVI, 1 (spring 1972), 120-35.

_____. "The Polls: The Population Explosion, Birth Control, and Sex Education," Public Opinion Quarterly, XXX, 3 (fall 1966), 490-501.

Gallup International, Inc. "Air and Water Pollution, Quality of Education—New 'Causes' on Campus," The Gallup Opinion Index, Vol. XX, Report 55 (January 1970).

Gallup Organization, Inc. "The U.S. Public Considers its Environment." Mimeo. Washington, D.C.: National Wildlife Federation, February 1969.

Harris, Louis, and Associates, Inc. "A Study of the Attitudes of the American Public Toward Improvement of the National Environment." Mimeo. Washington, D.C.: National Wildlife Federation, 1969.

_____. "A Survey of Public Attitudes Toward Urban Problems and Toward the Impact of Scientific and Technical Developments." Study No. 2044, prepared for the Public Broadcasting Environment Center, November 1970.

_____. "The Public's View of Environmental Problems in the State of Washington." Study No. 1990, prepared for Pacific Northwest Bell Telephone Company, February 1970.

Ibsen, Charles A., and John A. Ballweg. "Public Perception of Water Resource Problems." Bulletin 29, Water Resources Research Center, Virginia Polytechnic Institute (Blacksburg), September 1969.

Kaplan, Max, and Paul Lazarsfeld. "The Mass Media and Man's
    Orientation to Nature." In Trends In American Living and Out-
    door Recreation, A Report to the Outdoor Recreation Resources
    Review Commission, Study Report No. 22, Washington, D.C.,
    1962.

Lingwood, David A. "Environmental Education Through Information
    Seeking: The Case of an 'Environmental Teach-In.'" Mimeo.,
    Center for Research on Utilization of Scientific Knowledge,
    University of Michigan, 1971.

Madigan, Dennis P. "Special Interest Group Ratings of Conservation
    Issues." Unpublished M.S. thesis, University of Wisconsin
    (Madison), 1969.

Medalia, N. Z., and A. L. Finkner. "Community Perception of Air
    Quality: An Opinion Study in Clarkston, Washington." U.S.
    Public Health Service, 999-10, Cincinnati, 1965.

Morrison, Denton E.; Kenneth E. Hornback; and W. Keith Warner.
    "The Environment Movement: Some Preliminary Observations."
    In William Burch, Neil Cheek, and Lee Taylor, eds., Social
    Behavior, Natural Resources and the Environment. New York:
    Harper & Row, 1972.

Murch, Arvin W. "Public Concern for Environmental Pollution,"
    Public Opinion Quarterly, XXXV, 1 (spring 1971), 100-6.

Patterson, Joye; Laurel Booth; and Russell Smith. "Who Reads About
    Science?" Journalism Quarterly, XLVI, 3 (fall 1969) 599-602.

Public Opinion Surveys, Inc. "Who Litters—and Why?" Mimeo.
    New York: Keep American Beautiful, Inc., November 1968.

Research Triangle Institute of North Carolina. "A National Study of
    Roadside Litter." Mimeo., New York: Keep America Beautiful,
    Inc., October 1969.

Sewell, W. R. Derrick. "Environmental Perceptions and Attitudes of
    Engineers and Public Health Officials." Paper presented at
    annual meeting of the American Psychological Association,
    Miami Beach, September 5, 1970.

Shaw, Donald L., and Paul Van Nevel. "The Informative Value of
    Medical Science Stories," Journalism Quarterly, XLIV, 3
    (autumn 1967), 548.

Simon, Rita James. "Public Attitudes Toward Population and Pollution," Public Opinion Quarterly, XXXV, 1 (spring 1971), 93-99.

Smith, W. S.; J. J. Schueneman; and L. Zeidberg. "Public Reaction to Air Pollution in Nashville, Tennessee," Journal of Air Pollution Control Association, XIV (1964), pp. 418-23.

Stamm, Keith R., and John Ross. "The Rationality of Opinions on a Controversy in Conservation," Journalism Quarterly, XLIII, 4 (winter 1966), 762-65.

Swan, James A. "Response to Air Pollution: A Study of Attitudes and Coping Strategies of High School Youth," Environment and Behavior, ii, 2, (September 1970), 127-52.

Swinehart, James W., and Jack M. McLeod. "News About Science: Channels, Audiences, and Effects," Public Opinion Quarterly, XXIV, 4 (winter 1961), 583-89.

Tichenor, Phillip J., et al. "Environment and Public Opinion," The Journal of Environmental Education, II, 4 (summer 1971), 38-42.

_____. "Environment and Public Opinion in Minnesota." Mimeo., Institute of Agriculture and Department of Sociology, University of Minnesota (St. Paul), n. d.

Wade, Serena, and Wilbur Schramm. "The Mass Media as Sources of Public Affairs, Science, and Health Knowledge." Public Opinion Quarterly, XXXIII, 2 (summer 1969) 197-209.

Willeke, Gene E. "Effects of Water Pollution in San Francisco Bay." Unpublished Report EEP-29, Program in Engineering-Economic Planning, Stanford University, Stanford, Calif., October 1968.

Williams, J. D., and F. L. Bunyard. "Opinion Surveys and Air Quality Statistical Relationships." Interstate Air Pollution Study Phase II Project Report. Cincinnati: U.S. Public Health Service, 1966.

Withey, S. B. "Public Opinion About Science and Scientists," Public Opinion Quarterly, XXIII, 3 (fall 1959), 382-88.

Environmental Advertising

"Advertising—Promoting Nature's Friends," Time, August 17, 1970, pp. 58, 61.

Asher, Thomas. "Smoking Out Smokey The Bear," MORE, II, 3 (March 1972), 12-13.

Baum, Daniel J. "Self-Regulation and Anti-Trust: Suppression of Deceptive Advertising by the Publishing Media," Syracuse Law Review, XII, 3 (spring 1961), 289-304.

Beley, Gene R. "This Ad Was Unacceptable," Columbia Journalism Review, V, 4 (winter 1966/1967), 48-49.

"A Case to Watch," The Nation, October 6, 1969, pp. 332-33.

Council on Economic Priorities. Economic Priorities Report, "Corporate Advertising and the Environment," September/October 1971.

"Deceptive Advertising," Harvard Law Review, LXXX, 5 (March 1967), 1008-1163.

Diamond, Sidney A. "Courts Test Whether Publisher Is Responsible for Seal of Approval," Advertising Age, February 9, 1970, pp. 59-60.

Dorfman, Ron. "Freedom of Press Belongs to Man Who Owns One," Chicago Journalism Review, November 1969, p. 7.

Giges, Nancy. "Pollution—It's Today's Bonanza for Advertisers," Advertising Age, April 20, 1970, pp. 1, 216-18.

Greyser, Stephen A., and Raymond A. Bauer. "Americans and Advertising: Thirty Years of Public Opinion," Public Opinion Quarterly, XXX, 1 (spring 1966), 69-78.

Gwyn, Robert J. "Opinion Advertising and the Free Market of Ideas," Public Opinion Quarterly, XXXIV, 2 (summer 1970), 246-55.

Hamilton, David C. "Advertising: The Right to Refuse." Freedom of Information Center Report No. 187, School of Journalism, University of Missouri (Columbia), September 1967.

Lawson, Herbert G. "Chevron's F-310 Gas: A Lesson in How Not to Promote a Product," Wall Street Journal, January 7, 1971, pp. 1,6.

Lukas, J. Anthony. "Life in These United States," MORE, I, 1 (June 1971), 3-4.

Mander, Jerry. "Six Months and Nearly a Billion Dollars Later, Advertising Owns Ecology," Scanlan's, June 1970, pp. 54-61.

_____. "The Media and Environmental Awareness." In Garrett De
Bell, ed., The Environmental Handbook. New York: Ballantine,
1970.

Moore, Richard L. "Environment—A New PR Crisis," Public Relations
Journal, XXVI, 3 (March 1970), 6-9.

Pollock, Francis. "Consumer Reporting: Underdeveloped Region,"
X, 1 (May/June 1971), 37-43.

"Pollution: Puffery or Progress," Newsweek, December 28, 1970,
pp. 49-51.

Ramey, Carl R. "The Federal Communications Commission and
Broadcast Advertising: An Analytical Review," Federal Communications Bar Journal, XX, 2 (1966), 71-116.

Reeves, Clifford B. "Ecology Adds a New PR Dimension," Public
Relations Journal, XXVI, 6 (June 1970), 6-9.

Resneck, William A. "The Duty of Newspapers To Accept Political
Advertising—An Attack on Tradition," Indiana Law Journal,
XLIV (winter 1969), 222-41.

Ridgeway, James. "Exploits of 'The New Adventurers,'" MORE, II,
7 (July 1972), 1, 18-20.

Sandman, Peter M. "Who Should Police Environmental Advertising?"
Columbia Journalism Review, X, 5 (January/February 1972),
41-47.

Simon, Morton J. The Law for Advertising and Marketing. New York:
W. W. Norton, 1956.

Turner, Thomas. "Eco-Pornography or How to Spot an Ecological
Phony." In Garrett De Bell, ed., The Environmental Handbook.
New York: Ballantine, 1970.

_____. "Eco-Pornography Revisited." In Garrett De Bell, ed.,
The Voter's Guide to Environmental Politics. New York:
Ballantine, 1970.

Watkins, Mark E. "Implications of the Extension of the Fairness Doctrine to Editorial Expressions Implied in Commercial Advertising," Albany Law Review, XXXIV (winter 1970), 452-64.

Weiss, E. B. "Management: Don't Kid the Public with Those Noble Anti-Pollution Ads," Advertising Age, August 3, 1970, pp. 35, 36, 38.

Whiteside, Thomas. "Selling Death," New Republic, March 27, 1971, pp. 15-17.

The Press and the Growth Establishment

Banfield, Edward C. Political Influence. New York: Free Press, 1965.

_____, and James Q. Wilson. City Politics. New York: Vintage Books, 1963.

Bellush, Jewel, and Maurray Hausknecht. Urban Renewal: People, Politics and Planning. Garden City, N.Y.: Doubleday Anchor, 1967.

Bishop, Bruce A. "Socio-economic and Community Factors in Planning Urban Freeways." Unpublished Report EEP-33, Program in Engineering-Economic Planning, Stanford University, Stanford, Calif., October 1969.

Chandler, Otis. "A Publisher's View of Credibility." In Richard W. Lee, ed., Politics and the Press. Washington, D.C.: Acropolis Books, 1970.

Donohew, Lewis. "Newspaper Gatekeepers and Forces in the News Channel," Public Opinion Quarterly, XXXI, 1 (spring 1967), 61-68.

_____. "Publishers and their Influence Groups," Journalism Quarterly, XLII, 1 (winter 1965), 112-13.

Hunter, Floyd. Community Power Structure. Chapel Hill: University of North Carolina Press, 1953.

Janowitz, Morris. The Community Press. Chicago: University of Chicago Press, 1967.

Paletz, David L.; Peggy Reichert; and Barbara McIntrye. "How the Media Support Local Governmental Authority," Public Opinion Quarterly, XXXV, 1 (spring 1971), 80-92.

Rivers, William L. The Adversaries. Boston: Beacon Press, 1970.

Ecological Medicine

Bates, Marston. The Forest and the Sea. New York: Random House, 1960.

Brown, Harrison. The Challenge of Man's Future. New York: Viking Compass Books, 1970.

Ehrlich, Paul, and Ann Ehrlich. Population, Resources, and Environment. 2nd ed. San Francisco: W. H. Freeman, 1972.

Guidotti, Tee Lamont. "Environmental Quality and Community Planning: A Medical Concern," The Pharos of Alpha Omega Alpha, XXXV, 3, (July 1972), 112-16.

Hardin, Garrett. Nature and Man's Fate. New York: The New American Library, 1961.

Perloff, Harvey S. The Quality of the Urban Environment. Washington, D.C.: Resources for the Future/Johns Hopkins Press, 1969.

Roueche, Berton. "The Fog." In Eleven Blue Men. New York: Berkeley Medallion Paperbacks, 1953.

Sachs, David Peter. "Saving San Francisco Bay—In Sacramento," In Ecotactics: The Sierra Club Handbook for Environment Activists. New York: Pocket Books, 1970.

_____. "Toward a Comprehensive Program of Ecological Medicine," _____, and David M. Rubin. Mass Media and the Environment: San Francisco and Monterey Bay Water Resources. Bethesda, Md.: Educational Resources Information Center (ERIC), 1971 (ED-058-710).
The Pharos of Alpha Omega Alpha, XXXIV, 4 (October 1971), 147-50.

Welsh, Joseph E.; Adrian Arima; and Daniel Green. The Politics of
     Pollution Control in Monterey Bay. Stanford, Calif.: Environ-
     mental Research Project/Stanford Workshops on Political and
     Social Issues, 1971.

DAVID M. RUBIN is Assistant Professor of Journalism at New York University, Washington Square. He has worked as a newspaper reporter for the San Francisco Chronicle and the Elyria (Ohio) Chronicle-Telegram and has published articles in Columbia Journalism Reveiw, Seminar, and California Newspaper Publisher. He has co-authored three other books about journalism, including an introductory textbook on the mass media and a study of San Francisco Bay Area journalism.

A 1967 graduate of Columbia College, he received his Ph.D. from the Department of Communication, Stanford University, in 1972.

DAVID PETER SACHS has written about environmental subjects in McCall's magazine and Saturday Review. His interest in the environment began in 1958 with a study of pollution and eutrophication in Lake Erie. While a medical student at Stanford University, he headed the Stanford Population and Environment Forum and taught numerous undergraduate seminars on environmental subjects.

Dr. Sachs received his M.D. degree from Stanford University in 1972 and is presently an intern at Case Western Reserve University in Cleveland. He intends to do research in environmental medicine.